THE GUINNESS BOOK OF SPORTS RECORDS 1993

EDITOR
MARK YOUNG

Facts On File
New York

THE GUINNESS BOOK OF SPORTS RECORDS 1993

Copyright © 1993 by Guinness Publishing Ltd.

Facts On File, Inc.
460 Park Avenue South
New York NY 10016
USA

This book is taken in part from *The Guinness Book of Records* © 1992

Facts On File books are available at special discounts when purchased in bulk quantities for businesses, associations, institutions or sales promotions. Please contact the Special Sales Department of our New York office at 212/683-2244 or 1-800/322-8755.

ISBN 0-8160-2653-X (hardcover)
ISBN 0-8160-2654-8 (paperback)
ISSN 1054-4178

"Guinness" is a registered trademark of Guinness PLC for Publications

Text design by Ron Monteleone
Jacket design by Ron Monteleone
Composition by Ron Monteleone/Facts On File, Inc.
Production by Michael Braunschweiger
Manufactured by R. R. Donnelley & Sons, Inc.
Printed in the United States of America

10 9 8 7 6 5 4 3 2 1

This book is printed on acid-free paper.

CONTENTS

ILLUSTRATION CREDITS

Sam Moore: 10, 11, 18, 39, 133, 162, 188, 203, 205

PHOTOGRAPH CREDITS

t=top b=bottom m=middle l=left r=right

Atlanta Hawks: 40bl
APT: 199

Nancie Battaglia: 54tl, 54tr, 55, 56, 62, 64, 70, 73tl, 73br, 156, 171, 172, 173, 174tl, 179, 180, 210, 234br
Bruce Bennett: 132b
Kenny Bernstein's Budweiser King Racing: 7, 13
Tim Boggan: 186
Steve Brown: 214
Boston Bruins: 129
Allsport/Simon Bruty: 155, 166, 201, 234bl
Buffalo Bills: 77br

California Angels: 18, 23tm
Allsport/David Cannon: 170
CART, Inc.: 8
Allsport/Russell Cheyne: 181tl
Cincinnati Reds: 15
Cleveland Indians: 23tl

Daytona International Speedway: 10
Drake University: 50
Allsport/Tony Duffy: 204tl

Allsport/Tom Ewart: 209

Georgetown University: 46
Golden State Warriers: 45tl
Allsport/Jim Gund: 218

Hartford Whalers: 128
Houston Oilers: 80tl

Indiana University: 97b
Kansas City Chiefs: 80br
Stephen Koschal: 16
Ladies Professional Golfers Association: 116, 119
Allsport/Ken Levine: 211, 213, 215br
Loudon International Speedway: 151
Allsport/Bob Martin: 181, 183, 188, 245
Montreal Canadiens: 132t, 133t
Allsport/G. Mortimore: 198, 199, 204tr
Naismith Memorial Basketball Hall of Fame: 38
National Association for Stock Car Auto Racing: 11
New Orleans Saints: 88
Carol Newsom: 198
New York Islanders: 139br
New York Racing Association: 141, 142
New York Yankees: 34tr, 34tl

Oakland Athletics: 30
Allsport/C.J. Olivares Jr.: 208
Oklahoma State University: 49

Philadelphia Flyers: 127
Photography Ink: 39, 42
Pool & Billiards Magazine: 160
Professional Bowlers Association: 58

Professional Rodeo Cowboy Association: 164
Providence College: 45br
Allsport/Mike Powell: 204, 233, 234tr, 234tl

William S. Romano: 1, 110, 114, 115
Allsport/Pascal Rondeau: 157

San Francisco 49ers: 85
Seattle Mariners: 23tr
Dr. Ted Siciliano: 159
Allsport/Paul Souders: 174br

Texas Rangers: 19
Toronto Argonauts: 102
Toronto Maple Leafs: 139tl

United States Hang Gliding Association: 122
United States Soaring Association: 176
United States Synchronized Swimming Association: 185
United States Trotting Association: 123
University of Houston: 96
University of Kansas: 91
University of Maryland: 149
University of Pittsburgh: 97t
Utah Jazz: 40br

Allsport/Vandystadt/Bernard Asset: 154

Washington Redskins: 77bl
Women's Tennis Association: 189t, 189b
World Footbag Association: 76

ACKNOWLEDGMENTS

The goal of this book is to provide the most comprehensive and accurate account of the records established in the world of sports. Accumulating such a vast and disparate array of information has required the cooperation, patience and expertise of many organizations and individuals. I would like to thank the media representatives, librarians and historians of the following organizations for their help: National Championship Air Races, U.S. National Archery Assoc., Championship Auto Racing Teams, Indianapolis Motor Speedway, National Assoc. for Stock Car Auto Racing, National Hot Rod Association, U.S. Badminton Assoc., International Badminton Federation, Major League Baseball, The National Baseball Hall of Fame and Museum, Elias Sports Bureau, Little League Baseball, National Collegiate Athletic Assoc., Naismith Memorial Basketball Hall of Fame, National Basketball Assoc., U.S. Biathlon Assoc., U.S. Bobsled and Skeleton Fed., Professional Bowling Assoc., Ladies Professional Bowling Tour, American Bowling Congress, Women's Int'l Bowling Congress, USA Boxing, U.S. Canoe and Kayak Team, U.S. Croquet Assoc., U.S. Curling Assoc., U.S. Cycling Assoc., Ultra Marathon Cycling Assoc., U.S. Diving, American Horse Shows Assoc., U.S. Fencing Assoc., U.S. Field Hockey Assoc., U.S. Figure Skating Assoc., National Football League, Canadian Football League, World Flying Disc Federation, World Footbag Assoc., PGA Tour, LPGA Tour, European PGA Tour, U.S. Gymnastics Fed., U.S. Hang Gliding Assoc., U.S. Trotting Assoc., National Hockey League, Montreal Canadiens, Daily Racing Form, Churchill Downs, Breeders' Cup, New York Racing Assoc., Maryland Jockey Club, National Horseshoe Pitchers Assoc., U.S. Judo, USA Karate Fed., U.S. Modern Pentathlon Assoc., U.S. Olympic Committee, U.S. Orienteering Fed., U.S. Polo Assoc., Billiard Congress of America, American Powerboat Assoc., American Amateur Racquetball Assoc., Professional Rodeo Cowboys Assoc., U.S. Amateur Confederation of Roller Skating, U.S. Rowing Assoc., National Rifle Assoc., U.S. Skiing, Iditarod Trail Committee, Amateur Softball Assoc., U.S. Int'l Speedskating Assoc., Assoc. of Surfing Professionals, U.S. Swimming, U.S. Synchronized Swimming, U.S. Table Tennis Assoc., U.S. Taekwondo Union, U.S. Team Handball Fed., Women's Tennis Assoc., I.B.M./A.P.T. Tour, The Athletics Congress, New York Road Runners Club, American Trampoline and Tumbling Assoc., Triathlon Fed. USA, Assoc. of Volleyball Professionals, U.S. Water Polo, American Water Ski Assoc., U.S. Weightlifting, USA Wrestling, America's Cup Organizing Committee.

Regrettably, space prevents me from mentioning all the individuals who have helped me compile this book; however, I must mention certain people whose contributions have added immensely to this project: at Guinness Publishing in Enfield, England, Peter Matthews, Michelle Dunkley McCarthy, Stewart Newport and Debbie Collings. Special thanks is extended to Ken Park and Andrew Young for allowing me access to their encyclopedic knowledge of the world of sports records.

As I write in this space each year, publishing, as with sports, requires the efforts of many people to produce the on-field performance. I am once again indebted to the talented and professional team of people who have assisted me in producing this book: Jo Stein, Ron Monteleone, Grace M. Ferrara, Sam Moore, Joe Reilly, Virginia Rubens, Marjorie Bank, John W. Hansen, Linda Palamara. . . and *"danke schön"* to Michael Braunschweiger, who this year overcame the despair of seeing his beloved soccer team, FC Lucerne, relegated from the Swiss first division to make sure the book was "on schedule."

Mark Young
New York City

Editor's Note: FC Lucerne did win the Swiss Cup in 1992, thus becoming the first Swiss soccer team to win the national cup and be relegated from the first division in the same season. Can anyone associated with this book escape sports records?

AEROBATICS

ORIGINS The first aerobatic "maneuver" is generally considered to be the sustained inverted flight in a Blériot flown by Célestin-Adolphe Pégoud (France, 1889–1915), at Buc, France on September 21, 1913.

WORLD CHAMPIONSHIPS First held in 1960, the world championships are a biennial event.

Most titles Petr Jirmus (Czechoslovakia) is the only man to have won two world titles: 1984 and 1986. Betty Stewart (U.S.) is the only woman to have won two world titles: 1980 and 1982.

AIR RACING

Air racing, or airplane racing, consists of piloted aircraft racing a specific number of laps over a closed circuit marked by pylons. As with auto racing, the first plane to cross the finish line is the winner. Air races are divided into several categories, depending on the type of plane and engine. The top level of the sport is the unlimited class.

ORIGINS The first international airplane racing competition, the Bennett Trophy, was held at Rheims, France from August 22–28, 1909.

United States The first international air race staged in the United States was the second Bennett Trophy competition, held at Belmont Park, N.Y. in 1910. Air racing became very popular in the 1920s. Competitions, such as the National Air Races (inaugurated in 1924) and the Thompson Trophy

LOOPS ☛ JOANN OSTERUD (U.S.) PERFORMED 208 CONTINUOUS OUTSIDE LOOPS IN A "SUPERNOVA" HYPERBIPE OVER NORTH BEND, ORE., ON JULY 13, 1989.

OVERPASS ■ AIR RACING DATES TO THE 1930S. THE NATIONAL AIR RACING CHAMPIONSHIPS ARE STAGED IN RENO, NEV., ANNUALLY.

(inaugurated in 1930), drew enormous crowds—500,000 people attended the 1929 National Air Races in Cleveland, Ohio. Following World War II the popularity of the sport declined. During the mid-1950s, enthusiasts revived the sport, racing smaller World War II military planes. In 1964 Bill Stead staged the first National Championship Air Races (NCAR) at Reno, Nev.; this is now the premier air racing event in the United States.

NATIONAL CHAMPIONSHIP AIR RACES (NCAR)

Staged annually in Reno, Nev., since 1964, the NCAR has been held at its present site, the Reno/Stead Airport, since 1986. Races are staged in four categories: Unlimited class, AT-6 class, Formula One class and Biplane class.

Unlimited class In this class the aircraft must use piston engines, be propeller-driven and be capable of pulling six G's. The planes race over a pylon-marked 9.128 mile course.

Most titles Darryl Greenmyer has won seven unlimited NCAR titles: 1965–69, 1971 and 1977.

Fastest average speed (race) Lyle Shelton won the 1991 NCAR title recording the fastest average speed at 481.618 mph in his "Rare Bear."

Fastest qualifying speed The one-lap NCAR qualifying record is 482.892 mph, by Lyle Shelton in 1992.

ARCHERY

ORIGINS The exact date of the invention of the bow is unknown, but historians agree that it was at least 50,000 years ago. The origins of archery as a competitive sport are also unclear. It is believed that the ancient Olympic Games (776 B.C. to 393 A.D.) featured archery, using tethered doves as targets. The legends of Robin Hood and William Tell indicate that archery prowess was highly regarded in Europe by the 13th century. Archery became an official event in the modern Olympics in 1900. In 1931, the *Fédération Internationale de Tir à l'Arc* (FITA) was founded as the world governing body of the sport.

United States The date of the first use of the bow as a weapon in North America is unknown; however, it is believed that Native American tribes in the eastern part of North America were familiar with the bow by the 11th century. The National Archery Association was founded in 1879 in Crawfordsville, Ind. and is the oldest amateur sports organization in continuous existence in the United States.

TARGET ARCHERY

The most widely practiced discipline in archery is Olympic-style target archery (also known as FITA style). Olympic-style target archery competition is based on the Single FITA round system of scoring. A Single FITA round consists of 36 arrows shot from four distances: 90, 70, 50 and 30 meters for men; 70, 60, 50 and 30 for women, for a total of 144 arrows. Scoring ranges from 10 in the center gold circle to 1 in the outer white ring. The maximum possible score for a Single FITA round is 1,440 points. Competition varies from accumulated scores based on two or more Single FITA rounds to single elimination rounds in which each archer's score reverts to zero at each stage of the tournament.

OLYMPIC GAMES Archery made its first appearance in the 1900 Games in Paris, France. It was also featured in 1904, 1908 and 1920, but then was

WORLD RECORDS (Single FITA Rounds)

Men

Event	Archer	Country	Points	Year
FITA	Vladimir Esheev	USSR	1,352	1990
90 m	Vladimir Esheev	USSR	330	1990
70 m	Hiroshi Yamamoto	Japan	344	1990
50 m	Rick McKinney	U.S.	345	1982
30 m	Antonio Vazquez Megldo	Spain	358	1992
Final	Vladimir Esheev	USSR	345	1989

Women

Event	Archer	Country	Points	Year
FITA	Cho Youn-Jeong	S. Korea	1,375	1992
70 m	Cho Youn-Jeong	S. Korea	338	1992
60 m	Kim Soo-nyung	S. Korea	347	1989
50 m	Cho Youn-Jeong	S. Korea	338	1992
30 m	Joanne Edens	Great Britain	357	1990
Final	Kim Soo-nyung	S. Korea	346	1990

Source: U.S. National Archery Association

FLIGHT SHOOTING WORLD RECORDS

The object in flight shooting is to fire the arrow the greatest distance possible. There are two flight shooting classifications: regular flight and broadhead flight.

Regular Flight

Men

Bow Type	Distance	Archer	Date
Crossbow	2,047 yds 0 ft 2 in	Harry Drake	July 30, 1988
Unlimited Footbow	2,028 yds 0 ft 0 in	Harry Drake	Oct. 24, 1971
Conventional Footbow	1,542 yds 2 ft 10 in	Harry Drake	Oct. 6, 1979
Unlimited Recurve Bow	1,336 yds 1 ft 3 in	Don Brown	Aug. 2, 1987
Unlimited Compound Bow	1,320 yds 1 ft 3 in	Kevin Strother	July 31, 1992
Unlimited Longbow	356 yds 1 ft 2 in	Don Brown	July 29, 1989
Unlimited Primitive Bow	283 yds 2 ft 7 in	Daniel Perry	July 31, 1988

Women

Bow Type	Distance	Archer	Date
Unlimited Recurve Bow	1,039 yds 1 ft 1 in	April Moon	Sept. 13, 1981
Conventional Footbow	1,113 yds 2 ft 6 in	Arlyne Rhode	Sept. 10, 1978
Compound Bow (25kg)	904 yds 0 ft 5 in	April Moon	Oct. 5, 1989

Broadhead Flight

Men

Bow Type	Distance	Archer	Date
Unlimited Compound Bow	784 yds 2 ft 9 in	Bert McCune Jr.	Aug. 2, 1992
Unlimited Recurve Bow	526 yds 0 ft 5 in	Don Brown	June 26, 1988
Unlimited Longbow	332 yds 2 ft 0 in	Don Brown	Aug. 2, 1992
Unlimited Primitive Bow	244 yds 2 ft 7 in	Daniel Perry	June 24, 1990

Women

Bow Type	Distance	Archer	Date
Unlimited Compound Bow	481 yds 0 ft 7 in	April Moon	June 24, 1989
Unlimited Recurve Bow	364 yds 0 ft 4 in	April Moon	June 28, 1987
Unlimited Longbow	237 yds 2 ft 3 in	April Moon	Aug. 2, 1992
Unlimited Primitive Bow	107 yds 1 ft 5 in	Gwen Perry	June 24, 1990

Source: U.S. National Archery Association

omitted until 1972, when enough countries had adopted FITA standardized rules to allow for a meaningful international competition.

Most gold medals Hubert van Innis (Belgium) has won six gold medals (au cordon dore—33 meters, au chapelet—33 meters, 1900; moving bird target, 28 meters, 33 meters, moving bird target [team], 33 meters, 50 meters, 1920).

Most medals Hubert van Innis has won nine medals in all: six gold (see above), and three silver (au cordon dore—50 meters, 1900; moving bird target, 50 meters, moving bird target [team] 28 meters, 1920).

United States The most successful American archer at the Olympic Games has been Darrell Pace, who won gold medals in 1976 and 1984. Lida Howell (née Scott) won two gold medals in individual events in 1904; however, only American archers competed in the women's events that year.

WORLD CHAMPIONSHIPS Target archery world championships were first held in 1931 in Lvov, Poland. The championships are staged biennially.

Most titles (archer) The most titles won is seven, by Janina Spychajowa-Kurkowska (Poland) in 1931–34, 1936, 1939 and 1947. The most titles won by a man is four, by Hans Deutgen (Sweden) in 1947–50.

Most titles (country) The United States has a record 14 men's and eight women's team titles.

United States The most individual world titles won by a U.S. archer is three, by Rick McKinney:

1977, 1983 and 1985. Jean Lee, 1950 and 1952, is the only U.S. woman to have won two individual world titles.

UNITED STATES NATIONAL CHAMPIONSHIPS The U.S. national championships were first held in Chicago, Ill. from August 12–14, 1879, and are staged annually.

Most titles The most archery titles won is 17, by Lida Howell between 1883 and 1907. The most men's titles is nine (three individual, six pairs), by Rick McKinney, 1977, 1979–83, and 1985–87.

AUTO RACING

The nationality of the competitors in this section is U.S. unless noted otherwise.

ORIGINS The site of the first automobile race is open to debate. There is a claim that the first race was held in the United States in 1878, from Green Bay to Madison, Wis., won by an Oshkosh steamer. However, France discounts this, claiming that *La Velocipede*, a 19.3-mile race in Paris on April 20, 1887, was the first race. The first organized race did take place in France: 732 miles from Paris to Bordeaux and back, on June 11–14, 1895. The first closed-circuit race was held over five laps of a one-mile dirt track at Narragansett Park, Cranston, R.I. on September 7, 1896. Grand Prix racing started in 1906, also in France. The Indianapolis 500 was first run on May 30, 1911 (see below).

INDIANAPOLIS 500

The first Indianapolis 500 was held on May 30, 1911 at the Indianapolis Motor Speedway, where the event is still run. The Speedway was opened on August 19, 1909. The original track surface was crushed stone and tar, but several accidents during its initial races convinced the owners to install a paved surface, a project that required 3.2 million bricks and was completed by December 1909. In 1937, parts of the track were resurfaced with asphalt, and the track was completely resurfaced in 1976. The race track is a 2½ mile square oval that has two straightaways of 3,300 feet and two of 660 feet, all 50 feet wide. The four turns are each 1,320 feet, all 60 feet wide and banked 9 degrees, 12

BIGGEST PULL ☛ GARY SENTMAN (U.S.) DREW A LONGBOW WEIGHING A RECORD 176 LB TO THE MAXIMUM DRAW ON THE ARROW OF 28¼ INCHES AT FORKSVILLE, PA., ON SEPTEMBER 20, 1975.

minutes. A 36-inch strip of original brick marks the start–finish line.

VICTORY LANE

Most wins Three drivers have won the race four times: A. J. Foyt Jr., in 1961, 1964, 1967 and 1977; Al Unser, in 1970–71, 1978 and 1987; and Rick Mears, in 1979, 1984, 1988 and 1991.

Fastest win The record time is 2 hours 41 minutes 18.404 seconds (185.981 mph) by Arie Luyendyk (Netherlands) driving a 1990 Lola-Chevrolet on May 27, 1990.

Slowest win The slowest time is 6 hours 42 minutes 8 seconds (74.602 mph) by Ray Harroun in the inaugural race in 1911.

Consecutive wins Four drivers have won the race in consecutive years: Wilbur Shaw, 1939–40; Mauri Rose, 1947–48; Bill Vukovich, 1953–54; and Al Unser, 1970–71.

Oldest winner Al Unser became the oldest winner when he won the 1987 race at age 47 years 11 months.

Youngest winner Troy Ruttman became the youngest winner when he won the 1952 race at age 22 years 2 months.

Closest finish The closest margin of victory was 0.043 seconds in 1992 when Al Unser Jr. edged Scott Goodyear (Canada).

Lap leader Al Unser has led the race for a cumulative 629 laps during his 26 starts, 1965–92.

Highest earnings The record prize fund is $7,527,450, and the individual prize record is $1,244,184, by Al Unser Jr., both in 1992. Rick Mears leads the field in career earnings at $4,299,392 from 15 starts, 1978–92.

INDIANAPOLIS 500 WINNERS (1911–1952)

Year	Driver	Av. Speed (mph)	Year	Driver	Av. Speed (mph)
1911	Ray Harroun	74.602	1932	Fred Frame	104.144
1912	Joe Dawson	78.719	1933	Louis Meyer	104.162
1913	Jules Goux	75.933	1934	William Cummings	104.863
1914	Rene Thomas	82.474	1935	Kelly Petillo	106.240
1915	Ralph DePalma	89.840	1936	Louis Meyer	109.069
1916	Dario Resta	84.001	1937	Wilbur Shaw	113.580
1917	(not held)		1938	Floyd Roberts	117.200
1918	(not held)		1939	Wilbur Shaw	115.035
1919	Howard Wilcox	88.050	1940	Wilbur Shaw	114.277
1920	Gaston Chevrolet	88.618	1941	Floyd Davis & Mauri Rose	115.117
1921	Tommy Milton	89.621	1942	(not held)	
1922	Jimmy Murphy	94.484	1943	(not held)	
1923	Tommy Milton	90.954	1944	(not held)	
1924	L.L. Corum & Joe Boyer	98.234	1945	(not held)	
1925	Peter DePaolo	101.127	1946	George Robson	114.820
1926	Frank Lockhart	95.904	1947	Mauri Rose	116.338
1927	George Souders	97.545	1948	Mauri Rose	119.814
1928	Louis Meyer	99.482	1949	Bill Holland	121.327
1929	Ray Keech	97.585	1950	Johnnie Parsons	124.002
1930	Billy Arnold	100.448	1951	Lee Wallard	126.244
1931	Louis Schneider	96.629	1952	Troy Ruttman	128.922

QUALIFYING

Official time trials are held on the two weekends prior to the race to allow entrants to qualify for the 33 starting positions. A completed trial consists of four consecutive laps around the track with the course cleared of all other traffic. Pole position is determined at the "first day" trials. Qualifiers on each subsequent day are lined up behind the qualifiers of previous days. In 1991 Rick Mears gained pole position with an average speed of 224.113 mph, but Gary Bettenhausen recorded the fastest overall average speed of 224.468 mph on the following day, yet only gained a spot on Row 5 of the starting grid. This was the fourteenth time that this paradox had happened since the introduction of speed time trials in 1915.

Most starts A. J. Foyt Jr. has started a record 35 races (1958–92).

Pole position Rick Mears has gained a record six poles, in 1979, 1982, 1986, 1988–89 and 1991.

Fastest qualifier The record average speed for four laps qualifying is 232.482 mph by Roberto Guerrero (Colombia) in a Lola-Buick on May 9, 1992. On the same day he set the one-lap record of 233.433 mph.

INDY CAR RACING

The first Indy Car Championship was held in 1909 under the sponsorship of the American Automobile Association (AAA). In 1956 the United States Automobile Club (USAC) took over the running of the Indy series. Since 1979, Championship Auto Racing Teams Inc. (CART) has organized the Indy Championship, which has been called the PPG Indy Car World Series Championship since 1979.

INDIANAPOLIS 500 WINNERS (1953–1992)

Year	Driver	Av. Speed (mph)	Year	Driver	Av. Speed (mph)
1953	Bill Vukovich	128.740	1973	Gordon Johncock	159.036
1954	Bill Vukovich	130.840	1974	Johnny Rutherford	158.589
1955	Bob Sweikert	128.209	1975	Bobby Unser	149.213
1956	Pat Flaherty	128.490	1976	Johnny Rutherford	148.725
1957	Sam Hanks	135.601	1977	A. J. Foyt Jr.	161.331
1958	Jim Bryan	133.791	1978	Al Unser	161.363
1959	Rodger Ward	135.857	1979	Rick Mears	158.899
1960	Jim Rathmann	138.767	1980	Johnny Rutherford	142.862
1961	A. J. Foyt Jr.	139.131	1981	Bobby Unser	139.084
1962	Rodger Ward	140.293	1982	Gordon Johncock	162.029
1963	Parnelli Jones	143.137	1983	Tom Sneva	162.117
1964	A. J. Foyt Jr.	147.350	1984	Rick Mears	163.612
1965	Jim Clark*	150.686	1985	Danny Sullivan	152.982
1966	Graham Hill*	144.317	1986	Bobby Rahal	170.722
1967	A. J. Foyt Jr.	151.207	1987	Al Unser	162.175
1968	Bobby Unser	152.882	1988	Rick Mears	144.809
1969	Mario Andretti	156.867	1989	Emerson Fittipaldi*	167.581
1970	Al Unser	155.749	1990	Arie Luyendyk*	185.981
1971	Al Unser	157.735	1991	Rick Mears	176.457
1972	Mark Donohue	162.962	1992	Al Unser Jr.	134.477

* Nationality: Jim Clark (Great Britain), Graham Hill (Great Britain), Emerson Fittipaldi (Brazil), Arie Luyendyk (Netherlands).

POLE-AXED ■ ROBERTO GUERRERO SET THE INDY 500 QUALIFYING RECORD AT 232.482 MPH IN 1992, BUT SPUN ON THE PACE LAP AND FAILED TO START THE RACE.

VICTORY LANE

Most championships A.J. Foyt Jr. has won seven Indy Car National Championships: 1960–61, 1963–64, 1967, 1975 and 1979.

Most consecutive championships Ted Horn won three consecutive national titles from 1946–48.

Most wins (career) A.J. Foyt Jr. has won a career record 67 Indy car races, 1957–92. Foyt's first victory came at the DuQuoin 100 in 1960 and his latest at the Pocono 500 in 1981.

Most wins (season) The record for most victories in a season is 10, shared by two drivers: A.J. Foyt Jr. in 1964 and Al Unser in 1970.

Consecutive winning seasons Bobby Unser won at least one race per season for 11 seasons from 1966–76.

Most wins (road course) Mario Andretti has won a record 21 road course races, 1964–92.

Most wins (500-mile races) A. J. Foyt Jr. has won nine 500-mile races: Indianapolis 500 in 1961, 1964, 1967 and 1977; Pocono 500 in 1973, 1975, 1979 and 1981; California 500 in 1975.

Closest races The closest margin of victory in an Indy car race was 0.02 seconds on April 10, 1921 when Ralph DePalma edged Roscoe Sarles to win the Beverly Hills 25. The closest finish in a 500-mile event was Al Unser Jr.'s 0.043-second victory in the 1992 Indianapolis 500. Mario Andretti pulled off the closest finish in an Indy road race, when he won the Portland 200 by 0.07 seconds on June 15, 1986. The loser in this memorable showdown was his son, Michael. (Well, it was Father's Day!)

Highest earnings (season) The single-season record is $2,461,734, set in 1991 by Michael Andretti.

Highest earnings (career) Through the 1992 season, Bobby Rahal has the highest career earnings for Indy drivers with $11,166,578.

QUALIFYING

Most starts Mario Andretti has made a record 375 starts in Indy car racing, 1964–92.

Most poles (career) Mario Andretti has earned a record 65 pole positions, 1964–92.

Most poles (season) A.J. Foyt Jr. earned 10 poles in 1965.

Most poles (road courses) Mario Andretti has earned 26 poles on road courses.

Most poles (500-mile races) Rick Mears has earned a record 16 poles in 500-mile races.

FASTEST INDY CAR RACES

Distance	Race	Driver	Av. Speed (mph)	Year
100 miles	Ontario 100	Wally Dallenbach	179.910	1973
150 miles	Atlanta 150	Rick Mears	182.094	1979
200 miles	Michigan 200	Rick Mears	182.325	1983
250 miles	Michigan 250	Bobby Rahal	181.701	1986
500 miles	Michigan 500	Al Unser Jr.	189.727	1990

Source: CART

CART CASH ■ BOBBY RAHAL WON THE 1992 CART PPG WORLD SERIES AND MOVED TO THE HEAD OF THE ALL-TIME EARNINGS LIST AT $11,166,578.

Fastest qualifiers The fastest qualifying lap ever for an Indy car race was 232.482 mph by Roberto Guerrero (Colombia) on May 9, 1992 in qualifying for the Indianapolis 500.

NASCAR (NATIONAL ASSOCIATION FOR STOCK CAR AUTO RACING)

The National Association for Stock Car Auto Racing, Inc., was founded by Bill France Sr. in 1947. The first NASCAR-sanctioned race was held on February 15, 1948 on Daytona's beach course. The first NASCAR championship, the Grand National series, was held in 1949. Since 1970, the championship series has been called the Winston Cup Championship. The Winston Cup is won by the driver who accumulates the most points during the 29-race series.

VICTORY LANE

Most championships Richard Petty has won a record seven NASCAR titles: 1964, 1967, 1971–72, 1974–75 and 1979.

Most consecutive titles Cale Yarborough is the only driver to "threepeat" as NASCAR champion, winning in 1976–78.

Most wins (career) Richard Petty has won 200 NASCAR Winston Cup races out of 1,185 in which he competed, 1958–92.

Most wins (season) Richard Petty won a record 27 races in 1967.

Fastest average speed The fastest average speed in a Winston Cup race is 186.288 mph, set by Bill Elliott at Talladega Superspeedway, Ala. on May 5, 1985.

Highest earnings (season) Dale Earnhardt earned a record $3,083,056 in 1990.

Highest earnings (career) Dale Earnhardt also holds the career earnings mark at $16,094,782, 1975–92.

DAYTONA 500

The Daytona 500 has been held at the 2½ mile oval Daytona International Speedway in Daytona

Beach, Fla. since 1959. The Daytona 500 is the most prestigious event on the NASCAR calendar.

VICTORY LANE

Most wins Richard Petty has won a record seven times: 1964, 1966, 1971, 1973–74, 1979 and 1981.

Consecutive wins Richard Petty and Cale Yarborough are the only drivers to have repeated as Daytona 500 winners in consecutive years. Petty's double was in 1973–74 and Yarborough's in 1983–84.

Oldest winner Bobby Allison became the oldest winner of the race in 1988 at age 50 years 2 months 11 days.

Youngest winner Richard Petty became the youngest winner in 1964, at age 26 years 4 months 18 days.

Fastest win The record average speed for the race is 177.602 mph, by Buddy Baker in 1980.

Slowest win The slowest average speed is 124.740 mph, by Junior Johnson in 1960.

Highest earnings The individual race earnings record is $244,050, by Davey Allison in 1992. The career earnings record is $920,260, by Bill Elliott in 14 races, 1978–92.

QUALIFYING

Most starts Richard Petty has competed in 32 Daytona 500 races, 1959–92.

Fastest qualifying time The record average speed for qualifying for the race is 210.364 mph, set by Bill Elliott in 1987.

Most poles Cale Yarborough has earned a record four poles at the Daytona 500, in 1968, 1970, 1978 and 1984.

FORMULA ONE (GRAND PRIX)

The World Drivers' Championship was inaugurated in 1950. Currently the championship is contested over 16 races in 16 different countries worldwide. Points are awarded to the first six finishers in each race; the driver with the most points at the end of the season is the champion.

DAYTONA 500 WINNERS (1959–1992)

Year	Driver	Av. Speed (mph)	Year	Driver	Av. Speed (mph)
1959	Lee Petty	135.521	1976	David Pearson	152.181
1960	Junior Johnson	124.740	1977	Cale Yarborough	153.218
1961	Marvin Panch	149.601	1978	Bobby Allison	159.730
1962	Fireball Roberts	152.529	1979	Richard Petty	143.977
1963	Tiny Lund	151.566	1980	Buddy Baker	177.602
1964	Richard Petty	154.334	1981	Richard Petty	169.651
1965	Fred Lorenzen	141.539	1982	Bobby Allison	153.991
1966	Richard Petty	160.627	1983	Cale Yarborough	155.979
1967	Mario Andretti	149.926	1984	Cale Yarborough	150.994
1968	Cale Yarborough	143.251	1985	Bill Elliott	172.265
1969	LeeRoy Yarborough	157.950	1986	Geoff Bodine	148.124
1970	Pete Hamilton	149.601	1987	Bill Elliott	176.263
1971	Richard Petty	144.462	1988	Davey Allison	137.531
1972	A. J. Foyt Jr.	161.550	1989	Darrell Waltrip	148.466
1973	Richard Petty	157.205	1990	Derrike Cope	165.761
1974	Richard Petty	140.894	1991	Ernie Irvan	148.148
1975	Benny Parsons	153.649	1992	Davey Allison	160.256

RICHARD PETTY

The 1992 season marked the final spin for NASCAR's most successful driver and its most flamboyant character, "The King"—Richard Petty. The starting line of Petty's NASCAR career was at Toronto, Canada on July 18, 1958, and he took his final checkered flag at Atlanta, Ga., on November 15, 1992. Petty's final race was his 1,185th start, the most of any NASCAR driver. Records are not unusual for Petty; he dominates the NASCAR record book much as he dominated the track, holding numerous records, including most Winston Cup titles, race wins and starts.

DAYTONA 500

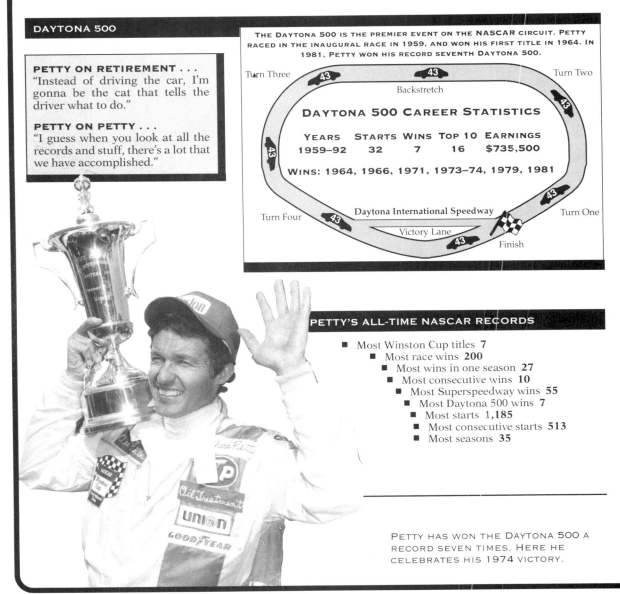

PETTY ON RETIREMENT . . .
"Instead of driving the car, I'm gonna be the cat that tells the driver what to do."

PETTY ON PETTY . . .
"I guess when you look at all the records and stuff, there's a lot that we have accomplished."

THE DAYTONA 500 IS THE PREMIER EVENT ON THE NASCAR CIRCUIT. PETTY RACED IN THE INAUGURAL RACE IN 1959, AND WON HIS FIRST TITLE IN 1964. IN 1981, PETTY WON HIS RECORD SEVENTH DAYTONA 500.

Turn Three
Turn Two
Backstretch

DAYTONA 500 CAREER STATISTICS

YEARS	STARTS	WINS	TOP 10	EARNINGS
1959–92	32	7	16	$735,500

WINS: 1964, 1966, 1971, 1973–74, 1979, 1981

Daytona International Speedway

Turn Four
Turn One
Victory Lane
Finish

PETTY'S ALL-TIME NASCAR RECORDS

- Most Winston Cup titles **7**
- Most race wins **200**
- Most wins in one season **27**
- Most consecutive wins **10**
- Most Superspeedway wins **55**
- Most Daytona 500 wins **7**
- Most starts **1,185**
- Most consecutive starts **513**
- Most seasons **35**

PETTY HAS WON THE DAYTONA 500 A RECORD SEVEN TIMES. HERE HE CELEBRATES HIS 1974 VICTORY.

SOURCES: ■ NASCAR, RICHARD PETTY 1992 FAN APPRECIATION TOUR GUIDE.

NASCAR CAREER STATISTICS, 1958–92

Year	Races	Wins	Earnings $
1958	9	0	760
1959	22	0	7,630
1960	40	3	35,180
1961	42	2	22,696
1962	52	8	52,885
1963	54	14	47,765
1964†	61	9	98,810
1965	14	4	16,450
1966	39	8	78,930
1967†	48	27*	130,275
1968	49	16	89,103
1969	50	10	109,180
1970	40	18	138,969
1971†	46	21	309,225
1972†	31	8	227,015
1973	28	6	159,655
1974†	30	10	299,175
1975†	30	13	378,865
1976	30	3	338,265
1977	30	5	345,886
1978	30	0	215,491
1979†	31	5	531,292
1980	31	2	374,092
1981	31	3	389,214
1982	30	0	453,832
1983	30	3	491,122
1984	30	2	251,226
1985	28	0	306,142
1986	29	0	280,657
1987	29	0	468,602
1988	29	0	190,155
1989	25	0	133,050

RICHARD PETTY IS THE MOST SUCCESSFUL DRIVER IN NASCAR HISTORY, HAVING WON THE MOST RACES, 200, AND THE MOST WINSTON CUP TITLES, 7.

Year	Races	Wins	Earnings $
1990	29	0	169,465
1991	29	0	268,035
1992	33	0	348,870
Totals	1,185*	200*	7,757,964

* NASCAR record

† Winston Cup Series winner

CONSECUTIVE WIN STREAK

From August 12 through October 1, 1967, Petty won a record 10 consecutive Winston Cup races.

	Venue	Date	Races
❶	Winston-Salem, N.C.	August 12	Myers Bros. Memorial
❷	Columbia, S.C.	August 17	Race #38
❸	Savannah, Ga.	August 25	Race #39
❹	Darlington, S.C.	September 4	Southern 500
❺	Hickory, N.C.	September 8	Buddy Shuman Memorial
❻	Richmond, Va.	September 10	Capital City 300
❼	Beltsville, Md.	September 15	Maryland 300
❽	Hillsborough, N.C.	September 17	Hillsborough 150
❾	Martinsville, Va.	September 24	Old Dominion 500
❿	North Wilkesboro, N.C.	October 1	Wilkes 400

VICTORY LANE

Most championships Juan-Manuel Fangio (Argentina) has won the drivers' championship five times, 1951 and 1954–57. He also holds the record for consecutive titles with four straight, 1954–57.

Oldest champion Juan-Manuel Fangio is the oldest world champion, winning the 1957 title at age 46 years 41 days.

Youngest champion Emerson Fittipaldi (Brazil) became the youngest champion in 1972, at age 25 years 273 days.

Most wins (career) Alain Prost (France) has won 44 Formula One races, the most of any driver.

Most wins (season) Nigel Mansell (Great Britain) won a record nine races in 1992. His victories came in South Africa, Mexico, Brazil, Spain, San Marino, France, Great Britain, Germany and Portugal.

Oldest winner The oldest driver to win an official race was Luigi Fagioli (Italy), who was 53 years 22 days old when he won the 1951 French Grand Prix.

Youngest winner The youngest driver to win an official race was Troy Ruttman, who was 22 years 2 months old when he won the 1952 Indianapolis 500, which counted in the World Drivers' Championship that year.

Closest finish The narrowest margin of victory in a Formula One race was when Ayrton Senna (Brazil) held off Nigel Mansell by 0.014 seconds to win the Spanish Grand Prix on April 13, 1986.

United States Two Americans have won the Formula One title—Phil Hill in 1961 and Mario Andretti in 1978.

QUALIFYING

Most starts Riccardo Patrese (Italy) has raced in a record 240 Grand Prix races from 1977–92.

Most poles Ayrton Senna has earned a record 61 poles in 142 races, 1985–92.

Fastest qualifying time Keke Rosberg (Finland) set the fastest qualifying lap in Formula One history, when he qualified for the British Grand Prix at Silverstone with an average speed of 160.817 mph on July 20, 1985.

DRAG RACING

Drag racing is an acceleration contest between two cars racing from a standing start over a precisely measured, straight-line, quarter-mile course. Competition is based on two-car elimination heats culminating in a final round. The fastest elapsed time wins the race. Elapsed time is measured over the distance of the course; the top speed is a measurement of the last 66 feet of the track, where a special speed trap electronically computes the speed of the dragster. There are several classifications in drag racing, based on the engine size, type of fuel and vehicle weight limitations of the car. The most prominent drag racing organization is the National Hot Rod Association (NHRA), which was founded in 1951. The NHRA recognizes 12 categories of racers, with the three main categories being Top Fuel, Funny Car and Pro Stock.

TOP FUEL

Top Fuel dragsters are 4,000-horsepower machines that are powered by nitromethane. The engines are mounted behind the driver, and parachutes are the primary braking system.

SPEED RECORDS

Quickest elapsed time in an NHRA event The quickest elapsed time recorded by a Top Fuel dragster from a standing start for 440 yards is 4.779 seconds by Eddie Hill at the Winston National Finals at Pomona, Calif., on October 29, 1992.

Fastest top speed in an NHRA event The fastest speed recorded in a Top Fuel race is 301.70 mph by Kenny Bernstein on March 20, 1992 at the Motorcraft Gatornationals, Gainesville, Fla.

VICTORIES

Most wins (career) Don Garlits has won a record 35 Top Fuel races (1975–92).

Most wins (season) Five drivers have won six Top Fuel races in a season: Don Garlits, 1985; Darrel Gwynn, 1988; Gary Ormsby, 1989; Joe Amato, 1990; and Kenny Bernstein, 1991.

FUNNY CAR

A Funny Car is a short-wheelbase version of the Top Fuel dragster. Funny Cars mount a fiberglass

VROOM ■ ON MARCH 20, 1992, KENNY BERNSTEIN BECAME THE FIRST DRAG RACER TO BREAK THE 300 MPH BARRIER. HE RECORDED A SPEED OF 301.70 MPH.

replica of a production car with the engine located in front of the driver.

SPEED RECORDS

Quickest elapsed time in an NHRA event The quickest elapsed time recorded in the Funny Car class is 5.076 seconds, by Cruz Pedregon on September 20, 1992 at the Sunoco Keystone Nationals, Mohnton, Pa.

Fastest top speed in an NHRA event Mark Oswald was timed at 293.06 mph at the Winston National Finals at Pomona Raceway, Calif. on October 18, 1992.

VICTORIES

Most wins (career) Don Prudhomme has won a record 35 Funny Car races (1975–89).

Most wins (season) Two drivers have won seven races in a season: Don Prudhomme in 1976, and Kenny Bernstein in 1985.

PRO STOCK

Pro Stock dragsters look like their oval-racing counterparts, but feature extensive engine modifications. A maximum 500-cubic-inch displacement

and a minimum vehicle weight of 2,350 pounds are allowed under NHRA rules.

SPEED RECORDS

Quickest elapsed time in an NHRA event The quickest elapsed time in the Pro Stock class is 7.099 seconds by Scott Geoffrion on September 19, 1992 at the Sunoco Keystone Nationals, Mohnton, Pa.

Fastest top speed in an NHRA event The fastest speed in a Pro Stock race is 194.51 mph by Warren Johnson on July 31, 1992 at the Autolite California Nationals, Sonoma, Calif.

VICTORIES

Most wins (career) Bob Glidden has won a record 81 races (1972–92), the most victories of any driver in NHRA events.

Most wins (season) Darrell Alderman won a record 11 races in 1991.

NHRA WINSTON DRAG RACING SERIES The NHRA World Championship Series was inaugurated in 1951. Since 1975 the series has been known as the NHRA Winston Drag Racing Series.

MOST TITLES

Top Fuel Joe Amato has won a record four national titles: 1984, 1988 and 1990–91.

Funny Car Two drivers have won a record four national titles: Don Prudhomme, 1975–78, and Kenny Bernstein, 1985–88.

Pro Stock Bob Glidden has won a record 10 national titles, in 1974–75, 1978–80 and 1985–89.

BADMINTON

ORIGINS Badminton is a descendant of the children's game of battledore and shuttlecock. It is believed that a similar game was played in China more than 2,000 years ago. Badminton takes its name from Badminton House in England, where the Duke of Beaufort's family and guests popularized the game in the 19th century. British army officers took the game to India in the 1870s, where the first modern rules were codified in 1876. The world governing body is the International Badminton Federation, formed in 1934.

United States The earliest known reference to badminton in the United States is a description of battledore shuttlecock in the 1864 *American Boy's Book of Sports and Games*. The first badminton club formed in the United States was the Badminton Club of New York, founded in 1878. The game was not organized at the national level until 1935, when the American Badminton Association (ABA) was founded in Boston, Mass. In 1978 the ABA was renamed the United States Badminton Association.

OLYMPIC GAMES Badminton was included in the Olympic Games as an official sport for the first time at the Barcelona Games in 1992. The game was included as a demonstration sport at the Munich Games in 1972.

Most medals No player in Barcelona won more than one medal. The four gold medals awarded were shared equally between players from Indonesia and South Korea.

WORLD CHAMPIONSHIPS The first championships were staged in Malmo, Sweden in 1977. Since 1983 the event has been held biennially.

Most titles (overall) Park Joo-bong (South Korea) has won a record five world titles: men's doubles in 1985 and 1991; mixed doubles in 1985, 1989 and 1991. Two women have won three titles: Lin Ying (China), ladies' doubles 1983, 1987 and 1989; Li Lingwei (China), ladies' singles in 1983 and 1989, ladies' doubles in 1985.

Most titles (singles) Yang Yang (China) is the only man to have won two world singles titles, in 1987 and 1989. Two women have won two singles titles: Li Lingwei (China), 1983 and 1989; Han Aiping (China), 1985 and 1987.

UNITED STATES NATIONAL CHAMPIONSHIPS The first competition was held in 1937.

Most titles Judy Hashman (née Devlin) has won a record 31 titles: 12 women's singles, 1954, 1956–63 and 1965–67; 12 women's doubles, 1953–55, 1957–63 and 1966–67 (10 with her sister Susan); and seven mixed doubles, 1956–59, 1961–62 and 1967. David G. Freeman has won a record seven men's singles titles: 1939–42, 1947–48 and 1953.

BASEBALL

ORIGINS In 1907, baseball's national commission appointed a committee to research the history of the game. The report, filed in 1908, concluded that Abner Doubleday had invented the game in 1839 at Cooperstown, N.Y. At the time, the report was viewed with some skepticism because of the friendship between Doubleday and the committee chairman, A. G. Mills; however, in 1939, major league baseball celebrated its centennial and cemented the legend of Doubleday's efforts in American folklore. Sports historians today discount the Doubleday theory, claiming that baseball in North America evolved from such English games as cricket, paddleball and rounders.

TIMEOUT

WINNING STREAK ☛ BADMINTON'S LONGEST WINNING STREAK IS HELD BY MILLER PLACE HIGH SCHOOL, N.Y. THE TEAM HAS BEEN UNBEATEN SINCE MARCH 1973. AT THE END OF THE 1992 SEASON THE TEAM HAD WON 304 CONSECUTIVE GAMES.

Uncontested is that Alexander Cartwright Jr. formulated the rules of the modern game in 1845, and that the first match under these rules was played on June 19, 1846 when the New York Nine defeated the New York Knickerbockers, 23–1, in four innings. On March 17, 1871 the National Association of Professional Base Ball Players was formed, the first professional league in the United States. Today there are two main professional baseball associations, the National League (organized in 1876) and the American League (organized in 1901, recognized in 1903), which together form the major leagues, along with approximately 20 associations that make up the minor leagues. The champions of the two leagues first played a World Series in 1903 and have played one continuously since 1905. (For further details on World Series history, see page 28.)

MAJOR LEAGUE RECORDS

Records listed in this section are for the all-time major league record. Where an all-time record is dated prior to 1900, the modern record (1900–present) is also listed.

GAMES PLAYED

Career 3,562, by Pete Rose, Cincinnati Reds (NL), 1963–78, 1984–86; Philadelphia Phillies (NL), 1979–83; Montreal Expos (NL), 1984.

HIT LEADER ■ PETE ROSE SINGLES OFF ERIC SHOW FOR HIT NUMBER 4,192, BREAKING TY COBB'S ALL-TIME HIT RECORD. ROSE LATER EXTENDED THE RECORD TO 4,256 HITS.

Consecutive 2,130, by Lou Gehrig, New York Yankees (AL), June 1, 1925 through April 30, 1939.

BATTING RECORDS

BATTING AVERAGE

Career .367, by Ty Cobb, Detroit Tigers (AL), 1905–26; Philadelphia Athletics (AL), 1927–28. Cobb compiled his record from 4,191 hits in 11,429 at-bats.

Season .438, by Hugh Duffy, Boston (American Association) in 1894. Duffy compiled 236 hits in 539 at-bats. The modern record is .424, by Rogers Hornsby, St. Louis Cardinals (NL), in 1924. Hornsby compiled 227 hits in 536 at-bats.

HITS

Career 4,256, by Pete Rose, Cincinnati Reds (NL), 1963–78, 1984–86; Philadelphia Phillies (NL), 1979–83; Montreal Expos (NL), 1984. Rose compiled his record hits total from 14,053 at-bats.

Season 257, by George Sisler, St. Louis Browns (AL), in 1920, from 631 at-bats.

Game Nine, by John Burnett, Cleveland Indians (AL), during an 18-inning game on July 10, 1932. The record for a nine-inning game is seven hits, by two players: Wilbert Robinson, Baltimore Orioles (NL), on June 10, 1892; Rennie Stennett, Pittsburgh Pirates (NL), on September 16, 1975.

SINGLES

Career 3,215, by Pete Rose, Cincinnati Reds (NL), 1963–78, 1984–86; Philadelphia Phillies, 1979–83, Montreal Expos, 1984.

TIMEOUT

BIGGEST SLUGGER ☛ THE LARGEST BASEBALL BAT CARVED FROM WOOD IS 5 FEET 8¼ INCHES LONG, 22¾ INCHES WIDE AND WEIGHS 57½ LB. OWNED BY STEPHEN KOSCHAL OF BOYNTON BEACH, FLA., THE BAT TOOK THREE MONTHS TO CARVE AND ORIGINALLY WEIGHED MORE THAN 100 LBS.

Season 206, by Wee Willie Keeler, Baltimore Orioles (NL) in 1898. The modern-day record is 198, by Lloyd Waner, Pittsburgh Pirates, in 1927.

Game Seven, by John Burnett, Cleveland Indians (AL), in an 18-inning game on July 10, 1932. In regulation play the record for both the National and American leagues is six hits by several players.

DOUBLES

Career 793, by Tris Speaker, Boston Red Sox (AL), 1907–1915; Cleveland Indians (AL), 1916–1926; Washington Senators (AL), 1927; Philadelphia Athletics (AL), 1928.

Season 67, by Earl Webb, Boston Red Sox (AL), in 1931.

Game Four, by many players in both leagues.

TRIPLES

Career 312, by Sam Crawford, Cincinnati Reds (NL), 1899–1902; Detroit Tigers (AL), 1903–17.

Season 36, by Owen Wilson, Pittsburgh Pirates (NL), in 1912.

Game Four, by two players: George A. Strief, Philadelphia (American Association) on June 25, 1885; William Joyce, New York Giants (NL) on May 18, 1897. The modern-day record for both leagues is three, achieved by several players.

HOME RUNS

Career 755, by Hank Aaron, Milwaukee/Atlanta Braves (NL), 1954–74; Milwaukee Brewers (AL), 1975–76. Aaron hit his record dingers from 12,364 at-bats.

Season 61, Roger Maris, New York Yankees (AL), in 1961.

LONGEST HOME RUN ☞ THE LONGEST MEASURED HOME RUN IN A MAJOR LEAGUE GAME WAS A 573-FOOT SHOT BY DAVE NICHOLSON, CHICAGO WHITE SOX (AL) V. KANSAS CITY ATHLETICS ON MAY 6, 1964 AT COMISKEY PARK.

SLUGGER ■ THE WORLD'S LARGEST CARVED WOODEN BASEBALL BAT MEASURES 5 FEET 8¼ INCHES AND IS SIGNED BY ALL LIVING MEMBERS OF THE HALL OF FAME.

Game Four, by 11 players: Bobby Lowe, Boston (NL), May 30, 1894; Ed Delahanty, Philadelphia Phillies (NL), July 13, 1896; Lou Gehrig, New York Yankees (AL), June 3, 1932; Chuck Klein, Philadelphia Phillies (NL), July 10, 1936; Pat Seerey, Chicago White Sox (AL), July 18, 1948; Gil Hodges, Brooklyn Dodgers (NL), August 31, 1950; Joe Adcock, Milwaukee Braves (NL), July 31, 1954; Rocky Colavito, Cleveland Indians (AL), June 10, 1959; Willie Mays, San Francisco Giants (NL), April 30, 1961; Mike Schmidt, Philadelphia Phillies (NL), April 17, 1976; and Bob Horner, Atlanta Braves, July 6, 1986. Klein, Schmidt and Seerey matched the record in extra-inning games.

GRAND SLAMS

Career 23, by Lou Gehrig, New York Yankees (AL), 1923–39.

Season Six, by Don Mattingly, New York Yankees (AL), in 1987.

Game Two, by seven players: Tony Lazzeri, New York Yankees (AL), May 24, 1936; Jim Tabor, Boston Red Sox (AL), July 4, 1939; Rudy York,

Boston Red Sox (AL), July 27, 1946; Jim Gentile, Baltimore Orioles (AL), May 9, 1961; Tony Cloninger, Atlanta Braves (NL), July 3, 1966; Jim Northrup, Detroit Tigers (AL), June 24, 1968; and Frank Robinson, Baltimore Orioles (AL), June 26, 1970. Cloninger is the only player from the National League to achieve this feat, and he was a pitcher!

RUNS BATTED IN

Career 2,297, by Hank Aaron, Milwaukee/Atlanta Braves (NL), 1954–74; Milwaukee Brewers (AL), 1975–76.

Season 190, by Hack Wilson, Chicago Cubs (NL), in 1930.

Game 12, by Jim Bottomley, St. Louis Cardinals (NL), on September 16, 1924.

RUNS SCORED

Career 2,245, by Ty Cobb, Detroit Tigers (AL), 1905–26; Philadelphia Athletics (AL), 1927–28.

Season 196, by Billy Hamilton, Philadelphia Phillies (NL), in 1894. The modern-day record is 177 runs, scored by Babe Ruth, New York Yankees (AL), in 1921.

Game Seven, by Guy Hecker, Louisville (American Association), on August 15, 1886. The modern-day record is six runs scored, achieved by 12 players, 10 in the National League and two in the American League.

TOTAL BASES

Career 6,856, by Hank Aaron, Milwaukee/Atlanta Braves (NL), 1954–74; Milwaukee Brewers (AL), 1975–76. Aaron's record is comprised of 2,294 singles, 624 doubles, 98 triples and 755 home runs.

Season 457, by Babe Ruth, New York Yankees (AL) in 1921. Ruth's total comprised 85 singles, 44 doubles, 16 triples and 59 home runs.

Game 18, by Joe Adcock, Milwaukee Braves (NL) on July 31, 1954. Adcock hit four home runs and a double.

WALKS

Career 2,056, by Babe Ruth, Boston Red Sox (AL), 1914–19; New York Yankees (AL), 1920–34; Boston Braves (NL), 1935.

Season 170, by Babe Ruth, New York Yankees (AL) in 1923.

STRIKEOUTS

Career 2,597, by Reggie Jackson, Kansas City/Oakland Athletics (AL), 1967–75, 1987; Baltimore Orioles (AL), 1976; New York Yankees (AL), 1977–81; California Angels (AL), 1982–86.

Season 189, by Bobby Bonds, San Francisco Giants (NL), in 1970.

HIT BY PITCH

Career 267, by Don Baylor, Baltimore Orioles (AL), 1970–75; Oakland Athletics (AL), 1976, 1988; California Angels (AL), 1977–82; New York Yankees (AL), 1983–85; Boston Red Sox (AL), 1986–87; Minnesota Twins (AL), 1987.

Season 50, by Ron Hunt, Montreal Expos (NL) in 1971.

CONSECUTIVE BATTING RECORDS

Hits in a row 12, by two players: Pinky Higgins, Boston Red Sox (AL), over four games, June 19–21, 1938; and Moose Droppo, Detroit Tigers (AL), over three games, July 14–15, 1952.

Games batted safely 56, by Joe DiMaggio, New York Yankees (AL), May 15 through July 16, 1941. During the streak, DiMaggio gained 91 hits from 223 at-bats: 56 singles, 16 doubles, 4 triples and 15 home runs.

Home runs in a row Four, by four players: Bobby Lowe, Boston (NL), May 30, 1894; Lou Gehrig, New York Yankees (AL), June 3, 1932; Rocky Colavito, Cleveland Indians (AL), June 10, 1959; and Mike Schmidt, Philadelphia Phillies (NL), April 17, 1976.

Games hitting home runs Eight, by two players: Dale Long, Pittsburgh Pirates (NL), May 19–28, 1956; Don Mattingly, New York Yankees (AL), July 8–18, 1987.

Walks in a row Seven, by three players: Billy Rogell, Detroit Tigers (AL), August 17–19, 1938; Mel Ott, New York Giants (NL), June 16–18, 1943; Eddie Stanky, New York Giants (NL), August 29–30, 1950.

Games receiving a walk 22, by Roy Cullenbine, Detroit Tigers (AL), July 2 through July 22, 1947.

PITCHING RECORDS

GAMES PLAYED

Career 1,070, by Hoyt Wilhelm, New York Giants (NL), 1952–56; St. Louis Cardinals (NL), 1957;

NOLAN RYAN

The "Ryan Express" has toured the national pastime for 26 seasons. It has taken in the skyscrapers of New York, the sunshine of southern California and the Texas prairies, and along the way has picked up many of baseball's prized souvenirs: a World Series in 1969, a 300th win in 1990 and numerous major league records. Nolan Ryan won his first major league game on April 14, 1968 and his 319th in 1992. His blazing fastball, "the Ryan Express," has been his trademark. Ryan is baseball's strikeout leader, counting among his victims seven pairs of fathers and sons, 12 pairs of brothers, and Claudell Washington 39 times. While Ryan's fastball has awed batters, his endurance has also earned him a niche in baseball folklore. He struck out his 5,000th batter at age 42, won his 300th game at 43, and pitched his seventh no-hitter at 44. The final stop in this journey will undoubtedly be the Baseball Hall of Fame in Cooperstown, N.Y.

RYAN'S MAJOR LEAGUE RECORDS

STRIKEOUTS
- Most in a career **5,668**
- Most in a season **383**
- Avg. per 9 innings, career **9.59**
- Avg. per 9 innings, season **11.48**
- 10 or more in a game **215**
- Most years, 300 or more **6**
- Most years, 200 or more **15**
- Most years, 100+ strikeouts **24**

NO-HIT AND LOW-HIT GAMES
- Most no-hitters, career **7**
- Most no-hitters, season **2†**
- Most one-hitters, career **12†**

OTHER RECORDS
- Most walks, career **2,755**
- Most wild pitches **274**

† Tied record

RYAN STRUCK OUT A MODERN-DAY RECORD 383 BATTERS IN 1973 WHILE PITCHING FOR THE CALIFORNIA ANGELS.

STRIKEOUTS PER SEASON

In 1992 Ryan whiffed, fanned or plain struck out 157 batters to extend his career record total to 5,668.

Year	Strikeouts	Year	Strikeouts
1966	6	1980	200
1967	—	1981	140
1968	133	1982	245
1969	92	1983	183
1970	125	1984	197
1971	137	1985	209
1972	329	1986	194
1973	383	1987	270
1974	367	1988	228
1975	186	1989	301
1976	327	1990	232
1977	341	1991	203
1978	260	1992	157
1979	223		

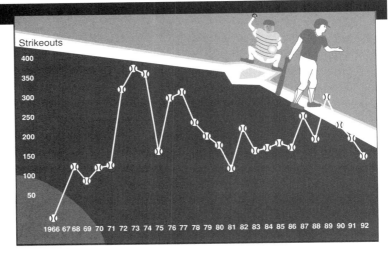

SOURCES: ■ TEXAS RANGERS, 1992 MEDIA GUIDE, THE BASEBALL ENCYCLOPEDIA.

Teams: New York Mets (NL), 1966–71; California Angels (AL), 1972–79; Houston Astros (NL), 1980–88; Texas Rangers (AL), 1989–92.

Year	W–L	ERA	G	CG	ShO	IP	H	BB	SO
1966	0–1	15.00	2	0	0	3.0	5	3	6
1968	6–9	3.09	21	3	0	134.0	93	75	133
1969	6–3	3.53	25	2	0	89.1	60	53	92
1970	7–11	3.41	27	5	2	132.0	86	97	125
1971	10–14	3.97	30	3	0	152.0	125	116	137
1972	19–16	2.28	39	20	9	284.0	166	157	329
1973	21–16	2.87	41	26	4	326.0	238	162	383†
1974	22–16	2.89	42	26	3	333.0	221	202	367
1975	14–12	3.45	28	10	5	198.0	152	132	186
1976	17–18	3.36	39	21	7	284.0	193	183	327
1977	19–16	2.77	37	22	4	299.0	198	204	341
1978	10–13	3.71	31	14	3	235.0	183	148	260
1979	16–14	3.59	34	17	5	223.0	169	114	223
1980	11–10	3.35	35	4	2	234.0	205	98	200
1981	11–5	1.69	21	5	3	149.0	99	68	140
1982	16–12	3.16	35	10	3	250.1	196	109	245
1983	14–9	2.98	29	5	2	196.1	134	101	183
1984	12–11	3.04	30	5	2	183.2	143	69	197
1985	10–12	3.80	35	4	0	232.0	205	95	209
1986	12–8	3.34	30	1	0	178.0	119	82	194
1987	8–16	2.76	34	0	0	211.2	154	87	270
1988	12–11	3.52	33	4	1	220.0	186	87	228
1989	16–10	3.20	32	6	2	239.1	162	98	301
1990	13–9	3.44	30	5	2	204.0	137	74	232
1991	12–6	2.91	27	2	2	173.0	102	72	203
1992	5–9	3.72	27	2	0	157.1	138	69	157
Totals	**319–287**	**3.17**	**794**	**222**	**61**	**5,321.0**	**3,869**	**2,755†**	**5,668†**

† Major league record

ON MAY 1, 1991 RYAN EXTENDED HIS ALL-TIME NO-HITTERS PITCHED RECORD TO SEVEN GAMES. AT AGE 44 YEARS, 3 MONTHS, 1 DAY HE ALSO BECAME THE OLDEST MAN TO THROW A NO-HITTER.

LEAGUE CHAMPIONSHIP SERIES

Teams: New York Mets, 1969; California Angels, 1979; Houston Astros, 1980, 1986

Year	W–L	ERA	G	CG	ShO	IP	H	BB	SO
1969	1–0	2.57	1	0	0	7.0	3	2	7
1979	0–0	1.29	1	0	0	7.0	4	3	8
1980	0–0	5.40	2	0	0	13.1	16	3	14
1986	0–1	3.86	2	0	0	14.0	9	1	17
Totals	**1–1**	**3.70**	**6**	**0**	**0**	**41.1**	**32**	**9**	**46†**

† Major league record (tied)

WORLD SERIES

Team: New York Mets, 1969

Year	W–L	ERA	G	CG	ShO	IP	H	BB	SO
1969	0–0	0.00	1	0	0	2.1	1	2	3

NO-HIT GAMES

Nolan Ryan pitched his first no-hitter for the California Angels *v.* Kansas City on May 15, 1973. His seventh no-hitter was pitched in his home state, Texas, playing for the Rangers *v.* Toronto on May 1, 1991. On this occasion Ryan also became the oldest man to throw a no-hitter: 44 years, 3 months, 1 day. Other no-hitter records held by Ryan are: pitching for three different teams—California (AL), Houston (NL) and Texas (AL); three different decades—1970s, 1980s and 1990s; and longest span between no-hitters—8 years, 8 months, 16 days.

Date	Game	Score
May 15, 1973	California at Kansas City	3–0
July 15, 1973	California at Detroit	6–0
Sept. 28, 1974	California *v.* Minnesota	4–0
June 1, 1975	California *v.* Baltimore	1–0
Sept. 26, 1981	Houston *v.* Los Angeles	5–0
June 11, 1990	Texas at Oakland	5–0
May 1, 1991	Texas *v.* Toronto	3–0

Cleveland Indians (AL), 1957–58; Baltimore Orioles (AL), 1958–62; Chicago White Sox (AL), 1963–68; California Angels (AL), 1969; Atlanta Braves (NL), 1969–70; Chicago Cubs (NL), 1970; Atlanta Braves (NL), 1971; Los Angeles Dodgers (NL), 1971–72.

Season 106, by Mike Marshall, Los Angeles Dodgers (NL), in 1974.

VICTORIES

Career 511, by Cy Young, Cleveland Spiders (NL), 1890–98; St. Louis Cardinals (NL), 1899–1900; Boston Red Sox (AL), 1901–08; Cleveland Indians (AL), 1909–11; Boston Braves (NL), 1911.

Season 60, by "Old Hoss" Radbourn, Providence Grays (NL), in 1884. The modern-day record is 41, by Jack Chesbro, New York Yankees (AL), in 1904.

LOSSES

Career 313, by Cy Young, Cleveland Spiders (NL), 1890–98; St. Louis Cardinals (NL), 1899–1900; Boston Red Sox (AL), 1901–08; Cleveland Indians (AL), 1909–11; Boston Braves (NL), 1911.

Season 48, by John Coleman, Philadelphia Phillies (NL), in 1883. The modern-day record is 29, by Vic Willis, Boston Braves (NL), in 1905.

EARNED RUN AVERAGE (ERA)

Career (min. 2,000 innings) 1.82, by Ed Walsh, Chicago White Sox (AL), 1904–16; Boston Braves (NL), 1917.

Season (min. 200 innings) 1.01, by Dutch Leonard, Boston Red Sox (AL), in 1914.

INNINGS PITCHED

Career 7,356, by Cy Young, Cleveland Spiders (NL), 1890–98; St. Louis Cardinals (NL), 1899–1900; Boston Red Sox (AL), 1901–08; Cleveland Indians (AL), 1909–11; Boston Braves (NL), 1911.

Season 680, by Will White, Cincinnati Reds (NL), in 1879. The modern-day record is 464, by Ed Walsh, Chicago White Sox (AL), in 1908.

NO-HITTERS

On September 4, 1991, baseball's Committee for Statistical Accuracy defined a no-hit game as "one in which a pitcher or pitchers complete a game of nine innings or more without allowing a hit." All previously considered no-hit games that did not fit into this definition—such as rain-shortened games; eight-inning, complete game no-hitters hurled by losing pitchers; and games in which hits were recorded in the tenth inning or later—would be considered "notable achievements," not no-hitters.

The first officially recognized no-hitter was pitched by Joe Borden for Philadelphia of the National Association v. Chicago on July 28, 1875. Through the 1992 season 235 no-hitters have been pitched. The most no-hitters pitched in one season is seven, on two occasions: 1990 and 1991.

Career Seven, by Nolan Ryan: California Angels v. Kansas City Royals (3–0), on May 15, 1973; California Angels v. Detroit Tigers (6–0), on July 15, 1973; California Angels v. Minnesota Twins (4–0), on September 28, 1974; California Angels v. Baltimore Orioles (1–0), on June 1, 1975; Houston Astros v. Los Angeles Dodgers (5–0), on September 26, 1981; Texas Rangers v. Oakland Athletics (5–0), on June 11, 1990; and Texas Rangers v. Toronto Blue Jays (3–0), on May 1, 1991.

Season Two, by four players: Johnny Vander Meer, Cincinnati Reds (NL), in 1938; Allie Reynolds, New York Yankees (AL), in 1951; Virgil Trucks, Detroit Tigers (AL) in 1952; and Nolan Ryan, California Angels (AL), in 1973.

PERFECT GAMES

In a perfect game, no batter reaches base during a complete game of at least nine innings.

The first officially recognized perfect game was hurled by John Richmond on June 12, 1880 for Worcester v. Cleveland in a National League game. Through the 1991 season there have been 14 perfect games pitched: Richmond (see above); John Ward, Providence v. Buffalo (NL), June 17, 1880; Cy Young, Boston Red Sox v. Philadelphia Athletics (AL), May 5, 1904; Addie Joss, Cleveland Indians v. Chicago White Sox (AL), October 2, 1908; Ernie Shore, Boston Red Sox v. Washington Senators (AL), June 23, 1917; Charlie Robertson, Chicago White Sox v. Detroit Tigers (AL), April 30, 1922; Don Larsen, New York Yankees v. Brooklyn Dodgers (World Series game), October 8, 1956; Jim Bunning, Philadelphia Phillies v. New York Mets (NL), June 21, 1964; Sandy Koufax, Los Angeles Dodgers v. Chicago Cubs (NL), September 9, 1965; Catfish Hunter, Oakland Athletics v. Minnesota Twins (AL), May 8, 1968; Len Barker, Cleveland Indians v. Toronto Blue Jays (AL), May 15, 1981; Mike Witt, California Angels v. Texas

Rangers (AL), September 30, 1984; Tom Browning, Cincinnati Reds v. Los Angeles Dodgers (NL), September 16, 1988; and Dennis Martinez, Montreal Expos v. Los Angeles Dodgers (NL), July 28, 1991.

COMPLETE GAMES

Career 750, by Cy Young, Cleveland Spiders (NL), 1890–98; St. Louis Cardinals (NL), 1899–1900; Boston Red Sox (AL), 1901–08; Cleveland Indians (AL), 1909–11; Boston Braves (NL), 1911. The modern-day record is 531, by Walter Johnson, Washington Senators (AL), 1907–27.

Season 75, by Will White, Cincinnati Reds (NL) in 1879. The modern-day record is 48, by Jack Chesbro, New York Yankees (AL), in 1904.

SHUTOUTS

Career 110, by Walter Johnson, Washington Senators (AL), 1907–27.

Season 16, by two pitchers: George Bradley, St. Louis (NL), in 1876; and Grover Alexander, Philadelphia Phillies (NL), in 1916.

STRIKEOUTS

Career 5,668, by Nolan Ryan, New York Mets (NL), 1966–71; California Angels (AL), 1972–79; Houston Astros (NL), 1980–88; Texas Rangers (AL), 1989–92.

Season 513, by Matt Kilroy, Baltimore (American Association), in 1886. The modern-day record is 383, by Nolan Ryan, California Angels (AL), in 1973.

Game (extra innings) 21, by Tom Cheney, Washington Senators (AL), on September 12, 1962 in a 16-inning game.

Game (nine innings) 20, by Roger Clemens, Boston Red Sox (AL), on April 29, 1986.

WALKS

Career 2,755, by Nolan Ryan, New York Mets (NL), 1966–71; California Angels (AL), 1972–79; Houston Astros (NL), 1980–88; Texas Rangers (AL), 1989–92.

Season 218, by Amos Rusie, New York Giants (NL), in 1893. The modern-day record is 208, by Bob Feller, Cleveland Indians (AL), in 1938.

Game 16, by two pitchers: Bruno Haas, Philadelphia Athletics (AL), on June 23, 1915 in a nine-inning game; Tom Byrne, St. Louis Browns (AL) on August 22, 1951 in a 13-inning game.

SAVES

Career 357, by Jeff Reardon, New York Mets (NL), 1979–81; Montreal Expos (NL), 1981–86; Minnesota Twins (AL), 1987–89; Boston Red Sox (AL), 1990–92; Atlanta Braves (NL), 1992.

Season 57, by Bobby Thigpen, Chicago White Sox (AL), in 1990.

CONSECUTIVE PITCHING RECORDS

Games won 24, by Carl Hubbell, New York Giants (NL), 16 in 1936 and eight in 1937.

Starting assignments 544, by Steve Carlton, from May 15, 1971 through 1986 while playing for four teams: St. Louis Cardinals (NL), Philadelphia Phillies (NL), San Francisco Giants (NL), and Chicago White Sox (AL).

Scoreless innings 59, by Orel Hershiser, Los Angeles Dodgers (NL), from sixth inning, August 30 through tenth inning, September 28, 1988.

No-hitters Two, by Johnny Vander Meer, Cincinnati Reds (NL), on June 11 and June 15, 1938.

Shutouts Six, by Don Drysdale, Los Angeles Dodgers (NL), May 14 through June 4, 1968.

Strikeouts 10, by Tom Seaver, New York Mets (NL) on April 22, 1970.

BASERUNNING

STOLEN BASES

Career 1,042, by Rickey Henderson, Oakland Athletics (AL), 1979–84, 1989–92; New York Yankees (AL), 1985–89.

HEADING FOR HOME ☞ THE FASTEST RECORDED TIME FOR CIRCLING THE BASES IS 13.3 SECONDS, BY ERNIE SWANSON AT COLUMBUS, OHIO IN 1932. SWANSON'S AVERAGE SPEED WAS 18.45 MPH.

Season 130, by Rickey Henderson, Oakland Athletics (AL), in 1982.

Game Seven, by two players: George Gore, Chicago Cubs (NL), on June 25, 1881; Billy Hamilton, Philadelphia Phillies (NL), on August 31, 1894. The modern-day record is six, by two players: Eddie Collins, Philadelphia Athletics (AL), on September 11, 1912; Otis Nixon, Atlanta Braves (NL), on June 17, 1991.

40/40 Club The only player to steal at least 40 bases and hit at least 40 home runs in one season is Jose Canseco, Oakland Athletics (AL), in 1988, when he stole 40 bases and hit 42 home runs.

FIELDING

HIGHEST FIELDING PERCENTAGE

Career .995, by two players: Wes Parker, Los Angeles Dodgers (NL), 1964–72; and Jim Spencer, California Angels (AL), 1968–73; Texas Rangers (AL), 1973–75; Chicago White Sox (AL), 1976–77; New York Yankees (AL), 1978–81; Oakland Athletics (AL), 1981–82. Parker played 1,108 games at first base and 155 in the outfield. Spencer played 1,221 games at first base and 24 in the outfield.

ASSISTS

Career 8,133, by Bill Dahlen, Chicago Cubs (NL), 1891–98; Brooklyn Dodgers (NL), 1899–1903, 1910–11; New York Giants (NL), 1904–07; Boston Braves (NL), 1908–09. Dahlen played 2,132 games at shortstop, 223 at third base, 19 at second base and 58 in the outfield.

MANAGERS

Most games managed 7,755, by Connie Mack, Pittsburgh Pirates (NL), 1894–96; Philadelphia Athletics (AL), 1901–50. Mack's career record was 3,731 wins, 3,948 losses, 75 ties and one no-decision.

Most wins 3,731, by Connie Mack, Pittsburgh Pirates (NL), 1894–96; Philadelphia Athletics (AL), 1901–50.

Most losses 3,948, by Connie Mack, Pittsburgh Pirates (NL), 1894–96; Philadelphia Athletics (AL), 1901–50.

Highest winning percentage .615, by Joe McCarthy, Chicago Cubs (NL), 1926–30; New York Yankees (AL), 1931–46; Boston Red Sox (AL), 1948–50. McCarthy's career record was 2,125 wins, 1,333 losses, 26 ties and three no-decisions.

MISCELLANEOUS

Youngest player The youngest major league player of all time was the Cincinnati Reds (AL) pitcher Joe Nuxhall, who played one game in June 1944, at age 15 years 314 days. He did not play again in the National League until 1952.

Oldest player Satchel Paige pitched for the Kansas City A's (AL) at age 59 years 80 days on September 25, 1965.

Shortest and tallest players The shortest major league player was Eddie Gaedel, a 3-foot-7-inch, 65-pound midget, who pinch-hit for the St. Louis Browns (AL) v. the Detroit Tigers (AL) on August 19, 1951. Wearing number 1/8, the batter with the smallest-ever major league strike zone walked on four pitches. Following the game, major league rules were hastily rewritten to prevent any recurrence. The tallest major leaguer of all time is Randy Johnson, a 6-foot-10-inch pitcher, who played in his first game for the Montreal Expos (NL) on September 15, 1988.

Father and son On August 31, 1990, Ken Griffey Sr. and Ken Griffey Jr., of the Seattle Mariners (AL), became the first father and son to play for the same major league team at the same time. In 1989 the Griffeys had been the first father/son combination to play in the major leagues at the same time. Griffey Sr. played for the Cincinnati Reds (NL) during that season.

Father, son and grandson On August 19, 1992, Bret Boone made his major league debut for the Seattle Mariners (AL), making the Boone family the first three-generation family in major league history. Boone's father Bob Boone played 18 seasons in the majors, 1972–89, and his grandfather Ray Boone played from 1948–60.

Record attendances The all-time season record for attendance for both leagues is 56,813,730, set in 1991 (32,117,558 for the 14-team American League, and 24,696,172 for the 12-team National League). The American League record is 32,117,558, set in 1991; the National League record is 25,324,963, set in 1989. The record for home-team attendance is held by the Toronto Blue Jays (AL) at 4,028,318 in 1992. The National

FIRST FAMILY ■ THE BOONES ARE THE FIRST THREE-GENERATION BASEBALL FAMILY. RAY BOONE (LEFT) PLAYED 13 SEASONS IN THE MAJORS, HIS SON BOB (CENTER) PLAYED 18 SEASONS, AND GRANDSON BRET (RIGHT) MADE HIS DEBUT ON AUGUST 19, 1992.

League record is held by the Los Angeles Dodgers at 3,608,881 in 1982.

Shortest game The New York Giants (NL) beat the Philadelphia Phillies (NL), 6–1, in nine innings in 51 minutes on September 28, 1919.

Longest games The Brooklyn Dodgers (NL) and the Boston Braves (NL) played to a 1–1 tie after 26 innings on May 1, 1920. The Chicago White Sox (AL) played the longest ballgame in elapsed time— 8 hours 6 minutes—before beating the Milwaukee

Brewers, 7–6, in the 25th inning on May 9, 1984 in Chicago. The game started on a Tuesday night and was tied at 3–3 when the 1 A.M. curfew caused suspension until Wednesday night.

The actual longest game was a minor league game in 1981 that lasted 33 innings. At the end of nine innings the score was tied, 1–1, with the Rochester (N.Y.) Red Wings battling the home team Pawtucket (R.I.) Red Sox. At the end of 32 innings the score was still 2–2, when the game was

CHALMERS AWARD (1911–1914)

Most Valuable Player Award (MVP) There have been three different MVP Awards in baseball: the Chalmers Award (1911–14), the League Award (1922–29), and the Baseball Writers' Association of America Award (1931– present).

National League				American League			
Year	Player	Team	Position	Year	Player	Team	Position
1911	Wildfire Schulte	Chicago Cubs	OF	1911	Ty Cobb	Detroit Tigers	OF
1912	Larry Doyle	New York Giants	2B	1912	Tris Speaker	Boston Red Sox	OF
1913	Jake Daubert	Brooklyn Dodgers	1B	1913	Walter Johnson	Washington Senators	P
1914	Johnny Evers	Boston Braves	2B	1914	Eddie Collins	Philadelphia A's	2B

LEAGUE AWARD (1922–1924)

1922	no selection			1922	George Sisler	St. Louis Browns	1B
1923	no selection			1923	Babe Ruth	New York Yankees	OF
1924	Dazzy Vance	Brooklyn Dodgers	P	1924	Walter Johnson	Washington Senators	P

LEAGUE AWARD (1925–1929)

Year	Player (National League)	Team	Position		Year	Player (American League)	Team	Position
1925	Rogers Hornsby	St. Louis Cardinals	2B		1925	Roger Peckinpaugh	Washington Senators	SS
1926	Bob O'Farrell	St. Louis Cardinals	C		1926	George Burns	Cleveland Indians	1B
1927	Paul Waner	Pittsburgh Pirates	OF		1927	Lou Gehrig	New York Yankees	1B
1928	Jim Bottomley	St. Louis Cardinals	1B		1928	Mickey Cochrane	Philadelphia A's	C
1929	Rogers Hornsby	Chicago Cubs	2B		1929	no selection		

BASEBALL WRITERS' AWARD (1931–1952)

Most wins Three, by seven players: Jimmie Foxx, Philadelphia Athletics (AL), 1932–33, 1938; Joe DiMaggio, New York Yankees (AL), 1939, 1941, 1947; Stan Musial, St. Louis Cardinals (NL), 1943, 1946, 1948; Roy Campanella, Brooklyn Dodgers (NL), 1951, 1953, 1955; Yogi Berra, New York Yankees (AL), 1951, 1954–55; Mickey Mantle, New York Yankees (AL), 1956–57, 1962; and Mike Schmidt, Philadelphia Phillies (NL), 1980–81, 1986.
Wins, both leagues Frank Robinson, Cincinnati Reds (NL), in 1961; Baltimore Orioles (AL), in 1966.

Year	Player (National League)	Team	Position		Year	Player (American League)	Team	Position
1931	Frankie Frisch	St. Louis Cardinals	2B		1931	Lefty Grove	Philadelphia A's	P
1932	Chuck Klein	Philadelphia Phillies	OF		1932	Jimmie Foxx	Philadelphia A's	1B
1933	Carl Hubbell	New York Giants	P		1933	Jimmie Foxx	Philadelphia A's	1B
1934	Dizzy Dean	St. Louis Cardinals	P		1934	Mickey Cochrane	Detroit Tigers	C
1935	Gabby Hartnett	Chicago Cubs	C		1935	Hank Greenberg	Detroit Tigers	1B
1936	Carl Hubbell	New York Giants	P		1936	Lou Gehrig	New York Yankees	1B
1937	Joe Medwick	St. Louis Cardinals	OF		1937	Charlie Gehringer	Detroit Tigers	2B
1938	Ernie Lombardi	Cincinnati Reds	C		1938	Jimmie Foxx	Boston Red Sox	1B
1939	Bucky Walters	Cincinnati Reds	P		1939	Joe DiMaggio	New York Yankees	OF
1940	Frank McCormick	Cincinnati Reds	1B		1940	Hank Greenberg	Detroit Tigers	OF
1941	Dolf Camilli	Brooklyn Dodgers	1B		1941	Joe DiMaggio	New York Yankees	OF
1942	Mort Cooper	St. Louis Cardinals	P		1942	Joe Gordon	New York Yankees	2B
1943	Stan Musial	St. Louis Cardinals	OF		1943	Spud Chandler	New York Yankees	P
1944	Marty Marion	St. Louis Cardinals	SS		1944	Hal Newhouser	Detroit Tigers	P
1945	Phil Cavarretta	Chicago Cubs	1B		1945	Hal Newhouser	Detroit Tigers	P
1946	Stan Musial	St. Louis Cardinals	1B–OF		1946	Ted Williams	Boston Red Sox	OF
1947	Bob Elliott	Boston Braves	3B		1947	Joe DiMaggio	New York Yankees	OF
1948	Stan Musial	St. Louis Cardinals	OF		1948	Lou Boudreau	Cleveland Indians	SS
1949	Jackie Robinson	Brooklyn Dodgers	2B		1949	Ted Williams	Boston Red Sox	OF
1950	Jim Konstanty	Philadelphia Phillies	P		1950	Phil Rizzuto	New York Yankees	SS
1951	Roy Campanella	Brooklyn Dodgers	C		1951	Yogi Berra	New York Yankees	C
1952	Hank Sauer	Chicago Cubs	OF		1952	Bobby Shantz	Philadelphia A's	P

BASEBALL WRITERS' AWARD (1953–1987)

National League

Year	Player	Team	Position
1953	Roy Campanella	Brooklyn Dodgers	C
1954	Willie Mays	New York Giants	OF
1955	Roy Campanella	Brooklyn Dodgers	C
1956	Don Newcombe	Brooklyn Dodgers	P
1957	Hank Aaron	Milwaukee Braves	OF
1958	Ernie Banks	Chicago Cubs	SS
1959	Ernie Banks	Chicago Cubs	SS
1960	Dick Groat	Pittsburgh Pirates	SS
1961	Frank Robinson	Cincinnati Reds	OF
1962	Maury Wills	Los Angeles Dodgers	SS
1963	Sandy Koufax	Los Angeles Dodgers	P
1964	Ken Boyer	St. Louis Cardinals	3B
1965	Willie Mays	San Francisco Giants	OF
1966	Roberto Clemente	Pittsburgh Pirates	OF
1967	Orlando Cepeda	St. Louis Cardinals	1B
1968	Bob Gibson	St. Louis Cardinals	P
1969	Willie McCovey	San Francisco Giants	1B
1970	Johnny Bench	Cincinnati Reds	C
1971	Joe Torre	St. Louis Cardinals	3B
1972	Johnny Bench	Cincinnati Reds	C
1973	Pete Rose	Cincinnati Reds	OF
1974	Steve Garvey	Los Angeles Dodgers	1B
1975	Joe Morgan	Cincinnati Reds	2B
1976	Joe Morgan	Cincinnati Reds	2B
1977	George Foster	Cincinnati Reds	OF
1978	Dave Parker	Pittsburgh Pirates	OF
1979	Willie Stargell	Pittsburgh Pirates	1B*
	Keith Hernandez	St. Louis Cardinals	1B*
1980	Mike Schmidt	Philadelphia Phillies	3B
1981	Mike Schmidt	Philadelphia Phillies	3B
1982	Dale Murphy	Atlanta Braves	OF
1983	Dale Murphy	Atlanta Braves	OF
1984	Ryne Sandberg	Chicago Cubs	2B
1985	Willie McGee	St. Louis Cardinals	OF
1986	Mike Schmidt	Philadelphia Phillies	3B
1987	Andre Dawson	Chicago Cubs	OF

American League

Year	Player	Team	Position
1953	Al Rosen	Cleveland Indians	3B
1954	Yogi Berra	New York Yankees	C
1955	Yogi Berra	New York Yankees	C
1956	Mickey Mantle	New York Yankees	OF
1957	Mickey Mantle	New York Yankees	OF
1958	Jackie Jensen	Boston Red Sox	OF
1959	Nellie Fox	Chicago White Sox	2B
1960	Roger Maris	New York Yankees	OF
1961	Roger Maris	New York Yankees	OF
1962	Mickey Mantle	New York Yankees	OF
1963	Elston Howard	New York Yankees	C
1964	Brooks Robinson	Baltimore Orioles	3B
1965	Zoilo Versalles	Minnesota Twins	SS
1966	Frank Robinson	Baltimore Orioles	OF
1967	Carl Yastrzemski	Boston Red Sox	OF
1968	Denny McLain	Detroit Tigers	P
1969	Harmon Killebrew	Minnesota Twins	3–1B
1970	Boog Powell	Baltimore Orioles	1B
1971	Vida Blue	Oakland A's	P
1972	Dick Allen	Chicago White Sox	1B
1973	Reggie Jackson	Oakland A's	OF
1974	Jeff Burroughs	Texas Rangers	OF
1975	Fred Lynn	Boston Red Sox	OF
1976	Thurman Munson	New York Yankees	C
1977	Rod Carew	Minnesota Twins	1B
1978	Jim Rice	Boston Red Sox	OF-DH
1979	Don Baylor	California Angels	OF-DH
1980	George Brett	Kansas City Royals	3B
1981	Rollie Fingers	Milwaukee Brewers	P
1982	Robin Yount	Milwaukee Brewers	SS
1983	Cal Ripken Jr.	Baltimore Orioles	SS
1984	Willie Hernandez	Detroit Tigers	P
1985	Don Mattingly	New York Yankees	1B
1986	Roger Clemens	Boston Red Sox	P
1987	George Bell	Toronto Blue Jays	OF

* Tied vote

BASEBALL WRITERS' AWARD (1988–1992)

National League

Year	Player	Team	Position
1988	Kirk Gibson	Los Angeles Dodgers	OF
1989	Kevin Mitchell	San Francisco Giants	OF
1990	Barry Bonds	Pittsburgh Pirates	OF
1991	Terry Pendleton	Atlanta Braves	3B
1992	Barry Bonds	Pittsburgh Pirates	OF

American League

Year	Player	Team	Position
1988	Jose Canseco	Oakland A's	OF
1989	Robin Yount	Milwaukee Brewers	OF
1990	Rickey Henderson	Oakland A's	OF
1991	Cal Ripken Jr.	Baltimore Orioles	SS
1992	Dennis Eckersley	Oakland A's	P

CY YOUNG AWARD WINNERS (1956–1979)

Inaugurated in 1956, this award is given to the best pitcher in baseball as judged by the Baseball Writers' Association of America. From 1967 on, separate awards have been given to the best pitcher in each league.

Most wins Four, by Steve Carlton, Philadelphia Phillies, 1972, 1977, 1980 and 1982.

Wins, both leagues The only pitcher to win the Cy Young Award in both leagues is Gaylord Perry: Cleveland Indians (AL), 1972; San Diego Padres (NL), 1978.

Year	Pitcher	Team
1956	Don Newcombe	Brooklyn Dodgers (NL)
1957	Warren Spahn	Milwaukee Braves (NL)
1958	Bob Turley	New York Yankees (AL)
1959	Early Wynn	Chicago White Sox (AL)
1960	Vernon Law	Pittsburgh Pirates (NL)
1961	Whitey Ford	New York Yankees (AL)

Year	Pitcher	Team
1962	Don Drysdale	Los Angeles Dodgers (NL)
1963	Sandy Koufax	Los Angeles Dodgers (NL)
1964	Dean Chance	Los Angeles Angels (AL)
1965	Sandy Koufax	Los Angeles Dodgers (NL)
1966	Sandy Koufax	Los Angeles Dodgers (NL)

National League

Year	Pitcher	Team
1967	Mike McCormick	San Francisco Giants
1968	Bob Gibson	St. Louis Cardinals
1969	Tom Seaver	New York Mets
1970	Bob Gibson	St. Louis Cardinals
1971	Ferguson Jenkins	Chicago Cubs
1972	Steve Carlton	Philadelphia Phillies
1973	Tom Seaver	New York Mets
1974	Mike Marshall	Los Angeles Dodgers
1975	Tom Seaver	New York Mets
1976	Randy Jones	San Diego Padres
1977	Steve Carlton	Philadelphia Phillies
1978	Gaylord Perry	San Diego Padres
1979	Bruce Sutter	Chicago Cubs

American League

Year	Pitcher	Team
1967	Jim Lonborg	Boston Red Sox
1968	Denny McLain	Detroit Tigers
1969*	Mike Cuellar / Denny McLain	Baltimore Orioles / Detroit Tigers
1970	Jim Perry	Minnesota Twins
1971	Vida Blue	Oakland Athletics
1972	Gaylord Perry	Cleveland Indians
1973	Jim Palmer	Baltimore Orioles
1974	Jim "Catfish" Hunter	Oakland Athletics
1975	Jim Palmer	Baltimore Orioles
1976	Jim Palmer	Baltimore Orioles
1977	Sparky Lyle	New York Yankees
1978	Ron Guidry	New York Yankees
1979	Mike Flanagan	Baltimore Orioles

CY YOUNG AWARD WINNERS (1980–1992)

National League			American League		
Year	Pitcher	Team	Year	Pitcher	Team
1980	Steve Carlton	Philadelphia Phillies	1980	Steve Stone	Baltimore Orioles
1981	Fernando Valenzuela	Los Angeles Dodgers	1981	Rollie Fingers	Milwaukee Brewers
1982	Steve Carlton	Philadelphia Phillies	1982	Pete Vukovich	Milwaukee Brewers
1983	John Denny	Philadelphia Phillies	1983	LaMarr Hoyt	Chicago White Sox
1984	Rick Sutcliffe	Chicago Cubs	1984	Willie Hernandez	Detroit Tigers
1985	Dwight Gooden	New York Mets	1985	Bret Saberhagen	Kansas City Royals
1986	Mike Scott	Houston Astros	1986	Roger Clemens	Boston Red Sox
1987	Steve Bedrosian	Philadelphia Phillies	1987	Roger Clemens	Boston Red Sox
1988	Orel Hershiser	Los Angeles Dodgers	1988	Frank Viola	Minnesota Twins
1989	Mark Davis	San Diego Padres	1989	Bret Saberhagen	Kansas City Royals
1990	Doug Drabek	Pittsburgh Pirates	1990	Bob Welch	Oakland Athletics
1991	Tom Glavine	Atlanta Braves	1991	Roger Clemens	Boston Red Sox
1992	Greg Maddux	Chicago Cubs	1992	Dennis Eckersley	Oakland Athletics

* Tied vote

suspended. Two months later, play was resumed, and 18 minutes later, Pawtucket scored one run and won.

LEAGUE CHAMPIONSHIP SERIES RECORDS (1969–1992)

GAMES PLAYED

Most series played 11, by Reggie Jackson, Oakland Athletics (AL), 1971–75; New York Yankees (AL), 1977–78, 1980–81; California Angels (AL), 1982, 1986.

Most games played 45, by Reggie Jackson, Oakland Athletics (AL), 1971–75; New York Yankees (AL), 1977–78, 1980–81; California Angels (AL), 1982, 1986.

HITTING RECORDS (CAREER)

Batting average (minimum 50 at-bats) .386, by Mickey Rivers, New York Yankees (AL), 1976–78. Rivers collected 22 hits in 57 at-bats in 14 games.

Hits 45, by Pete Rose, Cincinnati Reds (NL), 1970, 1972–73, 1975–76; Philadelphia Phillies (NL), 1980, 1983.

Home runs Nine, by George Brett, Kansas City Royals (AL), 1976–78, 1980, 1984–85.

Runs batted in (RBIs) 21, by Steve Garvey, Los Angeles Dodgers (NL), 1974, 1977–78, 1981; San Diego Padres (NL), 1984.

Runs scored 22, by George Brett, Kansas City Royals (AL), 1976–78, 1980, 1984–85.

Walks 23, by Joe Morgan, Cincinnati Reds (NL), 1972–73, 1975–76, 1979; Houston Astros (NL), 1980; Philadelphia Phillies (NL), 1983.

Stolen bases 14, by Rickey Henderson, Oakland Athletics (AL), 1981, 1989–90, 1992.

PITCHING RECORDS (CAREER)

Most series pitched Eight, by Bob Welch, Los Angeles Dodgers (NL), 1978, 1981, 1983, 1985; Oakland Athletics (AL), 1988–90, 1992.

Most games pitched 15, by two pitchers: Tug McGraw, New York Mets (NL), 1969, 1973; Philadelphia Phillies (NL), 1976–78, 1980; Dennis Eckersley, Chicago Cubs (NL), 1984; Oakland Athletics (AL), 1988–90, 1992.

Wins Six, by Dave Stewart, Oakland Athletics (AL), 1988–90, 1992.

Losses Seven, by Jerry Reuss, Pittsburgh Pirates (NL), 1974–75; Los Angeles Dodgers (NL), 1981, 1983, 1985.

Innings pitched 69⅓, by Jim "Catfish" Hunter, Oakland Athletics (AL), 1971–74, New York Yankees (AL), 1976, 1978.

Complete games Five, by Jim Palmer, Baltimore Orioles (AL), 1969–71, 1973–74, 1979.

Strikeouts 46, by two players: Nolan Ryan, New York Mets (NL), 1969; California Angels (AL),

1979; Houston Astros (NL), 1980, 1986; and Jim Palmer, Baltimore Orioles (AL), 1969–71, 1973–74, 1979.

Saves 10, by Dennis Eckersley, Chicago Cubs (NL), 1984; Oakland Athletics (AL), 1988–90, 1992.

WORLD SERIES

ORIGINS Played annually between the champions of the National League and the American League, the World Series was first staged unofficially in

---

LEAGUE CHAMPIONSHIP SERIES (1969–1992)

League Championship Series (LCS) playoffs began in 1969 when the American and National Leagues expanded to 12 teams each and created two divisions, East and West. To determine the respective league pennant winners, the division winners played a best-of-five-games series, which was expanded to best-of-seven in 1985.

National League

Year	Winner	Loser	Series
1969	New York Mets (East)	Atlanta Braves (West)	3–0
1970	Cincinnati Reds (West)	Pittsburgh Pirates (East)	3–0
1971	Pittsburgh Pirates (East)	San Francisco Giants (West)	3–1
1972	Cincinnati Reds (West)	Pittsburgh Pirates (East)	3–2
1973	New York Mets (East)	Cincinnati Reds (West)	3–2
1974	Los Angeles Dodgers (West)	Pittsburgh Pirates (East)	3–1
1975	Cincinnati Reds (West)	Pittsburgh Pirates (East)	3–0
1976	Cincinnati Reds (West)	Philadelphia Phillies (East)	3–0
1977	Los Angeles Dodgers (West)	Philadelphia Phillies (East)	3–1
1978	Los Angeles Dodgers (West)	Philadelphia Phillies (East)	3–1
1979	Pittsburgh Pirates (East)	Cincinnati Reds (West)	3–0
1980	Philadelphia Phillies (East)	Houston Astros (West)	3–2
1981	Los Angeles Dodgers (West)	Montreal Expos (East)	3–2
1982	St. Louis Cardinals (East)	Atlanta Braves (West)	3–0
1983	Philadelphia Phillies (East)	Los Angeles Dodgers (West)	3–1
1984	San Diego Padres (West)	Chicago Cubs (East)	3–2
1985	St. Louis Cardinals (East)	Los Angeles Dodgers (West)	4–2
1986	New York Mets (East)	Houston Astros (West)	4–2
1987	St. Louis Cardinals (East)	San Francisco Giants (West)	4–3
1988	Los Angeles Dodgers (West)	New York Mets (East)	4–3
1989	San Francisco Giants (West)	Chicago Cubs (East)	4–1
1990	Cincinnati Reds (West)	Pittsburgh Pirates (East)	4–2
1991	Atlanta Braves (West)	Pittsburgh Pirates (East)	4–3
1992	Atlanta Braves (West)	Pittsburgh Pirates (East)	4–3

1903, and officially from 1905 on. On October 20, 1992 the Toronto Blue Jays hosted the first World Series game played outside the United States. The Blue Jays won the 1992 Series, thus becoming the first non-U.S. team to win the fall classic.

WORLD SERIES RECORDS (1903–1992)

TEAM RECORDS

Most wins 22, by the New York Yankees (AL), 1923, 1927–28, 1932, 1936–39, 1941, 1943, 1947, 1949–53, 1956, 1958, 1961– 62, 1977–78.

Most appearances 33, by the New York Yankees (AL), 1921–23, 1926–28, 1932, 1936–39, 1941–43, 1947, 1949–53, 1955–58, 1960–64, 1976–78, 1981.

INDIVIDUAL RECORDS

GAMES PLAYED

Most series 14, by Yogi Berra, New York Yankees (AL), 1947, 1949–53, 1955–58, 1960–63.

Most series (pitcher) 11, by Whitey Ford, New York Yankees (AL), 1950, 1953, 1955–58, 1960–64.

Most games 75, by Yogi Berra, New York Yankees (AL), 1947, 1949–53, 1955–58, 1960–63.

Most games (pitcher) 22, by Whitey Ford, New York Yankees (AL), 1950, 1953, 1955–58, 1960–64.

LEAGUE CHAMPIONSHIP SERIES (1969–1992)

American League

Year	Winner	Loser	Series
1969	Baltimore Orioles (East)	Minnesota Twins (West)	3–0
1970	Baltimore Orioles (East)	Minnesota Twins (West)	3–0
1971	Baltimore Orioles (East)	Oakland A's (West)	3–0
1972	Oakland A's (West)	Detroit Tigers (East)	3–2
1973	Oakland A's (West)	Baltimore Orioles (East)	3–2
1974	Oakland A's (West)	Baltimore Orioles (East)	3–1
1975	Boston Red Sox (East)	Oakland A's (West)	3–0
1976	New York Yankees (East)	Kansas City Royals (West)	3–2
1977	New York Yankees (East)	Kansas City Royals (West)	3–2
1978	New York Yankees (East)	Kansas City Royals (West)	3–1
1979	Baltimore Orioles (East)	California Angels (West)	3–1
1980	Kansas City Royals (West)	New York Yankees (East)	3–0
1981	New York Yankees (East)	Oakland A's (West)	3–0
1982	Milwaukee Brewers (East)	California Angels (West)	3–2
1983	Baltimore Orioles (East)	Chicago White Sox (West)	3–1
1984	Detroit Tigers (East)	Kansas City Royals (West)	3–0
1985	Kansas City Royals (West)	Toronto Blue Jays (East)	4–3
1986	Boston Red Sox (East)	California Angels (West)	4–3
1987	Minnesota Twins (West)	Detroit Tigers (East)	4–1
1988	Oakland A's (West)	Boston Red Sox (East)	4–0
1989	Oakland A's (West)	Toronto Blue Jays (East)	4–1
1990	Oakland A's (West)	Boston Red Sox (East)	4–0
1991	Minnesota Twins (West)	Toronto Blue Jays (East)	4–1
1992	Toronto Blue Jays (East)	Oakland A's (West)	4–2

SAVES ■ 1992 MVP AND CY YOUNG AWARD WIN-
NER DENNIS ECKERSLEY RECORDED HIS 10TH PLAY-
OFF SAVE IN THIS YEAR'S ALCS, EXTENDING HIS
OWN RECORD.

HITTING RECORDS

BATTING AVERAGE

Career (min. 20 games) .391, by Lou Brock, St. Louis Cardinals (NL), 1964, 1967–68. Brock collected 34 hits in 87 at-bats over 21 games.

Series (min. four games) .750, by Billy Hatcher, Cincinnati Reds (NL), in 1990. Hatcher collected nine hits in 12 at-bats in four games.

HITS

Career 71, by Yogi Berra, New York Yankees (AL), 1947–63. In 259 at-bats, Berra hit 12 home runs, 10 doubles and 49 singles.

Series 13, by three players: Bobby Richardson, New York Yankees (AL), in 1960; Lou Brock, St. Louis Cardinals (NL), in 1968; Marty Barrett, Boston Red Sox (AL), in 1986.

HOME RUNS

Career 18, by Mickey Mantle, New York Yankees (AL), 1951–53, 1955–58, 1960–64. Mantle hit his record 18 homers from 230 at-bats in 65 games.

Series Five, by Reggie Jackson, New York Yankees (AL), in 1977.

Game Three, by two players: Babe Ruth, New York Yankees (AL), who did it twice: on October 6, 1926 v. St. Louis Cardinals, and on October 9, 1928 v. St. Louis Cardinals; and Reggie Jackson, New York Yankees (AL), on October 18, 1977 v. Los Angeles Dodgers.

RUNS BATTED IN (RBIs)

Career 40, by Mickey Mantle, New York Yankees (AL), 1951–53, 1955–58, 1960–64.

Series 12, by Bobby Richardson, New York Yankees (AL), in 1960.

Game Six, by Bobby Richardson, New York Yankees (AL), on October 8, 1960 v. Pittsburgh Pirates.

PITCHING RECORDS

WINS

Career Ten, by Whitey Ford, New York Yankees (AL), in 11 series, 1950–64. Ford's career record was 10 wins, 8 losses in 22 games.

Series Three, by 12 pitchers. Only two pitchers have won three games in a five-game series: Christy Matthewson, New York Giants (NL) in 1905; Jack Coombs, Philadelphia Athletics (AL) in 1910.

STRIKEOUTS

Career 94, by Whitey Ford, New York Yankees (AL), in 11 series, 1950–64.

Series 35, by Bob Gibson, St. Louis Cardinals (NL) in 1968, from seven games.

Game 17, by Bob Gibson, St. Louis Cardinals (NL), on October 2, 1968 v. Detroit Tigers.

INNINGS PITCHED

Career 146, by Whitey Ford, New York Yankees (AL), in 11 series, 1950, 1953, 1955–58, 1960–64.

Series 44, by Deacon Phillippe, Pittsburgh Pirates (NL), in 1903 in an eight-game series.

Game 14, by Babe Ruth, Boston Red Sox (AL), on October 9, 1916 v. Brooklyn Dodgers.

SAVES

Career Six, by Rollie Fingers, Oakland Athletics (AL), 1972–74.

Series Three, by Kent Tekulve, Pittsburgh Pirates (NL), in 1979 in a seven-game series.

PERFECT GAME The only perfect game in World Series history was hurled by Don Larsen, New York Yankees (AL), on October 8, 1956 v. Brooklyn Dodgers.

WORLD SERIES (1903-1938)

Year	Winner	Loser	Series
1903	Boston Pilgrims (AL)	Pittsburgh Pirates (NL)	5–3
1904	no series		
1905	New York Giants (NL)	Philadelphia A's (AL)	4–1
1906	Chicago White Sox (AL)	Chicago Cubs (NL)	4–2
1907	Chicago Cubs (NL)	Detroit Tigers (AL)	4–0–1 *
1908	Chicago Cubs (NL)	Detroit Tigers (AL)	4–1
1909	Pittsburgh Pirates (NL)	Detroit Tigers (AL)	4–3
1910	Philadelphia A's (AL)	Chicago Cubs (NL)	4–1
1911	Philadelphia A's (AL)	New York Giants (NL)	4–2
1912	Boston Red Sox (AL)	New York Giants (NL)	4–3–1*
1913	Philadelphia A's (AL)	New York Giants (NL)	4–1
1914	Boston Braves (NL)	Philadelphia A's (AL)	4–0
1915	Boston Red Sox (AL)	Philadelphia Phillies (NL)	4–1
1916	Boston Red Sox (AL)	Brooklyn Robins (NL)	4–1
1917	Chicago White Sox (AL)	New York Giants (NL)	4–2
1918	Boston Red Sox (AL)	Chicago Cubs (NL)	4–2
1919	Cincinnati Reds (NL)	Chicago White Sox (AL)	5–3
1920	Cleveland Indians (AL)	Brooklyn Robins (NL)	5–2
1921	New York Giants (NL)	New York Yankees (AL)	5–3
1922	New York Giants (NL)	New York Yankees (AL)	4–0–1*
1923	New York Yankees (AL)	New York Giants (NL)	4–2
1924	Washington Senators (AL)	New York Giants (NL)	4–3
1925	Pittsburgh Pirates (NL)	Washington Senators (AL)	4–3
1926	St. Louis Cardinals(NL)	New York Yankees (AL)	4–3
1927	New York Yankees (AL)	Pittsburgh Pirates (NL)	4–0
1928	New York Yankees (AL)	St. Louis Cardinals (NL)	4–0
1929	Philadelphia A's (AL)	Chicago Cubs (NL)	4–1
1930	Philadelphia A's (AL)	St. Louis Cardinals (NL)	4–2
1931	St. Louis Cardinals (NL)	Philadelphia A's (AL)	4–3
1932	New York Yankees (AL)	Chicago Cubs (NL)	4–0
1933	New York Giants (NL)	Washington Senators (AL)	4–1
1934	St. Louis Cardinals (NL)	Detroit Tigers (AL)	4–3
1935	Detroit Tigers (AL)	Chicago Cubs (NL)	4–2
1936	New York Yankees (AL)	New York Giants (NL)	4–2
1937	New York Yankees (AL)	New York Giants (NL)	4–1
1938	New York Yankees (AL)	Chicago Cubs (NL)	4–0

* Tied game

WORLD SERIES (1939–1975)

Year	Winner	Loser	Series
1939	New York Yankees (AL)	Cincinnati Reds (NL)	4–0
1940	Cincinnati Reds (NL)	Detroit Tigers (AL)	4–3
1941	New York Yankees (AL)	Brooklyn Dodgers (NL)	4–1
1942	St. Louis Cardinals (NL)	New York Yankees (AL)	4–1
1943	New York Yankees (AL)	St. Louis Cardinals (NL)	4–1
1944	St. Louis Cardinals (NL)	St. Louis Browns (AL)	4–2
1945	Detroit Tigers (AL)	Chicago Cubs (NL)	4–3
1946	St. Louis Cardinals (NL)	Boston Red Sox (AL)	4–3
1947	New York Yankees (AL)	Brooklyn Dodgers (NL)	4–3
1948	Cleveland Indians (AL)	Boston Braves (NL)	4–2
1949	New York Yankees (AL)	Brooklyn Dodgers (NL)	4–1
1950	New York Yankees (AL)	Philadelphia Phillies (NL)	4–0
1951	New York Yankees (AL)	New York Giants (NL)	4–2
1952	New York Yankees (AL)	Brooklyn Dodgers (NL)	4–3
1953	New York Yankees (AL)	Brooklyn Dodgers (NL)	4–2
1954	New York Giants (NL)	Cleveland Indians (AL)	4–0
1955	Brooklyn Dodgers (NL)	New York Yankees (AL)	4–3
1956	New York Yankees (AL)	Brooklyn Dodgers (NL)	4–3
1957	Milwaukee Braves (NL)	New York Yankees (AL)	4–3
1958	New York Yankees (AL)	Milwaukee Braves (NL)	4–3
1959	Los Angeles Dodgers (NL)	Chicago White Sox (AL)	4–2
1960	Pittsburgh Pirates (NL)	New York Yankees (AL)	4–3
1961	New York Yankees (AL)	Cincinnati Reds (NL)	4–1
1962	New York Yankees (AL)	San Francisco Giants (NL)	4–3
1963	Los Angeles Dodgers (NL)	New York Yankees (AL)	4–0
1964	St. Louis Cardinals (NL)	New York Yankees (AL)	4–3
1965	Los Angeles Dodgers (NL)	Minnesota Twins (AL)	4–3
1966	Baltimore Orioles (AL)	Los Angeles Dodgers (NL)	4–0
1967	St. Louis Cardinals (NL)	Boston Red Sox (AL)	4–3
1968	Detroit Tigers (AL)	St. Louis Cardinals (NL)	4–3
1969	New York Mets (NL)	Baltimore Orioles (AL)	4–1
1970	Baltimore Orioles (AL)	Cincinnati Reds (NL)	4–1
1971	Pittsburgh Pirates (NL)	Baltimore Orioles (AL)	4–3
1972	Oakland A's (AL)	Cincinnati Reds (NL)	4–3
1973	Oakland A's (AL)	New York Mets (NL)	4–3
1974	Oakland A's (AL)	Los Angeles Dodgers (NL)	4–1
1975	Cincinnati Reds (NL)	Boston Red Sox (AL)	4–3

WORLD SERIES (1976–1992)

Year	Winner	Loser	Series
1976	Cincinnati Reds (NL)	New York Yankees (AL)	4–0
1977	New York Yankees (AL)	Los Angeles Dodgers (NL)	4–2
1978	New York Yankees (AL)	Los Angeles Dodgers (NL)	4–2
1979	Pittsburgh Pirates(NL)	Baltimore Orioles (AL)	4–3
1980	Philadelphia Phillies (NL)	Kansas City Royals (AL)	4–2
1981	Los Angeles Dodgers (NL)	New York Yankees (AL)	4–2
1982	St. Louis Cardinals (NL)	Milwaukee Brewers (AL)	4–3
1983	Baltimore Orioles (AL)	Philadelphia Phillies (NL)	4–1
1984	Detroit Tigers (AL)	San Diego Padres (NL)	4–1
1985	Kansas City Royals (AL)	St. Louis Cardinals (NL)	4–3
1986	New York Mets (NL)	Boston Red Sox (AL)	4–3
1987	Minnesota Twins (AL)	St. Louis Cardinals (NL)	4–3
1988	Los Angeles Dodgers (NL)	Oakland A's (AL)	4–1
1989	Oakland A's (AL)	San Francisco Giants (NL)	4–0
1990	Cincinnati Reds (NL)	Oakland A's (AL)	4–0
1991	Minnesota Twins (AL)	Atlanta Braves (NL)	4–3
1992	Toronto Blue Jays (AL)	Atlanta Braves (NL)	4–2

MOST VALUABLE PLAYER AWARD The World Series MVP award has been won a record two times by three players: Sandy Koufax, Los Angeles Dodgers (NL), 1963 and 1965; Bob Gibson, St. Louis Cardinals (NL), 1964 and 1967; and Reggie Jackson, Oakland Athletics (AL), 1973, New York Yankees (AL), 1977.

MANAGERS

Most series Ten, by Casey Stengel, New York Yankees (AL), 1949–53, 1955–58, 1960. Stengel's record was seven wins, three losses.

Most wins Seven, by two managers: Joe McCarthy, New York Yankees (AL), 1932, 1936–39, 1941, 1943; and Casey Stengel, New York Yankees (AL), 1949–53, 1956, 1958.

Most losses Six, by John McGraw, New York Giants (NL), 1911–13, 1917, 1923–24.

Wins, both leagues The only manager to lead a team from each league to a World Series title is Sparky Anderson, who skippered the Cincinnati Reds (NL) to championships in 1975–76, and the Detroit Tigers (AL) in 1984.

COLLEGE BASEBALL

ORIGINS Various forms of college baseball have been played throughout the 20th century; however, the NCAA did not organize a championship until 1947 and did not begin to keep statistical records until 1957.

NCAA DIVISION I

HITTING RECORDS (CAREER)

Home runs 100 by Pete Incaviglia, Oklahoma State, 1983–85.

Hits 418, by Phil Stephenson, Wichita State, 1979–82.

PITCHING RECORDS (CAREER)

Wins 51, by Don Heinkel, Wichita State, 1979–82.

Strikeouts 541, by Derek Tatsumo, University of Hawaii, 1977–79.

COLLEGE WORLD SERIES The first College World Series was played in 1947 at Kalamazoo, Mich. The University of California at Berkeley defeated Yale University in a best-of-three-game series, 2–0.

In 1949 the series format was changed to a championship game. Since 1950 the College World Series has been played at Rosenblatt Stadium, Omaha, Nebr.

Most championships The most wins is 11, by Southern Cal., in 1948, 1958, 1961, 1963, 1968, 1970–74 and 1978.

COLLEGE WORLD SERIES (1947–1968)

Year	Winner	Loser	Score	Year	Winner	Loser	Score
1947	California	Yale	2–0 *	1958	Southern Cal.	Missouri	8–7
1948	Southern Cal.	Yale	2–1 *	1959	Oklahoma St.	Arizona	5–3
1949	Texas	Wake Forest	10–3	1960	Minnesota	Southern Cal.	2–1
1950	Texas	Washington St.	3–0	1961	Southern Cal.	Oklahoma St.	1–0
1951	Oklahoma	Tennessee	3–2	1962	Michigan	Santa Clara	5–4
1952	Holy Cross	Missouri	8–4	1963	Southern Cal.	Arizona	5–2
1953	Michigan	Texas	7–5	1964	Minnesota	Missouri	5–1
1954	Missouri	Rollins	4–1	1965	Arizona St.	Ohio St.	2–1
1955	Wake Forest	Western Mich.	7–6	1966	Ohio St.	Oklahoma St.	8–2
1956	Minnesota	Arizona	12–1	1967	Arizona St.	Houston	11–2
1957	California	Penn State	1–0	1968	Southern Cal.	Southern Ill.	4–3

* Series score

HITTING RECORDS (CAREER)

Home runs Four, by five players: Bud Hollowell, Southern Cal., 1963; Pete Incaviglia, Oklahoma State, 1983–85; Ed Sprague, Stanford, 1987–88; Gary Hymel, Louisiana State, 1990–91; and Lyle Mouton, Louisiana State, 1990–91.

Hits 23, by Keith Moreland, Texas, 1973–75.

PITCHING RECORDS (CAREER)

Wins Four, by nine players: Bruce Gardner, Southern Cal., 1958, 1960; Steve Arlin, Ohio State, 1965–66; Bert Hooten, Texas at Austin, 1969–70; Steve Rogers, Tulsa, 1969, 1971; Russ McQueen, Southern Cal., 1972–73; Mark Bull, Southern Cal., 1973–74; Greg Swindell, Texas, 1984–85; Kevin Sheary, Miami (Fla.), 1984–85; Greg Brummett, Wichita State, 1988–89.

Strikeouts 64, by Carl Thomas, Arizona, 1954–56.

LITTLE LEAGUE BASEBALL

ORIGINS Little League Baseball was founded in 1939 in Williamsport, Pa., by Carl Stotz and George and Bert Bebble. In 1947, the inaugural Little League World Series was played—Maynard, Pa. defeating Lock Haven, Pa. 16–7. By this time there were 12 leagues throughout Pennsylvania, and Little League had expanded beyond the state borders to Hammonton, N.J. By 1950, there were 307 leagues throughout the United States, and Little League Baseball was

quickly establishing itself as an American institution. In 1957 Monterrey, Mexico became the first international team to win the title. In 1989 Carl Yastrzemski became the first Little League graduate to be inducted into the Baseball Hall of Fame.

LITTLE LEAGUE WORLD SERIES

Most championships Taiwan (Chinese Taipei), 15 (1969, 1971–74, 1977–81, 1986–88, 1990–91).

Most championships (U.S.—state) Four, from two states: Pennsylvania (Maynard–1947, Lock Haven–1948, Morrisville–1955, Levittown–1960); Connecticut (Stamford–1951, Norwalk–1952, Windsor Locks–1965, Trumbull–1989).

BASKETBALL

ORIGINS Basketball was invented by the Canadian-born Dr. James Naismith at the Training School of the International YMCA College at Springfield, Mass. in mid-December 1891. The first game played under modified rules was on January 20, 1892. The International Amateur Basketball Federation (FIBA) was founded in 1932; it has now dropped the word Amateur from its title.

COLLEGE WORLD SERIES (1969–1992)

Year	Winner	Loser	Score	Year	Winner	Loser	Score
1969	Arizona St.	Tulsa	10–1	1981	Arizona St.	Oklahoma St.	7–4
1970	Southern Cal.	Florida St.	2–1	1982	Miami (Fla.)	Wichita St.	9–3
1971	Southern Cal.	Southern Ill.	7–2	1983	Texas	Alabama	4–3
1972	Southern Cal.	Arizona St.	1–0	1984	Cal. St. Fullerton	Texas	3–1
1973	Southern Cal.	Arizona St.	4–3	1985	Miami (Fla.)	Texas	10–6
1974	Southern Cal.	Miami (Fla.)	7–3	1986	Arizona	Florida St.	10–2
1975	Texas	South Carolina	5–1	1987	Stanford	Oklahoma St.	9–5
1976	Arizona	Eastern Mich.	7–1	1988	Stanford	Arizona St.	9–4
1977	Arizona St.	South Carolina	2–1	1989	Wichita St.	Texas	5–3
1978	Southern Cal.	Arizona St.	10–3	1990	Georgia	Oklahoma St.	2–1
1979	Cal. St. Fullerton	Arkansas	2–1	1991	Louisiana St.	Wichita St.	6–3
1980	Arizona	Hawaii	5–3	1992	Pepperdine	Cal. State Fullerton	3–2

NBA INDIVIDUAL RECORDS

Games Played

		Player(s)	Team(s)	Date(s)
Season	88	Walt Bellamy	New York Knicks, Detroit Pistons	1968–69
Career	1,560	Kareem Abdul-Jabbar	Milwaukee Bucks, Los Angeles Lakers	1969–89

Minutes Played

Game	69	Dale Ellis	Seattle SuperSonics v. Milwaukee Bucks	Nov 9, 1989 (OT)
Season	3,882	Wilt Chamberlain	Philadelphia Warriors	1961–62
Career	57,446	Kareem Abdul-Jabbar	Milwaukee Bucks, Los Angeles Lakers	1969–89

Points

Game	100	Wilt Chamberlain	Philadelphia Warriors v. New York Knicks	March 2, 1962
Season	4,029	Wilt Chamberlain	Philadelphia Warriors	1961–62
Career	38,387	Kareem Abdul-Jabbar	Milwaukee Bucks, Los Angeles Lakers	1969–89

Field Goals

Game	36	Wilt Chamberlain	Philadelphia Warriors v. New York Knicks	March 2, 1962
Season	1,597	Wilt Chamberlain	Philadelphia Warriors	1961–62
Career	15,837	Kareem Abdul-Jabbar	Milwaukee Bucks, Los Angeles Lakers	1969–89

Three-Point Field Goals

Game	9	Dale Ellis	Seattle SuperSonics v. Los Angeles Clippers	April 20, 1990
		Michael Adams	Denver Nuggets v. Los Angeles Clippers	April 12, 1991
Season	172	Vernon Maxwell	Houston Rockets	1990–91
Career	810	Michael Adams	Sacramento Kings, Washington Bullets, Denver Nuggets	1985–93*

Free Throws

Game	28	Wilt Chamberlain Adrian Dantley	Philadelphia Warriors v. New York Knicks Utah Jazz v. Houston Rockets	March 2, 1962 January 4, 1984
Season	840	Jerry West	Los Angeles Lakers	1965–66
Career	8,395	Moses Malone	Buffalo Braves, Houston Rockets, Philadelphia 76ers, Washington Bullets, Atlanta Hawks, Milwaukee Bucks	1976–93*

* As of January 11, 1993

Source: NBA

NBA INDIVIDUAL RECORDS

Assists

		Player(s)	Team(s)	Date(s)
Game	30	Scott Skiles	Orlando Magic v. Denver Nuggets	December 30, 1990
Season	1,164	John Stockton	Utah Jazz	1990–91
Career	9,921	Magic Johnson	Los Angeles Lakers	1979–91

Rebounds

Game	55	Wilt Chamberlain	Philadelphia Warriors v. Boston Celtics	November 24, 1960
Season	2,149	Wilt Chamberlain	Philadelphia Warriors	1960–61
Career	23,924	Wilt Chamberlain	Philadelphia/San Francisco Warriors, Philadelphia 76ers, Los Angeles Lakers	1959–73

Steals

Game	11	Larry Kenon	San Antonio Spurs v. Kansas City Kings	December 26, 1976
Season	301	Alvin Robertson	San Antonio Spurs	1985–86
Career	2,277	Maurice Cheeks	Philadelphia 76ers, San Antonio Spurs, New York Knicks, Atlanta Hawks, New Jersey Nets	1978–93*

Blocked Shots †

Game	17	Elmore Smith	Los Angeles Lakers v. Portland Trail Blazers	October 28, 1973
Season	456	Mark Eaton	Utah Jazz	1984–85
Career	3,189	Kareem Abdul-Jabbar	Milwaukee Bucks, Los Angeles Lakers	1973–89

Personal Fouls

Game	8	Don Otten	Tri-Cities v. Sheboygan	November 24, 1989
Season	386	Darryl Dawkins	New Jersey Nets	1983–84
Career	4,657	Kareem Abdul-Jabbar	Milwaukee Bucks, Los Angeles Lakers	1969–89

Disqualifications ††

Season	26	Don Meineke	Fort Wayne Pistons	1952–53
Career	127	Vern Mikkelsen	Minneapolis Lakers	1950–59

---

* As of January 11, 1993

† Compiled since 1973–74 season.

†† Through January 11, 1993, Moses Malone (Houston Rockets, Philadelphia 76ers, Washington Bullets, Atlanta Hawks, Milwaukee Bucks) has played 1,129 consecutive games without fouling out.

WILT CHAMBERLAIN

A prolific scorer, Wilt Chamberlain is one of the NBA's all-time great "big men." A highly touted high school player in Philadelphia, Chamberlain was recruited by the University of Kansas in 1955. His first professional experience was with the famed Harlem Globetrotters before joining the NBA's Philadelphia Warriors in 1959. Chamberlain's dazzling offensive play was highlighted by his 100-point game against the New York Knicks in 1962. His legendary match-ups with Bill Russell of the Boston Celtics defined the NBA in the 1960s. A 13-time All-Star, Chamberlain retired in 1973 holding the remarkable distinction of never having fouled out of any of the 1,045 NBA games he played in. He was elected to the Basketball Hall of Fame in 1978.

CHAMBERLAIN'S NBA RECORDS

REGULAR SEASON RECORDS

POINTS
- Most in a season **4,029**
- Average per game, season **50.4**
- Most consecutive 50+ games **7**
- Most points in a game **100**
- Most points in a half **53**

FIELD GOALS
- Most scored in a season **1,597**
- Most scored in a game **36**
- Most scored in a half **22**
- Consecutive field goals scored **35**
- Most attempts in a season **3,159**
- Most attempts in a game **63**

FREE THROWS
- Most made in a game **28**[†]
- Most attempts, career **11,862**
- Most attempts, season **1,363**
- Most attempts, game **34**

REBOUNDS
- Most in a career **23,924**
- Highest game average, career **22.9**
- Most in a season **2,149**
- Highest game average, season **27.2**
- Most in a game **55**

PLAYOFF RECORDS

MINUTES PLAYED
- Most in a series (4 games) **195**[†]
- Most in a series (6 games) **296**

FIELD GOALS
- Most scored, series (7 games) **113**
- Most scored, game **24**[†]

REBOUNDS
- Most in a game **41**
- Average per game, series **32.0**
- Most in a series (5 games) **160**
- Most in a series (6 games) **171**
- Most in a series (7 games) **220**

† Tied Record

IN HIS FINAL SEASON, 1972–73, CHAMBERLAIN SET AN NBA RECORD FOR HIGHEST FIELD GOAL PERCENTAGE, .727. CHAMBERLAIN HIT 426 OF 586 ATTEMPTS.

100-POINT GAME

Wilt Chamberlain's 100-point performance ranks as one of the greatest feats in NBA history. The historic game took place on March 2, 1962 at Hershey, Pa.; the Philadelphia Warriors defeated the New York Knicks 169–147. Many of the records Chamberlain set that day still stand, among them: the most points (100), most points in a half (59), most field goals (36), most field goals in a half (22), most attempts (63), most attempts in a half (37) and in a quarter (21). There were 4,124 people in attendance at the game, but tens of thousands have laid claim to being there.

CHAMBERLAIN'S SCORING BY PERIODS

Period	Min.	FGA	FGM	FTA	FTM	Reb	Ast	Pts
1st	12	14	7	9	9	10	0	23
2nd	12	12	7	5	4	4	1	18
3rd	12	16	10	8	8	6	1	28
4th	12	21	12	10	7	5	0	31
Totals	48	63	36	32	28	25	2	100

SOURCES: ■ THE SPORTING NEWS OFFICIAL NBA GUIDE, THE SPORTING NEWS OFFICIAL NBA REGISTER, THE PHILADELPHIA 76ERS MEDIA GUIDE AND STATISTICAL YEARBOOK, GOLDEN STATE WARRIORS MEDIA GUIDE

Teams: Philadelphia/San Francisco Warriors, 1959–65; Philadelphia 76ers, 1965–68; Los Angeles Lakers, 1968–73.

Season	G	FGA	FGM	FTA	FTM	Reb.	Ast.	Pts.	Avg.
59–60	72	2,311	1,065	991	577	1,941*	168	2,707*	37.6
60–61	79	2,457	1,251	1,054	531	2,149*	148	3,033	38.4
61–62	80	3,159*	1,597*	1,363*	835	2,052	192	4,029*	50.4*
62–63	80	2,770	1,463	1,113	660	1,946	275	3,586	44.8
63–64	80	2,298	1,204	1,016	540	1,787	403	2,948	36.9
64–65	73	2,083	1,063	880	408	1,673	250	2,534	34.7
65–66	79	1,990	1,074	976	501	1,943	414	2,649	33.5
66–67	81	1,150	785	875	386	1,957	630	1,956	24.1
67–68	82	1,377	819	932	354	1,952	702	1,992	24.3
68–69	81	1,099	641	857	382	1,712	366	1,664	20.5
69–70	12	227	129	157	70	221	49	328	27.3
70–71	82	1,226	668	669	360	1,493	352	1,696	20.7
71–72	82	764	496	524	221	1,572	329	1,213	14.8
72–73	82	586	426	455	232	1,526	365	1,084	13.2
Totals	1,045	23,497	12,681	11,862*	6,057	23,924*	4,643	31,419	30.1

NBA Playoff Record

Season	G	FGA	FGM	FTA	FTM	Reb.	Ast.	Pts.	Avg.
59–60	9	252	125	110	49	232	19	999	33.2
60–61	3	96	45	38	21	69	6	111	37.0
61–62	12	347	162	151	96	319	37	420	35.0
63–64	12	322	175	139	66	302	39	416	34.7
64–65	11	232	123	136	76	299	48	322	29.3
65–66	5	110	56	68	28	151	15	140	28.0
66–67	15	228	132	160	62	437	135	326	21.7
67–68	13	232	124	158	60	321	85	308	23.7
68–69	18	176	96	148	58	444	46	250	13.9
69–70	18	288	158	202	82	399	81	398	22.1
70–71	12	187	85	97	50	242	53	220	18.3
71–72	15	142	80	122	60	315	49	220	14.7
72–73	17	116	64	98	49	383	60	177	10.4
Totals	160	2,728	1,425	1,627	757	3,913	673	3,607	22.5

* NBA record

CHAMBERLAIN SET NUMEROUS SCORING RECORDS WHILE PLAYING IN HIS HOME TOWN OF PHILADELPHIA, INCLUDING MOST POINTS IN A GAME (100) AND MOST IN A SEASON (4,029).

CHAIRMAN OF THE BOARDS

Known for his prodigious scoring, Chamberlain was also an all-time great rebounder. At his retirement Chamberlain had set numerous all-time NBA career records, of which "most career rebounds" is one of the few that still stand.

Season	Rebounds	Season	Rebounds
1959–60	1,941	1967–68	1,952
1960–61	2,149	1968–69	1,712
1961–62	2,052	1969–70	221
1962–63	1,946	1970–71	1,493
1963–64	1,787	1971–72	1,572
1964–65	1,673	1972–73	1,526
1965–66	1,943		
1966–67	1,957	**Total**	23,924

NATIONAL BASKETBALL ASSOCIATION (NBA)

ORIGINS The Amateur Athletic Union (AAU) organized the first national tournament in the United States in 1897. The first professional league was the National Basketball League (NBL), founded in 1898, but this league only lasted two seasons. The American Basketball League was formed in 1925, but declined, and the NBL was refounded in 1937. This organization merged with the Basketball Association of America in 1949 to form the National Basketball Association (NBA).

NBA TEAM RECORDS (1947–1992)

SCORING

Most points (one team) 186, by the Detroit Pistons, defeating the Denver Nuggets, 186–184, at Denver, on December 13, 1983 after three overtimes.

Most points, regulation (one team) 173, by two teams: Boston Celtics *v.* Minneapolis Lakers (139 points), at Boston, on February 27, 1959; Phoenix Suns *v.* Denver Nuggets (143 points), at Phoenix, on November 10, 1990.

Highest-scoring game (aggregate) 370 points, Detroit Pistons defeated the Denver Nuggets, 186–184, at Denver, on December 13, 1983 after three overtimes.

Highest-scoring game (aggregate), regulation 320 points, Golden State Warriors defeated the Denver Nuggets, 162–158, at Denver, on November 2, 1990.

Lowest-scoring game (aggregate) 37 points, Fort Wayne Pistons defeated the Minneapolis Lakers, 19–18, at Minneapolis, on November 22, 1950.

Greatest margin of victory 68 points, by the Cleveland Cavaliers, defeating the Miami Heat, 148–80, on December 17, 1991.

WINS AND LOSSES

Most wins (season) 69, by the Los Angeles Lakers in 1971–72.

BIG MEN ■ CENTERS MOSES MALONE (LEFT) AND MARK EATON (ABOVE) BOTH HOLD NBA RECORDS. MALONE HAS PLAYED IN 1,129 CONSECUTIVE GAMES WITHOUT FOULING OUT. EATON HOLDS THE SEASON BLOCKED SHOT RECORD AT 456.

NBA MOST VALUABLE PLAYER AWARD (1956–1992)

The Maurice Podoloff Trophy was instituted in 1956 to be awarded to the NBA's most valuable player. From 1956 to 1980 the award was decided by a vote of eligible NBA players; since 1980 the winner has been decided by a vote of eligible writers and broadcasters.

Most wins Six, by Kareem Abdul-Jabbar, Milwaukee Bucks, 1971–72, 1974; Los Angeles Lakers, 1976–77, 1980.

Year	Player	Team	Year	Player	Team
1956	Bob Pettit	St. Louis Hawks	1975	Bob McAdoo	Buffalo Braves
1957	Bob Cousy	Boston Celtics	1976	Kareem Abdul-Jabbar	Los Angeles Lakers
1958	Bill Russell	Boston Celtics	1977	Kareem Abdul-Jabbar	Los Angeles Lakers
1959	Bob Pettit	St. Louis Hawks	1978	Bill Walton	Portland Trail Blazers
1960	Wilt Chamberlain	Philadelphia Warriors	1979	Moses Malone	Houston Rockets
1961	Bill Russell	Boston Celtics	1980	Kareem Abdul-Jabbar	Los Angeles Lakers
1962	Bill Russell	Boston Celtics	1981	Julius Erving	Philadelphia 76ers
1963	Bill Russell	Boston Celtics	1982	Moses Malone	Houston Rockets
1964	Oscar Robertson	Cincinnati Royals	1983	Moses Malone	Philadelphia 76ers
1965	Bill Russell	Boston Celtics	1984	Larry Bird	Boston Celtics
1966	Wilt Chamberlain	Philadelphia 76ers	1985	Larry Bird	Boston Celtics
1967	Wilt Chamberlain	Philadelphia 76ers	1986	Larry Bird	Boston Celtics
1968	Wilt Chamberlain	Philadelphia 76ers	1987	Magic Johnson	Los Angeles Lakers
1969	Wes Unseld	Baltimore Bullets	1988	Michael Jordan	Chicago Bulls
1970	Willis Reed	New York Knicks	1989	Magic Johnson	Los Angeles Lakers
1971	Kareem Abdul-Jabbar	Milwaukee Bucks	1990	Magic Johnson	Los Angeles Lakers
1972	Kareem Abdul-Jabbar	Milwaukee Bucks	1991	Michael Jordan	Chicago Bulls
1973	Dave Cowens	Boston Celtics	1992	Michael Jordan	Chicago Bulls
1974	Kareem Abdul-Jabbar	Milwaukee Bucks			

Most consecutive wins 33, by the Los Angeles Lakers. The Lakers' streak began with a 110–106 victory over the Baltimore Bullets on November 5, 1971 in Los Angeles, and ended on January 9, 1972 when they were beaten 120–104 by the Milwaukee Bucks in Milwaukee.

Most losses (season) 73, by the Philadelphia 76ers in 1972–73.

Most consecutive losses 24, by the Cleveland Cavaliers. The Cavs' undesirable roll started on March 19, 1982 when they lost to the Milwaukee Bucks, 119–97, in Milwaukee, and ended on November 10, 1982 when they defeated the Golden State Warriors 132–120 in overtime on November 10, 1982. During the streak the Cavs lost the last 19 games of the 1981–82 season, and the first five of the 1982–83 season.

TIMEOUT

TRAVELING ☛ PETER DEL MASTO (U.S.) DRIBBLED A BASKETBALL 265.2 MILES, FROM NEAR LEE TO PROVINCETOWN, MASS., FROM AUGUST 12–25, 1989. HE MAY HAVE ALSO SET SOME KIND OF PARADOX RECORD, AS THE JOURNEY WAS COMPLETED WITHOUT "TRAVELING."

CONSECUTIVE RECORDS (INDIVIDUAL, 1937–1992)

Games played 906, by Randy Smith, from February 18, 1972 to March 13, 1983. During his streak, Smith played for the Buffalo Braves, San Diego Clippers (twice), Cleveland Cavaliers, and New York Knicks.

Games scoring 50+ points Seven, by Wilt Chamberlain, Philadelphia Warriors, December 16–29, 1961.

Games scoring 10+ points 787, by Kareem Abdul-Jabbar, Los Angeles Lakers, from December 4, 1977 through December 2, 1987.

Free throws 78, by Calvin Murphy, Houston Rockets, from December 27, 1980 through February 28, 1981.

Free throws (game) 23, by Dominique Wilkins, Atlanta Hawks on December 8, 1992.

COACHES (1947–1992)

Most wins 938, by Red Auerbach, Washington Capitols (115 wins, 1946–49); Tri-Cities Blackhawks (28 wins, 1949–50); Boston Celtics (795 wins, 1950–66).

Highest winning percentage .722, by Pat Riley, Los Angeles Lakers, 1981–90, New York Knicks, 1991–92. Riley's record is 584 wins, 225 losses.

MOST POINTS ■ ELGIN BAYLOR SCORED 61 POINTS V. THE BOSTON CELTICS ON APRIL 14, 1962 TO SET THE NBA CHAMPIONSHIP GAME RECORD.

NBA CHAMPIONSHIP FINALS (1947–1968)

Year	Winner	Loser	Series	Year	Winner	Loser	Series
1947	Philadelphia Warriors	Chicago Stags	4–1	1958	St. Louis Hawks	Boston Celtics	4–2
1948	Baltimore Bullets	Philadelphia Warriors	4–2	1959	Boston Celtics	Minneapolis Lakers	4–0
1949	Minneapolis Lakers	Washington Capitols	4–2	1960	Boston Celtics	St. Louis Hawks	4–3
1950	Minneapolis Lakers	Syracuse Nationals	4–2	1961	Boston Celtics	St. Louis Hawks	4–1
1951	Rochester Royals	New York Knicks	4–3	1962	Boston Celtics	Los Angeles Lakers	4–3
1952	Minneapolis Lakers	New York Knicks	4–3	1963	Boston Celtics	Los Angeles Lakers	4–2
1953	Minneapolis Lakers	New York Knicks	4–1	1964	Boston Celtics	San Francisco Warriors	4–1
1954	Minneapolis Lakers	Syracuse Nationals	4–3	1965	Boston Celtics	Los Angeles Lakers	4–1
1955	Syracuse Nationals	Fort Wayne Pistons	4–3	1966	Boston Celtics	Los Angeles Lakers	4–3
1956	Philadelphia Warriors	Fort Wayne Pistons	4–1	1967	Philadelphia 76ers	San Francisco Warriors	4–2
1957	Boston Celtics	St. Louis Hawks	4–3	1968	Boston Celtics	Los Angeles Lakers	4–2

Most games 1,722, by Bill Fitch, Cleveland Cavaliers, 1970–79; Boston Celtics, 1979–83; Houston Rockets, 1983–88; New Jersey Nets, 1989–92. Fitch's career totals are 845 wins, 877 losses.

NBA CHAMPIONSHIP

The NBA recognizes the 1946–47 season as its first championship; however, at that time the league was known as the Basketball Association of America (BAA).

Most titles 16, by the Boston Celtics, 1957, 1959–66, 1968–69, 1974, 1976, 1981, 1984, 1986.

Consecutive titles Eight, by the Boston Celtics, 1959–66.

Most titles (coach) Nine, by Red Auerbach, Boston Celtics, 1957, 1959–66.

NBA CHAMPIONSHIP RECORDS (FINALS SERIES) (1947–1992)

INDIVIDUAL RECORDS (GAME)

Most points scored 61, by Elgin Baylor, Los Angeles Lakers v. Boston Celtics on April 14, 1962 in Boston.

Most field goals made 22, by two players: Elgin Baylor, Los Angeles Lakers v. Boston Celtics on April 14, 1962 in Boston; Rick Barry, San Francisco Warriors v. Philadelphia 76ers on April 18, 1967 in San Francisco.

Most free throws made 19, by Bob Pettit, St. Louis Hawks v. Boston Celtics on April 9, 1958 in Boston.

Most rebounds 40, by Bill Russell, Boston Celtics, who has performed this feat twice: v. St. Louis Hawks on March 29, 1960; v. Los Angeles Lakers on April 18, 1962, in an overtime game.

Most assists 21, by Magic Johnson, Los Angeles Lakers v. Boston Celtics on June 3, 1984.

Most steals Six, by four players: John Havlicek, Boston Celtics v. Milwaukee Bucks, May 3, 1974; Steve Mix, Philadelphia 76ers v. Portland Trail Blazers, May 22, 1977; Maurice Cheeks, Philadelphia 76ers v. Los Angeles Lakers, May 7, 1980; Isiah Thomas, Detroit Pistons v. Los Angeles Lakers, June 19, 1988.

Most blocked shots Eight, by two players: Bill Walton, Portland Trail Blazers v. Philadelphia 76ers, June 5, 1977; Hakeem Olajuwon, Houston Rockets v. Boston Celtics, June 5, 1986.

TEAM RECORDS (GAME)

Most points (one team) 148, by the Boston Celtics v. Los Angeles Lakers (114 points) on May 27, 1985.

NBA CHAMPIONSHIP FINALS (1969–1992)

Year	Winner	Loser	Series	Year	Winner	Loser	Series
1969	Boston Celtics	Los Angeles Lakers	4–3	1981	Boston Celtics	Houston Rockets	4–2
1970	New York Knicks	Los Angeles Lakers	4–3	1982	Los Angeles Lakers	Philadelphia 76ers	4–2
1971	Milwaukee Bucks	Baltimore Bullets	4–0	1983	Philadelphia 76ers	Los Angeles Lakers	4–0
1972	Los Angeles Lakers	New York Knicks	4–1	1984	Boston Celtics	Los Angeles Lakers	4–3
1973	New York Knicks	Los Angeles Lakers	4–1	1985	Los Angeles Lakers	Boston Celtics	4–2
1974	Boston Celtics	Milwaukee Bucks	4–3	1986	Boston Celtics	Houston Rockets	4–2
1975	Golden State Warriors	Washington Bullets	4–0	1987	Los Angeles Lakers	Boston Celtics	4–2
1976	Boston Celtics	Phoenix Suns	4–2	1988	Los Angeles Lakers	Detroit Pistons	4–3
1977	Portland Trail Blazers	Philadelphia 76ers	4–2	1989	Detroit Pistons	Los Angeles Lakers	4–0
1978	Washington Bullets	Seattle SuperSonics	4–3	1990	Detroit Pistons	Portland Trail Blazers	4–1
1979	Seattle SuperSonics	Washington Bullets	4–1	1991	Chicago Bulls	Los Angeles Lakers	4–1
1980	Los Angeles Lakers	Philadelphia 76ers	4–2	1992	Chicago Bulls	Portland Trail Blazers	4–2

NBA PLAYOFF RECORDS (1947–1992)

Points

		Player(s)	Team(s)	Date(s)
Game	63	Michael Jordan	Chicago Bulls v. Boston Celtics	April 20, 1986 (2 OT)
	61	Elgin Baylor	Los Angeles Lakers v. Boston Celtics	April 14, 1962*
Series	284	Elgin Baylor	Los Angeles Lakers v. Boston Celtics	1962
Career	5,762	Kareem Abdul-Jabbar	Milwaukee Bucks, Los Angeles Lakers	1969–89

Field Goals

Game	24	Wilt Chamberlain	Philadelphia Warriors v. Syracuse Nationals	March 14, 1960
		John Havlicek	Boston Celtics v. Atlanta Hawks	April 1, 1973
		Michael Jordan	Chicago Bulls v. Cleveland Cavaliers	May 1, 1988
Series	113	Wilt Chamberlain	San Francisco Warriors v. St. Louis	1964
Career	2,356	Kareem Abdul-Jabbar	Milwaukee Bucks, Los Angeles Lakers	1970–89

Free Throws

Game	30	Bob Cousy	Boston Celtics v. Syracuse Nationals	March 21, 1953 (4 OT)
	23	Michael Jordan	Chiacgo Bulls v. New York Knicks	May 14, 1989*
Series	86	Jerry West	Los Angeles Lakers v. Baltimore Bullets	1965
Career	1,213	Jerry West	Los Angeles Lakers	1960–74

Assists

Game	24	Magic Johnson	Los Angeles Lakers v. Phoenix Suns	May 15, 1984
		John Stockton	Utah Jazz v. Los Angeles Lakers	May 17, 1988
Series	115	John Stockton	Utah Jazz v. Los Angeles Lakers	1988
Career	2,320	Magic Johnson	Los Angeles Lakers	1979–91

Rebounds

Game	41	Wilt Chamberlain	Philadelphia 76ers v. Boston Celtics	April 5, 1967
Series	220	Wilt Chamberlain	Philadelphia 76ers v. Boston Celtics	1965
Career	4,104	Bill Russell	Boston Celtics	1956–69

Steals

Game	8	Rick Barry	Golden State Warriors v. Seattle SuperSonics	April 14, 1975
		Lionel Hollins	Portland Trail Blazers v. Los Angeles Lakers	May 8, 1977
		Maurice Cheeks	Philadelphia 76ers v. New Jersey Nets	April 11, 1979
		Craig Hodges	Milwaukee Bucks v. Philadelphia 76ers	May 9, 1986
		Tim Hardaway	Golden State Warriors v. Los Angeles Lakers	May 8, 1991
		Tim Hardaway	Golden State Warriors v. Seattle SuperSonics	April 30, 1992
Series	28	John Stockton	Utah Jazz v. Los Angeles Lakers	1988
Career	358	Magic Johnson	Los Angeles Lakers	1979–91

* Regulation play
Source: NBA

PICKPOCKET ■ TIM HARDAWAY IS THE ONLY PLAYER TO HAVE STOLEN THE BALL EIGHT TIMES IN A PLAYOFF GAME ON TWO OCCASIONS.

Highest-scoring game (aggregrate) 276 points, Philadelphia 76ers defeated the San Francisco Warriors, 141–135, in overtime, on April 14, 1967.

Highest-scoring game, regulation (aggregate) 263 points, Los Angeles Lakers defeated the Boston Celtics, 141–122, on June 4, 1987.

Greatest margin of victory 35 points, Washington Bullets shot down the Seattle SuperSonics, 117–82, on June 4, 1978.

NCAA COLLEGE BASKETBALL

MEN'S BASKETBALL (NCAA)

The National Collegiate Athletic Association (NCAA) has compiled statistics for its men's basketball competitions since the 1937–38 season. NCAA men's basketball is classified by three divisions: I, II and III.

NCAA CAREER INDIVIDUAL RECORDS (DIVISIONS I, II, III, 1937–1992)

POINTS SCORED

Game 113, by Clarence "Bevo" Francis, Rio Grande (Division II), *v.* Hillsdale on February 2, 1954.

Season 1,381, by Pete Maravich, Louisiana State (Division I) in 1970. Pistol Pete hit 522 field goals and 337 free throws in 31 games.

Career 4,045, by Travis Grant, Kentucky State (Division II), 1969–72.

FIELD GOALS MADE

Game 41, by Frank Selvy, Furman (Division I), *v.* Newberry on February 13, 1954. Selvy amassed his record total from 66 attempts.

Season 539, by Travis Grant, Kentucky State (Division II) in 1972. Grant's season record was gained from 869 attempts.

DEFENSE ■ ERIC MURDOCK HOLDS THE ALL-TIME NCAA DIVISION I RECORD FOR STEALS AT 376.

HIGHEST HOYA ■ GEORGETOWN CENTER ALONZO MOURNING SET THE NCAA DIVISION I RECORD FOR MOST BLOCKED SHOTS AT 453.

Career 1,760, by Travis Grant, Kentucky State (Division II), 1969–72. Grant achieved his career record from 2,759 attempts.

ASSISTS

Game 26, by Robert James, Kean (Division III), *v.* New Jersey Tech on March 11, 1989.

Season 406, by Mark Wade, UNLV (Division I) in 1987. Wade played in 38 games.

Career 1,038, by Chris Corchiani, North Carolina State (Division I), 1988–91. During his record-setting career Corchiani played in 124 games.

REBOUNDS

Game 51, by Bill Chambers, William & Mary (Division I), *v.* Virginia on February 14, 1953.

Season 799, by Elmore Smith, Kentucky State (Division II) in 1971. Smith played in 33 games.

Career 2,334, by Jim Smith, Steubenville (Division II), 1955–58. Smith amassed his record total from 112 games.

NCAA TEAM RECORDS (DIVISION I, 1937–1992)

Most points scored (one team) 186, by Loyola Marymount (Cal.) *v.* U.S. International (140 points), on January 5, 1991.

Highest-scoring game (aggregate) 331 points, Loyola Marymount (Cal.) defeating U.S. International, 181–150, on January 31, 1989.

Fewest points scored (team) Six, by two teams: Temple *v.* Tennessee (11 points), on December 15, 1973; Arkansas State *v.* Kentucky (75 points), on January 8, 1945.

Lowest-scoring game (aggregate) 17 points, Tennessee defeating Temple, 11–6, on December 15, 1973.

Widest margin of victory 95 points, Oklahoma defeating Northeastern Illinois, 146–51, on December 2, 1989.

Greatest deficit overcome 29 points, Duke defeating Tulane, 74–72, on December 30, 1950, after trailing 27–56 at half-time.

Most wins (season) 37, by two teams: Duke in 1986 (37 wins, 3 losses); UNLV in 1987 (37 wins, 2 losses).

Most losses (season) 28, by Prairie View in 1992 (0 wins, 28 losses).

CONSECUTIVE RECORDS (INDIVIDUAL, DIVISION I)

Games scoring 10+ points 115, by Lionel Simmons, La Salle, 1987–90.

Games scoring 50+ points Three, by Pete Maravich, Louisiana State, February 10 to February 15, 1969.

Field goals 25, by Ray Voelkel, American, over nine games from November 24 through December 16, 1978.

Field goals (game) 16, by Doug Grayson, Kent *v.* North Carolina on December 6, 1967.

Three-point field goals 15, by Todd Leslie, Northwestern, over four games from December 15 through December 28, 1990.

NCAA DIVISION I MEN'S RECORDS (1937–1992)

Points

		Player(s)	Team(s)	Date(s)
Game	100	Frank Selvy	Furman v. Newberry	February 13, 1954
	72	Kevin Bradshaw	U.S. International v. Loyola–Marymount	January 5, 1991*
Season	1,381	Pete Maravich	Louisiana State	1970
Career	3,667	Pete Maravich	Lousiana State	1968–70

Field Goals

Game	41	Frank Selvy	Furman v. Newberry	February 13, 1954
Season	522	Pete Maravich	Lousiana State	1970
Career	1,387	Pete Maravich	Lousiana State	1968–70

Free Throws

Game	30	Pete Maravich	Louisiana State v. Oregon State	December 22, 1969
Season	355	Frank Selvy	Furman	1954
Career	905	Dickie Hemric	Wake Forest	1952–55

Assists

Game	22	Tony Fairly	Baptist CS v. Armstrong State	February 9, 1987
		Avery Johnson	Southern-B.R. v. Texas Southern	January 25, 1988
		Sherman Douglas	Syracuse v. Providence	January 28, 1989
Season	406	Mark Wade	UNLV	1987
Career	1,038	Chris Corchiani	North Carolina State	1988–91

Rebounds

Game	51	Bill Chambers	William & Mary v. Virginia	February 14, 1953
Season	734	Walt Dukes	Seton Hall	1953
Career	2,243	Tom Gola	La Salle	1952–55

Blocked Shots

Game	14	David Robinson	Navy v. N.C.–Wilmington	January 4, 1986
		Shawn Bradley	BYU v. Eastern Kentucky	December 7, 1990
Season	207	David Robinson	Navy	1986
Career	453	Alonzo Mourning	Georgetown	1989–92

Steals

Game	13	Mookie Blaylock	Oklahoma v. Centenary	December 12, 1987
		Mookie Blaylock	Oklahoma v. Loyola–Marymount	December 17, 1988
Season	150	Mookie Blaylock	Oklahoma	1988
Career	376	Eric Murdock	Providence	1988–91

* Game between two Division I teams
Source: NCAA

Three-point field goals (game) 11, by Gary Bossert, Niagara *v.* Sienna, January 7, 1987.

Free throws 64, by Joe Dykstra, Western Illinois, over eight games, December 1, 1981 through January 4, 1982.

Free throws (game) 24, by Arlen Clark, Oklahoma State *v.* Colorado, March 7, 1959.

Wins (regular season) 76, by UCLA, from January 30, 1971 through January 17, 1974. The streak was ended on January 19, 1974 when the Bruins were defeated by Notre Dame, 71–70.

Wins (regular season and playoffs) 88, by UCLA, from January 30, 1971 through January 17, 1974.

NCAA DIVISION I CHAMPIONS (1939–1992)

Year	Winner	Loser	Score	Year	Winner	Loser	Score
1939	Oregon	Ohio State	46–33	1966	UTEP	Kentucky	72–65
1940	Indiana	Kansas	60–42	1967	UCLA	Dayton	79–64
1941	Wisconsin	Washington State	39–34	1968	UCLA	North Carolina	78–55
1942	Stanford	Dartmouth	53–38	1969	UCLA	Purdue	92–72
1943	Wyoming	Georgetown	46–34	1970	UCLA	Jacksonville	80–69
1944	Utah	Dartmouth	42–40†	1971	UCLA	Villanova*	68–62
1945	Oklahoma State	NYU	49–45	1972	UCLA	Florida State	81–76
1946	Oklahoma State	North Carolina	43–40	1973	UCLA	Memphis State	87–66
1947	Holy Cross	Oklahoma	58–47	1974	N. Carolina State	Marquette	76–64
1948	Kentucky	Baylor	58–42	1975	UCLA	Kentucky	92–85
1949	Kentucky	Oklahoma State	46–36	1976	Indiana	Michigan	86–68
1950	CCNY	Bradley	71–68	1977	Marquette	North Carolina	67–59
1951	Kentucky	Kansas State	68–58	1978	Kentucky	Duke	94–88
1952	Kansas	St. John's	80–63	1979	Michigan State	Indiana State	75–64
1953	Indiana	Kansas	69–68	1980	Louisville	UCLA*	59–54
1954	LaSalle	Bradley	92–76	1981	Indiana	North Carolina	63–50
1955	San Francisco	LaSalle	77–63	1982	North Carolina	Georgetown	63–62
1956	San Francisco	Iowa	83–71	1983	N. Carolina State	Houston	54–52
1957	North Carolina	Kansas	54–53‡	1984	Georgetown	Houston	84–75
1958	Kentucky	Seattle	84–72	1985	Villanova	Georgetown	66–64
1959	California	West Virginia	71–70	1986	Louisville	Duke	72–69
1960	Ohio State	California	75–55	1987	Indiana	Syracuse	74–73
1961	Cincinnati	Ohio State	70–65†	1988	Kansas	Oklahoma	83–79
1962	Cincinnati	Ohio State	71–59	1989	Michigan	Seton Hall	80–79†
1963	Loyola (Ill.)	Cincinnati	60–58†	1990	UNLV	Duke	103–73
1964	UCLA	Duke	98–83	1991	Duke	Kansas	72–65
1965	UCLA	Michigan	91–80	1992	Duke	Michigan	71–51

* These teams were disqualified by the NCAA for rules violations uncovered following the completion of the tournament.
† Overtime
‡ Triple overtime

Losses 37, by Citadel, from January 16, 1954 through December 12, 1955.

Winning seasons 46, by Louisville, 1945–90.

COACHES (DIVISION I)

Most wins 875, by Adolph Rupp, Kentucky, 1931–72.

Highest winning percentage .837, by Jerry Tarkanian, Long Beach State, 1969–73; UNLV, 1974–92. The shark's career record was 625 wins, 122 losses.

Most games 1,105, by Henry Iba, Northwest Missouri State, 1930–33; Colorado, 1934; Oklahoma State, 1935–70. Iba's career record was 767 wins, 338 losses.

Most years 48, by Phog Allen, Baker, 1906–08; Kansas, 1908–09; Haskell, 1909, Central Missouri State, 1913–19, Kansas, 1920–56.

NCAA CHAMPIONSHIP TOURNAMENT (1939–1992)

The NCAA finals were first contested in 1939 at Northwestern University, Evanston, Ill. The University of Oregon, University of Oklahoma, Villanova University and Ohio State University were the first "final four." Oregon defeated Ohio State 46–33 to win the first NCAA title.

Most wins (team) 10, by UCLA, 1964–65, 1967–73, 1975.

Most wins (coach) 10, by John Wooden. Wooden coached UCLA to each of its NCAA titles.

CHAMPIONSHIP GAME RECORDS (INDIVIDUAL, 1939–1992)

Most points 44, by Bill Walton, UCLA *v*. Memphis State in 1973.

Most field goals 21, by Bill Walton, UCLA *v*. Memphis State in 1973.

Most rebounds 27, by Bill Russell, San Francisco *v*. Iowa in 1956.

Most assists 11, by Rumeal Robinson, Michigan *v*. Seton Hall, 1989.

WOMEN'S BASKETBALL

ORIGINS Senda Berenson and Clara Baer are generally credited as the pioneers of women's basketball. In 1892, Berenson, a physical education instructor at Smith College, adapted James Naismith's rules of basketball to create a "divided-court" version, which required the players to remain in their assigned sections of the court, making the game less physically demanding and thus, presumably, more suitable for women. Clara Baer introduced women's basketball to Sophie Newcomb Memorial College in her native New Orleans, La., in 1893. Baer also adapted the style of

MOST GAMES ■ THE LEGENDARY HENRY IBA COACHED A RECORD 1,105 NCAA GAMES.

MOST POINTS ☞ THIRTEEN-YEAR-OLD SWEDISH SCHOOLBOY MATS WERMELIN SCORED ALL 272 POINTS IN HIS TEAM'S 272–0 VICTORY IN A TOURNAMENT IN STOCKHOLM, SWEDEN ON FEBRUARY 5, 1974.

Naismith's game, and published her own set of rules in 1895; these became known as the Newcomb College rules.

The game spread rapidly in the late 19th century, with the first women's collegiate game being played between California and Stanford on April 4, 1896. Women's basketball was unable to sustain its growth in the 20th century, however, due to controversy over whether it was safe for women to play the game. It wasn't until after World War II that attitudes changed and women's basketball began to organize itself on a national level and bring its rules into line with the men's game.

In 1969, Carol Eckman, coach at West Chester University, Pa., organized the first national invitation tournament. Under the auspices of the Association for Intercollegiate Athletics for Women (AIAW) the national tournament was expanded, and in 1982 the NCAA was invited to take over the tournament.

NCAA INDIVIDUAL RECORDS (DIVISIONS I, II, III, 1982–1992)

POINTS SCORED

Game 67, by Jackie Givens, Fort Valley State (Division II), *v.* Knoxville on February 22, 1991. Givens hit 19 field goals, six three-point field goals, and 11 free throws.

Season 1,075, by Jackie Givens, Fort Valley State (Division II), in 1991. Givens' record-setting season consisted of 249 field goals, 120 three-point field goals, and 217 free throws in 28 games.

Career 3,171, by Jeannie Demers, Buena Vista (Division III), 1983–87. Demers' career totals are 1,386 field goals and 399 free throws in 105 games.

FIELD GOALS MADE

Game 28, by Ann Gilbert, Oberlin (Division III), *v.* Allegheny on February 6, 1991.

Season 392, by Barbara Kennedy, Clemson (Division I) in 1982. Kennedy set her record total from 760 attempts.

Career 1,386, by Jeannie Demers, Buena Vista (Division III), 1983–87. Demers made her record total from 2,838 attempts.

ASSISTS

Game 23, by Michelle Burden, Kent (Division I), *v.* Ball State on February 6, 1991.

Season 355, by Suzie McConnell, Penn State (Division I), in 1987.

Career 1,307, by Suzie McConnell, Penn State (Division I), 1984–88.

REBOUNDS

Game 40, by Deborah Temple, Delta State (Division I), *v.* Alabama–Birmingham, on February 14, 1983.

Season 635, by Francine Perry, Quinnipac (Division II), in 1982.

Career 1,887, by Wanda Ford, Drake (Division I), 1983–86.

NCAA TEAM RECORDS (DIVISION I)

Most points scored (one team) 149, by Long Beach State *v.* San Jose State (69 points), on February 16, 1987.

OFF THE GLASS ■ DRAKE'S WANDA FORD HOLDS THE WOMEN'S ALL-TIME REBOUND MARK AT 1,887.

NCAA DIVISION I WOMEN'S RECORDS (1982–1992)

Points

		Player(s)	Team(s)	Date(s)
Game	60	Cindy Brown	Long Beach State v. San Jose State	February 16, 1987
Season	974	Cindy Brown	Long Beach State	1987
Career	3,122	Patricia Hoskins	Mississippi Valley	1985–89

Field Goals

Game	27	Lorri Bauman	Drake v. Southwest Missouri State	January 6, 1984
Season	392	Barbara Kennedy	Clemson	1982
Career	1,259	Joyce Walker	Louisiana State	1981–84

Free Throws

Game	22	Lorri Bauman	Drake v. Northern Illinois	November 26, 1982
		Tammy Hinchee	Northern Illinois v. Marquette	February 25, 1989
Season	275	Lorri Bauman	Drake	1982
Career	907	Lorri Bauman	Drake	1981–84

Assists

Game	23	Michelle Burden	Kent v. Ball State	February 6, 1991
Season	355	Suzie McConnell	Penn State	1987
Career	1,307	Suzie McConnell	Penn State	1984–88

Rebounds

Game	40	Deborah Temple	Delta State v. Alabama– Birmingham	February 14, 1983
Season	534	Wanda Ford	Drake	1985
Career	1,887	Wanda Ford	Drake	1983–86

Blocked Shots

Game	13	Stefanie Kasperski	Oregon v. Western Kentucky	December 29, 1987
		Suzanne Johnson	Monmouth v. Delaware	December 13, 1990
Season	151	Michelle Wilson	Texas Southern	1989
Career	428	Genia Miller	Cal. St. Fullerton	1987–91

Steals

Game	14	Natalie White	Florida A&M v. South Alabama	December 13, 1991
		Ann Thomas	Tennessee St. v. Monmouth	November 25, 1989
Season	160	Shelly Barton	Florida A&M	1990
Career	454	Dawn Staley	Virginia	1988–92

Source: NCAA

Highest-scoring game (aggregate) 243 points, Virginia defeating North Carolina State, 123–120, after three overtimes on January 12, 1991.

Fewest points scored (one team) 12, by Bennett *v.* North Carolina A&T (85 points), on November 21, 1990.

Lowest-scoring game (aggregate) 72 points, Virginia defeating San Diego State, 38–34, on December 29, 1981.

Most wins (season) 35, by three teams: Texas, 1982; Louisiana Tech, 1982; Tennessee, 1989.

Most losses (season) 28, by Charleston South in 1991.

COACHES (DIVISION I)

Most wins 598, by Jody Conradt, Texas, 1970–92.

Highest winning percentage .859, by Leon Barmore, Louisiana Tech, 1983–92. Barmore's career record through the 1990–91 season is 281 wins, 46 losses.

NCAA CHAMPIONSHIP TOURNAMENT (1982–1992)

The NCAA instituted a women's basketball championship in 1982.

Most wins (team) Three, by Tennessee, 1987, 1989 and 1991.

Most wins (coach) Three, by Pat Summitt. Summitt coached Tennessee to all three NCAA titles.

CHAMPIONSHIP GAME RECORDS (INDIVIDUAL, 1982–1992)

Most points 28, by two players in the 1991 championship game between Virginia and Tennessee: Dawn Staley (Virginia); Dena Head (Tennessee).

Most field goals 12, by Erica Westbrooks, Louisiana Tech *v.* Auburn, in 1988.

Most rebounds 20, by Tracy Claxton, Old Dominion *v.* Georgia, in 1985.

Most assists 10, by two players: Kamie Ethridge, Texas *v.* Southern Cal, in 1986; Melissa McCray, Tennessee *v.* Auburn, in 1989.

OLYMPIC GAMES The men's basketball competition was introduced at the Berlin Olympics in 1936. In April 1989, the International Olympic Committee voted to allow professional players to compete in the Games. The women's basketball competition was introduced at the Montreal Olympics in 1976.

Most gold medals (men) The United States has won 10 gold medals in Olympic basketball competition: 1936, 1948, 1952, 1956, 1960, 1964, 1968, 1976, 1984 and 1992.

NCAA CHAMPIONS (1982–1992)

Year	Winner	Loser	Score
1982	Louisiana Tech.	Cheyney	76–62
1983	Southern Cal.	Louisiana Tech.	69–67
1984	Southern Cal.	Tennessee	72–61
1985	Old Dominion	Georgia	70–65
1986	Texas	Southern Cal.	97–81
1987	Tennessee	Louisiana Tech.	67–44
1988	Louisiana Tech.	Auburn	56–54
1989	Tennessee	Auburn	76–60
1990	Stanford	Auburn	88–81
1991	Tennessee	Virginia	70–67*
1992	Stanford	Western Kentucky	78–62

* Overtime

Most gold medals (women) In the women's basketball tournament the gold medal has been won three times by the USSR/Unified Teams: 1976, 1980 and 1992.

WORLD CHAMPIONSHIPS An official men's world championship was first staged in 1950 in Buenos Aires, Argentina, and has been held quadrennially since. A women's world championship was first staged in 1953 and is now also staged as a quadrennial event.

Most titles (men) Two countries have won the men's title three times: USSR, 1967, 1974 and 1982; Yugoslavia, 1970, 1978 and 1990.

Most titles (women) The USSR has won the women's event a record six times: 1959, 1964, 1967, 1971, 1975 and 1983.

United States The United States has won the women's title five times: 1953, 1957, 1979, 1986 and 1990; and the men's title twice: 1954 and 1986.

BIATHLON

The biathlon is a composite test of cross-country skiing and rifle marksmanship. Competitors ski over a prepared course carrying a small-bore rifle; at designated ranges the skiers stop and complete the shooting assignment for the race. Time penalties are assessed for missed shots; the winner of the event is the one with the fastest time.

ORIGINS The sport reflects one of the earliest techniques of human survival; rock carvings in Roedoey, Norway dating to 3000 B.C. seem to depict hunters stalking their prey on skis. Biathlon as a modern sport evolved from military ski patrol maneuvers, which tested the soldier's ability as a fast skier and accurate marksman. In 1958 the *Union Internationale de Pentathlon Moderne et Biathlon* (UIPMB) was formed as the international governing body of biathlon and modern pentathlon. Biathlon was included in the Olympic Games for the first time in 1960.

United States The 1960 Olympic Games at Squaw Valley, Calif. introduced biathlon to this country. National championships were first held in 1965. The current governing body of the sport is the United States Biathlon Association, founded in 1980 and based in Essex Junction, Vt.

OLYMPIC GAMES "Military patrol," the forerunner to biathlon, was included in the Games of 1924, 1928, 1936 and 1948. Biathlon was included in the Winter Games for the first time at Squaw Valley, Calif. in 1960. Women's events were included for the first time at the 1992 Games at Albertville, France.

Most gold medals Aleksandr Tikhonov (USSR) has won four gold medals as a member of the Soviet relay team that won the 4 x 7,500 meter races in 1968, 1972, 1976 and 1980. Magnar Solberg (Norway) and Franz-Peter Rotsch (East Germany) have both won two gold medals in individual events. Solberg won the 20,000 meters in 1968 and 1972; Rotsch won the 10,000 meters and 20,000 meters in 1988.

Most medals Aleksandr Tikhonov has won a record five medals in Olympic competition. In addition to his four gold medals (see above), he won the silver medal in the 20,000 meters in 1968.

WORLD CHAMPIONSHIPS First held in 1958 for men and in 1984 for women, the world championships are an annual event. In Olympic years, the Games are considered the world championships; therefore, records in this section include results from the Games.

Most titles (overall) Aleksandr Tikhonov (USSR) has won 14 world titles: 10 in the 4 x 7,500 meter relay, 1968–74, 1976–77 and 1980; four individual events, 10,000 meter in 1977 and 20,000 meter in 1969–70 and 1973. In women's events, Kaya Parve (USSR) has won a record six gold medals: four in the 3 x 5,000 meter relay, 1984–86, 1988; two individual titles, the 5,000 meter in 1986 and the 10,000 meter in 1985.

Most titles (individual) Frank Ullrich (East Germany) has won a record six individual titles: 10,000 meter, 1978–81; 20,000 meter, 1982–83.

UNITED STATES NATIONAL CHAMPIONSHIPS In this competition, first held in 1965 in Rosendale, N.Y., men's events have been staged annually. Women's events were included in 1985.

Most titles Lyle Nelson has won seven national championships: five in the 10,000 meter, 1976, 1979, 1981, 1985 and 1987; two in the 20,000 meter, 1977 and 1985. Anna Sonnerup holds the women's record with five titles: two in the 10,000 meter, 1986–87; two in the 15,000 meter, 1989 and 1991; and one in the 7,500 meter in 1989.

BOBSLED AND LUGE

BOBSLED

ORIGINS The earliest known sled is dated c. 6500 B.C. and was found at Heinola, Finland. There are references to sled racing in Norwegian folklore dating from the 15th century. The first tracks built for sled racing were constructed in the mid-18th century in St. Petersburg, Russia. The modern sport of bobsled dates to the late 19th century, when British enthusiasts organized competitions in Switzerland. The first run built for bobsled racing was constructed in St. Moritz, Switzerland in 1902. The *Federation Internationale de Bobsleigh de Tobagganing* (FIBT) was founded in 1923 and is the world governing body of bobsled racing.

United States The United States Bobsled & Skeleton Federation was founded in 1941 and is still the governing body for the sport in this country.

OLYMPIC GAMES A four-man bob competition was included in the first Winter Games in 1924 at Chamonix, France. Bobsled events have been included in every Games except 1960, when the Squaw Valley organizing committee refused to build a bobsled track.

Four-man bob Switzerland has won a record five Olympic titles: 1924, 1936, 1956, 1972 and 1988.

Two-man bob Switzerland has won a record three Olympic titles: 1948, 1980 and 1992.

Most gold medals Meinhard Nehmer and Bernhard Germeshausen (both East Germany) have both won a record three gold medals. They were both members of the 1976 two-man and four-man winning crews and the 1980 four-man winning crews.

Most medals Eugenio Monti (Italy) has won six medals: two gold, two silver and two bronze, 1956–68.

WORLD CHAMPIONSHIPS A world championship staged independently of the Olympic Games was first held in 1930 for four-man bob, and from 1931 for two-man bob. In Olympic years the Games are considered the world championship; therefore, records in this section include the Games of 1924 and 1928.

Four-man bob Switzerland has won the world title a record 19 times: 1924, 1936, 1939, 1947, 1954–57, 1971–73, 1975, 1982–83 and 1986–90.

Two-man bob Italy has won the world title 14 times: 1954, 1956–63, 1966, 1968–69, 1971 and 1975.

Most titles Eugenio Monti (Italy) has won 11 bobsled world championships: eight in the two-man, 1957–1961, 1963, 1966 and 1968; three in the four-man, 1960–61 and 1968.

LUGE

In luge the rider adopts a supine as opposed to a sitting position.

ORIGINS The first international luge race took place in 1883. Organized by the hotel keepers of Davos, Switzerland to promote their town, the race attracted 21 entrants from seven countries,

GOLDEN MOMENT ■ GUSTAV WEDER AND DONAT ACKLIN CELEBRATE THEIR 1992 TWO-MAN OLYMPIC BOBSLED WIN.

including the United States. The course was 2½ miles, from St. Wolfgang to Klosters. The FIBT governed luge racing until 1957, when the *Fédération Internationale de Luge* (FIL) was formed.

United States The United States has participated in all Olympic luge events since the sport was sanctioned for the 1964 Games, but there was no organized governing body for the sport in this country until 1979, when the United States Luge Association was formed. The only luge run in the United States accredited for international competition is the refrigerated run used for the Lake Placid Olympics in 1980.

OLYMPIC GAMES One-man skeleton races were included in the 1928 and 1948 Games; however, in skeleton races riders race face down rather than lying on their backs as in luge. Luge was included in the Games for the first time in 1964 in Innsbruck, Austria.

Most gold medals Thomas Kohler, Hans Rinn, Norbert Hahn and Steffi Martin-Walter (all East Germany) have each won two Olympic titles: Kohler won the single-seater in 1964 and the two-seater in 1968; Rinn and Hahn won the two-seater in 1976 and 1980; Martin-Walter won the women's single-seater in 1984 and 1988.

United States No American luger has won a medal at the Olympic Games. In the skeleton sled races held in 1928 and 1948, the United States won one gold and two silvers out of six races. Jennison Heaton was the winner of the 1928 single skeleton sled event.

WORLD CHAMPIONSHIPS First held in 1955, the world championships have been staged biennially

FEET FIRST ■ FOUR LUGERS HAVE WON TWO OLYMPIC TITLES. STEFFI MARTIN-WALTER IS THE ONLY WOMAN TO ACHIEVE THIS FEAT.

since 1981. In Olympic years the Games are considered the world championships; therefore, records in this section include results from the Games.

Most titles Thomas Kohler and Hans Rinn (both East Germany) have both won six world titles: Kohler won the single-seater in 1962, 1964 and 1966–67, and the two-seater in 1967–68; Rinn won the single-seater in 1973 and 1977, and the two-seater in 1976–77 and 1980 (two world championships were held in 1980, with Rinn winning each time). Margit Schumann (East Germany) holds the women's mark with five world titles, 1973–77.

UNITED STATES NATIONAL CHAMPIONSHIPS This competition was inaugurated in 1974.

Most titles Frank Masley has won a record six men's championships: 1979, 1981–83 and 1987–

TIMEOUT

FASTEST LUGER ☛ THE FASTEST RECORDED PHOTO-TIMED SPEED IS 85.38 MPH, BY ASLE STRAND (NORWAY) AT TANDADALENS LINBANA, SÄLEN, SWEDEN ON MAY 1, 1982.

88. Bonny Warner has won a record five women's titles: 1983–84, 1987–88 and 1990.

BOWLING

ORIGINS The ancient German game of nine-pins (*Heidenwerfen*—"knock down pagans") was exported to the United States in the early 17th century. In 1841, the Connecticut state legislature prohibited the game, and other states followed. Eventually a tenth pin was added to evade the ban. The first body to standardize rules was the American Bowling Congress (ABC), established in New York City on September 9, 1895.

PROFESSIONAL BOWLERS ASSOCIATION (PBA)

The PBA was founded in 1958 by Eddie Elias and is based in Akron, Ohio.

Most titles (career) Earl Anthony of Dublin, Calif. has won a career record 41 PBA titles, 1970–83.

Most titles (season) The record number of titles won in one PBA season is eight, by Mark Roth of North Arlington, N.J., in 1978.

TRIPLE CROWN The United States Open, the PBA National Championship and the Firestone Tournament of Champions comprise the Triple Crown of men's professional bowling. No bowler has won all three titles in the same year, and only three have managed to win all three during a career. The first bowler to accumulate the three legs of the triple crown was Billy Hardwick: National Championship (1963); Firestone Tournament of Champions (1965); U.S. Open (1969). Hardwick's feat was matched by Johnny Petraglia: Firestone (1971); U.S. Open (1977); National (1980); and by Pete Weber: Firestone (1987); U.S. Open (1988 and 1991); National (1989).

U.S. OPEN In this tournament, inaugurated in 1942, the most wins is four, by two bowlers: Don Carter in 1953–54 and 1957–58, and Dick Weber in 1962–63 and 1965–66.

PBA NATIONAL CHAMPIONSHIP In this contest, inaugurated in 1960, the most wins is six, by Earl Anthony in 1973–75 and 1981–83.

FIRESTONE TOURNAMENT OF CHAMPIONS In this tournament, inaugurated in 1965, the most wins is three, by Mike Durbin in 1972, 1982 and 1984.

PEFECT GAMES

A total of 162 perfect (300 score) games were bowled in PBA tournaments in 1992, the most ever for one year.

Most perfect games (career) Since 1977, when the PBA began to keep statistics on perfect games, Wayne Webb has bowled 33 in tournament play.

Most perfect games (season) Amleto Monacelli rolled seven perfect games on the 1989 tour.

Highest earnings Marshall Holman has won a career record $1,592,966 in PBA competitions through 1992. Mike Aulby of Indianapolis, Ind. set a single-season earnings mark of $298,237 in 1989.

LADIES PROFESSIONAL BOWLERS TOUR (LPBT)

Founded in 1981, the LPBT is based in Rockford, Ill.

Most titles (career) Lisa Wagner has won 26 tournaments in her twelve-year career, 1980–92.

Most titles (season) Patty Costello won a season record seven tournaments in 1976.

PERFECT GAMES

Most bowled (career) Jeanne Maiden has bowled an LPBT-approved record 19 perfect games (300 score) in her career.

Most bowled (season) The record for most perfect games in a season is four, bowled by three bowlers: Betty Morris, 1986; Nikki Gianulias, 1986; and Debbie McMullen in 1991.

Highest earnings Lisa Wagner has won a career record $489,469 in prize money, 1980–92. Robin Romeo won a season record $113,750 in 1989.

AMERICAN BOWLING CONGRESS (ABC)

SCORING RECORDS

Highest individual score (three games) The highest individual score for three games is 899, by Thomas Jordan at Union, N.J. on March 7, 1989.

PBA TOUR SCORING RECORDS

Games	Score	Bowler	Site	Year
6	1,615	Walter Ray Williams Jr.	Beaumont, Tex.	1991
8	2,165	Billy Hardwick	Japan	1968
12	3,052	Walter Ray Williams Jr.	Beaumont, Tex.	1991
16	4,015	Carmen Salvino	Sterling Heights, Mich.	1980
18	4,515	Earl Anthony	New Orleans, La.	1977
24	5,825	Earl Anthony	Seattle, Wash.	1970

Source: PBA Tour

Highest team score (one game) The all-time ABC-sanctioned two-man single-game record is 600, held jointly by four teams: John Cotta and Steve Larson, May 1, 1981 at Manteca, Calif.; Jeff Mraz and Dave Roney, November 8, 1987 at Canton, Ohio.; William Gruner and Dave Conway, February 27, 1990 at Oceanside, Calif.; Scott Williams and Willie Hammar, June 7, 1990 at Utica, N.Y.

Highest team score (three games) The highest three-game team score is 3,858, by Budweisers of St. Louis on March 12, 1958.

Highest season average The highest season average attained in sanctioned competition is 245.63, by Doug Vergouven of Harrisonville, Mo. in the 1989–90 season.

Juniors Brentt Arcement, at age 16, bowled a three-game series of 888, the highest ever bowled in a league or tournament sanctioned by the Young American Bowling Alliance, which is the national organization serving junior bowlers (age 21 and under).

Consecutive strikes The record for consecutive strikes in sanctioned play is 33, by two bowlers: John Pezzin at Toledo, Ohio on March 4, 1976, and Fred Dusseau at Yuma, Ariz., on March 3, 1992.

PERFECT GAMES

Most bowled (career) The highest number of sanctioned 300 games is 42, by Bob Learn Jr. of Erie, Pa.

Consecutive Two perfect games were rolled back-to-back *twice* by two bowlers: Al Spotts of West Reading, Pa. on March 14, 1982 and again on February 1, 1985, and Jerry Wright of Idaho Falls, Idaho on January 9, 1992 and again on February 26, 1992.

PERFECT SEASON ■ IN 1989 AMLETO MONACELLI BOWLED A PBA TOUR RECORD SEVEN PERFECT GAMES.

BOWLING DU JOUR ■ THE BRUNSWICK THURSDAY NITE STARS SCORED A RECORD 209,072 POINTS IN 24 HOURS ON JUNE 20–21, 1991.

WOMEN'S INTERNATIONAL BOWLING CONGRESS (WIBC)

SCORING RECORDS

Highest individual score (three games) The highest individual score for three games is 864, by Jeanne Maiden at Sodon, Ohio on November 23, 1986.

Highest team score (one game) Jeanette Betts and Veronica Wilson bowled the all-time two-woman single-game highest score of 566 in Flint, Mich., on February 11, 1991.

Highest team score (three games) The highest three-game team score is 3,437, by Goebel Beer of Detroit, Mich., on November 23, 1988.

TIMEOUT

HIGHEST SCORE IN 24 HOURS ☞ THE BRUNSWICK THURSDAY NITE STARS, A SIX-MAN TEAM, SCORED 209,072 AT BRUNSWICK SHARPTOWN LANES, HOUSTON, TEX., ON JUNE 20–21, 1991.

Highest season average The highest season average attained in sanctioned WIBC-competition is 232.0, by Patty Ann of Appleton, Wis., in the 1983–84 season.

Consecutive strikes Jeanne Maiden bowled a record 40 consecutive strikes during her record-breaking 864 performance on November 23, 1986.

PERFECT GAMES

Most bowled (career) The highest number of WIBC-sanctioned perfect games (300) is 20, by Jeanne Maiden.

Oldest The oldest woman to bowl a perfect game was Helen Duval of Berkeley, Calif., at age 65 in 1982.

Bowled, lowest average Of all the women who have rolled a perfect game, the one with the lowest average was Diane Ponza of Santa Cruz, Calif., who had a 112 average in the 1977–78 season.

BOXING

The nationality of the competitors in this section is U.S. unless stated otherwise.

ORIGINS Boxing with gloves is depicted on a fresco from the Isle of Thera, Greece that has been dated to 1520 B.C. The earliest prize-ring code of rules was formulated in England on August 16, 1743 by the champion pugilist Jack Broughton, who reigned from 1734 to 1750. In 1867, boxing came under the Queensberry Rules, formulated for John Sholto Douglas, 8th Marquess of Queensberry.

United States New York was the first state to legalize boxing, in 1896. Today professional boxing is regulated in each state by athletic or boxing commissions.

Longest fights The longest recorded fight with gloves was between Andy Bowen and Jack Burke at New Orleans, La. on April 6–7, 1893. It lasted 110 rounds, 7 hours 19 minutes (9:15 P.M.–4:34 A.M.) and was declared a no contest (later changed to a draw). The longest bare-knuckle fight was 6 hours 15 minutes between James Kelly and Jack Smith at Fiery Creek, Dalesford, Victoria, Australia on December 3, 1855.

The greatest number of rounds was 276 in 4 hours 30 minutes when Jack Jones beat Patsy Tunney in Cheshire, England in 1825.

Shortest fights The shortest fight on record appears to be one in a Golden Gloves tournament at Minneapolis, Minn. on November 4, 1947, when Mike Collins floored Pat Brownson with the first punch and the contest was stopped, without a count, 4 seconds after the bell. The World Boxing Council reports that the shortest fight in the history of professional boxing occured on June 19, 1991, when Paul Rees (Australia) scored a technical knockout over Charlie Hansen (Australia) in five seconds in a junior- middleweight bout in Brisbane, Australia.

The shortest world title fight was 45 seconds, when Lloyd Honeyghan (Great Britain) beat Gene Hatcher in an IBF welterweight bout at Marbella, Spain on August 30, 1987. Some sources also quote the Al McCoy first-round knockout of George Chip in a middleweight contest on April 7, 1914 as being in 45 seconds.

Most fights without loss Of boxers with complete records, Packey McFarland had 97 fights (five draws) from 1905 to 1915 without a defeat.

Consecutive wins Pedro Carrasco (Spain) won 83 consecutive fights from April 22, 1964 to September 3, 1970.

Most knockouts The greatest number of finishes classified as "knockouts" in a career is 145 (129 in professional bouts), by Archie Moore.

Consecutive knockouts The record for consecutive knockouts is 44, by Lamar Clark from 1958 to January 11, 1960.

HEAVYWEIGHT DIVISION

Long accepted as the first world heavyweight title fight, with gloves and three-minute rounds, was that between John L. Sullivan and James J. "Gentleman Jim" Corbett in New Orleans, La. on September 7, 1892. Corbett won in 21 rounds.

Longest reign Joe Louis was champion for 11 years 252 days, from June 22, 1937, when he knocked out James J. Braddock in the eighth round at Chicago, Ill., until announcing his retirement on March 1, 1949. During his reign, Louis defended his title a record 25 times.

Shortest reign The shortest reign was 64 days for IBF champion Tony Tucker, May 30–August 1, 1987.

Most recaptures Muhammad Ali is the only man to have regained the heavyweight championship twice. Ali first won the title on February 25, 1964, defeating Sonny Liston. He defeated George Foreman on October 30, 1974, having been stripped of the title by the world boxing authorities on April 28, 1967. He won the WBA title from Leon Spinks on September 15, 1978, having previously lost to him on February 15, 1978.

Undefeated Rocky Marciano is the only world champion at any weight to have won every fight of his entire professional career (1947–56); 43 of his 49 fights were by knockouts or stoppages.

Oldest successful challenger Jersey Joe Walcott was 37 years 168 days when he knocked out Ezzard Charles on July 18, 1951 in Pittsburgh, Pa.

Lightest champion Bob Fitzsimmons (Great Britain) weighed 167 pounds when he won the title by knocking out James J. Corbett at Carson City, Nev. on March 17, 1897.

Heaviest champion Primo Carnera (Italy) weighed in at 270 pounds for the defense of his title *v.* Tommy Loughran on March 1, 1934. Carnera won a unanimous point decision.

Quickest knockout The quickest knockout in a heavyweight title fight was 55 seconds, by James J. Jeffries over Jack Finnegan at Detroit, Mich. on April 6, 1900.

WORLD CHAMPIONS (ANY WEIGHT)

Reign (longest) Joe Louis's heavyweight duration record of 11 years 252 days stands for all divisions.

Reign (shortest) Tony Canzoneri was world light welterweight champion for 33 days, May 21 to June 23, 1933, the shortest period for a boxer to have won and lost the world title in the ring.

Most recaptures The only boxer to win a world title five times at one weight is Sugar Ray Robinson, who beat Carmen Basilio in Chicago Stadium, Ill. on March 25, 1958 to regain the world middleweight title for the fourth time.

Greatest weight difference Primo Carnera (Italy) outweighed his opponent, Tommy Loughran, by 86 pounds (270 pounds to 184 pounds) when they fought for the heavyweight title on March 1, 1934 in Miami, Fla. Surprisingly, the bout went the distance, with Carnera winning on points.

Greatest tonnage The greatest tonnage recorded in any fight is 700 pounds, when Claude "Humphrey" McBride, 340 pounds, knocked out Jimmy Black, 360 pounds, in the third round of their bout at Oklahoma City, Okla. on June 1, 1971. The greatest combined weight for a world title fight is 488¾ pounds, when Primo Carnera (Italy), 259½ pounds, fought Paolino Uzcudun (Spain), 229¼ pounds, in Rome, Italy on October 22, 1933.

AMATEUR

OLYMPIC GAMES Boxing contests were included in the ancient games, and were included in the modern Games in 1904.

Most gold medals Two boxers have won three gold medals: Laszlo Papp (Hungary) won the middleweight title in 1948, and the light middleweight in 1952 and 1956; Teofilo Stevenson (Cuba) won the heavyweight division in 1972, 1976 and 1980. The only man to win two titles at the same Games was Oliver L. Kirk, who won both the bantamweight and featherweight titles in 1904. It should be noted that Kirk only had to fight one bout in each class.

WORLD CHAMPIONSHIPS The world championships were first staged in 1974, and are held quadrennially.

Most titles Three boxers have won three world championships: Teofilo Stevenson (Cuba), heavyweight champion in 1974 and 1978 and superheavyweight champion in 1986; Adolfo Horta (Cuba), bantamweight champion in 1978, featherweight champion in 1982 and lightweight champion in 1986; Félix Savon (Cuba), heavyweight champion in 1986, 1989 and 1991.

UNITED STATES NATIONAL CHAMPIONSHIPS U.S. amateur championships were first staged in 1888.

Most titles The most titles won is five, by middleweight W. Rodenbach, 1900–04.

CANOEING

ORIGINS The most influential pioneer of canoeing as a sport was John MacGregor, a British attorney, who founded the Canoe Club in Surrey, England in 1866. The sport's world governing body is the International Canoe Federation, founded in 1924.

United States The New York Canoe Club, founded in Staten Island, N.Y., in 1871, is the oldest in the United States. The American Canoe Association was formed on August 3, 1880.

OLYMPIC GAMES Canoeing was first included in the Games as a demonstration sport in 1924. At the 1936 Games, canoeing was included as an official Olympic sport for the first time.

Most gold medals Gert Fredriksson (Sweden) won a record six Olympic gold medals: 1,000 meter Kayak Singles (K1), 1948, 1952 and 1956; 10,000 meter K1, 1948 and 1956; 1,000 meter Kayak Pairs (K2), 1960. In women's competition, Birgit Schmidt (née Fischer; East Germany/Germany) has won four golds: 500 meter K1, 1980 and 1992; 500 meter K2, 1988; 500 meter K4, 1988.

United States Greg Barton is the only American canoeist to win two gold medals: 1,000 meter K1, 1,000 meter K2 in 1988.

WORLD CHAMPIONSHIPS In Olympic years, the Games also serve as the world championship.

Most titles Birgit Schmidt (East Germany) has won a record 24 titles, 1978–92. The men's record is 13, by three canoeists: Gert Fredriksson (Sweden), 1948–60; Rudiger Helm (East Germany),

TIMEOUT

24-HOUR PADDLING ☛ THE GREATEST DISTANCE PADDLED IN 24 HOURS IS 157.1 MILES, BY ZDZISLAW SZUBSKI (POLAND). SZUBSKI TRAVELED FROM WLOCKLAWEK TO GDANSK, POLAND ALONG THE VISTULA RIVER ON SEPTEMBER 11–12, 1987.

K-1 ■ THE MOST SUCCESSFUL AMERICAN CANOE-IST IS GREG BARTON. HE WON TWO GOLD MEDALS AT THE 1988 OLYMPIC GAMES.

1976–83; and Ivan Patzaichin (Romania), 1968–84.

UNITED STATES NATIONAL CHAMPIONSHIPS

Most titles Marcia Ingram Jones Smoke won 35 national titles from 1962–81. The men's record is 33, by Ernest Riedel from 1930–48.

CRICKET

ORIGINS Cricket originated in England in the Middle Ages. It is impossible to pinpoint its exact origin; however, historians believe that the modern game developed in the mid-16th century. The earliest surviving scorecard is from a match played between England and Kent on June 18, 1744. The Marylebone Cricket Club (MCC) was founded in 1787 and, until 1968, was the world governing body for the sport. The International Cricket Conference (ICC) is responsible for international (Test) cricket, while the MCC remains responsible for the laws of cricket.

INTERNATIONAL (TEST) CRICKET

Test match cricket is the highest level of the sport. The Test playing nations are Australia, England, India, New Zealand, Pakistan, South Africa, Sri Lanka and the West Indies. Test matches are generally played over five days. The result is decided by which team scores the most runs in two full innings (one inning sees all 11 members of a team come to bat; their opponents must achieve 10 outs to end the inning). If, at the end of the allotted time period, one or either team has not completed two full innings, the game is declared a tie. The first Test match was played at Melbourne, Australia on March 15–19, 1877 between Australia and England.

NATIONAL CRICKET CHAMPIONSHIPS

Australia The premier event in Australia is the Sheffield Shield, an interstate competition contested since 1891–92. New South Wales has won the title a record 40 times.

England The major championship in England is the County Championship, an intercounty competition officially recognized since 1890. Yorkshire has won the title a record 30 times.

India The Ranji Trophy is India's premier cricket competition. Established in 1934 in memory of K. S. Ranjitsinhji, it is contested on a zonal basis, culminating in a playoff competition. Bombay has won the tournament a record 30 times.

New Zealand Since 1975, the major championship in New Zealand has been the Shell Trophy. Otago and Wellington have each won the competition four times.

Pakistan Pakistan's national championship is the Quaid-e-Azam Trophy, established in 1953. Karachi has won the trophy a record seven times.

South Africa The Currie Cup, donated by Sir Donald Currie, was first contested in 1889. Transvaal has won the competition a record 28 times.

West Indies The Red Stripe Cup, established in 1966, is the premier prize played for by the association of Caribbean islands (plus Guyana) that form the West Indies Cricket League. Barbados has won the competion a record 13 times.

CROQUET

ORIGINS Its exact beginnings are unknown; however, it is believed that croquet developed from the French game *jeu de mail*. A game resembling croquet was played in Ireland in the 1830s and introduced to England 20 years later. Although croquet was played in the United States for a number of years, a national body was not established until the formation of the United States Croquet Association (USCA) in 1976. The first United States championship was played in 1977.

USCA NATIONAL CHAMPIONSHIPS J. Archie Peck has won the singles title a record four times (1977, 1979–80, 1982). Ted Prentis has won the doubles title four times with three different partners (1978, 1980–81, 1988). The teams of Ted Prentis and Ned Prentis (1980–81) and Dana Dribben and Ray Bell (1985–86) have each won the doubles title twice. The New York Croquet Club has won a record six National Club Championships (1980–83, 1986, 1988).

CROSS-COUNTRY RUNNING

ORIGINS The earliest recorded international cross-country race took place on March 20, 1898 between England and France. The race was staged at Ville d'Avray, near Paris, France over a course 9 miles 18 yards long.

WORLD CHAMPIONSHIPS The first international cross-country championships were staged in Glasgow, Scotland on March 28, 1903. Since 1973 the event has been an official world championship organized by the International Amateur Athletic Federation.

Most titles England has won the men's team event a record 45 times, 1903–14, 1920–21, 1924–25, 1930–38, 1951, 1953–55, 1958–60, 1962, 1964–72, 1976, 1979–80. The women's competition has been won eight times by two countries: United States, 1968–69, 1975, 1979, 1983–85, 1987; USSR, 1976–77, 1980–82, 1988–90.

Most titles (individual) Grete Waitz (Norway) has won a record five women's titles, 1978–81 and 1983. John Ngugi (Kenya) has won the men's title a record five times, 1986–89 and 1992.

United States The United States has never won either of the team events. Craig Virgin has won the men's individual title twice, 1980–81, and Lynn Jennings has won the women's title three times, 1990–92.

UNITED STATES NATIONAL CHAMPIONSHIPS This competition was first staged in 1890 for men, and in 1972 for women.

Most titles Pat Porter has won the men's event a record eight times, 1982–89. Lynn Jennings has won the women's event seven times, 1985 and 1987–92.

NCAA CHAMPIONSHIPS The first NCAA cross-country championship was held in 1938, and was open only to men's teams. A women's event was not staged until 1981.

Most titles (team) In men's competition, Michigan State has won the team title a record eight times: 1939, 1948–49, 1952, 1955–56, 1958–59.

Most titles (individuals) Three athletes have won the men's individual title three times: Gerry Lindgren (Washington State), 1966–67 and 1969; Steve Prefontaine (Oregon), 1970–71 and 1973; Henry Rono (Washington State), 1976–77 and 1979.

Most titles (team) In women's competition, Villanova has won the team title four times, 1989–92.

Most titles (individual) Two runners have won the title twice: Betty Springs (North Carolina State), 1981 and 1983; Sonia O'Sullivan (Villanova), 1990 and 1991.

CURLING

ORIGINS The traditional home of curling is Scotland; some historians, however, believe that the sport originated in the Netherlands in the 15th century. There is evidence of a curling club in Kilsyth, Scotland in 1716, but the earliest recorded club is the Muthill Curling Club, Tayside, Scotland, formed in 1739, which produced the first known written rules of the game on November 17, 1739. The Grand (later Royal) Caledonian Curling

Club was founded in 1838 and was the international governing body of the sport until 1966, when the International Curling Federation was formed; this was renamed the World Curling Federation in 1991.

United States and Canada Scottish immigrants introduced curling to North America in the 18th century. The earliest known club was the Royal Montreal Curling club, founded in 1807. The first international game was between Canada and the United States in 1884—the inaugural Gordon International Medal series. In 1832, Orchard Lake Curling Club, Mich., was founded, the first in the United States. The oldest club in continuous existence in the U.S. is the Milwaukee Curling Club, Wis., formed *c.* 1850. Regional curling associations governed the sport in the U.S. until 1947, when the United States Women's Curling Association was formed, followed in 1958 by the Men's Curling Association. In 1986, the United States Curling Association was formed and is the current governing body for the sport. In Canada, the Dominion Curling Association was formed in 1935, renamed the Canadian Curling Association in 1968.

OLYMPIC GAMES Curling has been a demonstration sport at the Olympic Games of 1924, 1932, 1964 and 1988.

WORLD CHAMPIONSHIPS First held in 1959, these championships are held annually. Women's competition was introduced in 1979.

Most titles (men) Canada has dominated this event, winning 20 titles: 1959–64, 1966, 1968–72,

SKIPS AND STONES ■ CURLING DEVELOPED IN CANADA IN THE 19TH CENTURY. CANADIAN TEAMS HAVE WON 20 MEN'S WORLD TITLES AND SIX WOMEN'S.

1980, 1982–83, 1985–87 and 1989–90. Ernie Richardson (Canada) has been winning skip a record four times, 1959–60, 1962–63.

Most titles (women) Canada has won six championships, in 1980, 1984–87 and 1989. Djordy Nordby (Norway) has been skip of two winning teams, 1990–91.

UNITED STATES NATIONAL CHAMPIONSHIPS A men's tournament was first held in 1957. A women's event was introduced in 1977.

Men Two curlers have been skips on five championship teams: Bud Somerville (Superior Curling Club, Wis. in 1965, 1968–69, 1974 and 1981), and Bruce Roberts (Hibbing Curling Club, Minn. in 1966–67, 1976–77 and 1984).

Women In this competition, Nancy Langley of Seattle, Wash. has been the skip of a record four championship teams: 1979, 1981, 1983 and 1988.

THE LABATT BRIER (FORMERLY THE MACDONALD BRIER 1927–79) The Brier is the Canadian men's curling championship. The competition was first held at the Granite Club, Toronto in 1927. Sponsored by Macdonald Tobacco Inc., it had been known as the Macdonald Brier; since 1980 Labatt Brewery has sponsored the event.

Most titles The most wins is 23, by Manitoba (1928–32, 1934, 1936, 1938, 1940, 1942, 1947, 1949, 1952–53, 1956, 1965, 1970–72, 1979, 1981, 1984 and 1992). Ernie Richardson (Saskatche-

TIMEOUT

LONG THROW ☛ THE LONGEST THROW OF A CURLING STONE WAS 576 FEET 4 INCHES BY EDDIE KULBACKI (CANADA) AT PARK LAKE, NEEPAWA, CANADA ON JANUARY 29, 1989.

wan) has been winning skip a record four times (1959–60 and 1962–63).

Perfect game Stu Beagle, of Calgary, Alberta, played a perfect game (48 points) against Nova Scotia in the Canadian Championships (Brier) at Fort William (now Thunder Bay), Ontario on March 8, 1960. Andrew McQuiston skipped the Scotland team to a perfect game v. Switzerland at the Uniroyal Junior Men's World Championship at Kitchener, Ontario, Canada in 1980.

Bernice Fekete, of Edmonton, Alberta, Canada, skipped her rink to two consecutive eight-enders on the same ice at the Derrick Club, Edmonton on January 10 and February 6, 1973.

Two eight-enders in one bonspiel were scored at the Parry Sound Curling Club, Ontario, Canada from January 6–8, 1983.

CYCLING

ORIGINS The forerunner of the bicycle, the *celerifere*, was demonstrated in the garden of the Palais Royale, Paris, France in 1791. The velocipede, the first practical pedal-propelled vehicle, was built in March 1861 by Pierre Michaux and his son Ernest and demonstrated in Paris. The first velocipede race occurred on May 31, 1868 at the Parc St. Cloud, Paris, over a distance of 1.24 miles. The first international organization was the International Cyclist Association (ICA), founded in 1892, which launched the first world championships in 1893. The current governing body, the *Union Cycliste Internationale* (UCI), was founded in 1900.

OLYMPIC GAMES Cycling was included in the first modern Games held in 1896, and has been part of every Games since, with the exception of 1904. Women's events were first staged in 1984.

Most gold medals Four men have won three gold medals: Paul Masson (France), 1,000 meter time-trial, 1,000 meter sprint, 10,000 meter track in 1896; Francesco Verri (Italy), 1,000 meter time-trial, 1,000 meter sprint, 5,000 meter track in 1906; Robert Charpentier (France), individual road race, team road race, 4,000 meter team pursuit in 1936; Daniel Morelon (France), 1,000 meter sprint in 1968 and 1972, 2,000 meter tandem in 1968.

Most medals Daniel Morelon (France) has won five Olympic medals: three gold (see above); one silver, 1,000 meter sprint in 1972; one bronze, 1,000 meter sprint in 1964.

TRANSCONTINENTAL CYCLING RECORDS

Men's Records (United States Crossing)

Event	Rider(s)	Start/Finish	Days: Hrs: Min	Av. mph	Year
Solo (time)	Michael Secrest	HB–NYC	7:23:16	15.24	1990
Solo (av. mph)	Pete Penseyres	HB–AC	8:09:47	15.40	1986
Tandem	Lon Halderman & Pete Penseyres	HB–AC	7:14:15	15.97	1987

Men's Records (Canada Crossing)

Event	Rider(s)	Start/Finish	Days: Hrs: Min	Av. mph	Year
Solo	William Narasnek	Van–Hal	13:09:06	11.68	1991

Women's Records (United States Crossing)

Event	Rider(s)	Start/Finish	Days: Hrs: Min	Av. mph	Year
Solo	Susan Notorangelo	CM–NYC	9:09:09	12.93	1989
Tandem	Estelle Grey & Cheryl Marek	SM–NYC	10:22:48	11.32	1984

HB: Huntington Beach Calif.; NYC: New York City; AC: Atlantic City N.J.; Van: Vancouver; Hal: Halifax, Nova Scotia; CM: Costa Mesa, Calif.; SM: Santa Monica, Calif.

Source: Ultra Marathon Cycling Association (UMCA), The Guinness Book of Records, 1993

TOUR DE FRANCE CHAMPIONS (1903–1946)

Year	Winner	Country	Year	Winner	Country
1903	Maurice Garin	France	1925	Ottavio Bottecchia	Italy
1904	Henri Cornet	France	1926	Lucien Buysse	Belgium
1905	Louis Trousselier	France	1927	Nicholas Frantz	Luxembourg
1906	Rene Pottier	France	1928	Nicholas Frantz	Luxembourg
1907	Lucien Petit-Breton	France	1929	Maurice Dewaele	Belgium
1908	Lucien Petit-Breton	France	1930	Andre Leducq	France
1909	Francois Faber	Luxembourg	1931	Antonin Magne	France
1910	Octave Lapize	France	1932	Andre Leducq	France
1911	Gustave Garrigou	France	1933	Georges Speicher	France
1912	Odile Defraye	Belgium	1934	Antonin Magne	France
1913	Philippe Thys	Belgium	1935	Romain Maes	Belgium
1914	Philippe Thys	Belgium	1936	Sylvere Maes	Belgium
1915	not held		1937	Roger Lapebie	France
1916	not held		1938	Gino Bartali	Italy
1917	not held		1939	Sylvere Maes	Belgium
1918	not held		1940	not held	
1919	Firmin Labot	Belgium	1941	not held	
1920	Philippe Thys	Belgium	1942	not held	
1921	Leon Scieur	Belgium	1943	not held	
1922	Firmin Labot	Belgium	1944	not held	
1923	Henri Pelissier	France	1945	not held	
1924	Ottavio Bottecchia	Italy	1946	Jean Lazarides	France

WORLD CHAMPIONSHIPS World championships are contested annually. They were first staged for amateurs in 1893 and for professionals in 1895.

Most titles (one event) The most wins in one event is 10, by Koichi Nakano (Japan), professional sprint 1977–86. The most wins in a men's amateur event is seven, by two cyclists: Daniel Morelon (France), sprint, 1966–67, 1969–71, 1973, 1975; and Leon Meredith (Great Britain), 100 kilometer motor-paced, 1904–05, 1907–09, 1911 and 1913.

The most women's titles is eight, by Jeannie Longo (France), pursuit 1986 and 1988–89 and road 1985–87 and 1989–90.

United States The most world titles won by a U.S. cyclist is four, in women's 3 kilometer pursuit by Rebecca Twigg, 1982, 1984–85 and 1987. The most successful man has been Greg LeMond, winner of the individual road race in 1983 and 1989.

UNITED STATES NATIONAL CHAMPIONSHIPS National cycling championships have been held annually since 1899. Women's events were first included in 1937.

Most titles Leonard Nitz has won 16 titles: five pursuit (1976 and 1980–83); eight team pursuit (1980–84, 1986 and 1988–89); two 1 kilometer time-trial (1982 and 1984); one criterium (1986). Connie Carpenter has won 11 titles in women's events: four road race (1976–77, 1979 and 1981); three pursuit (1976–77 and 1979); two criterium (1982–83); two points (1981–82).

TOUR DE FRANCE CHAMPIONS (1947–1992)

Year	Winner	Country	Year	Winner	Country
1947	Jean Robic	France	1970	Eddy Merckx	Belgium
1948	Gino Bartali	Italy	1971	Eddy Merckx	Belgium
1949	Fausto Coppi	Italy	1972	Eddy Merckx	Belgium
1950	Ferdinand Kubler	Switzerland	1973	Luis Ocana	Spain
1951	Hugo Koblet	Switzerland	1974	Eddy Merckx	Belgium
1952	Fausto Coppi	Italy	1975	Bernard Thevenet	France
1953	Louison Bobet	France	1976	Lucien van Impe	Belgium
1954	Louison Bobet	France	1977	Bernard Thevenet	France
1955	Louison Bobet	France	1978	Bernard Hinault	France
1956	Roger Walkowiak	France	1979	Bernard Hinault	France
1957	Jacques Anquetil	France	1980	Joop Zoetemilk	Netherlands
1958	Charly Gaul	Luxembourg	1981	Bernard Hinault	France
1959	Federico Bahamontes	Spain	1982	Bernard Hinault	France
1960	Gastone Nencini	Italy	1983	Laurent Fignon	France
1961	Jacques Anquetil	France	1984	Laurent Fignon	France
1962	Jacques Anquetil	France	1985	Bernard Hinault	France
1963	Jacques Anquetil	France	1986	Greg LeMond	U.S.
1964	Jacques Anquetil	France	1987	Stephen Roche	Ireland
1965	Felice Gimondi	Italy	1988	Pedro Delgado	Spain
1966	Lucien Aimar	France	1989	Greg LeMond	U.S.
1967	Roger Pingeon	France	1990	Greg LeMond	U.S.
1968	Jan Janssen	Netherlands	1991	Miguel Indurain	Spain
1969	Eddy Merckx	Belgium	1992	Miguel Indurain	Spain

TOUR DE FRANCE

First staged in 1903, the Tour meanders throughout France and sometimes neighboring countries over a four-week period.

Most wins Three riders have each won the event five times: Jacques Anquetil (France), 1957, 1961–64; Eddy Merckx (Belgium), 1969–72, 1974; Bernard Hinault (France), 1978–79, 1981–82, 1985.

Longest race The longest race held was 3,569 miles in 1926.

Closest race The closest race ever was in 1989, when after 2,030 miles over 23 days (July 1–23) Greg LeMond (U.S.), who completed the Tour in 87 hours 38 minutes 35 seconds, beat Laurent Fignon (France) in Paris by only 8 seconds.

Fastest speed The fastest average speed was 24.547 mph by Miguel Indurain (Spain) in 1992.

Longest stage The longest-ever stage was the 486 kilometers (302 miles) from Les Sables d'Olonne to Bayonne in 1919.

Most participants The most participants was 210 starters in 1986.

United States Greg LeMond became the first American winner in 1986; he returned from serious injury to win again in 1989 and 1990.

WOMEN'S TOUR DE FRANCE

The inaugural women's Tour de France was staged in 1984.

Most wins Jeannie Longo (France) has won the event a record four times, 1987–90.

RACE ACROSS AMERICA

ORIGINS An annual transcontinental crossing of the United States from west to east, the Race Across America was first staged in 1982. A women's division was introduced in 1984. The start and finish lines have varied, but currently the race starts in Irvine, Ca., and finishes in Savannah, Ga. The race must travel a minimum distance of 2,900 miles.

Most wins Three cyclists have won two men's titles: Lon Haldeman, 1982–83; Pete Penseyres, 1984, 1986; Bob Fourney, 1990–91. In the women's division Susan Notorangelo has won two titles, 1985 and 1989.

DARTS

ORIGINS Darts, or dartes (heavily weighted 10-inch throwing arrows) were first used in Ireland in the 16th century, as a weapon for self-defense. The Pilgrims played darts for recreation aboard the *Mayflower* in 1620. The modern game dates to 1896, when Brian Gamlin of Bury, England devised the present board numbering system. The first recorded score of 180, the maximum with three darts, was by John Reader at the Highbury Tavern, Sussex, England in 1902.

WORLD CHAMPIONSHIP This competition was instituted in 1978.

Most titles Eric Bristow of England has won the title a record five times (1980–81, 1984–86).

DIVING

ORIGINS Diving traces its roots to the gymnastics movement that developed in Germany and Sweden in the 17th century. During the summer, gymnasts would train at the beach, and acrobatic techniques would be performed over water as a safety measure. From this activity the sport of diving developed. The world governing body for diving is the *Fédération Internationale de Natation Amateur* (FINA), founded in 1980. FINA is also the governing body for swimming and water polo.

United States Ernst Bransten and Mike Peppe are considered the two main pioneers of diving in the United States. Bransten, a Swede, came to the United States following World War I. He introduced Swedish training methods and diving techniques, which revolutionized the sport in this country. Peppe's highly successful program at Ohio State University, 1931–68, produced several Olympic medalists and helped promote the sport here.

OLYMPIC GAMES Men's diving events were introduced at the 1904 Games, and women's events in 1912.

DARTS SCORING RECORDS (FEWEST THROWN)

Scores of 201 in four darts, 301 in six darts, 401 in seven darts and 501 in nine darts have been achieved on many occasions.

Score	Darts Thrown	Player(s)	Date
1,001	19	Cliff Inglis (England)	Nov. 11, 1975
	19	Jocky Wilson (Scotland)	March 23, 1989
2,001	52	Alan Evans (Wales)	Sept. 3, 1976
3,001	73	Tony Benson (England)	July 12, 1986
100,001	3,732	Alan Downie (Scotland)	Nov. 21, 1986
1,000,001	36,583	Eight-man team (U.S.)*	Oct. 19–20, 1991

* An eight-man team set the record at Buzzy's Pub and Grub in Lynn, Mass.

Most gold medals Two divers have won four gold medals: Pat McCormick (U.S.), who won both the women's springboard and the highboard events in 1952 and 1956; and Greg Louganis (U.S.), who performed the highboard/springboard double in 1984 and 1988.

Most medals Two divers have won five medals: Klaus Dibiasi (Italy), three golds, highboard in 1968, 1972 and 1976, and two silver, highboard in 1964 and springboard in 1968; and Greg Louganis, four golds (see above) and one silver, highboard in 1976.

WORLD CHAMPIONSHIPS Diving events were included in the first world aquatic championships staged in 1973.

Most titles Greg Louganis (U.S.) has won a record five world titles—highboard in 1978 and the highboard/springboard double in 1982 and 1986. Philip Boggs (U.S.) is the only diver to win three gold medals at one event, springboard, in 1973, 1975 and 1978.

UNITED STATES NATIONAL CHAMPIONSHIPS The Amateur Athletic Union (AAU) organized the first national diving championships in 1909. Since 1981, United States Diving has been the governing body of the sport in this country, and thus responsible for the national championships.

Most titles Greg Louganis has won a record 47 national titles: 17, one-meter springboard; 17, three-meter springboard; 13, platform. In women's competition, Cynthia Potter has won a record 28 titles.

EQUESTRIAN SPORTS

ORIGINS Evidence of horseback riding dates from a Persian engraving dated *c.* 3000 B.C. The three separate equestrian competitions recognized at the Olympic level are show jumping, the three-day event and dressage. The earliest known show jumping competition was in Ireland, when the Royal Dublin Society held its first "Horse Show" on April 15, 1864. Dressage competition derived from the exercises taught at 16th century Italian and French horsemanship academies, while the three-day event developed from cavalry endurance rides. The world governing body for all three disciplines is the *Fédération Equestre Internationale* (FEI), founded in Brussels, Belgium in 1921.

OLYMPIC GAMES In the ancient games, chariot races featured horses, and later riding contests were included. Show jumping was included in the 1900 Games; the three-day event and dressage disciplines were not added until 1912. In 1956 the equestrian events were held in Stockholm, Sweden, separate from the main Games in Melbourne, Australia, because of the strict Australian quarantine laws.

Most medals (all events) Germany has dominated the equestrian events, winning 64 medals overall: 27 gold, 17 silver and 20 bronze.

SHOW JUMPING

OLYMPIC GAMES

Most gold medals (rider) Hans-Gunther Winkler (West Germany) has won five titles, 1956, 1960, 1964 and 1972 in the team competition, and the individual championship in 1956. The only rider to win two individual titles is Pierre Jonqueres d'Oriola (France), in 1952 and 1964.

Most gold medals (horse) The most successful horse is Halla, ridden by Hans-Gunther Winkler during his individual and team wins in 1956, and during the team win in 1960.

Most medals Hans-Gunther Winkler has won a record seven medals: five gold (see above), one silver and one bronze in the team competition in 1976 and 1968.

United States Two American riders have won the individual event: Bill Steinkraus in 1968, and Joe

Fargis in 1984. The United States won the team event in 1984.

WORLD CHAMPIONSHIPS The men's world championship was inaugurated in 1953. In 1965, 1970

HIGHEST JUMP ☛ HUASÓ, RIDDEN BY CAPT. ALBERTO LARRAGUIBEL MORALES (CHILE), LEAPED OVER AN 8-FOOT-1¼-INCH FENCE AT VIÑA DEL MAR, CHILE ON FEBRUARY 5, 1949.

and 1974 separate women's championships were held. An integrated championship was first held in 1978 and is now held every four years.

Most titles Two riders share the record for most men's championships with two victories: Hans-Gunther Winkler (West Germany), 1954–55, and Raimondo d'Inzeo (Italy), 1956 and 1960. The women's title was won twice by Janou Tissot (née Lefebvre) of France, in 1970 and 1974. No rider has won the integrated competition more than once.

THREE-DAY EVENT

OLYMPIC GAMES

Most gold medals Charles Pahud de Mortanges (Netherlands) has won four gold medals—the individual title in 1928 and 1932, and the team event in 1924 and 1928. Mark Todd (New Zealand) is the only other rider to have won the individual title twice, in 1984 and 1988.

Most medals (rider) Charles Pahud de Mortanges has won five medals: four gold (see above) and one silver in the 1932 team event.

Most gold medals (horse) Marcroix was ridden by Charles Pahud de Mortanges in three of his four medal rounds, 1928–32.

United States The most medals won for the U.S. is six, by J. Michael Plumb: team gold, 1976 and 1984, and four silver medals, team 1964, 1968 and 1972, and individual 1976. Tad Coffin is the only U.S. rider to have won both team and individual gold medals, in 1976.

WORLD CHAMPIONSHIP First held in 1966, the event is held quadrenially and is open to both men and women.

Most titles (rider) Bruce Davidson (U.S.) is the only rider to have won two world titles, on Irish Cap in 1974, and on Might Tango in 1978.

Most titles (country) Great Britain has won the team title a record three times, 1970, 1982 and 1986. The United States won the team event in 1974.

DRESSAGE

OLYMPIC GAMES

Most gold medals (rider) Reiner Klimke (West Germany) has won six gold medals: one individual in 1984, and five team in 1964, 1968, 1976, 1984 and 1988. Henri St. Cyr (Sweden) is the only rider to have won two individual titles, in 1952 and 1956.

Most gold medals (horse) Ahlerich was ridden by Reiner Klimke in three of his gold medal rounds, individual in 1984, and team in 1984 and 1988.

Most medals Reiner Klimke won eight medals: six gold (see above), and two bronze in the individual event in 1968 and 1976.

United States The United States has never won a gold medal in dressage. In the team event the United States has won one silver, 1948, and three bronze, in 1932, 1976, and 1992. Hiram Tuttle is the only rider to have won an individual medal, earning the bronze in 1932.

WORLD CHAMPIONSHIPS This competition was instituted in 1966.

Most titles (country) West Germany has won a record six times: 1966, 1974, 1978, 1982, 1986 and 1990.

Most titles (rider) Reiner Klimke (West Germany) is the only rider to have won two individual titles, on Mehmed in 1974 and on Ahlerich in 1982.

FENCING

ORIGINS Evidence of swordsmanship can be traced back to Egypt as early as *c.* 1360 B.C., where it was demonstrated during religious ceremonies. Fencing, "fighting with sticks," gained popularity as a sport in Europe in the 16th century.

The modern foil, a light court sword, was introduced in France in the mid-17th century; in the late 19th century, the fencing "arsenal" was expanded to include the épée, a heavier dueling weapon, and the sabre, a light cutting sword.

The *Fédération Internationale d'Escrime* (FIE), the world governing body, was founded in Paris, France in 1913. The first European championships were held in 1921 and were expanded into world championships in 1935.

United States In the United States, the Amateur Fencers League of America (AFLA) was founded on April 22, 1891 in New York City. This group assumed supervision of the sport in the U.S., staging the first national championship in 1892. In June 1981, the AFLA changed its name to the United States Fencing Association (USFA).

OLYMPIC GAMES Fencing was included in the first Olympic Games of the modern era at Athens in 1896, and is one of only six sports to be featured in every Olympiad.

Most gold medals Aladar Gerevich (Hungary) has won a record seven gold medals, all in sabre: individual, 1948; team, 1932, 1936, 1948, 1952, 1956 and 1960. In individual events, two fencers have won three titles: Ramon Fonst (Cuba), épée, 1900 and 1904, and foil, 1904; Nedo Nadi (Italy), foil, 1912 and 1920, and sabre, 1920. The most golds won by a woman is four, by Yelena Novikova (née Belova; USSR), all in foil: individual, 1968; team, 1968, 1972 and 1976.

Most medals Edoardo Mangiarotti (Italy) has won a record 13 medals in fencing: six gold, five silver and two bronze in foil and épée events from 1936 to 1960.

United States Albertson Van Zo Post is the only American to have won an Olympic title. He won the single sticks competition and teamed with two Cubans to win the team foil title in 1904. In overall competition the United States has won 19 medals (both Cuba and the United States are credited with a gold medal for the 1904 team foil): two gold, six silver and 11 bronze—all in men's events.

WORLD CHAMPIONSHIPS The first world championships were staged in Paris, France in 1937. Foil, épée and sabre events were held for men and just foil for women. In 1989, a women's épée event was added. The tournament is staged annually.

Most titles The greatest number of individual world titles won is five, by Aleksandr Romankov (USSR), at foil, 1974, 1977, 1979, 1982 and 1983. Five women foilists have won three world titles: Hélène Mayer (Germany), 1929, 1931 and 1937; Ilona Schacherer-Elek (Hungary), 1934–35, 1951; Ellen Müller-Preis (Austria), 1947, 1949–50; Cornelia Hanisch (West Germany), 1979, 1981 and 1985; and Anja Fichtel (West Germany), 1986, 1988 and 1990.

UNITED STATES NATIONAL CHAMPIONSHIPS

Most titles The most U.S. titles won at one weapon is 12 at sabre, by Peter Westbrook, in 1974, 1975, 1979–86, 1988 and 1989. The women's record is 10 at foil, by Janice Romary in 1950–51, 1956–57, 1960–61, 1964–66 and 1968.

The most individual foil championships won is seven, by Michael Marx in 1977, 1979, 1982, 1985–87 and 1990. L. G. Nunes won the most épée championships, with six—1917, 1922, 1924, 1926, 1928 and 1932. Vincent Bradford won a record number of women's épée championships with four in 1982–84 and 1986.

NCAA CHAMPIONSHIP DIVISION I (TEAM) A men's championship was first staged in 1941. A women's championship was not introduced until 1982. In 1990 these two tournaments were replaced by a combined team event. In the now-defunct separate events, New York University won the men's title 12 times, 1947–76; and Wayne State (Mich.), won the women's event three times, 1982, 1988–89.

Most wins Penn State has won two titles: 1990–91.

Most titles (fencer) Michael Lofton, New York University, has won the most titles in a career, with four victories in the sabre, 1984–87. In women's competition, Caitlin Bilodeaux, Columbia–Barnard, and Molly Sullivan, Notre Dame, have both won the individual title twice: Bilodeaux in 1985 and 1987, and Sullivan in 1986 and 1988.

FIELD HOCKEY

ORIGINS Hitting a ball with a stick is a game that dates back to the origins of the human race. Bas-reliefs and frescoes discovered in Egypt and Greece depict hockey-like games. A drawing of a "bully" on the walls of a tomb at Beni Hassan in the Nile Valley has been dated to c. 2050 B.C. The birthplace of modern hockey is Great Britain, where the first definitive code of rules was established in 1886. The *Fédération Internationale de Hockey* (FIH), the world governing body, was founded on January 7, 1924.

United States The sport was introduced to this country in 1921 by a British teacher, Constance M. K. Applebee. The Field Hockey Association of America (FHAA) was founded in 1928 by Henry Greer. The first game was staged between the Germantown Cricket Club and the Westchester Field Hockey Club, also in 1928.

OLYMPIC GAMES Field hockey was added to the Olympic Games in 1908 and became a permanent feature in 1928; a women's tournament was added in 1980.

Most gold medals (team) In the men's competition, India has won eight gold medals: 1928, 1932, 1936, 1948, 1952, 1956, 1964 and 1980. In the women's competition, no team has won the event more than once.

United States The United States has never won either the men's or women's events; the best result has been a bronze in 1932 (men), and in 1984 (women).

SCORING RECORDS

Highest score The highest score in an international game was India's 24–1 defeat of the United States at Los Angeles, Calif., in the 1932 Olympic Games. In women's competition, England hammered France 23–0 at Merton, England on February 3, 1923.

Most goals Paul Litjens (Netherlands) holds the record for most goals by one player in international play. He scored 267 goals in 177 games.

Fastest goal The fastest goal scored in an international game was netted only seven seconds after the bully by John French for England *v.* West Germany at Nottingham, England on April 25, 1971.

NCAA DIVISION I (WOMEN) The women's championship was inaugurated in 1981.

Most titles Old Dominion has won the most championships with seven titles: 1982–84, 1988 and 1990–92.

FIGURE SKATING

ORIGINS The earliest reference to ice skating is in Scandinavian literature dating to the 2nd century A.D. Jackson Haines, a New Yorker, is regarded as the pioneer of the modern concept of figure skating, a composite of skating and dancing. Although his ideas were not initially favored in the United States, Haines moved to Europe in the mid-1860s, where his "International Style of Figure Skating" was warmly received and promoted. The first artificial rink was opened in London, England on January 7, 1876. The world governing body is the International Skating Union (ISU), founded in 1892. The sport functioned informally in the United States until 1921, when the United States Figure Skating Association (USFSA) was formed to oversee skating in this country—a role it still performs.

OLYMPIC GAMES Figure skating was first included in the 1908 Summer Games in London, and has been featured in every Games since 1920. Uniquely, both men's and women's events have been included in the Games from the first introduction of the sport.

Most gold medals Three skaters have won three gold medals: Gillis Grafstrom (Sweden) in 1920, 1924 and 1928; Sonja Henie (Norway) in 1928, 1932 and 1936; Irina Rodnina (USSR), with two different partners, in the pairs in 1972, 1976 and 1980.

SKATING DYNASTY ■ SKATERS FROM THE FORMER SOVIET UNION WON NINE CONSECUTIVE OLYMPIC PAIRS TITLES, 1970–92. GORDAYEVICH AND GRINKO WON THE 1988 TITLE.

United States Dick Button is the only American skater to win two gold medals, in 1948 and 1952. American skaters have won the men's title six times and the women's five. No American team has won either the pairs or dance titles.

WORLD CHAMPIONSHIPS This competition was first staged in 1896.

Most titles (individual) The greatest number of men's individual world figure skating titles is 10, by Ulrich Salchow (Sweden), in 1901–05 and 1907–11. The women's record (instituted 1906) is also 10 individual titles, by Sonja Henie (Norway) between 1927 and 1936.

Most titles (pairs) Irina Rodnina (USSR) has won 10 pairs titles (instituted 1908), four with Aleksey Ulanov, 1969–72, and six with her husband, Aleksandr Zaitsev, 1973–78.

Most titles (ice dance) The most ice dance titles (instituted 1952) won is six, by Lyudmila Pakhomova and her husband, Aleksandr Gorshkov (USSR), 1970–74 and 1976.

United States Dick Button won five world titles, 1948–52. Five women's world titles were won by Carol Heise, 1956–60.

UNITED STATES NATIONAL CHAMPIONSHIPS The U.S. championships were first held in 1914.

Most titles The most titles won by an individual is nine, by Maribel Y. Vinson, 1928–33 and 1935–37. She also won six pairs titles, and her aggregate of 15 titles is equaled by Therese Blanchard (née

Weld), who won six individual and nine pairs titles between 1914 and 1927. The men's individual record is seven, by Roger Turner, 1928–34, and by Dick Button, 1946–52.

HIGHEST MARKS The highest tally of maximum six marks awarded in an international championship was 29, to Jayne Torvill and Christopher Dean (Great Britain) in the World Ice Dance Championships at Ottawa, Canada on March 22–24, 1984. They previously gained a perfect set of nine sixes for artistic presentation in the free dance at the 1983 World Championships in Helsinki, Finland and at the 1984 Winter Olympic Games in Sarajevo, Yugoslavia. In their career, Torvill and Dean received a record total of 136 sixes.

The highest tally by a soloist is seven, by Donald Jackson (Canada) in the World Men's Championship at Prague, Czechoslovakia in 1962; and by Midori Ito (Japan) in the World Ladies' Championships at Paris, France in 1989.

BACKFLIP ■ 1980 OLYMPIC CHAMPION ROBIN COUSINS PERFORMED AN 18-FOOT-LONG BACKFLIP ON NOVEMBER 16, 1983.

FISHING

Oldest existing club The Ellem fishing club was formed by a number of Edinburgh and Berwickshire gentlemen in Scotland in 1829. Its first annual general meeting was held on April 29, 1830.

Largest single catch The largest officially ratified fish ever caught on a rod was a man-eating great white shark (*Carcharodon carcharias*) weigh-

FRESHWATER AND SALT WATER ALL-TACKLE CLASS WORLD RECORDS

A selection of records ratified by the International Game Fish Association to January 1, 1993.

Species	Weight	Caught By	Location	Date
Arawana	10 lb 2 oz	Gilberto Fernandes	Brazil	Feb. 3, 1990
Barracuda, California	6 lb 3 oz	James A. Seibert	Point Loma, Calif.	April 4, 1992
Barracuda, great	83 lb 0 oz	K. Hackett	Nigeria	Jan. 13, 1952
Bass, kelp	13 lb 4 oz	Larry Skiles	Laguna Beach, Calif.	July 1, 1991
Bass, largemouth	22 lb 4 oz	George W. Perry	Montgomery Lake, Ga.	June 2, 1932
Bass, smallmouth	11 lb 15 oz	David L. Hayes	Dale Hollow Lake, Ky.	July 9, 1955
Bass, striped	78 lb 8 oz	Albert Reynolds	Atlantic City, N.J.	Sept. 21, 1982
Bluefish	31 lb12 oz	James M. Hussey	Hatteras, N.C.	Jan. 30, 1972
Carp	75 lb 11 oz	Leo van der Gugten	France	May 21, 1987
Carp, grass	62 lb 0 oz	Craig Bass	Pinson, Ala.	May 13, 1991
Catfish, blue	109 lb 4 oz	George A. Lijewski	Moncks Corner, S.C.	March 14, 1991
Chub	5 lb 12 oz	Luis Rasmussen	Sweden	July 26, 1987
Cod, Atlantic	98 lb 12 oz	Alphonse Bielevich	Isle of Shoals, N.H.	June 8, 1969
Cod, estuary rock	263 lb 7 oz	Peter Norris	Australia	Sept. 9, 1988
Conger	110 lb 8 oz	Hans Clausen	English Channel	Aug. 20, 1991
Eel, American	8 lb 8 oz	Gerald Lapierre	Brewster, Mass.	May 17, 1992
Flounder, summer	22 lb 7 oz	Charles Nappi	Montauk, N.Y.	Sept. 15, 1975
Geelbek	14 lb 15 oz	Hester Wessels	South Africa	Feb. 15, 1992
Goldfish	3 lb 0 oz	Kenneth Kinsey	Livingston, Tex.	May 8, 1988
Grouper, black	113 lb 6 oz	Donald Bone	Dry Tortugas, Fla.	Jan. 27, 1990
Grouper, broomtail	83 lb 0 oz	Enrique Weisson	Ecuador	June 28, 1992
Haddock	11 lb 11 oz	Jim Mailea	Ogunquit, Me.	Sept. 12, 1991
Halibut, Atlantic	255 lb 4 oz	Sonny Manley	Gloucester, Mass.	July 28, 1989
Halibut, Pacific	368 lb 0 oz	Celia Dueitt	Gustavus, Alaska	July 5, 1991
Houndfish	14 lb 0 oz	Deborah Dunaway	Costa Rica	July 18, 1992
Mackerel, broad barred	12 lb 2 oz	Ben Pugh	Australia	March 14, 1992
Marlin, black	1,560 lb 0 oz	Alfred Glassell Jr.	Peru	Aug. 4, 1953
Marlin, blue (Atlantic)	1,402 lb 2 oz	Roberto A. Amorim	Brazil	Feb. 29, 1992
Marlin, blue (Pacific)	1,376 lb 0 oz	Jay deBeaubien	Kona, Hawaii	May 31, 1982

ing 2,664 lb and measuring 16 ft 10 in long, caught on a 130–lb test line by Alf Dean at Denial Bay, near Ceduna, South Australia on April 21, 1959. A great white shark weighing 3,388 lb was caught by Clive Green off Albany, Western Australia on April 26, 1976 but will remain unratified, as whale meat was used as bait.

In June 1978, a great white shark measuring 20 ft 4 in in length and weighing more than 5,000 lb

FRESHWATER AND SALT WATER ALL-TACKLE CLASS WORLD RECORDS

A selection of records ratified by the International Game Fish Association to January 1, 1993.

Species	Weight	Caught By	Location	Date
Perch, Nile	191 lb 8 oz	Andy Davison	Kenya	Sept. 5, 1991
Pike, northern	55 lb 1 oz	Lothar Louis	Germany	Oct. 16, 1986
Piranha, black	3 lb 0 oz	Doug Olander	Brazil	Nov. 23, 1991
Roosterfish	114 lb 0 oz	Abe Sackheim	Mexico	June 1, 1960
Sailfish, Atlantic	135 lb 5 oz	Ron King	Nigeria	Nov. 10, 1991
Sailfish, Pacific	221 lb 0 oz	C.W. Stewart	Ecuador	Feb. 12, 1947
Salmon, Atlantic	79 lb 2 oz	Henrik Henriksen	Norway	1928
Salmon, chinook	97 lb 4 oz	Les Anderson	Kenai River, Alaska	May 17, 1985
Salmon, pink	12 lb 9 oz	Steven Lee	Kenai River, Alaska	Aug. 17, 1974
Samson fish	24 lb 11 oz	Clive Johnson	Australia	April 12, 1992
Shad, American	11 lb 4 oz	Bob Thibodo	S. Hadley, Mass.	May 19, 1986
Shark, blue	437 lb 0 oz	Peter Hyde	Australia	Oct. 2, 1976
Shark, Greenland	1,708 lb 9 oz	Terje Nordtvedt	Norway	Oct. 18, 1987
Shark, hammerhead	991 lb 0 oz	Allen Ogle	Sarasota, Fla.	May 30, 1982
Shark, mako	1,115 lb 0 oz	Patrick Guillanton	Mauritius	Nov. 16, 1988
Shark, tiger	1,780 lb 0 oz	Walter Maxwell	Cherry Grove, S.C.	June 14, 1964
Shark, white	2,664 lb 0 oz	Alfred Dean	Australia	April 21, 1959
Snapper, red	46 lb 8 oz	E. Lane Nichols	Destin, Fla.	Oct. 1, 1985
Stingray, southern	229 lb 0 oz	David Anderson	Galveston Bay, Tex.	June 2, 1991
Sturgeon, lake	92 lb 4 oz	James DeOtis	Kettle River, Minn.	Sept. 11, 1986
Sturgeon, white	468 lb 0 oz	Joey Pallotta III	Benica, Calif.	July 9, 1983
Swordfish	1,182 lb 0 oz	L. Marron	Chile	May 7, 1953
Tarpon	283 lb 4 oz	Yvon Sebag	Sierra Leone	April 16, 1991
Trout, brook	14 lb 8 oz	W.J. Cook	Canada	July 1916
Trout, brown	40 lb 4 oz	Howard L. Collins	Heber Springs, Ark.	May 9, 1992
Trout, rainbow	42 lb 2 oz	David White	Bell Island, Alaska	June 22, 1970
Tuna, bluefin	1,496 lb 0 oz	Ken Fraser	Canada	Oct. 26, 1979
Wahoo	155 lb 8 oz	William Bourne	Bahamas	April 3, 1990

was harpooned and landed by fishermen in the harbor of San Miguel, Azores.

The largest marine animal killed by hand harpoon was a blue whale 97 ft in length, by Archer Davidson in Twofold Bay, New South Wales, Australia in 1910. Its tail flukes measured 20 ft across and its jawbone 23 ft 4 in.

Casting The longest freshwater cast ratified under ICF (International Casting Federation) rules is 574 ft 2 in, by Walter Kummerow (West Germany), for the Bait Distance Double-Handed 30 g event held at Lenzerheide, Switzerland in the 1968 Championships.

At the currently contested weight of 17.7 g, the longest Double-Handed cast is 457 ft ½ in by Kevin Carriero (U.S.) at Toronto, Canada on July 24, 1984.

The longest Fly Distance Double-Handed cast is 319 ft 1 in by Wolfgang Feige (West Germany) at Toronto, Canada on July 23, 1984.

FOOTBAG

A footbag is a small, pliable, pellet-filled ball-like object with little or no bounce. The concept of the game is to keep the footbag in the air for the longest possible time. Both the time and the number of consecutive hacks (kicks) are recorded.

ORIGINS The sport of footbag was invented by John Stalberger (U.S.) in 1972.

TIMEOUT

FOOTBAG CIRCLE ☛ THE LARGEST CONTINUOUS CIRCLE OF PEOPLE PLAYING FOOTBAG IS 862. THIS GATHERING OF WELL-ROUNDED PEOPLE WAS STAGED AT COLORADO STATE UNIVERSITY IN FORT COLLINS ON JUNE 25, 1986.

UP IN THE AIR ■ TED MARTIN AND ANDY LINDER KEPT A FOOTBAG ALOFT FOR A PAIRS RECORD 83,453 KICKS ON SEPTEMBER 26, 1992.

CONSECUTIVE RECORDS

Men's singles 48,825 hacks by Ted Martin (U.S.) on June 4, 1988 in Memphis, Tenn. Martin kept the footbag aloft for 8 hours 11 minutes 25 seconds.

Women's singles 15,458 hacks by Francine Beaudry (Canada) on July 28, 1987 in Golden, Colo. Beaudry kept the footbag aloft for 2 hours 35 minutes 13 seconds.

Men's doubles 83,453 hacks by Andy Linder and Ted Martin (both U.S.) on September 26, 1992 in Mount Prospect, Ill. The pair kept the footbag aloft for 12 hours 39 minutes 15 seconds.

Women's doubles 21,025 hacks by Constance Reed and Marie Elsner (both U.S.) on July 31, 1986. The pair kept the footbag aloft for 3 hours 6 minutes 37 seconds.

FOOTBALL

ORIGINS On November 6, 1869, Princeton and Rutgers staged what is generally regarded as the first intercollegiate football game at New Brunswick, N.J. In October 1873 the Intercollegiate Football Association was formed (Columbia, Princeton, Rutgers and Yale), with the purpose of standardizing rules. At this point football was a modified version of soccer. The first significant move toward today's style of play came when Harvard accepted an invitation to play McGill University (Montreal, Canada) in a series of three challenge matches, the first being in May 1874, under modified rugby rules. Walter Camp is credited with organizing the basic format of the current game. Between 1880 and 1906, Camp sponsored the concepts of scrimmage lines, 11-man teams, reduction in field size, "downs" and "yards to gain" and a new scoring system.

NATIONAL FOOTBALL LEAGUE (NFL)

ORIGINS William (Pudge) Heffelfinger became the first professional player on November 12, 1892, when he was paid $500 by the Allegheny Athletic Association (AAA) to play for them against the Pittsburgh Athletic Club (PAC). In 1893, PAC signed one of its players, believed to have been Grant Dibert, to the first known professional contract. The first game to be played with admitted professionals participating was played at Latrobe, Pa., on August 31, 1895, with Latrobe YMCA defeating the Jeanette Athletic Club 12–0. Professional leagues existed in Pennsylvania and Ohio at the turn of the 20th century; however, the major breakthrough for professional football was the formation of the American Professional Football Association (APFA), founded in Canton, Ohio on September 17, 1920. Reorganized a number of times, the APFA was renamed the National Football League (NFL) on June 24, 1922. Since 1922, several rival leagues have challenged the NFL, the most significant being the All-America Football Conference (AAFL) and the American Football League (AFL). The AAFL began play in 1946 but after four seasons merged with the NFL for the 1950 season. The AFL challenge was stronger and more acrimonious. Formed in 1959, it had its inaugural season in 1960. The AFL–NFL "war" was halted on June 4, 1966, when an agreement to merge the leagues was announced. The leagues

WELL RECEIVED ■ DURING THE 1992 SEASON, ART MONK (LEFT) SET THE LEAGUE RECORD FOR ALL-TIME RECEPTIONS AT 847. JAMES LOFTON (RIGHT) BROKE THE NFL MARK FOR YARDAGE GAINED, EXTENDING IT TO 13,821 YARDS.

NFL INDIVIDUAL RECORDS (1920–1992)

POINTS SCORED

		Player(s)	Team(s)	Date(s)
Game	40	Ernie Nevers	Chicago Cardinals v. Chicago Bears	Nov. 18, 1929
Season	176	Paul Hornung	Green Bay Packers	1960
Career	2,002	George Blanda	Chicago Bears, Baltimore Colts, Houston Oilers, Oakland Raiders	1949–75

TOUCHDOWNS SCORED

Game	6	Ernie Nevers	Chicago Cardinals v. Chicago Bears	Nov. 28, 1929
		Dub Jones	Cleveland Browns v. Chicago Bears	Nov. 25, 1951
		Gale Sayers	Chicago Bears v. San Francisco 49ers	Dec. 12, 1965
Season	24	John Riggins	Washington Redskins	1983
Career	126	Jim Brown	Cleveland Browns	1957–65

PASSING

Yards Gained

Game	554	Norm Van Brocklin	Los Angeles Rams v. New York Yankees	Sept. 28, 1951
Season	5,084	Dan Marino	Miami Dolphins	1984
Career	47,003	Fran Tarkenton	Minnesota Vikings, New York Giants	1961–78

Completions

Game	42	Richard Todd	New York Jets v. San Francisco 49ers	Sept. 21, 1980
Season	404	Warren Moon	Houston Oilers	1991
Career	3,686	Fran Tarkenton	Minnesota Vikings, New York Giants	1961–78

Attempts

Game	68	George Blanda	Houston Oilers v. Buffalo Bills	Nov. 1, 1964
Season	655	Warren Moon	Houston Oilers	1991
Career	6,467	Fran Tarkenton	Minnesota Vikings, New York Giants	1961–78

Touchdowns Thrown

Game	7	Sid Luckman	Chicago Bears v. New York Giants	Nov. 14, 1943
		Adrian Burk	Philadelphia Eagles v. Washington Redskins	Oct. 17, 1954
		George Blanda	Houston Oilers v. New York Titans	Nov. 19, 1961
		Y. A. Tittle	New York Giants v. Washington Redskins	Oct. 28, 1962
		Joe Kapp	Minnesota Vikings v. Baltimore Colts	Sept. 28, 1969
Season	48	Dan Marino	Miami Dolphins	1984
Career	342	Fran Tarkenton	Minnesota Vikings, New York Giants	1961–78

NFL INDIVIDUAL RECORDS (1920–1992)

PASSING (cont.)

Average Yards Gained

		Player(s)	Team(s)	Date(s)
Game (min. 20 attempts)	18.58	Sammy Baugh	Washington Redskins v. Boston Yanks (24–446)	Oct. 31, 1948
Season (qualifiers)	11.17	Tommy O'Connell	Cleveland Browns (110–1,229)	1957
Career (min. 1,500 attempts)	8.63	Otto Graham	Cleveland Browns (1,565–13,499)	1950–55

PASS RECEIVING

Receptions

Game	18	Tom Fears	Los Angeles Rams v. Green Bay Packers	Dec. 3, 1950
Season	108	Sterling Sharpe	Green Bay Packers	1992
Career	847	Art Monk	Washington Redskins	1980–92

Yards Gained

Game	336	Willie Anderson	Los Angeles Rams v. New Orleans Saints	Nov. 26, 1989*
Season	1,746	Charley Hennigan	Houston Oilers	1961
Career	13,821	James Lofton	Green Bay Packers, Los Angeles Raiders, Buffalo Bills	1978–92

Touchdown Receptions

Game	5	Bob Shaw	Chicago Cardinals v. Baltimore Colts	Oct. 2, 1950
		Kellen Winslow	San Diego Chargers v. Oakland Raiders	Nov. 22, 1981
		Jerry Rice	San Francisco 49ers v. Atlanta Falcons	Oct. 14, 1990
Season	22	Jerry Rice	San Francisco 49ers	1987
Career	103	Jerry Rice	San Francisco 49ers	1985–92

Average Yards Gained

Game (min. 3 catches)	60.67	Bill Groman	Houston Oilers v. Denver Broncos (3–182)	Nov. 20, 1960
		Homer Jones	New York Giants v. Washington Redskins (3–182)	Dec. 12, 1965
Season (min. 24 catches)	32.58	Don Currivan	Boston Yanks (24–782)	1947
Career (min. 200 catches)	22.26	Homer Jones	New York Giants, Cleveland Browns (224–4,986)	1964–70

* Overtime

Table continued on page 81

PASS PLAY ■ WARREN MOON HOLDS THE NFL SEASON RECORD FOR MOST PASS ATTEMPTS, 655, AND MOST COMPLETIONS, 404.

finally merged for the 1970 season, but an AFL–NFL championship game, the Super Bowl, was first played in January 1967.

NFL INDIVIDUAL RECORDS (1922–1992)

ENDURANCE

Most games played (career) George Blanda played in a record 340 games in a record 26 seasons in the NFL, for the Chicago Bears (1949, 1950–58), the Baltimore Colts (1950), the Houston Oilers (1960–66), and the Oakland Raiders (1967–75).

Most consecutive games played Jim Marshall played 282 consecutive games from 1960–79 for two teams: the Cleveland Browns, 1960, and the Minnesota Vikings, 1961–79.

LONGEST PLAYS

Run from scrimmage Tony Dorsett, Dallas Cowboys, ran through the Minnesota Vikings defense for a 99-yard touchdown on January 3, 1983.

Pass completion The longest pass completion, all for touchdowns, is 99 yards, performed by six

quarterbacks: Frank Filchock (to Andy Farkas), Washington Redskins *v*. Pittsburgh Steelers, October 15, 1939; George Izo (to Bobby Mitchell), Washington Redskins *v*. Cleveland Browns, September 15, 1963; Karl Sweetan (to Pat Studstill), Detroit Lions *v*. Baltimore Colts, October 16, 1966; Sonny Jurgensen (to Gerry Allen), Washington Redskins *v*. Chicago Bears, September 15, 1968; Jim Plunkett (to Cliff Branch), Los Angeles Raiders *v*. Washington Redskins, October 2, 1983; Ron Jaworski (to Mike Quick), Philadelphia Eagles *v*. Atlanta Falcons, November 10, 1985.

Field goal The longest was 63 yards, by Tom Dempsey, New Orleans Saints *v*. Detroit Lions, on November 8, 1970.

Punt Steve O'Neal, New York Jets, boomed a 98-yard punt on September 21, 1969 *v*. Denver Broncos.

Interception return The longest interception return, both for touchdowns, is 103 yards, by two players: Vencie Glenn, San Diego Chargers *v*. Denver Broncos, November 29, 1987; and Louis Oliver, Miami Dolphins *v*. Buffalo Bills, October 4, 1992.

Kickoff return Three players share the record for a kickoff return at 106 yards: Al Carmichael, Green Bay Packers *v*. Chicago Bears, October 7, 1956; Noland Smith, Kansas City Chiefs *v*. Denver Broncos, December 17, 1967; and Roy Green, St.

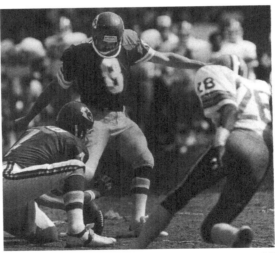

LONG DISTANCE ■ NICK LOWERY IS THE ONLY KICKER TO MAKE TWO 50 YARDERS IN A GAME ON THREE OCCASIONS.

NFL INDIVIDUAL RECORDS (1920–1992)

RUSHING

Yards Gained

		Player(s)	Team(s)	Date(s)
Game	275	Walter Payton	Chicago Bears *v.* Minnesota Vikings	Nov. 20, 1977
Season	2,105	Eric Dickerson	Los Angeles Rams	1984
Career	16,726	Walter Payton	Chicago Bears	1975–87

Attempts

Game	45	Jamie Morris	Washington Redskins *v.* Cincinnati Bengals	Dec. 17, 1988*
Season	407	James Wilder	Tampa Bay Buccaneers	1984
Career	3,838	Walter Payton	Chicago Bears	1975–87

Touchdowns Scored

Game	6	Ernie Nevers	Chicago Cardinals *v.* Chicago Bears	Nov. 28, 1929
Season	24	John Riggins	Washington Redskins	1983
Career	110	Walter Payton	Chicago Bears	1975–87

Average Yards Gained

Game (min. 10 attempts)	17.09	Marion Mottley	Cleveland Browns *v.* Pittsburgh Steelers (11–188)	Oct. 29, 1950
Season (qualifiers)	9.94	Beattie Feathers	Chicago Bears (101–1,004)	1934
Career (min. 700 attempts)	5.22	Jim Brown	Cleveland Browns (2,359–12,312)	1957–65

INTERCEPTIONS

Game	4	16 players have achieved this feat.		
Season	14	Dick "Night Train" Lane	Los Angeles Rams	1952
Career	81	Paul Krause	Washington Redskins, Minnesota Vikings	1964–79

Interceptions Returned for Touchdowns

Game	2	15 players have achieved this feat.		
Season	4	Ken Houston	Houston Oilers	1971
		Jim Kearney	Kansas City Chiefs	1972
Career	9	Ken Houston	Houston Oilers, Washington Redskins	1967–80

* Overtime

NFL INDIVIDUAL RECORDS (1920–1992)

SACKS
(compiled since 1982)

		Player(s)	Team(s)	Date(s)
Game	7	Derrick Thomas	Kansas City v. Seattle Seahawks	Nov. 11, 1990
Season	22	Mark Gastineau	New York Jets	1984
Career	136.5	Lawrence Taylor	New York Giants	1982–92

KICKING

Field Goals

Game	7	Jim Bakken	St. Louis Cardinals v. Pittsburgh Steelers	Sept. 24, 1967
		Rich Karlis	Minnesota Vikings v. Los Angeles Rams	Nov. 5, 1989*
Season	35	Ali Haji-Sheikh	New York Giants	1983
Career	373	Jan Stenerud	Kansas City Chiefs, Green Bay Packers, Minnesota Vikings	1967–85

Highest Percentage

Game	100.00	This has been achieved by many kickers. The most field goals kicked with no misses is 7, by Rich Karlis, Minnesota Vikings v. Los Angeles Rams on Nov. 5, 1989 in an overtime game.
Season (qualifiers)	100.00	Tony Zendejas — Los Angeles Rams (17–17) — 1991
Career (min. 100 field goals)	80.08	Pete Stoyanovich — Miami Dolphins — 1989–92

Field Goals 50 or More Yards

Game	2	This record has been achieved 24 times; Nick Lowery, Kansas City Chiefs, is the only kicker to have done it 3 times.
Season	6	Dean Biasucci — Indianapolis Colts — 1988
Career	21	Morten Andersen — New Orleans Saints — 1982–92

Points After Touchdown (PATs)

		Player(s)	Team(s)	Date(s)
Game	9	Pat Harder	Chicago Cardinals v. New York Giants	Oct. 17, 1948
		Bob Waterfield	Los Angeles Rams v. Baltimore Colts	Oct. 22, 1950
		Charlie Gogolak	Washington Redskins v. New York Giants	Nov. 27, 1966
Season	66	Uwe von Schamann	Miami Dolphins	1984
Career	943	George Blanda	Chicago Bears, Baltimore Colts, Houston Oilers, Oakland Raiders	1949–75

* Overtime

NFL INDIVIDUAL RECORDS (1920–1992)

PUNTING

Punts

		Player(s)	Team(s)	Date(s)
Game	15	John Teltschik	Philadelphia Eagles v. New York Giants	Dec. 6, 1987*
Season	114	Bob Parsons	Chicago Bears	1981
Career	1,154	Dave Jennings	New York Giants, New York Jets	1974–87

Average Yards Gained

Game (min. 4 punts)	61.75	Bob Cifers	Detroit Lions v. Chicago Bears (4–247)	Nov. 24, 1946
Season (qualifiers)	51.40	Sammy Baugh	Washington Redskins (35–1,799)	1940
Career (min. 300 punts)	45.10	Sammy Baugh	Washington Redskins (338–15,245)	1937–52

SPECIAL TEAMS

Punt Returns for Touchdowns

Game	2	Jack Christiansen	Detroit Lions v. Los Angeles Rams	Oct. 14, 1951
		Jack Christiansen	Detroit Lions v. Green Bay Packers	Nov. 22, 1951
		Dick Christy	New York Titans v. Denver Broncos	Sept. 24, 1961
		Rick Upchurch	Denver Broncos v. Cleveland Browns	Sept. 26, 1976
		LeRoy Irvin	Los Angeles Rams v. Atlanta Falcons	Oct. 11, 1981
		Vai Sikahema	St. Louis Cardinals v. Tampa Bay Buccaneers	Dec. 21, 1986
Season	4	Jack Christiansen	Detroit Lions	1951
		Rick Upchurch	Denver Broncos	1976
Career	8	Jack Christiansen	Detroit Lions	1951–58
		Rick Upchurch	Denver Broncos	1975–83

Kickoff Returns for Touchdowns

Game	2	Timmy Brown	Philadelphia Eagles v. Dallas Cowboys	Nov. 6, 1966
		Travis Williams	Green Bay Packers v. Cleveland Browns	Nov. 12, 1967
		Ron Brown	Los Angeles Rams v. Green Bay Packers	Nov. 24, 1985
Season	4	Travis Williams	Green Bay Packers	1967
		Cecil Turner	Chicago Bears	1970
Career	6	Ollie Matson	Chicago Cardinals, Los Angeles Rams, Detroit Lions, Philadelphia Eagles	1952–64
		Gale Sayers	Chicago Bears	1965–71
		Travis Williams	Green Bay Packers, Los Angeles Rams	1967–71

* Overtime
Source: NFL

Louis Cardinals *v.* Dallas Cowboys, October 21, 1979. All three players scored touchdowns.

Missed field goal return Al Nelson, Philadelphia Eagles, returned a Dallas Cowboys' missed field goal 101 yards for a touchdown on September 26, 1971.

Punt return Four players share the record for the longest punt return at 98 yards: Gil LeFebvre, Cincinnati Reds *v.* Brooklyn Dodgers, December 3, 1933; Charlie West, Minnesota Vikings *v.* Washington Redskins, November 3, 1968; Dennis Morgan, Dallas Cowboys *v.* St. Louis Cardinals, October 13, 1974; Terance Mathis, New York Jets *v.* Dallas Cowboys, November 4, 1990. All four players scored touchdowns.

Fumble return Jack Tatum, Oakland Raiders, returned a Green Bay Packers fumble 104 yards for a touchdown on September 24, 1972.

CONSECUTIVE RECORDS

Scoring (games) 186, Jim Breech, Oakland Raiders, 1979; Cincinnati Bengals, 1980–92.

Scoring touchdowns (games) 18, Lenny Moore, Baltimore Colts, 1963–65.

Points after touchdown (PATs), consecutive kicked 234, Tommy Davis, San Francisco 49ers, 1959–65.

Field goals, consecutive kicked 24, Kevin Butler, Chicago Bears, 1988–89.

Field goals (games) 31, Fred Cox, Minnesota Vikings, 1968–70.

100+ yards rushing (games) 11, Marcus Allen, Los Angeles Raiders, 1985–86.

200+ yards rushing (games) 2, by two players: O.J. Simpson, Buffalo Bills, 1973, 1976; Earl Campbell, Houston Oilers, 1980.

Touchdown passes (games) 47, Johnny Unitas, Baltimore Colts, 1956–60.

Touchdown rushes (games) 13, by two players: John Riggins, Washington Redskins, 1982–83; George Rogers, Washington Redskins, 1985–86.

Touchdown receptions (games) 13, Jerry Rice, San Francisco 49ers, 1986–87.

Passes completed (consecutive) 22, Joe Montana, San Francisco 49ers *v.* Cleveland Browns, November 29, 1987 (5); *v.* Green Bay Packers, December 6, 1987 (17).

300+ yards passing (games) 5, Joe Montana, San Francisco 49ers, 1982.

Four or more touchdown passes (games) 4, Dan Marino, Miami Dolphins, 1984.

Pass receptions (games) 177, Steve Largent, Seattle Seahawks, 1977–89.

NFL TEAM RECORDS (1920–92)

WINS AND LOSSES

Most consecutive games won The Chicago Bears won 17 straight regular-season games, covering the 1933–34 seasons.

Most consecutive games unbeaten The Canton Bulldogs played 25 regular-season games without a defeat, covering the 1921–23 seasons. The Bulldogs won 22 games and tied three.

Most games won in a season Two teams have compiled 15-win seasons: the San Francisco 49ers in 1984, and the Chicago Bears in 1985.

Most consecutive games lost This most undesirable of records is held by the Tampa Bay Buccaneers, who lost 26 straight games from 1976–77.

Most games lost in a season Four teams hold the dubious honor of having lost 15 games in one season: the New Orleans Saints in 1980, the Dallas Cowboys in 1989, the New England Patriots in 1990 and the Indianapolis Colts in 1991.

SCORING

Most points scored, game The Washington Redskins scored 72 points *v.* the New York Giants on November 27, 1966 to set the single-game NFL regular-season record for most points scored by one team.

Highest aggregate score On November 27, 1966, the Washington Redskins defeated the New York Giants 72–41 in Washington, D.C. The Redskins' total was an NFL record for most points (see above).

Largest deficit overcome On January 3, 1993, the Buffalo Bills, playing at home in the AFC Wild Card game, trailed the Houston Oilers 35-3 with 28 minutes remaining. The Bills rallied to score 35 unanswered points and take the lead with 3:08 left. The Bills eventually won the game in overtime, overcoming a deficit of 32 points—the largest in NFL history.

TOUCHDOWN LEADER ∎ IN 1992 JERRY RICE ECLIPSED THE NFL CAREER MARK FOR TOUCHDOWNS BY A RECEIVER. RICE HAS 103 NFL TD'S.

TRADES

Largest in NFL history Based on the number of players and/or draft choices involved, the largest trade in NFL history is 15, which has happened twice. On March 26, 1953 the Baltimore Colts and the Cleveland Browns exchanged 15 players; and on January 28, 1971, the Washington Redskins and the Los Angeles Rams completed the transfer of seven players and eight draft choices.

COACHES

Most seasons 40, George Halas, Decatur/Chicago Staleys/Chicago Bears: 1920–29, 1933–42, 1946–55, 1958–67.

Most wins (including playoffs) 325, George Halas, Decatur/Chicago Staleys/Chicago Bears: 1920–29, 1933–42, 1946–55, 1958–67.

NFL CHAMPIONSHIP

The first NFL championship was awarded in 1920 to the Akron Pros, as the team with the best record. From 1920 to 1931, the championship was based on regular-season records. The first championship game was played in 1932.

In 1966, the National Football League (NFL) and the American Football League (AFL) agreed to merge their competing leagues to form an expanded NFL. Regular-season play would not begin until 1970, but the two leagues agreed to stage an annual AFL–NFL world championship game beginning in January 1967. The proposed championship game was dubbed the Super Bowl, and in 1969 the NFL officially recognized the title.

Most NFL titles The Green Bay Packers have won 11 NFL championships: 1929–31, 1936, 1939, 1944, 1961–62, 1965, and Super Bowls I and II (1966 and 1967 seasons).

THE SUPER BOWL (1967–1993)

Super Bowl I was played on January 15, 1967, with the Green Bay Packers (NFL) defeating the Kansas City Chiefs (AFL), 35–10.

Most wins Two teams have won the Super Bowl four times: the Pittsburgh Steelers, Super Bowls IX, X, XIII and XIV; and the San Francisco 49ers, XVI, XIX, XXIII and XXIV.

Consecutive wins Four teams have won Super Bowls in successive years: the Green Bay Packers, I and II; the Miami Dolphins, VII and VIII; the Pittsburgh Steelers (twice), IX and X, and XIII and

NFL CHAMPIONS (1920–1957)

Season	Winner	Loser	Score
1920	Akron Pros	—	—
1921	Chicago Staleys	—	—
1922	Canton Bulldogs	—	—
1923	Canton Bulldogs	—	—
1924	Cleveland Bulldogs	—	—
1925	Chicago Cardinals	—	—
1926	Frankford Yellowjackets	—	—
1927	New York Giants	—	—
1928	Providence Steam Roller	—	—
1929	Green Bay Packers	—	—
1930	Green Bay Packers	—	—
1931	Green Bay Packers	—	—
1932	Chicago Bears	Portsmouth Spartans	9–0
1933	Chicago Bears	New York Giants	23–21
1934	New York Giants	Chicago Bears	30–13
1935	Detroit Lions	New York Giants	26–7
1936	Green Bay Packers	Boston Redskins	21–6
1937	Washington Redskins	Chicago Bears	28–21
1938	New York Giants	Green Bay Packers	23–17
1939	Green Bay Packers	New York Giants	27–0
1940	Chicago Bears	Washington Redskins	73–0
1941	Chicago Bears	New York Giants	37–9
1942	Washington Redskins	Chicago Bears	14–6
1943	Chicago Bears	Washington Redskins	41–21
1944	Green Bay Packers	New York Giants	14–7
1945	Cleveland Rams	Washington Redskins	15–14
1946	Chicago Bears	New York Giants	24–14
1947	Chicago Cardinals	Philadelphia Eagles	28–21
1948	Philadelphia Eagles	Chicago Cardinals	7–0
1949	Philadelphia Eagles	Los Angeles Rams	14–0
1950	Cleveland Browns	Los Angeles Rams	30–28
1951	Los Angeles Rams	Cleveland Browns	24–17
1952	Detroit Lions	Cleveland Browns	17–7
1953	Detroit Lions	Cleveland Browns	17–16
1954	Cleveland Browns	Detroit Lions	56–10
1955	Cleveland Browns	Los Angeles Rams	38–14
1956	New York Giants	Chicago Bears	47–7
1957	Detroit Lions	Cleveland Browns	59–14

NFL CHAMPIONS (1958–1965)

Season	Winner	Loser	Score
1958	Baltimore Colts	New York Giants	23–17
1959	Baltimore Colts	New York Giants	31–16
1960	Philadelphia Eagles	Green Bay Packers	17–13
1961	Green Bay Packers	New York Giants	37–0
1962	Green Bay Packers	New York Giants	16–7
1963	Chicago Bears	New York Giants	14–10
1964	Cleveland Browns	Baltimore Colts	27–0
1965	Green Bay Packers	Cleveland Browns	23–12

SUPER BOWL RESULTS (1967–1993)

Bowl	Date	Winner	Loser	Score	Site
I	Jan. 15, 1967	Green Bay Packers	Kansas City Chiefs	35–10	Los Angeles, Calif.
II	Jan. 14, 1968	Green Bay Packers	Oakland Raiders	33–14	Miami, Fla.
III	Jan. 12, 1969	New York Jets	Baltimore Colts	16–7	Miami, Fla.
IV	Jan. 11, 1970	Kansas City Chiefs	Minnesota Vikings	23–7	New Orleans, La.
V	Jan. 17, 1971	Baltimore Colts	Dallas Cowboys	16–13	Miami, Fla.
VI	Jan. 16, 1972	Dallas Cowboys	Miami Dolphins	24–3	New Orleans, La.
VII	Jan. 14, 1973	Miami Dolphins	Washington Redskins	14–7	Los Angeles, Calif.
VIII	Jan. 13, 1974	Miami Dolphins	Minnesota Vikings	24–7	Houston, Tex.
IX	Jan. 12, 1975	Pittsburgh Steelers	Minnesota Vikings	16–6	New Orleans, La.
X	Jan. 18, 1976	Pittsburgh Steelers	Dallas Cowboys	21–17	Miami, Fla.
XI	Jan. 9, 1977	Oakland Raiders	Minnesota Vikings	32–14	Pasadena, Calif.
XII	Jan. 15, 1978	Dallas Cowboys	Denver Broncos	27–10	New Orleans, La.
XIII	Jan. 21, 1979	Pittsburgh Steelers	Dallas Cowboys	35–31	Miami, Fla.
XIV	Jan. 20, 1980	Pittsburgh Steelers	Los Angeles Rams	31–19	Pasadena, Calif.
XV	Jan. 25, 1981	Oakland Raiders	Philadelphia Eagles	27–10	New Orleans, La.
XVI	Jan. 24, 1982	San Francisco 49ers	Cincinnati Bengals	26–21	Pontiac, Mich.
XVII	Jan. 30, 1983	Washington Redskins	Miami Dolphins	27–17	Pasadena, Calif.
XVIII	Jan. 22, 1984	Los Angeles Raiders	Washington Redskins	38–9	Tampa, Fla.
XIX	Jan. 20, 1985	San Francisco 49ers	Miami Dolphins	38–16	Stanford. Calif.
XX	Jan. 26, 1986	Chicago Bears	New England Patriots	46–10	New Orleans, La.
XXI	Jan. 25, 1987	New York Giants	Denver Broncos	39–20	Pasadena, Calif.
XXII	Jan. 31, 1988	Washington Redskins	Denver Broncos	42–10	San Diego, Calif.
XXIII	Jan. 22, 1989	San Francisco 49ers	Cincinnati Bengals	20–16	Miami, Fla.
XXIV	Jan. 28, 1990	San Francisco 49ers	Denver Broncos	55–10	New Orleans, La.

BIG TOP ■ THE LOUISIANA SUPERDOME IS COVERED BY THE LONGEST ROOF SPAN IN THE WORLD. IT HAS HOSTED A RECORD SEVEN SUPER BOWLS.

XIV; and the San Francisco 49ers, XXIII and XXIV.

Most appearances The Dallas Cowboys have played in six Super Bowls: V, VI, X, XII, XIII and XXVII. The Cowboys have won three games and lost three.

SCORING RECORDS

Most points scored The San Francisco 49ers scored 55 points *v.* the Denver Broncos in Super Bowl XXIV.

Highest aggregate score The highest aggregate score is 69 points when the Dallas Cowboys beat the Buffalo Bills 52–17 in Super Bowl XXVII.

Greatest margin of victory The greatest margin of victory is 45 points, set by the San Francisco 49ers when they defeated the Denver Broncos 55–10 in Super Bowl XXIV.

Most MVP awards Joe Montana, quarterback of the San Francisco 49ers, has been voted the Super Bowl MVP on a record three occasions, XVI, XIX, XXIV.

COACHES

Most wins Chuck Noll led the Pittsburgh Steelers to four Super Bowl titles, IX, X, XIII and XIV.

Most appearances Don Shula has been the head coach of six Super Bowl teams: the Baltimore Colts, III; the Miami Dolphins, VI, VII, VIII, XVII and XIX. He won two games and lost four.

SUPER BOWL RECORDS (1967–1993)

POINTS SCORED

		Player(s)	Team(s)	Super Bowl
Game	18	Roger Craig	San Francisco 49ers	XIX
		Jerry Rice	San Francisco 49ers	XXIV
Career	24	Franco Harris	Pittsburgh Steelers	IX, X, XIII, XIV
		Roger Craig	San Francisco 49ers	XIX, XXIII, XXIV
		Jerry Rice	San Francisco 49ers	XXIII, XXIV

TOUCHDOWNS SCORED

Game	3	Roger Craig	San Francisco 49ers	XIX
		Jerry Rice	San Francisco 49ers	XXIV
Career	4	Franco Harris	Pittsburgh Steelers	IX, X, XIII, XIV
		Roger Craig	San Francisco 49ers	XIX, XXIII, XXIV
		Jerry Rice	San Francisco 49ers	XXIII, XXIV

PASSING

Yards Gained

Game	357	Joe Montana	San Francisco 49ers	XXIII
Career	1,142	Joe Montana	San Francisco 49ers	XVI, XIX, XXIII, XXIV

Completions

Game	29	Dan Marino	Miami Dolphins	XIX
Career	83	Joe Montana	San Francisco 49ers	XVI, XIX, XXIII, XXIV

Touchdowns Thrown

Game	5	Joe Montana	San Francisco 49ers	XXIV
Career	11	Joe Montana	San Francisco 49ers	XVI, XIX, XXIII, XXIV

Highest Completion Percentage

Game (min. 20 attempts)	88.0	Phil Simms	New York Giants (22–25)	XXI
Career (min. 40 attempts)	68.0	Joe Montana	San Francisco 49ers (83–122)	XVI, XIX, XXIII, XXIV

SUPER BOWL RECORDS (1967–1993)

PASS RECEIVING

		Player(s)	Team(s)	Super Bowl
Receptions				
Game	11	Dan Ross	Cincinnati Bengals	XVI
		Jerry Rice	San Francisco 49ers	XXIII
Career	21	Andre Reed	Buffalo Bills	XXV, XXVI, XXVII
Yards Gained				
Game	215	Jerry Rice	San Francisco 49ers	XXIII
Career	364	Lynn Swann	Pittsburgh Steelers	IX, X, XIII, XIV
Touchdown Receptions				
Game	3	Jerry Rice	San Francisco 49ers	XXIV
Career	4	Jerry Rice	San Francisco 49ers	XXIII, XXIV

RUSHING

Yards Gained				
Game	204	Timmy Smith	Washington Redskins	XXII
Career	354	Franco Harris	Pittsburgh Steelers	IX, X, XIII, XIV
Touchdowns Scored				
Game	2	This feat has been achieved by 9 players		
Career	4	Franco Harris	Pittsburgh Steelers	IX, X, XIII, XIV
Interceptions				
Game	3	Rod Martin	Oakland Raiders	XV
Career	3	Chuck Howley	Dallas Cowboys	V, VI
		Rod Martin	Oakland/Los Angeles Raiders	XV, XVIII

FIELD GOALS KICKED

Game	4	Don Chandler	Green Bay Packers	II
		Ray Wersching	San Francisco 49ers	XVI
Career	5	Ray Wersching	San Francisco 49ers	XVI, XIX

LONGEST PLAYS

Run from Scrimmage	74 yards	Marcus Allen	Los Angeles Raiders	XVIII
Pass Completion	80 yards	Jim Plunkett	(to Kenny King) Oakland Raiders	XV
		Doug Williams	(to Ricky Sanders) Washington Redskins	XXII
Field Goal	48 yards	Jan Stenerud	Kansas City Chiefs	IV
		Rich Karlis	Denver Broncos	XXI
Punt	63 yards	Lee Johnson	Cincinnati Bengals	XXIII

Source: NFL

COLLEGE FOOTBALL (NCAA)

ORIGINS At the turn of the 20th century, football's popularity was rising rapidly; however, with the increased participation came a rise in serious injuries and even some deaths. Many institutions, alarmed at the violent nature of the game, called for controls to be established.

In December 1905, 13 universities, led by Chancellor Henry M. MacCracken of New York University, outlined a plan to establish an organization to standardize playing rules. On December 28, the Intercollegiate Athletic Association of the United States (IAAUS) was founded in New York City with 62 charter members. The IAAUS was officially constituted on March 31, 1906, and was renamed the National Collegiate Athletic Association (NCAA) in 1910.

The NCAA first began to keep statistics for football in 1937, and the records in this section date from that time. In 1973, the NCAA introduced a classification system creating Divisions I, II, and III to identify levels of college play. In 1978, Division I was subdivided into I-A and I-AA.

INDIVIDUAL RECORDS (1937–1992)

NCAA OVERALL CAREER RECORDS (DIVISIONS I-A, I-AA, II AND III)

POINTS SCORED

Game Three players have scored 48 points in an NCAA game: Junior Wolf, Panhandle State (Div. II), set the mark on November 8, 1958 v. St. Mary's (Kans.); Paul Zaeske, North Park (Div. II), tied the record on October 12, 1968 v. North Central; Howard Griffith, Illinois (Div I-A), created a triumvirate on September 22, 1990.

Season The most points scored in a season is 234, by Barry Sanders, Oklahoma State (Div. I-A) in 1988, all from touchdowns, 37 rushing and two receptions.

Career The career record for most points scored is 474, by Joe Dudek, Plymouth State (Div. III), 1982–85. Dudek scored 79 touchdowns, 76 rushing and three receptions.

RUSHING (YARDS GAINED)

Game Tony Sands, Kansas (Div. I-A) rushed for an NCAA single-game record 396 yards v. Missouri on November 23, 1991.

Season The most yards gained in a season is 2,628, by Barry Sanders, Oklahoma State (Div. I-A), in 1988. Sanders played in 11 games and carried the ball 344 times for an average gain of 7.64 yards per carry.

Career The career record for most yards gained is 6,320, by Johnny Bailey, Texas A&I (Div. II), 1986–89. Bailey carried the ball 885 times for an average gain of 7.14 yards per carry.

PASSING (YARDS GAINED)

Game David Klingler, Houston (Div. I-A) threw for an NCAA single-game record 716 yards v. Arizona State on December 2, 1990.

Season The single-season NCAA mark is held by Ty Detmer, BYU, who threw for 5,188 yards in 1990.

Career The career passing record is 15,031 yards, set by Ty Detmer, BYU (Div. I-A).

RECEIVING (YARDS GAINED)

Game The most yards gained from pass receptions in a single game is 370, by Barry Wagner,

ON THE RUN ■ ON NOVEMBER 23, 1991, TONY SANDS GAINED AN NCAA GAME RECORD 396 YARDS RUSHING.

NCAA DIVISION I-A RECORDS

Points Scored

		Player(s)	Team(s)	Date(s)
Game	48	Howard Griffith	Illinois v. Southern Illinois (8 TDs)	Sept. 22, 1990
Season	234	Barry Sanders	Oklahoma State (39 TDs)	1988
Career	423	Roman Anderson	Houston (70 FGs, 213 PATs)	1988–91

Touchdowns Scored

Game	8	Howard Griffith	Illinois v. Southern Illinois (all rushing)	Sept. 22, 1990
Season	39	Barry Sanders	Oklahoma State	1988
Career	65	Anthony Thompson	Indiana (64 rushing, 1 reception)	1986–89

2-Point Conversions

Game	6	Jim Pilot	New Mexico State v. Hardin-Simmons	Nov. 25, 1961
Season	6	Pat McCarthy	Holy Cross	1960
		Jim Pilot	New Mexico State	1961
		Howard Twilley	Tulsa	1964
Career	13	Pat McCarthy	Holy Cross	1960–62

PASSING

Touchdown Passes

Game	11	David Klingler	Houston v. Eastern Washington	Nov. 17, 1990
Season	54	David Klingler	Houston	1990
Career	121	Ty Detmer	BYU	1988–91

Yards Gained

Game	716	David Klingler	Houston v. Arizona State	Dec. 1, 1990
Season	5,188	Ty Detmer	BYU	1990
Career	15,031	Ty Detmer	BYU	1988–91

Completions

Game	48	David Klingler	Houston v. SMU	Oct. 20, 1990
Season	374	David Klingler	Houston	1990
Career	958	Ty Detmer	BYU	1988–91

Attempts

Game	79	Matt Vogler	TCU v. Houston	Nov. 3, 1990
Season	643	David Klingler	Houston	1990
Career	1,530	Ty Detmer	BYU	1988–91

NCAA DIVISION I-A RECORDS

PASSING (cont.)

Average Yards Gained per Attempt

		Player(s)	Team(s)	Date(s)
Game (min. 40 attempts)	13.93	Marc Wilson	BYU v. Utah (41 for 571 yards)	Nov. 5, 1977
Season (min. 400 attempts)	11.07	Ty Detmer	BYU (412 for 4,560 yards)	1989
Career (min. 1,000 attempts)	9.82	Ty Detmer	BYU (1,530 for 15,031 yards)	1988–91

PASS RECEIVING

Touchdown Receptions

Game	6	Tim Delaney	San Diego State v. New Mexico State	Nov. 15, 1969
Season	22	Emmanuel Hazard	Houston	1989
Career	38	Clarkston Hines	Duke	1986–89

Receptions

Game	22	Jay Miller	BYU v. New Mexico	Nov. 3, 1973
Season	142	Emmanuel Hazard	Houston	1989
Career	263	Terance Mathis	New Mexico	1985–87

Yards Gained

Game	349	Chuck Hughes	UTEP v. North Texas	Sept. 18, 1965
Season	1,779	Howard Twilley	Tulsa	1965
Career	4,254	Terance Mathis	New Mexico	1985–87, 1989

Average Yards Gained per Reception

Game (min. 5 catches)	52.6	Alex Wright	Auburn v. Pacific (5 for 263 yards)	Sept. 9, 1989
Season (min. 50 catches)	24.4	Henry Ellard	Fresno State (62 for 1,510 yards)	1982
Career (min. 100 catches)	22.0	Herman Moore	Virginia (114 for 2,504 yards)	1988–90

NCAA DIVISION I–A RECORDS

RUSHING

Yards Gained

		Player(s)	Team(s)	Date(s)
Game	396	Tony Sands	Kansas *v.* Missouri	Nov. 23, 1991
Season	2,628	Barry Sanders	Oklahoma State	1988
Career	6,082	Tony Dorsett	Pittsburgh	1973–76

Attempts

		Player(s)	Team(s)	Date(s)
Game	58	Tony Sands	Kansas *v.* Missouri	Nov. 23, 1991
Season	403	Marcus Allen	Southern Cal.	1981
Career	1,215	Steve Bartalo	Colorado State	1983–86

Average Yards Gained per Attempt

		Player(s)	Team(s)	Date(s)
Game (min. 15 rushes)	21.40	Tony Jeffery	TCU *v.* Tulane (16 for 343 yards)	Sept. 13, 1986
Season (min. 250 rushes)	7.81	Mike Rozier	Nebraska (275 for 2,148 yards)	1983
Career (min. 600 rushes)	7.61	Mike Rozier	Nebraska (668 for 4,780 yards)	1981–83

Touchdowns Scored

		Player(s)	Team(s)	Date(s)
Game	8	Howard Griffith	Illinois *v.* Southern Illinois	Sept. 22, 1990
Season	37	Barry Sanders	Oklahoma State	1988
Career	64	Anthony Thompson	Indiana	1986–89

TOTAL OFFENSE (Rushing plus Passing)

Yards Gained

		Player(s)	Team(s)	Date(s)
Game	732	David Klingler	Houston *v.* Arizona State (716 passing, 16 rushing)	Dec. 2, 1990
Season	5,221	David Klingler	Houston (81 rushing, 5,140 passing)	1990
Career	14,665	Ty Detmer	BYU (–366 rushing, 15,031 passing)	1988–91

Interceptions

		Player(s)	Team(s)	Date(s)
Game	5	Lee Cook	Oklahoma State *v.* Detroit	Nov. 28, 1942
		Walt Pastuszak	Brown *v.* Rhode Island	Oct. 8, 1949
		Byron Beaver	Houston *v.* Baylor	Sept. 22, 1962
		Dan Rebsch	Miami (Ohio) *v.* Western Michigan	Nov. 4, 1972
Season	14	Al Worley	Washington	1968
Career	29	Al Brosky	Illinois	1950–52

NCAA DIVISION I–A RECORDS

KICKING

Field Goals Kicked

		Player(s)	Team(s)	Date(s)
Game	7	Mike Prindle	Western Michigan v. Marshall	Sept. 29, 1984
		Dale Klein	Nebraska v. Missouri	Oct. 19, 1985
Season	29	John Lee	UCLA	1984
Career	80	Jeff Jaeger	Washington	1983–86

Points Scored

Game	24	Mike Prindle	Western Michigan v. Marshall (7 FGs, 3 PATSs)	Sept. 29, 1984
Season	131	Roman Anderson	Houston (22 FGs, 65 PATs)	1989
Career	423	Roman Anderson	Houston (70 FGs, 213 PATs)	1988–91

Points After Touchdown (PATs)

Game	13	Terry Leiweke	Houston v. Tulsa	Nov. 23, 1968
		Derek Mahoney	Fresno State v. New Mexico	Oct. 5, 1991
Season	67	Cary Blanchard	Oklahoma State	1988
Career	213	Roman Anderson	Houston	1988–91

PUNTING

Most Punts

Game	36	Charlie Calhoun	Texas Tech v. Centenary	Nov. 11, 1939
Season	101	Jim Bailey	Virginia Military	1969
Career	320	Cameron Young	TCU	1976–79

Average Yards Gained

Game (min. 5 punts)	60.4	Lee Johnson	BYU v. Wyoming (5 for 302 yds)	Oct. 8, 1983
Season (min. 50 punts)	48.2	Ricky Anderson	Vanderbilt (58 for 2,793)	1984
Career (min. 200 punts)	44.7	Ray Guy	Southern Mississippi (200 for 8,934)	1970–72

Yards Gained

Game	1,318	Charlie Calhoun	Texas Tech v. Centenary	Nov. 11, 1939
Season	4,138	Johnny Pingel	Michigan State	1938
Career	12,947	Cameron Young	TCU	1976–79

Source: NCAA

Alabama A&M (Div. II), *v.* Clark Atlanta on November 4, 1989.

Season The single-season NCAA record is 1,812 yards, by Barry Wagner, Alabama A&M (Div. II). Wagner caught 106 passes for an average gain of 17.1 yards.

Career The all-time NCAA mark is held by Jerry Rice, Mississippi Valley (Div. I-AA), 1981–84. He gained 4,693 yards on 301 catches (also an NCAA career record), for an average gain of 15.6 yards.

FIELD GOALS (MOST MADE)

Game Goran Lingmerth, Northern Arizona (Div. I-AA) booted 8 out of 8 field goals *v.* Idaho on October 25, 1986. The distances were 39, 18, 20, 33, 46, 27, 22 and 35 yards each.

Season The most kicks made in a season is 29, by John Lee, UCLA (Div. I-A) from 33 attempts in 1984.

Career The NCAA all-time career record is 80, by Jeff Jaeger, Washington (Div. I-A) from 99 attempts, 1983–86.

LONGEST PLAYS (DIVISION I-A)

Run from scrimmage 99 yards, by four players: Gale Sayers (Kansas *v.* Nebraska), 1963; Max Anderson (Arizona State *v.* Wyoming), 1967; Ralph Thompson (West Texas State *v.* Wichita State), 1970; Kelsey Finch (Tennessee *v.* Florida), 1977.

Pass completion 99 yards, on eight occasions, performed by seven players (Terry Peel and Robert Ford did it twice): Fred Owens (to Jack Ford), Portland *v.* St. Mary's, Calif., 1947; Bo Burris (to Warren McVea), Houston *v.* Washington State, 1966; Colin Clapton (to Eddie Jenkins), Holy Cross *v.* Boston U, 1970; Terry Peel (to Robert Ford), Houston *v.* Syracuse, 1970; Terry Peel (to Robert Ford), Houston *v.* San Diego State, 1972; Cris Collingsworth (to Derrick Gaffney), Florida *v.*

ALL-TIME RUSHERS ■ TONY DORSETT (ABOVE) HOLDS THE ALL-TIME RUSHING MARK FOR YARDS GAINED AT 6,082. ANTHONY THOMPSON (BELOW) HAS SCORED THE MOST TD'S, 64, IN A COLLEGE CAREER.

Rice, 1977; Scott Ankrom (to James Maness), TCU *v.* Rice, 1984; Gino Torretta (to Horace Copeland), Miami *v.* Arkansas, 1991.

Field goal 67 yards, by three players: Russell Erxleben (Texas *v.* Rice), 1977; Steve Little (Arkansas *v.* Texas), 1977; Joe Williams (Wichita State *v.* Southern Illinois), 1978.

TIMEOUT

BIGGEST BOOT ☞ ON OCTOBER 16, 1976, OVE JOHANNSON, ABILENE CHRISTIAN, KICKED THE LONGEST FIELD GOAL IN FOOTBALL HISTORY. WITH A TAILWIND OF 18–20 MPH THE BALL TRAVELED AN AMAZING 69 YARDS FOR THE SCORE.

Punt 99 yards, by Pat Brady, Nevada–Reno *v.* Loyola, Calif. in 1950.

CONSECUTIVE RECORDS

REGULAR SEASON (INDIVIDUAL—DIVISION I-A)

Scoring touchdowns (games) 23, by Bill Burnett, Arkansas. Burnett amassed 47 touchdowns during his 23-game streak, which ran from October 5, 1968–October 31, 1970.

Touchdown passes (games) 35, by Ty Detmer, BYU, September 7, 1989–November 23, 1991.

Touchdown passes (consecutive) 6, by Brooks Dawson, UTEP *v.* New Mexico, October 28, 1967. Dawson completed his first 6 passes for touchdowns, which must rank as the greatest start to a game ever!

Passes completed 22, shared by two players: Steve Young, BYU *v.* Utah State, October 30, 1982, *v.* Wyoming, November 6, 1982; Chuck Long, Iowa *v.* Indiana, October 27, 1984.

100 yards+ rushing (games) 31, by Archie Griffin, Ohio State, September 15, 1973–November 22, 1975.

200 yards+ rushing (games) 5, shared by two players: Marcus Allen, Southern Calif., 1981; Barry Sanders, Oklahoma State, 1988.

Touchdown receptions (games) 12, Desmond Howard, Michigan, 1990–91.

Pass receptions (caught for touchdowns) 6, by Carlos Carson, Louisiana State, 1977. Carlson scored touchdowns on his last five receptions *v.* Rice on September 24, 1977, and from his first reception *v.* Florida on October 1, 1977. Amazingly, these were the first six receptions of his collegiate career!

Pass receptions (games) 44, by Gary Williams, Ohio State, 1979–82.

NCAA DIVISION I–A NATIONAL CHAMPIONS (1936–1963)

In 1936 the Associated Press introduced the AP poll, a ranking of college teams by a vote of sportswriters and broadcasters. In 1950 the United Press, later UPI, introduced a coaches' poll. The AP and UPI polls were still used as the basis for declaring the national college football champion until 1991. In 1992 the CNN/USA Today poll joined the AP as the main arbitrator of the National Championship. The polls have chosen different champions on nine occasions: 1954, 1957, 1965, 1970, 1973, 1974, 1978, 1990, and 1991. Notre Dame has been voted national champion a record eight times: 1943, 1946–47, 1949, 1966, 1973, 1977, 1988.

Year	Team	Record	Year	Team	Record
1936	Minnesota	7–1–0	1951	Tennessee	10–0–0
1937	Pittsburgh	9–0–1	1952	Michigan State	9–0–0
1938	TCU	11–0–0	1953	Maryland	10–1–0
1939	Texas A&M	11–0–0	1954	Ohio State (AP)	10–0–0
1940	Minnesota	8–0–0		UCLA (UPI)	9–0–0
1941	Minnesota	8–0–0	1955	Oklahoma	11–0–0
1942	Ohio State	9–1–0	1956	Oklahoma	10–0–0
1943	Notre Dame	9–1–0	1957	Auburn (AP)	10–0–0
1944	Army	9–0–0		Ohio State (UPI)	9–1–0
1945	Army	9–0–0	1958	LSU	11–0–0
1946	Notre Dame	8–0–1	1959	Syracuse	11–0–0
1947	Notre Dame	9–0–0	1960	Minnesota	8–2–0
1948	Michigan	9–0–0	1961	Alabama	11–0–0
1949	Notre Dame	10–0–0	1962	Southern Cal.	11–0–0
1950	Oklahoma	10–0–0	1963	Texas	11–0–0

Field goals (consecutive) 30, by Chuck Nelson, Washington, 1981–82. Nelson converted his last five kicks of the season *v.* Southern Cal on November 14, 1981, and then booted the first 25 of the 1982 season, missing an attempt *v.* Washington State on November 20, 1982.

Field goals (games) 19, shared by two players: Larry Roach, Oklahoma State (1983–84); Gary Gussman, Miami (Ohio) (1986–87).

TEAM RECORDS (DIVISION I-A)

Most wins Michigan has won 731 games out of 1,005 played, 1879–1992.

Highest winning percentage The highest winning percentage in college football history is .761 by Notre Dame. The Fighting Irish have won 712, lost 210 and tied 41 out of 963 games played, 1887–1992.

Longest winning streak The longest winning streak in Division I-A football, including bowl games, is 47 games by Oklahoma from 1953–57. Oklahoma's streak was stopped on November 16, 1957, when Notre Dame defeated them 7–0 in Norman.

Longest undefeated streak Including bowl games, Washington played 63 games, 1907–17, without losing a game. California ended the streak with a 27–0 victory on November 3, 1917. Washington's record during the streak was 59 wins and 4 ties.

Longest losing streak The most consecutive losses in Division I-A football is 34 games, by Northwestern. This undesirable streak started on September 22, 1979 and was finally snapped three years later on September 25, 1982 when Northern Illinois succumbed to the Wildcats 31–6.

Most points scored Wyoming crushed Northern Colorado 103–0 on November 5, 1949 to set the Division I-A mark for most points scored by one team in a single game. The Cowboys scored 15 touchdowns and converted 13 PATs.

Highest-scoring game The most points scored in a Division I-A game is 124, when Oklahoma defeated Colorado 82–42 on October 4, 1980.

Highest-scoring tie game BYU and San Diego State played a 52–52 tie on November 16, 1991.

NCAA DIVISION I-A NATIONAL CHAMPIONS (1964–1992)

Year	Team	Record	Year	Team	Record
1964	Alabama	10–1–0	1978	Alabama (AP)	11–1–0
1965	Alabama (AP)	9–1–1		Southern Cal. (UPI)	12–1–0
	Michigan State (UPI)	10–1–0	1979	Alabama	11–0–0
1966	Notre Dame	9–0–1	1980	Georgia	12–0–0
1967	Southern Cal.	10–1–0	1981	Clemson	12–0–0
1968	Ohio State	10–0–0	1982	Penn State	11–1–0
1969	Texas	11–0–0	1983	Miami, Fla.	11–1–0
1970	Nebraska (AP)	11–0–1	1984	BYU	13–0–0
	Texas (UPI)	10–1–0	1985	Oklahoma	11–1–0
1971	Nebraska	12–0–0	1986	Penn State	12–0–0
1972	Southern Cal.	12–0–0	1987	Miami, Fla.	12–0–0
1973	Notre Dame (AP)	11–0–0	1988	Notre Dame	12–0–0
	Alabama (UPI)	11–1–0	1989	Miami, Fla.	10–1–0
1974	Oklahoma (AP)	11–0–0	1990	Colorado (AP)	11–1–1
	Southern Cal. (UPI)	10–1–0		Georgia Tech (UPI)	11–0–1
1975	Oklahoma	11–1–0	1991	Miami, Fla. (AP)	12–0–0
1976	Pittsburgh	12–0–0		Washington (UPI)	12–0–0
1977	Notre Dame	11–1–0	1992	Alabama	13–0–0

BOWL GAMES

The oldest college bowl game is the Rose Bowl. It was first played on January 1, 1902 at Tournament Park, Pasadena, Calif., where Michigan defeated Stanford 49–0. The other three bowl games that make up the "big four" are the Orange Bowl, initiated in 1935; the Sugar Bowl, 1935; and the Cotton Bowl, 1937.

ROSE BOWL In the first game, played on January 1, 1902, Michigan blanked Stanford 49–0.

Most wins Southern Cal. has won the Rose Bowl 19 times: 1923, 1930, 1932–33, 1939–40, 1944–45, 1953, 1963, 1968, 1970, 1973, 1975, 1977, 1979–80, 1985, 1990.

Most appearances Southern Cal. has played in the Rose Bowl 27 times, with a record of 19 wins and 8 losses.

ORANGE BOWL In the first game, played on January 1, 1935, Bucknell shut out Miami (Fla.) 26–0.

Most wins Oklahoma has won the Orange Bowl 11 times: 1954, 1956, 1958–59, 1968, 1976, 1979–81, 1986–87.

Most appearances Oklahoma has played in the Orange Bowl 16 times, with a record of 11 wins and 5 losses.

SUGAR BOWL In the first game, played on January 1, 1935, Tulane defeated Temple 20–14.

Most wins Alabama has won the Sugar Bowl eight times: 1962, 1964, 1967, 1975, 1978–80, 1992.

Most appearances Alabama has played in the Sugar Bowl 12 times, with a record of 8 wins and 4 losses.

COTTON BOWL In the first game, played on January 1, 1937, Texas Christian defeated Marquette 16–6.

Most wins Texas has won the Cotton Bowl nine times: 1943, 1946, 1953, 1962, 1964, 1969–70, 1973, 1982.

Most appearances Texas has played in the Cotton Bowl 18 times, with a record of 9 wins, 8 losses and 1 tie.

BOWL GAME RECORDS Alabama, Georgia, Georgia Tech and Notre Dame are the only four teams to have won each of the "big four" bowl games.

Most wins Alabama has won a record 25 bowl games: Sugar Bowl, eight times, 1962, 1964, 1967, 1975, 1978–80, 1992; Rose Bowl, four times, 1926, 1931, 1935, 1946; Orange Bowl, four times, 1943, 1953, 1963, 1966; Sun Bowl (now John Hancock Bowl), three times, 1983, 1986, 1988; Cotton Bowl,

HEISMAN TROPHY WINNERS (1935–1962)

Year	Player	Team	Year	Player	Team
1935	Jay Berwanger	Chicago	1949	Leon Hart	Notre Dame
1936	Larry Kelley	Yale	1950	Vic Janowicz	Ohio State
1937	Clint Frank	Yale	1951	Dick Kazmaier	Princeton
1938	Davey O'Brien	TCU	1952	Billy Vessels	Oklahoma
1939	Nile Kinnick	Iowa	1953	Johnny Lattner	Notre Dame
1940	Tom Harmon	Michigan	1954	Alan Ameche	Wisconsin
1941	Bruce Smith	Minnesota	1955	Howard Cassady	Ohio State
1942	Frank Sinkwich	Georgia	1956	Paul Hornung	Notre Dame
1943	Angelo Bertelli	Notre Dame	1957	John David Crow	Texas A&M
1944	Les Horvath	Ohio State	1958	Pete Dawkins	Army
1945	Doc Blanchard	Army	1959	Billy Cannon	LSU
1946	Glenn Davis	Army	1960	Joe Bellino	Navy
1947	Johnny Lujack	Notre Dame	1961	Ernie Davis	Syracuse
1948	Doak Walker	SMU	1962	Terry Baker	Oregon State

twice, 1942, 1981; Liberty Bowl, twice, 1976, 1982; Aloha Bowl, once, 1985; Blockbuster Bowl, once, 1991.

Consecutive seasons UCLA won a bowl game for seven consecutive seasons: Rose Bowl, 1983–84; Fiesta Bowl, 1985; Rose Bowl, 1986; Freedom Bowl, 1986; Aloha Bowl, 1987; Cotton Bowl, 1989.

Bowl game appearances Alabama has played in 45 bowl games.

HEISMAN TROPHY

Awarded annually since 1935 by the Downtown Athletic Club of New York to the top college football player as determined by a poll of journalists, it was originally called the D.A.C. Trophy, but the name was changed in 1936. Its full title is the John W. Heisman Memorial Trophy and it is named after the first athletic director of the Downtown Athletic Club. The only double winner has been Archie Griffin of Ohio State, 1974–75. Notre Dame, with seven, has had more Heisman Trophy winners than any other school.

COACHES

Wins (Division I-A) In Division I-A competition, Paul "Bear" Bryant has won more games than any other coach, with 323 victories over 38 years. Bryant coached four teams: Maryland, 1945 (6–2–1); Kentucky, 1956–53 (60–23–5); Texas A&M, 1954–57 (25–14–2); and Alabama, 1958–82 (232–46–9). His completed record was 323 wins–85 losses–17 ties, for a .780 winning percentage.

Wins (all divisions) In overall NCAA competition, Eddie Robinson, Grambling (Division I-AA) holds the mark for most victories with 381.

Highest winning percentage (Division I-A) The highest winning percentage in Division I-A competition is .881, held by Knute Rockne of Notre Dame. Rockne coached the Irish from 1918 to 1930, for a record of 105 wins–12 losses–5 tied.

ATTENDANCES

Single game It has been estimated that crowds of 120,000 were present for two Notre Dame games played at Soldier Field, Chicago, Ill.: v. Southern Cal. (November 26, 1927); v. Navy (October 13, 1928). Official attendance records have been kept by the NCAA since 1948. The highest official crowd for a regular-season NCAA game was 106,255 Wolverine fans at Michigan Football Stadium, Ann Arbor, Mich., on October 23, 1983 for

HEISMAN TROPHY WINNERS (1963–1992)

Year	Player	Team	Year	Player	Team
1963	Roger Staubach	Navy	1978	Billy Sims	Oklahoma
1964	John Huarte	Notre Dame	1979	Charles White	Southern Cal.
1965	Mike Garrett	Southern Cal.	1980	George Rogers	South Carolina
1966	Steve Spurrier	Florida	1981	Marcus Allen	Southern Cal.
1967	Gary Beban	UCLA	1982	Herschel Walker	Georgia
1968	O. J. Simpson	Southern Cal.	1983	Mike Rozier	Nebraska
1969	Steve Owens	Oklahoma	1984	Doug Flutie	Boston College
1970	Jim Plunkett	Stanford	1985	Bo Jackson	Auburn
1971	Pat Sullivan	Auburn	1986	Vinny Testaverde	Miami, Fla.
1972	Johnny Rodgers	Nebraska	1987	Tim Brown	Notre Dame
1973	John Cappelletti	Penn State	1988	Barry Sanders	Oklahoma State
1974	Archie Griffin	Ohio State	1989	Andre Ware	Houston
1975	Archie Griffin	Ohio State	1990	Ty Detmer	BYU
1976	Tony Dorsett	Pittsburgh	1991	Desmond Howard	Michigan
1977	Earl Campbell	Texas	1992	Gino Torretta	Miami, Fla.

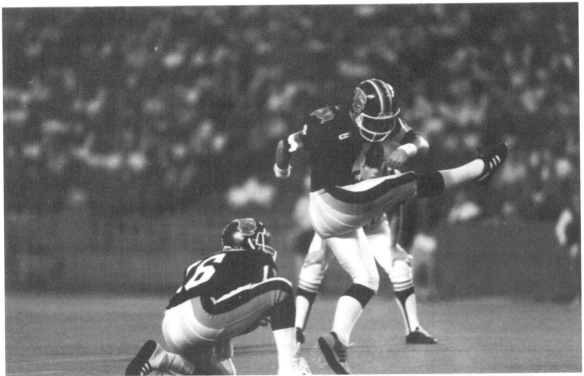

CFL RECORD ■ KICKER LANCE CHOMYC HOLDS THE CFL RECORD FOR MOST POINTS SCORED IN A SEASON AT 236.

the Michigan *v.* Ohio State game. As Michigan lost 18–15, a record may have been set for the greatest number of depressed people at a football game!

Bowl game The record attendance for a bowl game is 106,869 people at the 1973 Rose Bowl, where Southern Cal. defeated Ohio State 42–17.

Season average The highest average attendance for home games is 105,588 for the six games played by Michigan in 1985.

CANADIAN FOOTBALL LEAGUE (CFL)

ORIGINS The earliest recorded football game in Canada was an intramural contest between students of the University of Toronto on November 9, 1861. As with football in the U.S., the development of the game in Canada dates from a contest between two universities—McGill and Harvard, played in May 1874.

Canadian football differs in many ways from its counterpart in the U.S. The major distinctions are the number of players (CFL–12, NFL–11); size of field (CFL–110 yards x 65 yards, NFL–100 yards x 53 yards); number of downs (CFL–3, NFL–4); and a completely different system for scoring and penalties.

The current CFL is comprised of eight teams in two divisions, the Western and Eastern. The divisional playoff champions meet in the Grey Cup to decide the CFL champion.

CFL TEAM RECORDS

Longest winning streak The Calgary Stampeders won 22 consecutive games between August 25, 1948 and October 22, 1949 to set the CFL mark.

Longest winless streak The Hamilton Tiger-Cats hold the dubious distinction of being the CFL's most futile team, amassing a 20-game winless streak (0–19–1), from September 28, 1948 to September 2, 1950.

CFL INDIVIDUAL RECORDS

Games Played

		Player(s)	Team(s)	Date(s)
Most	288	Ron Lancaster	Ottawa/Saskatchewan Roughriders	1960–78
Consecutive	253	Dave Cutler	Edmonton Eskimos	1969–84

Points Scored

Game	36	Bob McNamara	Winnipeg Blue Bombers *v.* B.C. Lions	Oct. 13, 1956
Season	236	Lance Chomyc	Toronto Argonauts	1991
Career	2,653	Lui Passaglia	B.C. Lions	1976–92

Touchdowns Scored

Game	6	Eddie James	Winnipegs *v.* Winnipeg St. Johns	Sept. 28, 1932
		Bob McNamara	Winnipeg Blue Bombers *v.* B.C. Lions	Oct. 13, 1956
Season	20	Pat Abbruzzi	Montreal Alouettes	1956
		Darrell K. Smith	Toronto Argonauts	1990
		Blake Marshall	Edmonton Eskimos	1991
		Jon Volpe	B.C. Lions	1991
Career	137	George Reed	Saskatchewan Roughriders	1963–75

PASSING

Yards Gained

Game	586	Sam Etcheverry	Montreal Alouettes *v.* Hamilton Tiger-Cats	Oct. 16, 1954
Season	6,619	Doug Flutie	B.C. Lions	1991
Career	50,535	Ron Lancaster	Ottawa Roughriders/Saskatchewan Roughriders	1960–78

Touchdowns Thrown

Game	8	Joe Zuger	Hamilton Tiger-Cats	Oct. 15, 1962
Season	40	Peter Liske	Calgary Stampeders	1967
Career	333	Ron Lancaster	Ottawa/Saskatchewan Roughriders	1960–78

Completions

Game	41	Dieter Brock	Winnipeg Blue Bombers *v.* Ottawa Roughriders	Oct. 3, 1981
Season	466	Doug Flutie	B.C. Lions	1991
Career	3,384	Ron Lancaster	Ottawa Roughriders/Saskatchewan Roughriders	1960–78

CFL INDIVIDUAL RECORDS

PASS RECEIVING

Receptions

		Player(s)	Team(s)	Date(s)
Game	16	Terry Greer	Toronto Argonauts v. Ottawa Roughriders	Aug. 19, 1983
Season	118	Allen Pitts	Calgary Stampeders	1991
Career	706	Rocky DiPietro	Hamilton Tiger-Cats	1978–91

Yards Gained

Game	338	Hal Patterson	Montreal Alouettes v. Hamilton Tiger-Cats	Sept. 29, 1956
Season	2,003	Terry Greer	Toronto Argonauts	1983
Career	11,169	Brian Kelly	Edmonton Eskimos	1979–87

Touchdown Receptions

Game	5	Ernie Pitts	Winnipeg Blue Bombers v. Saskatchewan Roughriders	Aug. 29, 1959
Season	20	Darrell K. Smith	Toronto Argonauts	1990
Career	97	Brian Kelly	Edmonton Eskimos	1979–87

RUSHING

Yards Gained

Game	287	Ron Stewart	Ottawa Roughriders v. Montreal Alouettes	Oct. 10, 1960
Season	1,896	Willie Burden	Calgary Stampeders	1975
Career	16,116	George Reed	Saskatchewan Roughriders	1963–75

Touchdowns Scored

Game	5	Earl Lunsford	Calgary Stampeders v. Edmonton Eskimos	Sept. 3, 1962
Season	18	Gerry James	Winnipeg Blue Bombers	1957
		Jim Germany	Edmonton Eskimos	1981
Career	134	George Reed	Saskatchewan Roughriders	1963–75

Longest Plays (Yards)

Rushing	109	George Dixon	Montreal Alouettes	Sept. 2, 1963
		Willie Fleming	B.C. Lions	Oct. 17, 1964
Pass Completion	109	Sam Etcheverry to Hal Patterson	Montreal Alouettes	Sept. 22, 1956
		Jerry Keeling to Terry Evanshen	Calgary Stampeders	Sept. 27, 1966
Field Goal	60	Dave Ridgway	Saskatchewan Roughriders	Sept. 6, 1987
Punt	108	Zenon Andrusyshyn	Toronto Argonauts	Oct. 23, 1977

Source: CFL

Highest-scoring game The Toronto Argonauts defeated the B.C. Lions 68–43 on September 1, 1990 to set a CFL combined score record of 111 points.

Highest score by one team The Montreal Alouettes rolled over the Hamilton Tiger-Cats 82–14 on October 20, 1956 to set the CFL highest-score mark.

THE GREY CUP

In 1909, Lord Earl Grey, the governor general of Canada, donated a trophy that was to be awarded to the Canadian Rugby Football champion. The competition for the Grey Cup evolved during the first half of the 20th century from an open competition for amateurs, college teams and hybrid rugby teams to the championship of the professional Canadian Football League that was formed in 1958.

Most wins 12, Toronto Argonauts: 1914, 1921, 1933, 1937–38, 1945–47, 1950, 1952, 1983, 1991.

Most consecutive wins Five, Edmonton Eskimos: 1978–83.

GREY CUP RESULTS (1909–1935)

Year	Winner	Loser	Score
1909	University of Toronto	Toronto Parkdale	26–6
1910	University of Toronto	Hamilton Tigers	16–7
1911	University of Toronto	Toronto Argonauts	14–7
1912	Hamilton Alerts	Toronto Argonauts	11–4
1913	Hamilton Tigers	Toronto Parkdale	44–2
1914	Toronto Argonauts	University of Toronto	14–2
1915	Hamilton Tigers	Toronto Rowing	13–7
1916	not held		
1917	not held		
1918	not held		
1919	not held		
1920	University of Toronto	Toronto Argonauts	16–3
1921	Toronto Argonauts	Edmonton Eskimos	23–0
1922	Queen's University	Edmonton Elks	13–1
1923	Queen's University	Regina Roughriders	54–0
1924	Queen's University	Toronto Balmy Beach	11–3
1925	Ottawa Senators	Winnipeg Tammany Tigers	24–1
1926	Ottawa Senators	University of Toronto	10–7
1927	Toronto Balmy Beach	Hamilton Tigers	9–6
1928	Hamilton Tigers	Regina Roughriders	30–0
1929	Hamilton Tigers	Regina Roughriders	14–3
1930	Toronto Balmy Beach	Regina Roughriders	11–6
1931	Montreal AAA Winged Wheelers	Regina Roughriders	22–0
1932	Hamilton Tigers	Regina Roughriders	25–6
1933	Toronto Argonauts	Sarnia Imperials	4–3
1934	Sarnia Imperials	Regina Roughriders	20–12
1935	Winnipeg	Hamilton Tigers	18–12

GREY CUP RESULTS (1936–1972)

Year	Winner	Loser	Score
1936	Sarnia Imperials	Ottawa Rough Riders	26–20
1937	Toronto Argonauts	Winnipeg Blue Bombers	4–3
1938	Toronto Argonauts	Winnipeg Blue Bombers	30–7
1939	Winnipeg Blue Bombers	Ottawa Rough Riders	8–7
1940 (Nov.)	Ottawa Rough Riders	Toronto Balmy Beach	8–2
1940 (Dec.)	Ottawa Rough Riders	Toronto Balmy Beach	12–5
1941	Winnipeg Blue Bombers	Ottawa Rough Riders	18–16
1942	Toronto Hurricanes	Winnipeg Bombers	8–5
1943	Hamilton Flying Wildcats	Winnipeg Bombers	23–14
1944	St. Hyacinthe-Donnacona Navy	Hamilton Wildcats	7–6
1945	Toronto Argonauts	Winnipeg Blue Bombers	35–0
1946	Toronto Argonauts	Winnipeg Blue Bombers	28–6
1947	Toronto Argonauts	Winnipeg Blue Bombers	10–9
1948	Calgary Stampeders	Ottawa Rough Riders	12–7
1949	Montreal Alouettes	Calgary Stampeders	28–15
1950	Toronto Argonauts	Winnipeg Blue Bombers	13–0
1951	Ottawa Rough Riders	Saskatchewan Roughriders	21–14
1952	Toronto Argonauts	Edmonton Eskimos	21–11
1953	Hamilton Tiger-Cats	Winnipeg Blue Bombers	12–6
1954	Edmonton Eskimos	Montreal Alouettes	26–25
1955	Edmonton Eskimos	Montreal Alouettes	34–19
1956	Edmonton Eskimos	Montreal Alouettes	50–27
1957	Hamilton Tiger-Cats	Winnipeg Blue Bombers	32–7
1958	Winnipeg Blue Bombers	Hamilton Tiger-Cats	35–28
1959	Winnipeg Blue Bombers	Hamilton Tiger-Cats	21–7
1960	Ottawa Senators	Edmonton Eskimos	16–6
1961	Winnipeg Blue Bombers	Hamilton Tiger-Cats	21–14
1962	Winnipeg Blue Bombers	Hamilton Tiger-Cats	28–27
1963	Hamilton Tiger-Cats	B.C. Lions	21–10
1964	B.C. Lions	Hamilton Tiger-Cats	34–24
1965	Hamilton Tiger-Cats	Winnipeg Blue Bombers	22–16
1966	Saskatchewan Roughriders	Ottawa Senators	29–14
1967	Hamilton Tiger-Cats	Saskatchewan Roughriders	24–1
1968	Ottawa Rough Riders	Calgary Stampeders	24–21
1969	Ottawa Rough Riders	Saskatchewan Roughriders	29–11
1970	Montreal Alouettes	Calgary Stampeders	23–10
1971	Calgary Stampeders	Toronto Argonauts	14–11
1972	Hamilton Tiger-Cats	Saskatchewan Roughriders	13–10

GREY CUP RESULTS (1973–1992)

Year	Winner	Loser	Score
1973	Ottawa Rough Riders	Edmonton Eskimos	22–18
1974	Montreal Alouettes	Edmonton Eskimos	20–7
1975	Edmonton Eskimos	Montreal Alouettes	9–8
1976	Ottawa Rough Riders	Saskatchewan Roughriders	23–20
1977	Montreal Alouettes	Edmonton Eskimos	41–6
1978	Edmonton Eskimos	Montreal Alouettes	20–13
1979	Edmonton Eskimos	Montreal Alouettes	17–9
1980	Edmonton Eskimos	Hamilton Tiger-Cats	48–10
1981	Edmonton Eskimos	Ottawa Senators	26–23
1982	Edmonton Eskimos	Toronto Argonauts	32–16
1983	Toronto Argonauts	B.C. Lions	18–17
1984	Winnipeg Blue Bombers	Hamilton Tiger-Cats	47–17
1985	B.C. Lions	Hamilton Tiger-Cats	37–24
1986	Hamilton Tiger-Cats	Edmonton Eskimos	39–15
1987	Edmonton Eskimos	Toronto Argonauts	38–36
1988	Winnipeg Blue Bombers	B.C. Lions	22–21
1989	Saskatchewan Roughriders	Hamilton Tiger-Cats	43–40
1990	Winnipeg Blue Bombers	Edmonton Eskimos	50–11
1991	Toronto Argonauts	Calgary Stampeders	36–21
1992	Calgary Stampeders	Winnipeg Blue Bombers	24–10

FRISBEE (FLYING DISC THROWING)

ORIGINS The design of a carved plastic flying disc was patented in the United States by Fred Morrison in 1948. In 1957 Wham-O Inc. of San Gabriel, Calif. bought Morrison's patent and trademarked the name *FRISBEE* in 1958. In 1968 Wham-O helped form the International FRISBEE Association (IFA) as a vehicle for organizing the *FRISBEE* craze that had swept across the United States. The IFA folded in 1982 and it wasn't until 1986 that the World Flying Disc Federation was formed to organize and standardize rules for the sport.

FLYING DISC RECORDS

Distance thrown Sam Ferrans (U.S.) set the flying disc distance record at 623 feet 7 inches on July 2, 1988 at La Habra, Calif. The women's record is 426 feet 9½ inches by Amy Bekkan (U.S.) on June 25, 1990 at La Habra, Calif.

Throw, run, catch Hiroshi Oshima (Japan) set the throw, run, catch distance record at 303 feet 11 inches on July 20, 1988 at San Francisco, Calif. The women's record is 196 feet 11 inches by Judy Horowitz (U.S.) on June 29, 1985 at La Mirada, Calif.

Time aloft The record for maximum time aloft is 16.72 seconds, by Don Cain (U.S.) on May 26, 1984 at Philadelphia, Pa. The women's record is 11.81 seconds, by Amy Bekkan (U.S.) on August 1, 1991.

GOLF

The nationality of the competitors in this section is U.S. unless stated otherwise.

ORIGINS The Chinese Nationalist Golf Association claims that golf (*ch'ui wan*—"the ball-hitting game") was played in China in the 3rd or 2nd century B.C. There is evidence that a game resembling golf was played in the Low Countries (present-day Belgium, Holland and northern France) in the Middle Ages. Scotland, however, is generally regarded as the home of the modern game. The oldest club of which there is written evidence is the Honourable Company of Edinburgh Golfers, Scotland, founded in 1744. The Royal & Ancient Club of St. Andrews (R&A), has been in existence since 1754. The R&A is credited with formulating the rules of golf upon which the modern game is based. Gutta percha balls succeeded feather balls in 1848. In 1899 Coburn Haskell (U.S.) invented rubber-cored balls. Steal shafts were authorized in the United States in 1925.

United States There are claims that golf was played in this country as early as the 18th century in North Carolina and Virginia. The oldest recognized club in North America is the Royal Montreal Golf Club, Canada, formed on November 4, 1873. Two clubs claim to be the first established in the U.S.: the Foxberg Golf Club, Clarion County, Pa. (1887), and St. Andrews Golf Club of Yonkers, N.Y. (1888). The United States Golf Association (USGA) was founded in 1894 as the governing body of golf in the United States.

PROFESSIONAL GOLF (MEN)

GRAND SLAM CHAMPIONSHIPS (THE MAJORS)

GRAND SLAM In 1930, Bobby Jones won the U.S. and British Open Championships and the U.S. and British Amateur Championships. This feat was christened the "Grand Slam." In 1960, the professional Grand Slam (the Masters, U.S. Open, British Open, and Professional Golfers Association [PGA] Championships) gained recognition when Arnold Palmer won the first two legs, the Masters and the U.S. Open. However, he did not complete the set of titles, and the Grand Slam has still not been attained. Ben Hogan came the closest in 1951, when he won the first three legs, but didn't return to the U.S. from Great Britain in time for the PGA Championship.

Most grand slam titles Jack Nicklaus has won the most majors, with 18 professional titles (six Masters, four U.S. Opens, three British Opens, five PGA Championships).

THE MASTERS Inaugurated in 1934, this event is held annually at the 6,980-yd Augusta National Golf Club, Augusta, GA.

MASTERS CHAMPIONS (1934–1992)

Year	Champion	Year	Champion	Year	Champion	Year	Champion
1934	Horton Smith	1949	Sam Snead	1964	Arnold Palmer	1979	Fuzzy Zoeller
1935	Gene Sarazen	1950	Jimmy Demaret	1965	Jack Nicklaus	1980	Seve Ballesteros**
1936	Horton Smith	1951	Ben Hogan	1966	Jack Nicklaus	1981	Tom Watson
1937	Byron Nelson	1952	Sam Snead	1967	Jay Brewer	1982	Craig Stadler
1938	Henry Picard	1953	Ben Hogan	1968	Bob Goalby	1983	Seve Ballesteros**
1939	Ralph Guldahl	1954	Sam Snead	1969	George Archer	1984	Ben Crenshaw
1940	Jimmy Demaret	1955	Cary Middlecoff	1970	Billy Casper	1985	Bernhard Langer†
1941	Craig Wood	1956	Jack Burke Jr.	1971	Charles Coody	1986	Jack Nicklaus
1942	Byron Nelson	1957	Doug Ford	1972	Jack Nicklaus	1987	Larry Mize
1943	not held	1958	Arnold Palmer	1973	Tommy Aaron	1988	Sandy Lyle‡
1944	not held	1959	Art Wall Jr.	1974	Gary Player*	1989	Nick Faldo‡
1945	not held	1960	Arnold Palmer	1975	Jack Nicklaus	1990	Nick Faldo‡
1946	Herman Keiser	1961	Gary Player*	1976	Raymond Floyd	1991	Ian Woosnam‡
1947	Jimmy Demaret	1962	Arnold Palmer	1977	Tom Watson	1992	Fred Couples
1948	Claude Harmon	1963	Jack Nicklaus	1978	Gary Player		

* South Africa,   ** Spain,   † Germany,   ‡ Great Britain

Most wins Jack Nicklaus has won the coveted green jacket a record six times (1963, 1965–66, 1972, 1975, 1986).

Consecutive wins Jack Nicklaus (1965–66) and Nick Faldo (1989–90) are the only two players to have won back-to-back Masters.

Lowest 18-hole total (any round) 63, by Nick Price (Zimbabwe) in 1986.

Lowest 72-hole total 271, by Jack Nicklaus (67, 71, 64, 69) in 1965; and Raymond Floyd (65, 66, 70, 70) in 1976.

Oldest champion 46 years 81 days, Jack Nicklaus (1986).

Youngest champion 23 years 2 days, Severiano Ballesteros (1980).

THE UNITED STATES OPEN Inaugurated in 1895, this event is held on a different course each year. The Open was expanded from a three-day, 36-hole Saturday finish to four days of 18 holes of play in 1965.

Most wins Four players have won the title four times: Willie Anderson (1901, 1903–05); Bobby Jones (1923, 1926, 1929–30); Ben Hogan (1948, 1950–51, 1953); Jack Nicklaus (1962, 1967, 1972, 1980).

Most consecutive wins Three, by Willie Anderson (1903–05).

U.S. OPEN CHAMPIONS (1895–1992)

Year	Champion	Year	Champion	Year	Champion	Year	Champion
1895	Horace Rawlins	1919	Walter Hagen	1943	not held	1968	Lee Trevino
1896	James Foulis	1920	Edward Ray*	1944	not held	1969	Orville Moody
1897	Joe Lloyd	1921	Jim Barnes	1945	not held	1970	Tony Jacklin*
1898	Fred Herd	1922	Gene Sarazen	1946	Lloyd Mangrum	1971	Lee Trevino
1899	Willie Smith	1923	Bobby Jones	1947	Lew Worsham	1972	Jack Nicklaus
1900	Harry Vardon*	1924	Cyril Walker	1948	Ben Hogan	1973	Johnny Miller
1901	Willie Anderson	1925	Willie MacFarlane	1949	Cary Middlecoff	1974	Hale Irwin
1902	Laurie Auchterlonie	1926	Bobby Jones	1950	Ben Hogan	1975	Lou Graham
1903	Willie Anderson	1927	Tommy Armour	1951	Ben Hogan	1976	Jerry Pate
1904	Willie Anderson	1928	Johnny Farrell	1952	Julius Boros	1977	Hubert Green
1905	Willie Anderson	1929	Bobby Jones	1953	Ben Hogan	1978	Andy North
1906	Alex Smith	1930	Bobby Jones	1954	Ed Furgol	1979	Hale Irwin
1907	Alex Ross	1931	Billy Burke	1955	Jack Fleck	1980	Jack Nicklaus
1908	Fred McLeod	1932	Gene Sarazen	1956	Cary Middlecoff	1981	David Graham‡
1909	George Sargent	1933	Johnny Goodman	1957	Dick Mayer	1982	Tom Watson
1910	Alex Smith	1934	Olin Dutra	1958	Tommy Bolt	1983	Larry Nelson
1911	John McDermott	1935	Sam Parks Jr.	1959	Billy Casper	1984	Fuzzy Zoeller
1912	John McDermott	1936	Tony Manero	1960	Arnold Palmer	1985	Andy North
1913	Francis Ouimet	1937	Ralph Guldahl	1961	Gene Littler	1986	Raymond Floyd
1914	Walter Hagen	1938	Ralph Guldahl	1962	Jack Nicklaus	1987	Scott Simpson
1915	Jerome Travers	1939	Byron Nelson	1963	Julius Boros	1988	Curtis Strange
1916	Charles Evans Jr.	1940	Lawson Little	1964	Ken Venturi	1989	Curtis Strange
1917	not held	1941	Craig Wood	1965	Gary Player†	1990	Hale Irwin
1918	not held	1942	not held	1966	Billy Casper	1991	Payne Stewart
				1967	Jack Nicklaus	1992	Tom Kite

* Great Britain, † South Africa, ‡ Australia

HALE AND HEARTY ■ IN 1990 HALE IRWIN BECAME THE OLDEST MAN TO WIN THE U.S. OPEN AT AGE 45 YEARS 15 DAYS.

Lowest 18-hole total (any round) 63, by three players: Johnny Miller at Oakmont Country Club, Pa., on June 17, 1973; Jack Nicklaus and Tom Weiskopf, both at Baltusrol Country Club, Springfield, N.J., on June 12, 1980.

Lowest 72-hole total 272 (63, 71, 70, 68), by Jack Nicklaus at Baltusrol Country Club, Springfield, N.J., in 1980.

Oldest champion 45 years 15 days, Hale Irwin (1990).

Youngest champion 19 years 317 days, John J. McDermott (1911).

THE BRITISH OPEN In this event, inaugurated in 1860, the first dozen tournaments were staged at Prestwick, Scotland. Since 1873, the locations have varied, but all venues are coastal links courses.

Most wins Harry Vardon won a record six titles, in 1896, 1898–99, 1903, 1911, 1914.

Most consecutive wins Four, Tom Morris Jr. (1868–70, 1872; the event was not held in 1871).

TIMEOUT

LONGEST HOLE ☛ THE LONGEST HOLE IN THE WORLD IS THE SEVENTH HOLE OF THE SANO COURSE, SATSUKI GOLF CLUB, JAPAN. IT MEASURES 909 YARDS AND IS A FULL PAR 7.

Lowest 18-hole total (any round) 63, by five players: Mark Hayes at Turnberry, Scotland, on July 7, 1977; Isao Aoki (Japan) at Muirfield, Scotland, on July 19, 1980; Greg Norman (Australia) at Turnberry, Scotland, on July 18, 1986; Paul Broadhurst (Great Britain) at St. Andrews, Scotland, on July 21, 1990; Jodie Mudd at Royal Birkdale, England, on July 21, 1991.

Lowest 72-hole total 268 (68, 70, 65, 65) by Tom Watson at Turnberry, Scotland in 1977.

Oldest champion 46 years 99 days, Tom Morris Sr. (Great Britain) (1867).

Youngest champion 17 years 249 days, Tom Morris Jr. (Great Britain) (1868).

THE PROFESSIONAL GOLFERS ASSOCIATION (PGA) CHAMPIONSHIP Inaugurated in 1916, the tournament was a match-play event, but switched to a 72-hole stroke-play event in 1958.

Most wins Two players have won the title five times: Walter Hagen (1921, 1924–27); and Jack Nicklaus (1963, 1971, 1973, 1975, 1980).

Most consecutive wins Four, by Walter Hagen (1924–27).

Lowest 18-hole total (any round) 63, by two players: Bruce Crampton (Australia) at Firestone Country Club, Akron, Ohio, in 1975; Ray Floyd at Southern Hills, Tulsa, Okla., in 1982.

Lowest 72-hole total 271 (64, 71, 69, 67), by Bobby Nichols at Columbus Country Club, Ohio in 1964.

Oldest champion 48 years 140 days, Julius Boros (1968).

Youngest champion 20 years 173 days, Gene Sarazen (1922).

BRITISH OPEN CHAMPIONS (1860–1922)

Year	Champion	Country	Year	Champion	Country	Year	Champion	Country
1860	Willie Park Sr.	Great Britain	1881	Robert Ferguson	Great Britain	1902	Sandy Herd	Great Britain
1861	Tom Morris Sr.	Great Britain	1882	Robert Ferguson	Great Britain	1903	Harry Vardon	Great Britain
1862	Tom Morris Sr.	Great Britain	1883	Willie Fernie	Great Britain	1904	Jack White	Great Britain
1863	Willie Park Sr.	Great Britain	1884	Jack Simpson	Great Britain	1905	James Braid	Great Britain
1864	Tom Morris Sr.	Great Britain	1885	Bob Martin	Great Britain	1906	James Braid	Great Britain
1865	Andrew Strath	Great Britain	1886	David Brown	Great Britain	1907	Arnaud Massy	France
1866	Willie Park Sr.	Great Britain	1887	Willie Park Jr.	Great Britain	1908	James Braid	Great Britain
1867	Tom Morris Sr.	Great Britain	1888	Jack Burns	Great Britain	1909	John H. Taylor	Great Britain
1868	Tom Morris Jr.	Great Britain	1889	Willie Park Jr.	Great Britain	1910	James Braid	Great Britain
1869	Tom Morris Jr.	Great Britain	1890	John Ball	Great Britain	1911	Harry Vardon	Great Britain
1870	Tom Morris Jr.	Great Britain	1891	Hugh Kirkaldy	Great Britain	1912	Edward Ray	Great Britain
1871	not held		1892	Harold H. Hilton	Great Britain	1913	John H. Taylor	Great Britain
1872	Tom Morris Jr.	Great Britain	1893	William Auchterlonie	Great Britain	1914	Harry Vardon	Great Britain
1873	Tom Kidd	Great Britain	1894	John H. Taylor	Great Britain	1915	not held	
1874	Mungo Park	Great Britain	1895	John H. Taylor	Great Britain	1916	not held	
1875	Willie Park Sr.	Great Britain	1896	Harry Vardon	Great Britain	1917	not held	
1876	Bob Martin	Great Britain	1897	Harold H. Hilton	Great Britain	1918	not held	
1877	Jamie Anderson	Great Britain	1898	Harry Vardon	Great Britain	1919	not held	
1878	Jamie Anderson	Great Britain	1899	Harry Vardon	Great Britain	1920	George Duncan	Great Britain
1879	Jamie Anderson	Great Britain	1900	John H. Taylor	Great Britain	1921	Jock Hutchinson	U.S.
1880	Robert Ferguson	Great Britain	1901	James Braid	Great Britain	1922	Walter Hagen	U.S.

PROFESSIONAL GOLFERS ASSOCIATION (PGA) TOUR RECORDS

Most wins (season) Byron Nelson won a record 18 tournaments in 1945.

Most wins (career) Sam Snead won 81 official PGA tour events from 1936–65.

Most consecutive wins 11, Byron Nelson, 1945.

Most wins (same event) Sam Snead won the Greater Greensboro Open eight times to set the individual tournament win mark. His victories came in 1938, 1946, 1949–50, 1955–56, 1960, 1965.

Most consecutive wins (same event) Four, by Walter Hagen, PGA Championship, 1924–27.

Oldest winner 52 years 10 months, Sam Snead, 1965 Greater Greensboro Open.

Youngest winner 19 years 10 months, Johnny McDermott, 1911 U.S. Open.

Widest winning margin 16 strokes, by Bobby Locke (South Africa), 1948 Chicago Victory National Championship.

LOWEST SCORES

Nine holes 27, by two players: Mike Souchak at the Brackenridge Park Golf Course, San Antonio, Texas, on the back nine of the first round of the 1955 Texas Open; Andy North at the En-Joie Golf Club, Endicott, N.Y., on the back nine of the first round of the 1975 B.C. Open.

BRITISH OPEN CHAMPIONS (1923–1992)

Year	Champion	Country	Year	Champion	Country	Year	Champion	Country
1923	Arthur Havers	Great Britain	1947	Fred Daly	Great Britain	1971	Lee Trevino	U.S.
1924	Walter Hagen	U.S.	1948	Henry Cotton	Great Britain	1972	Lee Trevino	U.S.
1925	Jim Barnes	U.S.	1949	Bobby Locke	South Africa	1973	Tom Weiskopf	U.S.
1926	Bobby Jones	U.S.	1950	Bobby Locke	South Africa	1974	Gary Player	South Africa
1927	Bobby Jones	U.S.	1951	Max Faulkner	Great Britain	1975	Tom Watson	U.S.
1928	Walter Hagen	U.S.	1952	Bobby Locke	South Africa	1976	Johnny Miller	U.S.
1929	Walter Hagen	U.S.	1953	Ben Hogan	U.S.	1977	Tom Watson	U.S.
1930	Bobby Jones	U.S.	1954	Peter Thomson	Australia	1978	Jack Nicklaus	U.S.
1931	Tommy Armour	U.S.	1955	Peter Thomson	Australia	1979	Seve Ballesteros	Spain
1932	Gene Sarazen	U.S.	1956	Peter Thomson	Australia	1980	Tom Watson	U.S.
1933	Densmore Shute	U.S.	1957	Bobby Locke	South Africa	1981	Bill Rogers	U.S.
1934	Henry Cotton	Great Britain	1958	Peter Thomson	Australia	1982	Tom Watson	U.S.
1935	Alfred Perry	Great Britain	1959	Gary Player	South Africa	1983	Tom Watson	U.S.
1936	Alfred Padgham	Great Britain	1960	Kel Nagle	Australia	1984	Seve Ballesteros	Spain
1937	Henry Cotton	Great Britain	1961	Arnold Palmer	U.S.	1985	Sandy Lyle	Great Britain
1938	Reg Whitcombe	Great Britain	1962	Arnold Palmer	U.S.	1986	Greg Norman	Australia
1939	Dick Burton	Great Britain	1963	Bob Charles	New Zealand	1987	Nick Faldo	Great Britain
1940	not held		1964	Tony Lema	U.S.	1988	Seve Ballesteros	Spain
1941	not held		1965	Peter Thomson	Australia	1989	Mark Calcavecchia	U.S.
1942	not held		1966	Jack Nicklaus	U.S.	1990	Nick Faldo	Great Britain
1943	not held		1967	Roberto de Vicenzo	Argentina	1991	Ian Baker-Finch	Australia
1944	not held		1968	Gary Player	South Africa	1992	Nick Faldo	Great Britain
1945	not held		1969	Tony Jacklin	Great Britain			
1946	Sam Snead	U.S.	1970	Jack Nicklaus	U.S.			

18 holes 59, by two players: Al Geiberger at the Colonial Country Club, Memphis, Tenn., during the second round of the 1977 Danny Thomas Memphis Classic; Chip Beck at the Sunrise Golf Club, Las Vegas, Nev., during the third round of the 1991 Las Vegas Invitational.

36 holes 125, by two players: Ron Streck at the Oak Hills Country Club, San Antonio, Tex., during the third and fourth rounds of the 1978 Texas Open; Blaine McCallister at the Oakwood Country Club, Coal Valley, Ill., during the sec-

ond and third rounds of the 1988 Hardee's Golf Classic.

54 holes 189, by Chandler Harper at the Brackenridge Park Golf Course, San Antonio, Tex., during the last three rounds of the 1954 Texas Open.

72 holes 257, by Mike Souchak at the Brackenridge Park Golf Course, San Antonio, Tex., at the 1955 Texas Open.

Most shots under par 31, by two players: Andrew Magee and D.A. Weibring at the 90-hole

PGA CHAMPIONS (1916–1992)

Year	Champion	Year	Champion	Year	Champion
1916	Jim Barnes	1942	Sam Snead	1968	Julius Boros
1917	not held	1943	not held	1969	Raymond Floyd
1918	not held	1944	Bob Hamilton	1970	Dave Stockton
1919	Jim Barnes	1945	Byron Nelson	1971	Jack Nicklaus
1920	Jock Hutchinson	1946	Ben Hogan	1972	Gary Player *
1921	Walter Hagen	1947	Jim Ferrier	1973	Jack Nicklaus
1922	Gene Sarazen	1948	Ben Hogan	1974	Lee Trevino
1923	Gene Sarazen	1949	Sam Snead	1975	Jack Nicklaus
1924	Walter Hagen	1950	Chandler Harper	1976	Dave Stockton
1925	Walter Hagen	1951	Sam Snead	1977	Lanny Wadkins
1926	Walter Hagen	1952	Jim Turnesa	1978	John Mahaffey
1927	Walter Hagen	1953	Walter Burkemo	1979	David Graham **
1928	Leo Diegel	1954	Chick Harbert	1980	Jack Nicklaus
1929	Leo Diegel	1955	Doug Ford	1981	Larry Nelson
1930	Tommy Armour	1956	Jack Burke Jr.	1982	Raymond Floyd
1931	Tom Creavy	1957	Lionel Hebert	1983	Hal Sutton
1932	Olin Dutra	1958	Dow Finsterwald	1984	Lee Trevino
1933	Gene Sarazen	1959	Bob Rosburg	1985	Hubert Green
1934	Paul Runyan	1960	Jay Herbert	1986	Bob Tway
1935	Johnny Revolta	1961	Jerry Barber	1987	Larry Nelson
1936	Densmore Shute	1962	Gary Player *	1988	Jeff Sluman
1937	Densmore Shute	1963	Jack Nicklaus	1989	Payne Stewart
1938	Paul Runyan	1964	Bobby Nichols	1990	Wayne Grady**
1939	Henry Picard	1965	Dave Marr	1991	John Daly
1940	Byron Nelson	1966	Al Geiberger	1992	Nick Price†
1941	Vic Chezzi	1967	Don January		

* South Africa,   ** Australia,   † Zimbabwe

PRIZE MONEY ■ TOM KITE HOLDS THE PGA EARN-INGS MARK AT $7,612,919.

1991 Las Vegas Invitational. Magee won the tournament in a playoff. The most shots under par in a 72-hole tournament is 27, shared by two players: Mike Souchak, at the 1955 Texas Open; and Ben Hogan, at the 1945 Portland Invitational.

TIMEOUT

ONE-CLUB ☞ THE LOWEST SCORE RECORDED ON A REGULATION GOLF COURSE USING ONLY ONE CLUB IS 70, SHOT BY THAD DABER (U.S.). USING ONLY A SIX IRON, DABER SET HIS RECORD ROUND IN WINNING THE 1987 WORLD ONE-CLUB CHAMPIONSHIP AT THE 6,037-YARD LOCKMORE GOLF CLUB IN CARY, N.C.

TEED UP . . . AND UP ■ THIS TOWER OF SEVEN GOLF BALLS WAS BALANCED BY LANG MARTIN ON FEBRUARY 9, 1980.

Season Tom Kite, $1,359,278 in 1989.

Career Tom Kite, $7,612,919, 1971–92.

Most times leading money winner Eight, Jack Nicklaus, 1964–65, 1967, 1971–73, 1975–76.

SENIOR PGA TOUR

The Senior PGA tour was established in 1982. Players 50 years and older are eligible to compete on the tour. Tournaments vary between 54- and 72-hole stroke-play.

Most wins 24, by Miller Barber (1981–92).

Most wins (season) Nine, by Peter Thomson, 1985.

Most consecutive wins Three, by two players: Bob Charles and Chi Chi Rodriguez, both in 1987.

Senior Tour / Regular Tour win Ray Floyd (U.S.) is the only player to win a Senior Tour event and a

DOUBLE-DIPPING ■ IN 1992 RAYMOND FLOYD BE-
CAME THE FIRST PLAYER TO WIN EVENTS ON THE
PGA AND SENIOR TOURS IN THE SAME SEASON.

PGA Tour event in the same year. He won the Doral Open PGA event in March 1992, and won his first Senior event, the GTE Northern, in September 1992.

HIGHEST EARNINGS

Season $1,190,518, Lee Trevino in 1990.

Career $3,740,267, Chi Chi Rodriguez, 1985–92.

THE PGA EUROPEAN TOUR

Most wins (season) Seven, by two players: Norman von Nida (Australia), 1947; and Flory van Donck (Belgium), 1953.

Most wins (career) 51, by Severiano Ballesteros (Spain), 1976–92.

HIGHEST EARNINGS

Season £708,522, by Nick Faldo (Great Britain) in 1992.

Career £3,153,819, by Severiano Ballesteros (Spain), 1974–92.

Most times leading money winner Six, Severiano Ballesteros, 1976–78, 1986, 1988, 1991.

RYDER CUP A biennial match-play competition between professional representative teams of the United States and Europe (Great Britain and Ireland prior to 1979), this event was launched in 1927. The U.S. leads the series 22–5, with two ties.

Most individual wins Arnold Palmer has won the most matches in Ryder Cup competition with 22 victories out of 32 played.

Most selections Christy O'Connor Sr. (Great Britain and Ireland) has played in the most contests, with 10 selections 1955–73.

PROFESSIONAL GOLF (WOMEN)

GRAND SLAM CHAMPIONSHIPS

GRAND SLAM A Grand Slam in ladies' professional golf has been recognized since 1955. From 1955–66, the United States Open, Ladies Professional Golf Association (LPGA) Championship, Western Open and Titleholders Championship served as the "majors." From 1967–82 the Grand Slam events changed, as first the Western Open (1967) and then the Titleholders Championship (1972) were discontinued. Since 1983, the U.S. Open, LPGA Championship, du Maurier Classic and Nabisco Dinah Shore have comprised the Grand Slam events.

Most grand slam titles Patty Berg has won the most majors, with 15 titles (one U.S. Open, seven Titleholders, seven Western Open).

THE UNITED STATES OPEN In this competition, inaugurated in 1946, the first event was played as a match-play tournament; however, since 1947, the 72-hole stroke-play format has been used.

Most wins Two players have won the title four times: Betsy Rawls (1951, 1953, 1957, 1960); Mickey Wright (1958–59, 1961, 1964).

Most consecutive wins Two, by five players: Mickey Wright (1958–59); Donna Caponi (1969–70); Susie Berning (1972–73); Hollis Stacy (1977–78); Betsy King (1989–90).

Lowest 18-hole total 65, by three players: Sally Little at Country Club of Indianapolis, Ind., in 1978; Judy Dickinson at Baltusrol Golf Club, Springfield, N.J., in 1985; Ayako Okamoto (Japan) at Indian Wood Golf and Country Club, Lake Orion, Mich., in 1989.

LOW SCORE ■ LISELOTTE NEUMANN WON THE 1988 U.S. OPEN SHOOTING A TOURNAMENT RECORD SCORE OF 277.

U.S. OPEN CHAMPIONS (1946–1992)

Year	Champion	Year	Champion	Year	Champion
1946	Patty Berg	1962	Murle Lindstrom	1978	Hollis Stacy
1947	Betty Jameson	1963	Mary Mills	1979	Jerilyn Britz
1948	Babe Zaharias	1964	Mickey Wright	1980	Amy Alcott
1949	Louise Suggs	1965	Carol Mann	1981	Pat Bradley
1950	Babe Zaharias	1966	Sandra Spuzich	1982	Janet Alex
1951	Betsy Rawls	1967	Catherine Lacoste*	1983	Jan Stephenson
1952	Louise Suggs	1968	Susie Berning	1984	Hollis Stacy
1953	Betsy Rawls	1969	Donna Caponi	1985	Kathy Baker
1954	Babe Zaharias	1970	Donna Caponi	1986	Jane Geddes
1955	Fay Crocker	1971	JoAnne Carner	1987	Laura Davies**
1956	Kathy Cornelius	1972	Susie Berning	1988	Liselotte Neumann †
1957	Betsy Rawls	1973	Susie Berning	1989	Betsy King
1958	Mickey Wright	1974	Sandra Haynie	1990	Betsy King
1959	Mickey Wright	1975	Sandra Palmer	1991	Meg Mallon
1960	Betsy Rawls	1976	JoAnne Carner	1992	Patty Sheehan
1961	Mickey Wright	1977	Hollis Stacy		

* France, ** Great Britain, † Sweden

Lowest 72-hole total 277, by Liselotte Neumann (Sweden) at Baltimore Country Club, Md., in 1988.

Oldest champion 40 years 11 months, Fay Croker (1955).

Youngest champion 22 years 5 days, Catherine Lacoste (France; 1967).

LPGA CHAMPIONSHIP This event was inaugurated in 1955; since 1987, it has been officially called the Mazda LPGA Championship.

Most wins Mickey Wright has won the LPGA a record four times: 1958, 1960–61, 1963.

Most consecutive wins Two, by two players: Mickey Wright (1960–61); Patty Sheehan (1983–84).

Lowest 18-hole total 64, by Patty Sheehan at the Jack Nicklaus Sports Center, Kings Island, Ohio, in 1984.

Lowest 72-hole total 267, by Betsy King at the Bethesda Country Club, Md., in 1992.

NABISCO DINAH SHORE Inaugurated in 1972, this event was formerly called the Colgate-Dinah Shore (1972–82). The event was designated a "major" in 1983. Mission Hills Country Club, Rancho Mirage, Calif. is the permanent site.

NABISCO DINAH SHORE CHAMPIONS (1972–1992)

Year	Champion	Year	Champion
1972	Jane Blalock	1983	Amy Alcott
1973	Mickey Wright	1984	Juli Inkster
1974	Jo Ann Prentice	1985	Alice Miller
1975	Sandra Palmer	1986	Pat Bradley
1976	Judy Rankin	1987	Betsy King
1977	Kathy Whitworth	1988	Amy Alcott
1978	Sandra Post	1989	Juli Inkster
1979	Sandra Post	1990	Betsy King
1980	Donna Caponi	1991	Amy Alcott
1981	Nancy Lopez	1992	Dottie Mochrie
1982	Sally Little		

Most wins Amy Alcott has won the title three times: 1983, 1988 and 1991.

Most consecutive wins Two, by Sandra Post (1978–79).

Lowest 18-hole total 64, by two players: Nancy Lopez in 1981; Sally Little in 1982.

Lowest 72-hole total 273, by Amy Alcott in 1991.

LPGA CHAMPIONS (1955–1992)

Year	Champion	Year	Champion	Year	Champion
1955	Beverly Hanson	1968	Sandra Post	1981	Donna Caponi
1956	Marlene Hagge	1969	Betsy Rawls	1982	Jan Stephenson
1957	Louise Suggs	1970	Shirley Englehorn	1983	Patty Sheehan
1958	Mickey Wright	1971	Kathy Whitworth	1984	Patty Sheehan
1959	Betsy Rawls	1972	Kathy Ahem	1985	Nancy Lopez
1960	Mickey Wright	1973	Mary Mills	1986	Pat Bradley
1961	Mickey Wright	1974	Sandra Haynie	1987	Jane Geddes
1962	Judy Kimball	1975	Kathy Whitworth	1988	Sherri Turner
1963	Mickey Wright	1976	Betty Burfeindt	1989	Nancy Lopez
1964	Mary Mills	1977	Chako Higuchi	1990	Beth Daniel
1965	Sandra Haynie	1978	Nancy Lopez	1991	Meg Mallon
1966	Gloria Ehret	1979	Donna Caponi	1992	Betsy King
1967	Kathy Whitworth	1980	Sally Little		

du Maurier Classic Inaugurated in 1973, this event was formerly known as La Canadienne (1973) and the Peter Jackson Classic (1974–82). Granted "major" status in 1979, the tournament is held annually at different sites in Canada.

Most wins Pat Bradley has won this event a record three times, 1980, 1985–86.

Most consecutive wins Two, by Pat Bradley (1985–86).

Lowest 18-hole total 64, by two players: JoAnne Carner at St. George's Country Club, Toronto, Canada in 1978; Jane Geddes at Beaconsfield Country Club, Montreal, Canada in 1985.

Lowest 72-hole total 276, by three players. Pat Bradley and Ayako Okamato (Japan) tied in regulation play in 1986 at the Board of Trade Country Club, Toronto. Bradley defeated Okamoto for the title in a sudden-death playoff. Cathy Johnston matched Bradley and Okamoto in 1990 at Westmont Golf and Country Club, Kitchener, Ontario.

LADIES PROFESSIONAL GOLF ASSOCIATION (LPGA) TOUR

Origins In 1944, three women golfers, Hope Seignious, Betty Hicks and Ellen Griffin, launched the Women's Professional Golf Association (WPGA). By 1947 the WPGA was unable to sustain the tour at the level that was hoped, and it seemed certain that women's professional golf would fade away. However, Wilson Sporting Goods stepped in, overhauled the tour and called it the Ladies Professional Golf Association. In 1950, the LPGA received its official charter.

Most wins (career) 88, by Kathy Whitworth, 1962–85.

Most wins (season) 13, by Mickey Wright, in 1963.

Most consecutive wins (scheduled events) Four, by two players: Mickey Wright, on two occasions, 1962, 1963; Kathy Whitworth, 1969.

Most consecutive wins (in events participated in) Five, by Nancy Lopez between May and June 1978.

Most wins (same event) Seven, by Patty Berg, who won two tournaments, the Titleholders Championship and the Western Open, both now defunct, on seven occasions during her illustrious career. She won the Titleholders in 1937–39, 1948, 1953, 1955, 1957; and the Western in 1941, 1943, 1948, 1951, 1955, 1957–58.

Oldest winner 46 years 5 months 9 days, JoAnne Carner at the 1985 Safeco Classic.

Youngest winner 18 years 14 days, Marlene Hagge at the 1952 Sarasota Open.

Widest margin of victory 14 strokes, by two players: Louise Suggs in the 1949 U.S. Open; Cindy Mackey in the 1986 Mastercard International.

Highest Earnings

Season $863,578, by Beth Daniel in 1990.

Career $4,347,706 by Pat Bradley, 1974–92.

Most times leading money winner Eight, Kathy Whitworth, 1965–68, 1970–73.

Lowest Scores

Nine holes 28, by four players: Mary Beth Zimmerman at the Rail Golf Club, Springfield, Ill., during the 1984 Rail Charity Golf Classic; Pat Bradley at the Green Gables Country Club, Denver, Colo., during the 1984 Columbia Savings Classic; Muffin Spencer-Devlin at the Knollwood Country Club, Elmsford, N.Y., during the 1985 MasterCard International Pro-Am; Peggy Kirsch

DU MAURIER CLASSIC CHAMPIONS (1973–1992)

Year	Champion	Year	Champion	Year	Champion
1973	Jocelyne Bourassa	1980	Pat Bradley	1987	Jody Rosenthal
1974	Carole Jo Skala	1981	Jan Stephenson	1988	Sally Little
1975	JoAnne Carner	1982	Sandra Haynie	1989	Tammie Green
1976	Donna Caponi	1983	Hollis Stacy	1990	Cathy Johnston
1977	Judy Rankin	1984	Juli Inkster	1991	Nancy Scranton
1978	JoAnne Carner	1985	Pat Bradley	1992	Sherri Steinhauer
1979	Amy Alcott	1986	Pat Bradley		

at the Squaw-Creek Country Club, Vienna, Ohio during the 1991 Phar-Mar in Youngstown.

18 holes 62, by three players: Mickey Wright at Hogan Park Golf Club, Midland, Tex., in the first round of the 1964 Tall City Open; Vicki Fergon at Alamaden Golf & Country Club, San Jose, Calif., in the second round of the 1984 San Jose Classic; and Laura Davies (Great Britain) at the Rail Golf Club, Springfield, Ill., during the 1991 Rail Charity Golf Classic.

36 holes 129, by Judy Dickinson at Pasadena Yacht & Country Club, St. Petersburg, Fla., during the 1985 S&H Golf Classic.

54 holes 197, by Pat Bradley at the Rail Golf Club, Springfield, Ill., in the 1991 Rail Charity Golf Classic.

72 holes 267, by Betsy King at the Bethesda Country Club, Md., in the 1992 Mazda LPGA Championship.

AMATEUR GOLF (MEN)

UNITED STATES AMATEUR CHAMPIONSHIP Inaugurated in 1895, the initial format was match-play competition. In 1965, the format was changed to stroke-play; however, since 1972, the event has been played under the original match-play format.

Most wins Five, by Bobby Jones, 1924–25, 1927–28, 1930.

Lowest score (stroke-play) 279, Lanny Wadkins, 1970.

Biggest winning margin (match-play: final) 12 & 11, Charles Macdonald, 1895.

RICHEST SHOT ☛ ON NOVEMBER 1, 1992 JASON BOHN WON $1 MILLION WHEN HE MADE A HOLE-IN-ONE DURING A CHARITY CONTEST. HE ACED THE 136-YARD 2ND HOLE AT THE HARRY S. PRITCHETT GOLF COURSE IN TUSCALOOSA, ALA.

BEST 18 ■ THE LPGA LOWEST SCORE FOR 18 HOLES IS 62, ACHIEVED BY THREE PLAYERS. LAURA DAVIES (ABOVE) JOINED THIS ELITE CLUB IN 1991.

NCAA CHAMPIONSHIP The men's championship was initiated in 1897 as a match-play championship. In 1967 the format was switched to stroke-play.

Most titles (team) Yale has won the most team championships with 21 victories (1897–98, 1902, 1905–13, 1915, 1924–26, 1931–33, 1936, 1943).

Most titles (individual) Two golfers have won three individual titles: Ben Crenshaw (Texas), 1971–73, Phil Mickelson (Arizona State), 1989–90, 1992.

GYMNASTICS

ORIGINS The ancient Greeks and Romans were exponents of gymnastics, as shown by demonstration programs in the ancient Olympic Games (776 B.C. to A.D. 393). Modern training techniques were developed in Germany toward the end of the 18th century. Johann Friedrich Simon was the first teacher of the modern methods, at Basedow's School, Dessau, Germany in 1776. Friedrich Jahn, who founded the Turnverein in Berlin, Germany in 1811, is regarded as the most influential of the gymnastics pioneers. The International Gymnastics Federation (IGF) was formed in 1891.

United States Gymnastics was introduced to the United States in the 19th century. With the advent of the modern Olympic Games, interest in the sport grew in this country, and in 1920 the United States entered its first gymnastics team in the Games. The sport was governed by the Amateur Athletic Union (AAU) and then by the National Collegiate Athletic Association (NCAA) until 1963, when the United States Gymnastics Federation (USGF) was formed. The USGF is still the governing body for the sport, and has its headquarters in Indianapolis, Ind.

OLYMPIC GAMES Gymnastics was included in the first modern Olympic Games in 1896; however, women's competition was not included until 1928.

Most gold medals Larissa Latynina (USSR) has won nine gold medals: six individual—all-around title, 1956 and 1960; floor exercise, 1956, 1960 and 1964; vault, 1956; and three team titles—1956, 1960 and 1964. In men's competition, Sawao Kato (Japan) has won eight gold medals: five individual—all-around title, 1968 and 1972; floor exercise, 1968; and parallel bars, 1972 and 1976; and three team titles—1968, 1972 and 1976.

Vera Caslavska (Czechoslovakia) has won a record seven individual gold medals: all-around title, 1964 and 1968; uneven bars, 1968; beam, 1964; floor exercise, 1968; and vault, 1964 and 1968. In men's competition, Boris Shakhlin and Nikolai Andrianov (both USSR) have each won six individual titles. Shakhlin won the all-around title, 1960; parallel bars, 1960; pommel horse, 1956, 1960; horizontal bar, 1964; vault, 1960. Andrianov won the all-around title, 1976; floor exercise, 1972, 1976; pommel horse, 1976; and vault, 1976 and 1980.

Most medals Larissa Latynina (USSR) has won 18 medals, the most of any athlete in any sport. She has won nine gold (six in individual events [see above] and one team event, 1980); five silver—all-around title, 1964; uneven bars, 1956 and 1960; beam, 1960; vault, 1964; and four bronze—uneven bars, 1964; beam, 1964; vault, 1964; and the portable apparatus team event (now discontinued) in 1956. Nikolai Andrianov holds the men's record at 15, which is the most by any male athlete in any sport. He won seven gold (six in individual events [see above] and one team event, 1980); five silver—team event, 1972 and 1976; all-around title, 1980; floor exercise, 1980; parallel bars, 1976; and three bronze—pommel horse, 1976; horizontal bar, 1980; and vault, 1972.

WORLD CHAMPIONSHIPS First held in Antwerp, Belgium in 1903, the championships were discontinued in 1913. Reintroduced in 1922, the event was held quadrenially until 1979, when the format became biennial. Until 1979 the Olympic Games served as the world championships, and results from Olympic competition are included in world championship statistics.

Most titles Larissa Latynina (USSR) won 17 world titles: five team and 12 individual, 1956–64. In men's competition, Boris Shakhlin (USSR) has won 13 titles: three team and 10 individual, 1954–64.

United States The most successful American gymnasts have been Kurt Thomas and Kim Zmeskal, who have each won three gold medals. Thomas won the floor exercise in 1978 and 1979, and the horizontal bar in 1979. Zmeskal won the all-around title in 1991 and the beam and floor exercise in 1992.

UNITED STATES NATIONAL CHAMPIONSHIPS

Most titles Alfred A. Jochim won a record seven men's all-around U.S. titles, 1925–30 and 1933, and a total of 34 at all exercises between 1923 and 1934. The women's record is six all-around, 1945–46 and 1949–52, and 39 at all exercises, including 11 in succession at balance beam, 1941–51, by Clara Marie Schroth Lomady.

NCAA CHAMPIONSHIPS (MEN) The men's competition was first held in 1932.

Most team titles The most team championships won is nine, by two colleges: Illinois, 1939–42, 1950, 1955–56, 1958, 1989; Penn State, 1948, 1953–54, 1957, 1959–61, 1965, 1976.

INDIVIDUAL RECORDS, 1932–92

Most titles (one year) Four, by two gymnasts: Jean Cronstedt, Penn State, won the all-around title, parallel bar, horizontal bar and floor exercise in 1954; Robert Lynn, Southern Cal., won the all-around title, parallel bar, horizontal bar and floor exercise in 1962.

Most titles (career) Seven, by two gymnasts: Joe Giallombardo, Illinois, won the tumbling, 1938–40, all-around title, 1938–40; and floor exercise, 1938; Jim Hartung, Nebraska, won the all-around title, 1980–81; rings, 1980–82; and parallel bar, 1981–82.

NCAA CHAMPIONSHIPS (WOMEN) The women's competition was first held in 1982.

Most team titles The most team championships won is six, by Utah, 1982–86, 1990.

INDIVIDUAL RECORDS, 1982–92

Most titles (one year) Three, by two gymnasts: Kelly Garrison-Steves, Oklahoma, won the all-around title, balance beam and uneven bars in

1988; Hope Spivey, Georgia, won the all-around title, floor exercise and vault in 1991.

Most titles (career) Four, by three gymnasts: Kelly Garrison-Steves, Oklahoma, won the all-around title, 1987–88; balance beam, 1988; uneven bars, 1988; Kim Hamilton, UCLA, won the floor exercise, 1987–89, and vault, 1989; Penney Hauschild, Alabama, won the all-around title, 1985–86; uneven bars, 1985; and floor exercise, 1986.

MODERN RHYTHMIC GYMNASTICS

Modern rhythmic gymnastics involves complex body movements combined with handling of apparatus such as ropes, hoops, balls, clubs and ribbons. The performance must include required elements, and the choreography must cover the entire floor area and include elements such as jumps, pivots and leaps.

ORIGINS In 1962 the International Gymnastics Federation (IGF) officially recognized rhythmic gymnastics as a distinct sport. The first world championships were held in 1963 and the sport was included in the Olympic Games in 1984.

OLYMPIC GAMES No gymnast has won more than one medal in Olympic competition. Marina Lobach (USSR) won the 1988 Olympic title with perfect scores of 60.00 points in each of her events.

WORLD CHAMPIONSHIPS

Most titles (individual) Maria Gigova (Bulgaria) has won three individual world championships in 1969, 1971 and 1973 (tied).

Most titles (country) Bulgaria has won eight team championships: 1969, 1971, 1973, 1981, 1983, 1985, 1987 and 1989 (tie).

HANG GLIDING

ORIGINS In the 11th century the monk Eilmer is reported to have flown from the 60-foot tower of Malmesbury Abbey, Wiltshire, England. The earliest modern pioneer was Otto Lilienthal (Germany), with about 2,500 flights in gliders of his own construction between 1891 and 1896. In the 1950s, Professor Francis Rogallo of the National Space Agency developed a flexible "wing" from his space capsule reentry research.

TIMEOUT

ON A ROLL ☛ ASHRITA FURMAN (U.S.) PERFORMED 8,341 FORWARD ROLLS IN 10 HOURS 30 MINUTES ON APRIL 30, 1986. FURMAN SOMERSAULTED FROM LEXINGTON TO CHARLESTOWN, MASS., A DISTANCE OF 12 MILES 390 YARDS.

ABOVE IT ALL ■ HANG-GLIDER LARRY TUDOR SET AN ALTITUDE GAIN RECORD OF 14,250.69 FEET ON AUGUST 4, 1985.

WORLD RECORDS The *Fédération Aéronautique Internationale* recognizes world records for flexible-wing, rigid-wing, and multiplace flexible-wing.

FLEXIBLE WING—SINGLE PLACE DISTANCE RECORDS (MEN)

Straight line Larry Tudor (U.S.) piloted a Wills Wing HPAT 158 for a straight-line distance of 303.36 miles, from Hobbs, N. Mex. to Elkhart, Kans., on July 3, 1990.

Single turnpoint Christian Durif (France) piloted a La Mouette Compact 15 a single-turnpoint record 158.94 miles over Owens Valley, Calif. on July 3, 1990.

Triangular course James Lee Jr. (U.S.) piloted a Willis Wing HPAT 158 for a triangular course record 121.82 miles over Garcia, Colo. on July 4, 1991.

Out and return The out and return goal distance record is 192.818 miles, set by two pilots on the same day, July 26, 1988, over Lone Pine, Calif.: Larry Tudor, Wills Wing HPAT 158; Geoffrey Loyns (Great Britain), Enterprise Wings.

Altitude gain Larry Tudor set a height gain record of 14,250.69 feet flying a G2-155 over Horseshoe Meadows, Calif. on August 4, 1985.

FLEXIBLE WING—SINGLE PLACE DISTANCE RECORDS (WOMEN)

Straight line Kari Castle (U.S.) piloted a Wills Wing AT 145 a straight-line distance of 208.63 miles over Lone Pine, Calif. on July 22, 1991.

Single turnpoint Kari Castle piloted a Pacific Airwave Magic Kiss a single-turnpoint distance of 181.47 miles over Hobbs, N.Mex. on July 1, 1990.

Triangular course Judy Leden (Great Britain) flew a triangular course record 70.173 miles over Austria on June 22, 1991.

Out and return The out and return goal distance record is 81.99 miles, set by Tover Buas-Hansen (Norway), piloting an International Axis over Owens Valley, Calif. on July 6, 1989.

Altitude gain Tover Buas-Hansen set an altitude gain record of 11,998.62 feet, piloting an International Axis over Bishop Airport, Calif. on July 6, 1989.

RIGID WING—SINGLE PLACE DISTANCE RECORDS (MEN)

Straight line The straight-line distance record is 139.07 miles, set by William Reynolds (U.S), piloting a Wills Wing over Lone Pine, Calif. on June 27, 1988.

Out and return The out and return goal distance is 47.46 miles, set by Randy Bergum (U.S.), piloting an Easy Riser over Big Pine, Calif. on July 12, 1988.

Altitude gain Rainer Scholl (South Africa) set an altitude gain record of 12,532.80 feet on May 8, 1985.

FLEXIBLE WING—MULTIPLACE DISTANCE RECORDS (MEN)

Straight line The straight line distance record is 100.60 miles, set by Larry Tudor and Eri Fujita, flying a Comet II-185 on July 12, 1985.

Out and return The out and return goal distance record is 81.99 miles, set by Kevin and Tom Klinefelter (U.S.) on July 6, 1989.

Altitude gain Tom and Kevin Klinefelter set an altitude record of 10,997.30 feet on July 6, 1989 over Bishop Airport, Calif. flying a Moyes Delta Glider.

HARNESS RACING

Harness racing involves two styles of racing: trotting and pacing. The distinction between trotters and pacers is in the gait of the horses. The trotting gait requires the simultaneous use of the diagonally opposite legs, while pacers thrust out their fore and hind legs simultaneously on one side.

ORIGINS Trotting races are known to have been held in Valkenburg, the Netherlands in 1554.

There is also evidence of trotting races in England in the late 16th century.

United States Harness racing became popular in the United States in the mid-19th century. The National Trotting Association was founded, originally as the National Association for the Promotion of the Interests of the Trotting Turf, in 1870, and is still the governing body for the sport in the United States.

TROTTING

HORSES' RECORDS

VICTORIES

Career Goldsmith Maid won an all-time record 350 races (including dashes and heats) from 1864 through 1877.

HIGHEST EARNINGS ■ IN 1992, PEACE CORPS SET THE ALL TIME RECORD FOR EARNINGS BY A TROTTER AT $4,888,999.

Season Make Believe won a record 53 races in 1949.

HIGHEST EARNINGS

Career The greatest career earnings for any harness horse is $4,888,999, by Peace Corps, 1988–92.

Season The single-season earnings record for a trotter is $1,610,608, by Prakas in 1985.

Race The richest race in the trotting calendar is the Hambletonian. The richest Hambletonian was the 1992 event, with a total purse of $1,380,000. The record first-place prize was $673,000 for the 1990 race, won by Harmonious.

INDIVIDUAL RACES

THE TRIPLE CROWN The Triple Crown for trotters consists of three races: Hambletonian, Kentucky Futurity and Yonkers Trot. Six trotters have won the Triple Crown.

TRIPLE CROWN WINNERS—TROTTERS

Year	Horse	Driver
1955	Scott Frost	Joe O'Brien
1963	Speedy Scot	Ralph Baldwin
1964	Ayres	John Simpson Sr.
1968	Nevele Pride	Stanley Dancer
1969	Lindy's Pride	Howard Beissinger
1972	Super Bowl	Stanley Dancer

HAMBLETONIAN The most famous race in North American harness racing, the Hambletonian, was first run in 1926. The Hambletonian has been run at six venues: New York State Fairgrounds, Syracuse, N.Y. (1926 and 1928); The Red Mile, Lexington, Ky. (1927 and 1929); Good Time Park, Goshen, N.Y. (1930–42, 1944–56); Empire City, Yonkers, N.Y. (1943); Du Quoin State Fair, Du Quoin, Ill. (1957–80); and The Meadowlands, N.J. (1981–present). The Hambletonian is open to three-year-olds and is run over one mile.

Fastest time The fastest time is 1 minute 53⅗ seconds, by Mack Lobell, driven by John Campbell, in 1987.

Most wins (driver) Three drivers have won the Hambletonian four times: Ben White, 1933, 1936, 1942 and 1943; Stanley Dancer, 1968, 1972, 1975 and 1983; William Haughton, 1974, 1976–77 and 1980.

KENTUCKY FUTURITY First held in 1893, the Kentucky Futurity is a one-mile race for three-year-olds, raced at The Red Mile, Lexington, Ky.

Fastest time Two trotters hold the race record of 1 minute 54⅖ seconds: Peace Corps, driven by John Campbell, in 1989; and Star Mystic, driven by Jan Johnson, in 1990.

Most wins (driver) Ben White has driven the winning trotter seven times: 1916, 1922, 1924–25, 1933, 1936–37.

YONKERS TROT First run in 1955, when it was known as "The Yonkers," this race has been known since 1975 as the Yonkers Trot. Run over one mile for three-year-olds, the race is currently staged at Yonkers Raceway, N.Y.

Fastest time The fastest time is 1 minute 57⅘ seconds, by Mack Lobell, driven by John Campbell, in 1987.

Most wins (driver) Stanley Dancer has driven the winning trotter six times: 1959, 1965, 1968, 1971–72 and 1975.

PACERS

HORSES' RECORDS

VICTORIES

Career Single G won 262 races (including dashes and heats), 1918–26.

Career (modern record) Symbol Allen won 241 races from 1943 through 1958.

Season Victory Hy won a record 65 races in 1950.

Consecutive wins Carty Nagle won 41 consecutive races from 1937 through 1938.

HIGHEST EARNINGS

Career The all-time earnings record for a pacer is $3,225,653, by Nihilator, 1984–85.

Season The single-season record for a pacer is $2,217,222, by Precious Bunny in 1991.

Race The richest race in harness racing history was the 1984 Woodrow Wilson, which carried a total purse of $2,161,000. The winner, Nihilator, earned a record $1,080,500.

INDIVIDUAL RACES

THE TRIPLE CROWN The Triple Crown for pacers consists of three races: Cane Pace, Little Brown Jug and Messenger Stakes. Seven horses have won the Triple Crown.

TRIPLE CROWN WINNERS—PACERS

Year	Horse	Driver
1959	Adios Butler	Clint Hodgins
1965	Bret Hanover	Frank Ervin
1966	Romeo Hanover	Jerry Silverman
1968	Rum Customer	William Haughton
1970	Most Happy Fella	Stanley Dancer
1980	Niatross	Clint Galbraith
1983	Ralph Hanover	Ron Waples

CANE PACE First run in 1955, this race was originally known as the Cane Futurity. Since 1975, it has been called the Cane Pace. Run over one mile, the race is open to three-year-olds, and is run at Yonkers Raceway, N.Y.

Fastest time The fastest time is 1 minute 53⅗ seconds, by two pacers: Silky Stallone, driven by Jack Moiseyev, in 1991; and Western Hanover, driven by Bill Fahy, in 1992.

Most wins (driver) Stanley Dancer has driven the winning pacer four times: 1964, 1970–71 and 1976.

LITTLE BROWN JUG First run in 1946, the Jug is raced annually at Delaware County Fair, Delaware, Ohio. The race is for three-year-olds and is run over one mile.

Fastest time The fastest time is 1 minute 52⅕ seconds, by Nihilator, driven by Bill O'Donnell, in 1985.

Most wins (driver) William Haughton has driven five winning pacers, in 1955, 1964, 1968–69 and 1974.

MESSENGER STAKES First run in 1956, this race has been staged at various locations during its history. The race is run over one mile and is open to three-year-olds only.

Fastest time The fastest time is 1 minute 51⅕ seconds, by Die Laughing, driven by Richard Silverman, in 1991.

Most wins (drivers) William Haughton has driven the winning pacer seven times, in 1956, 1967–68, 1972 and 1974–76.

DRIVERS' RECORDS

Most wins (career) Herve Filion (Canada) has won 13,750 harness races as of January 12, 1993.

Most wins (season) Walter Case won a record 843 races in 1992.

Most wins (day) Mike Lachance won 12 races at Yonkers Raceway, N.Y. on June 23, 1987.

HIGHEST EARNINGS

Career John Campbell has won a career record $109,209,614 in prize money, 1972–92.

Season John Campbell won a season record $11,620,878 in 1990, when he won 543 races.

HOCKEY

ORIGINS There is pictorial evidence that a hockey-like game (*kalv*) was played on ice in the early 16th century in the Netherlands. The game was probably first played in North America on December 25, 1855 at Kingston, Ontario, Canada, but Halifax also lays claim to priority. The International Ice Hockey Federation was founded in 1908.

NATIONAL HOCKEY LEAGUE (NHL) (1917–1992)

ORIGINS The National Hockey League (NHL) was founded on November 22, 1917 in Montreal, Canada. The formation of the NHL was precipitated by the collapse of the National Hockey Association of Canada (NHA). Four teams formed the original league: the Montreal Canadiens, Montreal Wanderers, Ottawa Senators and Quebec Bulldogs. The Toronto Arenas were admitted as a fifth team, but the Bulldogs were unable to operate, and the league began as a four-team competition. The first NHL game was played on December 19, 1917. The NHL is now comprised of 22 teams, seven from Canada and 15 from the United States, divided into two divisions within two conferences: Adams and Patrick Divisions in the Wales Conference;

NATIONAL HOCKEY LEAGUE RECORDS (1917 –1992)

Goals

		Player(s)	Team(s)	Date(s)
Period	4	Busher Jackson	Toronto Maple Leafs v. St. Louis Eagles	November 20, 1934
		Max Bentley	Chicago Blackhawks v. New York Rangers	January 28, 1943
		Clint Smith	Chicago Blackhawks v. Montreal Canadiens	March 4, 1945
		Red Berenson	St. Louis Blues v. Philadelphia Flyers	November 7, 1968
		Wayne Gretzky	Edmonton Oilers v. St. Louis Blues	February 18, 1981
		Grant Mulvey	Chicago Blackhawks v. St. Louis Blues	February 3, 1982
		Bryan Trottier	New York Islanders v. Philadelphia Flyers	February 13, 1982
		Al Secord	Chicago Blackhawks v. Toronto Maple Leafs	January 7, 1987
		Joe Nieuwendyk	Calgary Flames v. Winnipeg Jets	January 11, 1989
Game	7	Joe Malone	Quebec Bulldogs v. Toronto St. Patricks	January 31, 1920
Season	92	Wayne Gretzky	Edmonton Oilers	1981–82
Career	801	Gordie Howe	Detroit Red Wings, Hartford Whalers	1946–71, 1979–80

Assists

Period	5	Dale Hawerchuk	Winnipeg Jets v. Los Angeles Kings	March 6, 1984
Game	7	Billy Taylor	Detroit Red Wings v. Chicago Blackhawks	March 16, 1947
		Wayne Gretzky	Edmonton Oilers v. Washington Capitals	February 15, 1980
		Wayne Gretzky	Edmonton Oilers v. Chicago Blackhawks	December 11, 1985
		Wayne Gretzky	Edmonton Oilers v. Quebec Nordiques	February 14, 1986
Season	163	Wayne Gretzky	Edmonton Oilers	1985–86
Career	1,520	Wayne Gretzky	Edmonton Oilers, Los Angeles Kings	1979–93*

Points

Period	6	Bryan Trottier	New York Islanders v. New York Rangers	December 23, 1978
Game	10	Darryl Sittler	Toronto Maple Leafs v. Boston Bruins	February 7, 1976
Season	215	Wayne Gretzky	Edmonton Oilers	1985–86
Career	2,271	Wayne Gretzky	Edmonton Oilers, Los Angeles Kings	1979–93*

Goaltenders
Shutouts

Season	22	George Hainsworth	Montreal Canadiens	1928–29
Career	103	Terry Sawchuk	Detroit Red Wings, Boston Bruins, Toronto Maple Leafs, Los Angeles Kings, New York Rangers	1949–70

Wins

Season	47	Bernie Parent	Philadelphia Flyers	1973–74
Career	435	Terry Sawchuk	Detroit Red Wings, Boston Bruins, Toronto Maple Leafs, Los Angeles Kings, New York Rangers	1949–70

* As of January 19, 1993
Source: NHL

WINS ■ THE FLYERS' BERNIE PARENT SET AN NHL SEASON MARK FOR VICTORIES IN 1973–74 WHEN HE WON 47 GAMES.

Norris and Smythe Division in the Campbell Conference. At the end of the regular season, 16 teams compete in the Stanley Cup playoffs to decide the NHL Championship. (For further details of the Stanley Cup, see below.)

TEAM RECORDS (1917–1992)

Most wins (season) The Montreal Canadiens won 60 games during the 1976–77 season. In 80 games, "the Habs" won 60, lost 8 and tied 12.

Highest winning percentage (season) The 1929–30 Boston Bruins set an NHL record .875 winning percentage. The Bruins' record was 38 wins, 5 losses and 1 tie.

Most points (season) The Montreal Canadiens accumulated 132 points during their record-setting campaign of 1976–77, when they won a record 60 games.

Most losses (season) The Washington Capitals hold the unenviable record of having lost the most games in one season. During the 1974–75 season, the first for the franchise, the Capitals lost 67 of 80 games played.

Most goals (game) The NHL record for goals in one game is 21, which has occurred on two occasions. The mark was set on January 10, 1920, when the Montreal Canadiens defeated the Toronto St. Patricks, 14–7, at Montreal. This record was matched on December 11, 1985, when the Edmonton Oilers beat the Chicago Blackhawks, 12–9, at Chicago.

Most goals (game—one team) The Montreal Canadiens pounded the Quebec Bulldogs 16–3 on March 3, 1920 to set the single-game scoring record. To make matters worse for Quebec, it was on home ice!

Most goals (season) The Edmonton Oilers scored 446 goals in 80 games during the 1983–84 season.

Most assists (season) The Edmonton Oilers recorded 737 assists during the 1985–86 season.

Most points (season) The Edmonton Oilers amassed 1,182 points (446 goals, 736 assists) during the 1983–84 season.

Most power-play goals scored (season) The Pittsburgh Penguins scored 120 power-play goals during the 1988–89 season.

Most shorthand goals scored (season) The Edmonton Oilers scored 36 shorthand goals during the 1983–84 season.

Most penalty minutes in one game At the Boston Garden on February 26, 1981, the Boston Bruins and the Minnesota North Stars received a combined 406 penalty minutes, a record for one game. The Bruins received 20 minors, 13 majors, three 10-minute misconducts and six game misconducts for a total of 195 penalty minutes; the North Stars received 18 minors, 13 majors, four 10-minute misconducts and seven game misconducts for a total of 211 penalty minutes. It is also reported that a hockey game broke out between the fights, which the Bruins won 5–1.

Longest winning streak The New York Islanders won 15 consecutive games from January 21–February 20, 1982.

Longest undefeated streak The longest undefeated streak in one season is 35 games by the Philadelphia Flyers. The Flyers won 25 games and tied 10 from October 14, 1979–January 6, 1980.

Longest losing streak The Washington Capitals lost 17 consecutive games from February 18–March 26, 1975.

Longest winless streak The Winnipeg Jets set the mark for the longest winless streak at 30 games. From October 19 to December 20, 1980, the Jets lost 23 games and tied seven.

Longest game The longest game was played between the Detroit Red Wings and the Montreal Maroons at the Forum Montreal and lasted 2 hours 56 minutes 30 seconds. The Red Wings won when Mud Bruneteau scored the only goal of the game in the sixth period of overtime at 2:25 A.M. on March 25, 1936. Norm Smith, the Red Wings

goaltender, turned aside 92 shots for the NHL's longest shutout.

INDIVIDUAL RECORDS (1917–1992)

Most games played Gordie Howe played 1,767 games over a record 26 seasons for the Detroit Red Wings (1946–71) and Hartford Whalers (1979–80). The most games played by a goaltender is 971, by Terry Sawchuk, who played 21 seasons for five teams: Detroit Red Wings, Boston Bruins, Toronto Maple Leafs, Los Angeles Kings and New York Rangers (1949–70).

Most consecutive games played Doug Jarvis played 964 consecutive games from October 8, 1975 to October 10, 1987. During the streak, Jarvis played for three teams: the Montreal Canadiens, Washington Capitals and Hartford Whalers.

Fastest goal The fastest goal from the start of a game is 5 seconds, a feat performed by three players: Doug Smail (Winnipeg Jets) v. St. Louis Blues at Winnipeg on December 20, 1981; Bryan Trottier (New York Islanders) v. Boston Bruins at Boston on March 22, 1984; and Alexander Mogilny (Buffalo Sabres) v. Toronto Maple Leafs at Toronto on December 21, 1991. The fastest goal from

SKATING STREAK ■ DEFENSEMAN DOUG JARVIS PLAYED **964** CONSECUTIVE NHL GAMES FROM **1975**

the start of any period was after 4 seconds by Claude Provost (Montreal Canadiens) *v.* Boston Bruins in the second period at Montreal on November 9, 1957, and by Denis Savard (Chicago Blackhawks) *v.* Hartford Whalers in the third period at Chicago on January 12, 1986.

Most hat tricks The most hat tricks (three or more goals in a game) in a career is 49, by Wayne Gretzky for the Edmonton Oilers and Los Angeles Kings in 13 seasons (1979–92). "The Great One" has recorded 36 three-goal games, nine four-goal games and four five-goal games. Gretzky also holds the record for most hat tricks in a season, 10, in both the 1981–82 and 1983–84 seasons for the Edmonton Oilers.

Longest consecutive goal-scoring streak The most consecutive games scoring at least one goal in a game is 16, by Harry (Punch) Broadbent (Ottawa Senators) in the 1921–22 season. Broadbent scored 25 goals during the streak.

Longest consecutive assist-scoring streak The record for most consecutive games recording at least one assist is 23 games, by Wayne Gretzky (Los Angeles Kings) in 1990–91. Gretzky was credited with 48 assists during the streak.

Most consecutive 50-or-more-goal seasons Mike Bossy (New York Islanders) scored at least 50 goals in nine consecutive seasons from 1977–78 through 1985–86.

Longest consecutive point-scoring streak The most consecutive games scoring at least one point is 51, by Wayne Gretzky (Edmonton Oilers) between October 5, 1983 and January 27, 1984. During the streak, Gretzky scored 61 goals, 92 assists for 153 points.

Longest shutout sequence by a goaltender Alex Connell (Ottawa Senators) played 461 minutes, 29 seconds without conceding a goal in the 1927–28 season.

Longest undefeated streak by a goaltender Gerry Cheevers (Boston Bruins) went 32 games (24 wins, 8 ties) undefeated during the 1971–72 season.

Defensemen On October 17, 1991, Paul Coffey (Edmonton Oilers, 1980–87; Pittsburgh Penguins, 1987–91) broke the career record for assists and points by a defenseman in the NHL, when he recorded two assists in the game *v.* the New York Islanders, increasing his totals to 744

ORR-SOME ■ IN 1970–71, BOBBY ORR SET THE SINGLE-SEASON MARKS FOR ASSISTS, 102, AND POINTS, 139, SCORED BY A DEFENSEMAN.

assists and 1,053 points. On November 8, 1991, Coffey surpassed the record for most goals by a defenseman when he scored his 311th goal *v.* the Winnipeg Jets. As of January 19, 1993, Coffey's career marks were 326 goals, 838 assists and 1,164 points. Coffey also holds the single-season record for goals scored by a defenseman, 48, which he scored in 1985–86 when he played for the Edmonton Oilers. Bobby Orr (Boston Bruins) holds the single-season marks for assists (102) and points (139), both of which were set in 1970–71.

COACHES

Most wins As of January 13, 1992, Scotty Bowman has coached his teams to 807 victories (110 wins, St. Louis Blues, 1967–71; 419 wins, Montreal Canadiens, 1971–79; 210 wins, Buffalo Sabres, 1979–87; 68 wins, Pittsburgh Penguins, 1991–92).

Most games coached Al Arbour has coached a record 1,438 games with two teams: St. Louis Blues, 1970–73; New York Islanders, 1973–86,

HART MEMORIAL TROPHY WINNERS (1924–1992)

The Hart Trophy has been awarded annually since the 1923–24 season by the Professional Hockey Writers Association to the Most Valuable Player of the NHL. Wayne Gretzky has won the award a record nine times, 1980–87 and 1989.

Year	Player	Team	Year	Player	Team
1924	Frank Nighbor	Ottawa Senators	1959	Andy Bathgate	New York Rangers
1925	Billy Burch	Hamilton Tigers	1960	Gordie Howe	Detroit Red Wings
1926	Nels Stewart	Montreal Maroons	1961	Bernie Geoffrion	Montreal Canadiens
1927	Herb Gardiner	Montreal Canadiens	1962	Jacques Plante	Montreal Canadiens
1928	Howie Morenz	Montreal Canadiens	1963	Gordie Howe	Detroit Red Wings
1929	Roy Worters	New York Americans	1964	Jean Beliveau	Montreal Canadiens
1930	Nels Stewart	Montreal Maroons	1965	Bobby Hull	Chicago Blackhawks
1931	Howie Morenz	Montreal Canadiens	1966	Bobby Hull	Chicago Blackhawks
1932	Howie Morenz	Montreal Canadiens	1967	Stan Mikita	Chicago Blackhawks
1933	Eddie Shore	Boston Bruins	1968	Stan Mikita	Chicago Blackhawks
1934	Aurel Joliat	Montreal Canadiens	1969	Phil Esposito	Boston Bruins
1935	Eddie Shore	Boston Bruins	1970	Bobby Orr	Boston Bruins
1936	Eddie Shore	Boston Bruins	1971	Bobby Orr	Boston Bruins
1937	Babe Siebert	Montreal Canadiens	1972	Bobby Orr	Boston Bruins
1938	Eddie Shore	Boston Bruins	1973	Bobby Clarke	Philadelphia Flyers
1939	Toe Blake	Montreal Canadiens	1974	Phil Esposito	Boston Bruins
1940	Ebbie Goodfellow	Detroit Red Wings	1975	Bobby Clarke	Philadelphia Flyers
1941	Bill Cowley	Boston Bruins	1976	Bobby Clarke	Philadelphia Flyers
1942	Tom Anderson	Brooklyn Americans	1977	Guy Lafleur	Montreal Canadiens
1943	Bill Cowley	Boston Bruins	1978	Guy Lafleur	Montreal Canadiens
1944	Babe Pratt	Toronto Maple Leafs	1979	Bryan Trottier	New York Islanders
1945	Elmer Lach	Montreal Canadiens	1980	Wayne Gretzky	Edmonton Oilers
1946	Max Bentley	Chicago Blackhawks	1981	Wayne Gretzky	Edmonton Oilers
1947	Maurice Richard	Montreal Canadiens	1982	Wayne Gretzky	Edmonton Oilers
1948	Buddy O'Connor	New York Rangers	1983	Wayne Gretzky	Edmonton Oilers
1949	Sid Abel	Detroit Red Wings	1984	Wayne Gretzky	Edmonton Oilers
1950	Charlie Rayner	New York Rangers	1985	Wayne Gretzky	Edmonton Oilers
1951	Milt Schmidt	Boston Bruins	1986	Wayne Gretzky	Edmonton Oilers
1952	Gordie Howe	Detroit Red Wings	1987	Wayne Gretzky	Edmonton Oilers
1953	Gordie Howe	Detroit Red Wings	1988	Mario Lemieux	Pittsburgh Penguins
1954	Al Rollins	Chicago Blackhawks	1989	Wayne Gretzky	Los Angeles Kings
1955	Ted Kennedy	Toronto Maple Leafs	1990	Mark Messier	Edmonton Oilers
1956	Jean Beliveau	Montreal Canadiens	1991	Brett Hull	St. Louis Blues
1957	Gordie Howe	Detroit Red Wings	1992	Mark Messier	New York Rangers
1958	Gordie Howe	Detroit Red Wings			

1988–92. Arbour's career record is 705 wins, 504 losses, 229 ties.

STANLEY CUP

The Stanley Cup is currently the oldest competition in North American professional sports. The cup was donated to the Canadian Amateur Hockey Association (AHA) by Sir Frederick Arthur Stanley, Lord Stanley of Preston in 1893. The inaugural championship was presented to the AHA champion, but since 1894 there has always been a playoff. The playoff format underwent several changes until 1926, when the National Hockey League (NHL) playoffs became the permanent forum to decide the Stanley Cup champion.

Most championships The Montreal Canadiens have won the Stanley Cup a record 23 times: 1916, 1924, 1930–31, 1944, 1946, 1953, 1956–60, 1965–66, 1968–69, 1971, 1973, 1976–79, 1986.

Most consecutive wins The Montreal Canadiens won the Stanley Cup for five consecutive years, 1956–60.

Most games played Larry Robinson has played in 227 Stanley Cup playoff games for the Montreal Canadiens (1973–89, 203 games) and the Los Angeles Kings (1990–92, 24 games).

GOAL SCORING RECORDS

Fastest goal The fastest goal from the start of any playoff game was scored by Don Kozak (Los Angeles Kings) past Gerry Cheevers (Boston Bruins) with 6 seconds elapsed. The Kings went on to win 7–4; the game was played on April 17, 1977. Kozak's goal shares the mark for fastest goal from the start of any period with one scored by Pelle Eklund (Philadelphia Flyers). Eklund scored in the second period of a game against the Pittsburgh Penguins in Pittsburgh on April 25, 1989; his effort was in vain, however, as the Penguins won 10–7.

STANLEY CUP CHAMPIONS (1893–1904)

Year	Champion	Loser	Series
1893	Montreal A.A.A.	(no challenger)	——
1894	Montreal A.A.A.	Ottawa Generals	3–1*
1895	Montreal Victorias	(no challenger)	——
1896	Winnipeg Victorias (February)	Montreal Victorias	2–0*
	Montreal Victorias (December)	Winnipeg Victorias	6–5*
1897	Montreal Victorias	Ottawa Capitals	15–2*
1898	Montreal Victorias	(no challenger)	——
1899	Montreal Victorias (February)	Winnipeg Victorias	2–0
	Montreal Shamrocks (March)	Queen's University	6–2*
1900	Montreal Shamrocks	Halifax Crescents	**
		Winnipeg Victorias	
1901	Winnipeg Victorias	Montreal Shamrocks	2–0
1902	Winnipeg Victorias (January)	Toronto Wellingtons	2–0
	Montreal A.A.A. (March)	Winnipeg Victorias	2–1
1903	Montreal A.A.A. (February)	Winnipeg Victorias	2–1
	Ottawa Silver Seven (March)	Rat Portage Thistles	**
		Montreal Victorias	
1904	Ottawa Silver Seven	Brandon Wheat Kings	**
		Montreal Wanderers	
		Toronto Marlboros	
		Winnipeg Rowing Club	

MONTREAL CANADIENS

A combination of legendary players, 23 Stanley Cups and its French-Canadian mystique have made the Montreal Canadiens the flagship franchise of the National Hockey League. Founded on December 4, 1909, the Canadiens were founder members of the National Hockey League in 1917, and won the first of a record 23 Stanley Cups in 1916. However, the Canadiens' dynasty is not simply a matter of cups won and records broken; there's something more—a certain mystique born of its French-Canadian heritage and its legendary players. The names Georges Vézina, Newsy Lalonde, George Hainsworth, Henri Richard, Maurice Richard, Jean Béliveau, Ken Dryden and Guy Lafleur grace both the pages of hockey history and the history of Canada and Quebec.

NHL TEAM RECORDS (1917–92)

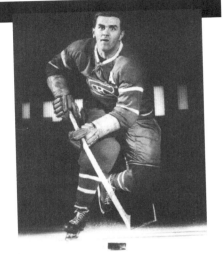

- Most wins, all-time **2,391**
- Most games played, all-time **4,512†**
- Most goals scored, all-time **15,328**
- Most points, all-time **5,488**
- Most points, season **132**
- Most wins, season **60**
- Fewest losses, season **5†**
- Longest home undefeated streak **34**
- Most shutouts, season **22**
- Most goals scored, game **16**
- Fewest losses, season (min. 70-games) **8**
- Most road wins, season **27****
- Fewest home losses, season **0†**
- Fewest home losses, season (min. 70 games) **1**
- Fewest road losses, season **3**
- Fewest road losses, season (min. 70 games) **6††**

† Tied record
** The 1967–77 and 1977–78 teams both won 27 road games.
†† The 1972–73, 1974–75 and 1977–78 teams all achieved this feat.

MAURICE ("THE ROCKET") RICHARD WAS THE FIRST NHL PLAYER TO SCORE 50 GOALS IN A SEASON AND 500 IN A CAREER. HE SET THE 50-GOAL STANDARD IN 1944–45, AND SCORED HIS 500TH GOAL ON OCTOBER 19, 1957.

MONTREAL CANADIENS TEAM RECORDS

Record	Player	Total	Years
Games	Henri Richard	1,256	1955–75
Games*	Jacques Plante	556	1952–63
Goals	Maurice Richard	544	1942–60
Assists	Guy Lafleur	728	1971–85
Points	Guy Lafleur	1,246	1971–85
Hat tricks	Maurice Richard	26	1942–60
Shutouts	George Hainsworth	74	1926–37

* Goaltenders

RIGHT WINGER GUY LAFLEUR HOLDS THE CANADIENS' CAREER RECORD FOR MOST POINTS (1,246) AND MOST ASSISTS (728).

SOURCES: NHL OFFICAL GUIDE & RECORD BOOK, 1992–93, MONTREAL CANADIENS MEDIA GUIDE.

STANLEY CUP RECORDS
1893–92

The Canadiens have won a record 23 Stanley Cups and dominate the playoff record books. The Canadiens might have won a 24th Cup in 1919, but the final versus the Seattle Metropolitans was cancelled because of an influenza epidemic. The series was tied at 2-2 and one tie, when the final was halted.

- Most championships **23**
- Consecutive championships **5**
- Most finals **32**
- Consecutive finals **10**
- Most years in playoffs **67**
- Most games **579**
- Most wins **351**
- Most losses **220**
- Most goals scored **1,806**

JACQUES PLANTE HOLDS THE STANLEY CUP CAREER RECORD FOR MOST SHUTOUTS, WITH 14.

A RECORD-BREAKING SEASON, 1976–77

Fans will always argue as to the greatest team in history. Statistically, the 1976–77 Canadiens have the strongest claim of all. They set NHL records for most wins, most points and fewest defeats in a season. Not surprisingly the season culminated in a 4–0 sweep of the Boston Bruins in the Stanley Cup final.

132 Most Points
60 Most Wins
8† Fewest Losses
27* Most Road Wins
38‡ Undefeated Home Streak

† 70–Game schedule
* Tie
‡ Including playoffs

STANLEY CUP CHAMPIONS (1905–1930)

Year	Champion	Loser	Series
1905	Ottawa Silver Seven	Rat Portage Thistles Dawson City Nuggets	** **
1906	Ottawa Silver Seven (February) Montreal Wanderers (March)	Queen's Unversity Smith's Falls New Glasgow Clubs Ottawa Silver Seven	** **
1907	Kenora Thistles (January) Montreal Wanderers (March)	Montreal Wanderers Kenora Thistles	2–0 1–1†
1908	Montreal Wanderers	Edmonton Eskimos Toronto Maple Leafs Winnipeg Maple Leafs Ottawa Victorias (no challenger)	**
1909	Ottawa Senators		
1910	Ottawa Senators (January) Montreal Wanderers (March)	Galt Edmonton Eskimos Berlin (Kitchener)	** 7–3*
1911	Ottawa Senators	Galt Port Arthur	**
1912	Quebec Bulldogs	Moncton Victorias	2–0
1913	Quebec Bulldogs	Sydney Miners	2–0
1914	Toronto Blueshirts	Victoria Cougars Montreal Canadiens	**
1915	Vancouver Millionaires	Ottawa Senators	3–0
1916	Montreal Canadiens	Portland Rosebuds	3–2
1917	Seattle Metropolitans	Montreal Canadiens	3–1
1918	Toronto Arenas	Vancouver Millionaires	3–2
1919	no decision		‡
1920	Ottawa Senators	Seattle Metropolitans	3–2
1921	Ottawa Senators	Vancouver Millionaires	3–2
1922	Toronto St. Patricks	Vancouver Millionaires	3–2
1923	Ottawa Senators	Vancouver Maroons Edmonton Eskimos	**
1924	Montreal Canadiens	Vancouver Maroons Calgary Tigers	**
1925	Victoria Cougars	Montreal Canadiens	3–1
1926	Montreal Maroons	Victoria Cougars	3–1
1927	Ottawa Senators	Boston Bruins	2–0
1928	New York Rangers	Montreal Maroons	3–2
1929	Boston Bruins	New York Rangers	2–0
1930	Montreal Canadiens	Boston Bruins	2–0

STANLEY CUP CHAMPIONS (1931–1968)

Year	Champion	Loser	Series
1931	Montreal Canadiens	Chicago Blackhawks	3–2
1932	Toronto Maple Leafs	New York Rangers	3–0
1933	New York Rangers	Toronto Maple Leafs	3–1
1934	Chicago Blackhawks	Detroit Red Wings	3–1
1935	Montreal Maroons	Toronto Maple Leafs	3–0
1936	Detroit Red Wings	Toronto Maple Leafs	3–1
1937	Detroit Red Wings	New York Rangers	3–2
1938	Chicago Blackhawks	Toronto Maple Leafs	3–1
1939	Boston Bruins	Toronto Maple Leafs	4–1
1940	New York Rangers	Toronto Maple Leafs	4–2
1941	Boston Bruins	Detroit Red Wings	4–0
1942	Toronto Maple Leafs	Detroit Red Wings	4–3
1943	Detroit Red Wings	Boston Bruins	4–0
1944	Montreal Canadiens	Chicago Blackhawks	4–0
1945	Toronto Maple Leafs	Detroit Red Wings	4–3
1946	Montreal Canadiens	Boston Bruins	4–1
1947	Toronto Maple Leafs	Montreal Canadiens	4–2
1948	Toronto Maple Leafs	Detroit Red Wings	4–0
1949	Toronto Maple Leafs	Detroit Red Wings	4–0
1950	Detroit Red Wings	New York Rangers	4–3
1951	Toronto Maple Leafs	Montreal Canadiens	4–1
1952	Detroit Red Wings	Montreal Canadiens	4–0
1953	Montreal Canadiens	Boston Bruins	4–1
1954	Detroit Red Wings	Montreal Canadiens	4–3
1955	Detroit Red Wings	Montreal Canadiens	4–3
1956	Montreal Canadiens	Detroit Red Wings	4–1
1957	Montreal Canadiens	Boston Bruins	4–1
1958	Montreal Canadiens	Boston Bruins	4–2
1959	Montreal Canadiens	Toronto Maple Leafs	4–1
1960	Montreal Canadiens	Toronto Maple Leafs	4–0
1961	Chicago Blackhawks	Detroit Red Wings	4–2
1962	Toronto Maple Leafs	Chicago Blackhawks	4–2
1963	Toronto Maple Leafs	Detroit Red Wings	4–1
1964	Toronto Maple Leafs	Detroit Red Wings	4–3
1965	Montreal Canadiens	Chicago Blackhawks	4–3
1966	Montreal Canadiens	Detroit Red Wings	4–2
1967	Toronto Maple Leafs	Montreal Canadiens	4–2
1968	Montreal Canadiens	St. Louis Blues	4–0

STANLEY CUP CHAMPIONS (1969–1992)

Year	Champion	Loser	Series
1969	Montreal Canadiens	St. Louis Blues	4–0
1970	Boston Bruins	St. Louis Blues	4–0
1971	Montreal Canadiens	Chicago Blackhawks	4–3
1972	Boston Bruins	New York Rangers	4–2
1973	Montreal Canadiens	Chicago Blackhawks	4–2
1974	Philadelphia Flyers	Boston Bruins	4–2
1975	Philadelphia Flyers	Buffalo Sabres	4–2
1976	Montreal Canadiens	Philadelphia Flyers	4–0
1977	Montreal Canadiens	Boston Bruins	4–0
1978	Montreal Canadiens	Boston Bruins	4–2
1979	Montreal Canadiens	New York Rangers	4–1
1980	New York Islanders	Philadelphia Flyers	4–2
1981	New York Islanders	Minnesota North Stars	4–1
1982	New York Islanders	Vancouver Canucks	4–0
1983	New York Islanders	Edmonton Oilers	4–0
1984	Edmonton Oilers	New York Islanders	4–1
1985	Edmonton Oilers	Philadelphia Flyers	4–1
1986	Montreal Canadiens	Calgary Flames	4–1
1987	Edmonton Oilers	Philadelphia Flyers	4–3
1988	Edmonton Oilers	Boston Bruins	4–0
1989	Calgary Flames	Montreal Canadiens	4–2
1990	Edmonton Oilers	Boston Bruins	4–1
1991	Pittsburgh Penguins	Minnesota North Stars	4–2
1992	Pittsburgh Penguins	Chicago Blackhawks	4–0

* Final score of single challenge game.

** Multiple challenger series.

† Series decided on total goals scored.

‡ The 1919 final between the Montreal Canadiens and the Seattle Metropolitans was canceled because of an influenza epidemic.

SHORTHANDED GOALS SCORED

Period The most shorthanded goals scored in a single period is two, shared by three players. Bryan Trottier was the first player to perform this feat on April 8, 1990 for the New York Islanders *v*. the Los Angeles Kings. His goals came in the second period of an 8–1 Islanders victory. Bobby Lalonde (Boston Bruins) matched Trottier on April 11, 1981. His double came in the third period of a Bruins 6–3 loss to the Minnesota North Stars. Jari Kurri (Edmonton Oilers) joined this club on April 24, 1983. His goals came in the third period of an Oilers 8–4 win over the Chicago Blackhawks.

Series The record for most shorthanded goals in a playoff series is three, shared by two players: Bill Barber (Philadelphia Flyers) in a Flyers 4–1 series victory over the Minnesota North Stars in 1980; and Wayne Presley (Chicago Blackhawks) in a series *v*. the Detroit Red Wings in 1989.

STANLEY CUP INDIVIDUAL RECORDS (1917–1992)

Records in this section are listed only from the formation of the National Hockey League in 1917.

Goals Scored

		Player(s)	Team(s)	Date(s)
Period	4	Tim Kerr	Philadelphia Flyers v. New York Rangers	April 13, 1985
		Mario Lemieux	Pittsburgh Penguins v. New York Rangers	April 25, 1989
Game	5	Newsy Lalonde	Montreal Canadiens v. Ottawa Senators	March 1, 1919
		Maurice Richard	Montreal Canadiens v. Toronto Maple Leafs	March 23, 1944
		Darryl Sittler	Toronto Maple Leafs v. Philadelphia Flyers	April 22, 1976
		Reggie Leach	Philadelphia Flyers v. Boston Bruins	May 6, 1976
		Mario Lemieux	Pittsburgh Penguins v. Philadelphia Flyers	April 25, 1989
Series (any round)	12	Jari Kurri	Edmonton Oilers v. Chicago Blackhawks	1985
Series (final)	9	Babe Dye	Toronto St. Patricks v. Vancouver Millionaires	1922
Season	19	Reggie Leach	Philadelphia Flyers	1976
		Jari Kurri	Edmonton Oilers	1985
Career	95	Wayne Gretzky	Edmonton Oilers, Los Angeles Kings	1979–92

Power-Play Goals Scored

Period	3	Tim Kerr	Philadelphia Flyers v. New York Rangers	April 13, 1985
Series	6	Chris Kontos	Los Angeles Kings v. Edmonton Oilers	1989
Season	9	Mike Bossy	New York Islanders	1981
		Cam Neely	Boston Bruins	1991
Career	35	Mike Bossy	New York Islanders	1977–87

Points Scored

Period	4	Maurice Richard	Montreal Canadiens v. Toronto Maple Leafs	March 29, 1945
		Dickie Moore	Montreal Canadiens v. Boston Bruins	March 25, 1954
		Barry Pederson	Boston Bruins v. Buffalo Sabres	April 8, 1982
		Peter McNab	Boston Bruins v. Buffalo Sabres	April 11, 1982
		Tim Kerr	Philadelphia Flyers v. New York Rangers	April 13, 1985
		Ken Linseman	Boston Bruins v. Montreal Canadiens	April 14, 1985
		Wayne Gretzky	Edmonton Oilers v. Los Angeles Kings	April 12, 1987
		Glenn Anderson	Edmonton Oilers v. Winnipeg Jets	April 6, 1988
		Mario Lemieux	Pittsburgh Penguins v. Philadelphia Flyers	April 25, 1989
		Dave Gagner	Minnesota North Stars v. Chicago Blackhawks	April 8, 1991
		Mario Lemieux	Pittsburgh Penguins v. Washington Capitals	April 23, 1992
Game	8	Patrik Sundstrom	New Jersey Devils v. Washington Capitals	April 22, 1988
		Mario Lemieux	Pittsburgh Penguins v. Philadelphia Flyers	April 25, 1989
Series (any round)	19	Rick Middleton	Boston Bruins v. Buffalo Sabres	1983
Series (final)	13	Wayne Gretzky	Edmonton Oilers v. Boston Bruins	1988
Season	47	Wayne Gretzky	Edmonton Oilers	1985
Career	306	Wayne Gretzky	Edmonton Oilers, Los Angeles Kings	1979–92

STANLEY CUP INDIVIDUAL RECORDS (1917–1992)

Assists

		Player(s)	Team(s)	Date(s)
Period	3	This feat has been achieved 56 times.		
Game	6	Mikko Leinonen	New York Rangers v. Philadelphia Flyers	April 8, 1982
		Wayne Gretzky	Edmonton Oilers v. Los Angeles Kings	April 9, 1987
Series (any round)	14	Rick Middleton	Boston Bruins v. Buffalo Sabres	1983
		Wayne Gretzky	Edmonton Oilers v. Chicago Blackhawks	1985
Series (final)	10	Wayne Gretzky	Edmonton Oilers v. Boston Bruins	1988
Season	31	Wayne Gretzky	Edmonton Oilers	1988
Career	211	Wayne Gretzky	Edmonton Oilers, Los Angeles Kings	1979–92

Goaltenders

Shutouts

Season	4	Clint Benedict	Montreal Maroons	1926
		Clint Benedict	Montreal Maroons	1928
		Dave Kerr	New York Rangers	1937
		Frank McCool	Toronto Maple Leafs	1945
		Terry Sawchuk	Detroit Tigers	1952
		Bernie Parent	Philadelphia Flyers	1975
		Ken Dyrden	Montreal Canadiens	1977
Career	15	Clint Benedict	Ottawa Senators, Montreal Maroons	1917–30

Minutes Played

Season	1,540	Ron Hextall	Philadelphia Flyers	1987
Career	7,645	Billy Smith	New York Islanders	1971–89

Wins

Season	16	Grant Fuhr	Edmonton Oilers	1988
		Mike Vernon	Calgary Flames	1989
		Bill Ranford	Edmonton Oilers	1990
		Tom Barrasso	Pittsburgh Penguins	1992
Career	88	Billy Smith	New York Islanders	1975–88

Penalty Minutes

Game	42	Dave Schultz	Philadelphia Flyers v. Toronto Maple Leafs	April 22, 1976
Career	564	Dale Hunter	Quebec Nordiques, Washington Capitals	1980–92

Source: NHL

HOT SHOT ■ FIVE PLAYERS HAVE SCORED FIVE GOALS IN A PLAYOFF GAME. DARRYL SITTLER (ABOVE) WAS THE THIRD PLAYER TO PERFORM THIS FEAT.

Season The record for shorthanded goals in one season is three, shared by five players: Derek Sanderson (Boston Bruins) in 1969; Bill Barber (Philadelphia Flyers) in 1980; Lorne Henning (New York Islanders) in 1980; Wayne Gretzky (Edmonton Oilers) in 1983; and Wayne Presley (Chicago Blackhawks) in 1989.

Career Mark Messier (Edmonton Oilers, New York Rangers) holds the mark for career playoff goals at 13 in 156 games (1979–92).

DEFENSEMEN RECORDS

GOAL SCORING

Game The most goals scored by a defenseman in a playoff game is three, by five players: Bobby Orr, Boston Bruins *v.* Montreal Canadiens, April 11, 1971; Dick Redmond, Chicago Blackhawks *v.* St. Louis Blues, April 4, 1973; Denis Potvin, New York Islanders *v.* Edmonton Oilers, April 17, 1981; Paul Reinhart, Calgary Flames, who performed the feat twice, *v.* Edmonton Oilers, April 14, 1983; *v.* Vancouver Canucks, April 8, 1984; and Doug Halward, Vancouver Canucks *v.* Calgary Flames, April 7, 1984.

Season Paul Coffey (Edmonton Oilers) scored 12 goals in 18 games during the 1985 playoffs.

Career Denis Potvin (New York Islanders, 1973–88) has scored a playoff record 56 goals.

POINT SCORING

Game Paul Coffey earned a record six points on one goal and five assists, for the Edmonton Oilers *v.* the Chicago Blackhawks on May 14, 1985.

Season Paul Coffey also holds the record for most points by a defenseman in a season, with 37 in 1985 for the Edmonton Oilers. Coffey's total comprised 12 goals and 25 assists in 18 games.

Career Denis Potvin (New York Islanders, 1973–88) has scored a playoff record 164 points. Potvin scored 56 goals and 108 assists in 185 games.

CONSECUTIVE RECORDS

Point-scoring streak Bryan Trottier (New York Islanders) scored a point in 27 consecutive playoff

CUP ANCHOR ■ GOALIE BILLY SMITH HOLDS THE PLAYOFF RECORD FOR MOST WINS, 88, AND THE MOST MINUTES PLAYED, 7,645.

games over three seasons (1980–82), scoring 16 goals and 26 assists for 42 points.

Goal-scoring streak Reggie Leach (Philadelphia Flyers) scored at least one goal in nine consecutive playoff games in 1976. The streak started on April 17 *v.* the Toronto Maple Leafs, and ended on May 9 when he was shut out by the Montreal Canadiens. Overall, Leach scored 14 goals during his record-setting run.

Consecutive wins by a goaltender Two goalies have won 11 straight playoff games: Ed Belfour (Chicago Blackhawks), and Tom Barrasso (Pittsburgh Penguins), both in 1992.

Longest shutout sequence In the 1936 semi-final contest between the Detroit Red Wings and the Montreal Maroons, Norm Smith, the Red Wings goaltender, shut out the Maroons for 248 minutes, 32 seconds. The Maroons failed to score in the first two games (the second game lasted 116 minutes, 30 seconds, the longest overtime game in playoff history), and finally breached Smith's defenses at 12:02 of the first period in game three. After such a stellar performance, it is no surprise that the Red Wings swept the series 3–0.

COACHES

Most championships Toe Blake coached the Montreal Canadiens to eight Stanley Cups, 1956–60, 1965–66, 1968.

Most playoff wins Through the 1991–92 season the record for playoff wins is 130 games by Scotty Bowman, St. Louis Blues, 1967–71 (26 wins), Montreal Canadiens, 1971–79 (70 wins), Buffalo

Sabres, 1979–87 (18 wins), Pittsburgh Penguins, 1992 (16 wins).

Most games Scotty Bowman holds the mark for most games coached, at 207 with four teams: St. Louis Blues, 1967–71; Montreal Canadiens, 1971–79; Buffalo Sabres, 1979–87; Pittsburgh Penguins, 1992.

OLYMPIC GAMES

Hockey was included in the 1920 Summer Olympics in Antwerp, Belgium, and has been an integral part of the Winter Olympics since its introduction in 1924.

Most gold medals (country) The USSR/Unified Team has won eight Olympic titles, in 1956, 1964, 1968, 1972, 1976, 1984, 1988 and 1992.

WORLD CHAMPIONSHIPS (MEN) The world championships were first held in 1920 in conjunction with the Olympic Games. Since 1930, the world championships have been held annually. Through the 1964 Olympics, the Games were considered the world championships, and records for those Games are included in this section. Since 1977, the championships have been open to professionals.

Most titles The USSR has won the world championship 22 times: 1954, 1956, 1963–71, 1973–75, 1978–79, 1981–83, 1986, 1989–90.

Most consecutive titles The USSR won nine consecutive championships from 1963–71.

WORLD CHAMPIONSHIPS (WOMEN) The inaugural tournament was held in 1990. Canada won the inaugural event, defeating the United States 5–2 in the final, staged in Ottawa, Canada on March 24, 1990.

NCAA CHAMPIONSHIPS A men's Division I hockey championship was first staged in 1948, and has been held annually since.

Most wins Michigan has won the title seven times: 1948, 1951–53, 1955–56 and 1964.

HORSE RACING

ORIGINS Horsemanship was an important part of the Hittite culture of Anatolia, Turkey, dating from 1400 B.C. The 33rd ancient Olympic Games of 648 B.C. in Greece featured horse racing. Horse races can be traced in England from the 3rd century. The

TIMEOUT

FASTEST HAT TRICK ☛ JORGAN PALMGREN ERICHSEN (NORWAY) SCORED THREE GOALS IN 10 SECONDS FOR FRISK V. HOLMEN IN A JUNIOR LEAGUE GAME IN NORWAY ON MARCH 17, 1991.

first sweepstakes race was originated by the 12th Earl of Derby at his estate in Epsom in 1780. The Epsom Derby is still run today and is the classic race of the English flat racing season.

United States Horses were introduced to the North American continent from Spain by Cortéz in 1519. In colonial America, horse racing was common. Colonel Richard Nicholls, commander of English forces in New York, is believed to have staged the first organized race at Salisbury Plain, Long Island, N.Y. in 1665. The first Jockey Club to be founded was at Charleston, S.C. in 1734. Thoroughbred racing was first staged at Saratoga Springs, N.Y. in 1863.

RACING RECORDS (UNITED STATES)

HORSES

CAREER RECORDS

Most wins The most wins in a racing career is 89, by Kingston, from 138 starts, 1886–94.

Most wins (graded stakes races) John Henry won 25 graded stakes races, including 16 Grade I races, 1978–84.

HIGHEST EARNINGS

Career The career record for earnings is $6,679,242, by Alysheba, 1986–88. Alysheba's career record was 11 wins, eight seconds and two thirds from 26 races.

Season The single-season earnings record is $4,578,454, by Sunday Silence, in 1989, from nine starts (seven wins and two seconds).

Single race The richest race in the United States is the Breeders' Cup Classic, which carries a purse of $3 million, with first-place prize money of $1,560,000 to the winner.

JOCKEYS

CAREER RECORDS

Most wins Bill Shoemaker rode a record 8,833 winners from 40,350 mounts. "The Shoe" made his debut aboard Waxahachie on March 19, 1949, and raced for the last time on Patchy Groundfog on February 3, 1990. His first victory came on April 20, 1949 aboard Shafter V, his last on January 20, 1990 aboard Beau Genius at Gulfstream Park, Fla.

FIRST PAST THE POST ■ THE MOST WINS BY A JOCKEY IN A SEASON IS 598, BY KENT DESORMEAUX (AT LEFT) IN 1989.

SEASON RECORDS

Most wins Kent Desormeaux rode a season record 598 winners, from 2,312 mounts, in 1989.

Most wins (stakes races) Pat Day rode a season record 60 stakes race winners in 1991.

DAILY RECORDS

Most wins (single day) The most winners ridden in one day is nine, by Chris Antley on October 31, 1987. Antley rode four winners in the afternoon at Aqueduct, N.Y. and five in the evening at The Meadowlands, N.J.

Most wins (one card) The most winners ridden on one card is eight, achieved by four jockeys:

TRIPLE CROWN WINNERS

Year	Horse	Jockey	Trainer	Owner
1919	Sir Barton	Johnny Loftus	H. Guy Bedwell	J. K. L. Ross
1930	Gallant Fox	Earle Sanders	J. E. Fitzsimmons	Belair Stud
1935	Omaha	Willie Saunders	J. E. Fitzsimmons	Belair Stud
1937	War Admiral	Chas. Kurtsinger	George Conway	Samuel Riddle
1941	Whirlaway	Eddie Arcaro	Ben A. Jones	Calumet Farm
1943	Count Fleet	Johnny Longden	Don Cameron	Mrs. J. D. Hertz
1946	Assault	Warren Mehrtens	Max Hirsch	King Ranch
1948	Citation	Eddie Arcaro	Ben A. Jones	Calumet Farm
1973	Secretariat	Ron Turcotte	Luciren Laurin	Meadow Stable
1977	Seattle Slew	Jean Cruguet	Billy Turner	Karen Taylor
1978	Affirmed	Steve Cauthen	Laz Barrera	Harbor View Farm

Jim Fitzsimmons and Ben Jones are the only trainers to have trained two Triple Crown winners. Eddie Arcaro is the only jockey to have ridden two Triple Crown winners.

FLAT OUT ■ HAVING WON OVER 2,539 RACES, JULIE KRONE IS THE MOST SUCCESSFUL WOMAN JOCKEY IN RACING HISTORY.

Hubert Jones, from 13 rides, at Caliente, Calif., on June 11, 1944; Dave Gall, from 10 rides, at Cahokia Downs, East St. Louis, Ill., on October 18, 1978; Robert Williams, from 10 rides, at Lincoln, Neb., on September 29, 1984; and Pat Day, from nine rides, at Arlington, Ill., on September 13, 1989.

Consecutive wins The longest consecutive winning streak by a jockey is nine races, by Albert Adams, at Marlboro Racetrack, Md., over three days, September 10–12, 1930. He won the last two races on September 10, all six races on September 11, and the first race on September 12.

HIGHEST EARNINGS

Career Laffit Pincay Jr. has won a career record $169,091,348 from 1964 through December 31, 1992.

Season The greatest prize money earned in a single season is $14,877,298, by Jose Santos in 1988.

KENTUCKY DERBY WINNERS (1875–1992)

Year	Horse	Year	Horse	Year	Horse	Year	Horse
1875	Aristides	1905	Agile	1935	Omaha	1964	Northern Dancer
1876	Vagrant	1906	Sir Huon	1936	Bold Venture	1965	Lucky Debonair
1877	Baden-Baden	1907	Pink Star	1937	War Admiral	1966	Kauai King
1878	Day Star	1908	Stone Street	1938	Lawrin	1967	Proud Clarion
1879	Lord Murphy	1909	Wintergreen	1939	Johnstown	1968	Forward Pass
1880	Fonso	1910	Donau	1940	Gallahadian	1969	Majestic Prince
1881	Hindoo	1911	Meridian	1941	Whirlaway	1970	Dust Commander
1882	Apollo	1912	Worth	1942	Shut Out	1971	Canonero II
1883	Leonatus	1913	Donerail	1943	Count Fleet	1972	Riva Ridge
1884	Buchanan	1914	Old Rosebud	1944	Pensive	1973	Secretariat
1885	Joe Cotton	1915	Regret	1945	Hoop Jr.	1974	Cannonade
1886	Ben Ali	1916	George Smith	1946	Assault	1975	Foolish Pleasure
1887	Montrose	1917	Omar Khayyam	1947	Jet Pilot	1976	Bold Forbes
1888	MacBeth II	1918	Exterminator	1948	Citation	1977	Seattle Slew
1889	Spokane	1919	Sir Barton	1949	Ponder	1978	Affirmed
1890	Riley	1920	Paul Jones	1950	Middleground	1979	Spectacular Bid
1891	Kingman	1921	Behave Yourself	1951	Count Turf	1980	Genuine Risk
1892	Azra	1922	Morvich	1952	Hill Gail	1981	Pleasant Colony
1893	Lookout	1923	Zev	1953	Dark Star	1982	Gato Del Sol
1894	Chant	1924	Black Gold	1954	Determine	1983	Sunny's Halo
1895	Halma	1925	Flying Ebony	1955	Swaps	1984	Swale
1896	Ben Brush	1926	Bubbling Over	1956	Needles	1985	Spend A Buck
1897	Typhoon II	1927	Whiskery	1957	Iron Liege	1986	Ferdinand
1898	Plaudit	1928	Reigh Count	1958	Tim Tam	1987	Alysheba
1899	Manuel	1929	Clyde Van Dusen	1959	Tomy Lee	1988	Winning Colors
1900	Lt. Gibson	1930	Gallant Fox	1960	Venetian Way	1989	Sunday Silence
1901	His Eminence	1931	Twenty Grand	1961	Carry Back	1990	Unbridled
1902	Alan-a-Dale	1932	Burgoo King	1962	Decidedly	1991	Strike the Gold
1903	Judge Himes	1933	Brokers Tip	1963	Chateaugay	1992	Lil E Tee
1904	Elwood	1934	Cavalcade				

JOCKEYS (WOMEN)

Most wins Julie Krone has won a record 2,539 races from 1980 through 1992.

Highest earnings Julie Krone has won a record $46,986,969 from 1980 through 1992.

THE TRIPLE CROWN The races that make up the Triple Crown are the Kentucky Derby, the Preakness Stakes and the Belmont Stakes. The Triple Crown is for three-year-olds only and has been achieved by 11 horses.

KENTUCKY DERBY This event is held on the first Saturday in May at Churchill Downs, Louisville, Ky. The first race was run in 1875 over 1½ miles; the distance was shortened to 1¼ miles in 1896 and is still run at that length.

PREAKNESS STAKES WINNERS (1873–1992)

Year	Horse	Year	Horse	Year	Horse	Year	Horse
1873	Survivor	1903	Flocarline	1933	Head Play	1963	Candy Spots
1874	Culpepper	1904	Bryn Mawr	1934	High Quest	1964	Northern Dancer
1875	Tom Ochiltree	1905	Cairngorm	1935	Omaha	1965	Tom Rolfe
1876	Shirley	1906	Whimsical	1936	Bold Venture	1966	Kauai King
1877	Cloverbrook	1907	Don Enrique	1937	War Admiral	1967	Damascus
1878	Duke of Magenta	1908	Royal Tourist	1938	Dauber	1968	Forward Pass
1879	Harold	1909	Effendi	1939	Challedon	1969	Majestic Prince
1880	Grenada	1910	Layminister	1940	Bimelech	1970	Personality
1881	Saunterer	1911	Watervale	1941	Whirlaway	1971	Canonero II
1882	Vanguard	1912	Colonel Holloway	1942	Alsab	1972	Bee Bee Bee
1883	Jacobus	1913	Buskin	1943	Count Fleet	1973	Secretariat
1884	Knight of Ellerslie	1914	Holiday	1944	Pensive	1974	Little Current
1885	Tecumseh	1915	Rhine Maiden	1945	Polynesian	1975	Master Derby
1886	The Bard	1916	Damrosch	1946	Assault	1976	Elocutionist
1887	Dunboyne	1917	Kalitan	1947	Faultless	1977	Seattle Slew
1888	Refund	1918	Jack Hare Jr.	1948	Citation	1978	Affirmed
1889	Buddhist	1919	Sir Barton	1949	Capot	1979	Spectacular Bid
1890	Montague	1920	Man o' War	1950	Hill Prince	1980	Codex
1891	not held	1921	Broomspun	1951	Bold	1981	Pleasant Colony
1892	not held	1922	Pillory	1952	Blue Man	1982	Aloma's Ruler
1893	not held	1923	Vigil	1953	Native Dancer	1983	Deputed Testamony
1894	Assignee	1924	Nellie Morse	1954	Hasty Road	1984	Gate Dancer
1895	Belmar	1925	Coventry	1955	Nashua	1985	Tank's Prospect
1896	Margrave	1926	Display	1956	Fabius	1986	Snow Chief
1897	Paul Kauvar	1927	Bostonian	1957	Bold Ruler	1987	Alysheba
1898	Sly Fox	1928	Victorian	1958	Tim Tam	1988	Risen Star
1899	Half Time	1929	Dr. Freeland	1959	Royal Orbit	1989	Sunday Silence
1900	Hindus	1930	Gallant Fox	1960	Bally Ache	1990	Summer Squall
1901	The Parader	1931	Mate	1961	Carry Back	1991	Hansel
1902	Old England	1932	Burgoo King	1962	Greek Money	1992	Pine Bluff

Most Wins

Jockey Five, by two jockeys: Eddie Arcaro (1938, 1941, 1945, 1948, 1952); Bill Hartack (1957, 1960, 1962, 1964, 1969).

Trainer Six, by Ben Jones (1938, 1941, 1944, 1948–49, 1952).

Owner Eight, by Calumet Farm (1941, 1944, 1948–49, 1952, 1957–58, 1968).

Fastest time 1 minute 59⅖ seconds, by Secretariat, 1973.

Largest field 23 horses in 1974.

BELMONT STAKES WINNERS (1867–1992)

Year	Horse	Year	Horse	Year	Horse	Year	Horse
1867	Ruthless	1899	Jean Bereaud	1931	Twenty Grand	1962	Jaipur
1868	General Duke	1900	Ildrim	1932	Faireno	1963	Chateaugay
1869	Fenian	1901	Commando	1933	Hurryoff	1964	Quadrangle
1870	Kingfisher	1902	Masterman	1934	Peace Chance	1965	Hail to All
1871	Harry Bassett	1903	Africander	1935	Omaha	1966	Amberoid
1872	Joe Daniels	1904	Delhi	1936	Granville	1967	Damascus
1873	Springbok	1905	Tanya	1937	War Admiral	1968	Stage Door Johnny
1874	Saxon	1906	Burgomaster	1938	Pasteurized	1969	Arts and Letters
1875	Calvin	1907	Peter Pan	1939	Johnstown	1970	High Echelon
1876	Algerine	1908	Colin	1940	Bimelech	1971	Pass Catcher
1877	Cloverbrook	1909	Joe Madden	1941	Whirlaway	1972	Riva Ridge
1878	Duke of Magenta	1910	Sweep	1942	Shut Out	1973	Secretariat
1879	Spendthrift	1911	not held	1943	Count Fleet	1974	Little Current
1880	Grenada	1912	not held	1944	Bounding Home	1975	Avatar
1881	Saunterer	1913	Prince Eugene	1945	Pavot	1976	Bold Forbes
1882	Forester	1914	Luke McLuke	1946	Assault	1977	Seattle Slew
1883	George Kinney	1915	The Finn	1947	Phalanx	1978	Affirmed
1884	Panique	1916	Friar Rock	1948	Citation	1979	Coastal
1885	Tyrant	1917	Hourless	1949	Capot	1980	Temperence Hill
1886	Inspector B	1918	Johren	1950	Middleground	1981	Summing
1887	Hanover	1919	Sir Barton	1951	Counterpoint	1982	Conquistador Cielo
1888	Sir Dixon	1920	Man o'War	1952	One Count	1983	Caveat
1889	Eric	1921	Grey Lag	1953	Native Dancer	1984	Swale
1890	Burlington	1922	Pillory	1954	High Gun	1985	Creme Fraiche
1891	Foxford	1923	Zev	1955	Nashua	1986	Danzig Connection
1892	Patron	1924	Mad Play	1956	Needles	1987	Bet Twice
1893	Comanche	1925	American Flag	1957	Gallant Man	1988	Risen Star
1894	Henry of Navarre	1926	Crusader	1958	Cavan	1989	Easy Goer
1895	Belmar	1927	Chance Shot	1959	Sword Dancer	1990	Go and Go
1896	Hastings	1928	Vito	1960	Celtic Ash	1991	Hansel
1897	Scottish Chieftain	1929	Blue Larkspur	1961	Sherluck	1992	A.P. Indy
1898	Bowling Brook	1930	Gallant Fox				

PREAKNESS STAKES Inaugurated in 1873, this event is held annually at Pimlico Race Course, Baltimore, Md. Originally run at 1½ miles, the distance was changed several times before being settled at the current length of 1³⁄₁₆ miles in 1925.

Most Wins

Jockey Six, by Eddie Arcaro (1941, 1948, 1950–51, 1955, 1957).

Trainer Seven, by Robert Wyndham Walden (1875, 1878–82, 1888).

Owner Five, by George Lorillard (1878–82).

Fastest time 1 minute 53⅕ seconds, by Tank's Prospect, 1985.

Largest field 18 horses in 1928.

BELMONT STAKES This race is the third leg of the Triple Crown, first run in 1867 at Jerome Park, N.Y. Since 1905 the race has been staged at Belmont Park, N.Y. Originally run over 1 mile 5 furlongs, the current distance of 1½ miles has been set since 1926.

Most Wins

Jockey Six, by two jockeys: Jim McLaughlin (1882–84, 1886–88); Eddie Arcaro (1941–42, 1945, 1948, 1952, 1955).

Trainer Eight, by James Rowe Sr. (1883–84, 1901, 1904, 1907–08, 1910, 1913).

Owner Five, by three owners: Dwyer Brothers (1883–84, 1886–88); James R. Keene (1901, 1904, 1907–08, 1910); and William Woodward Sr. (Belair Stud) (1930, 1932, 1935–36, 1939).

Fastest time 2 minutes 24 seconds, by Secretariat, 1973.

Largest field 15 horses, in 1983.

BREEDERS' CUP CHAMPIONSHIP

The Breeders' Cup Championship has been staged annually since 1984. It was devised by John R. Gaines, a leading thoroughbred owner and breeder, to provide a season-ending championship for each division of thoroughbred racing. The Breeders' Cup Championship consists of seven races: Juvenile, Juvenile Fillies, Sprint, Mile, Distaff, Turf and the Classic, with a record purse of $10 million.

CHAMPIONSHIP RECORDS

HORSES

Most wins Two horses have won two Breeders' Cup races: Bayakoa, which won the Distaff in 1989 and 1990, and Miesque, which won the Mile in 1987 and 1988.

Highest earnings Alysheba has won a record $2,133,000 in Breeders' Cup races, from three starts, 1986–88.

JOCKEYS

Most wins Three jockeys have ridden six winners in the Breeders' Cup Championship: Laffit Pincay Jr., Juvenile (1985, 1986, 1988), Classic (1986), Distaff (1989, 1990); Pat Day, Classic (1984, 1990), Distaff (1986, 1991), Juvenile Fillies (1987), Turf (1987); Pat Valenzuela, Juvenile (1991), Juvenile Fillies (1986, 1992), Sprint (1987), Turf (1991–92).

Highest earnings Pat Day has won a record $8,875,000 in Breeders' Cup racing, 1984–92.

BREEDERS' CUP CLASSIC This race, the principle event of the Breeders' Cup Championship, is run over 1¼ miles. The Classic offers a single-race record $3 million purse, with $1,560,000 to the winner.

Most wins (horse) The Classic has been won by a different horse on each occasion.

Most wins (jockey) Two jockeys have won the Classic twice: Pat Day, 1984 and 1990; Chris McCarron, 1988 and 1989.

INTERNATIONAL RACES

VRC Melbourne Cup This contest, Australia's most prestigious classic race, has been staged annually since 1861. The race is run over one mile at the Flemington Racetrack, Victoria.

Fastest time The fastest time is 3 minutes 16.3 seconds, by Kingston Rule, ridden by Darren Beadman in 1990.

Most wins (jockeys) Two jockeys have won the race four times: Bobby Lewis, 1902, 1915, 1919 and 1927; Harry White, 1974–75 and 1978–79.

Derby England's most prestigious classic race has been staged annually since 1780. The race is contested over 1 mile 4 furlongs at Epsom Downs, Surrey.

Fastest time The fastest time is 2 minutes 33.8 seconds, by Mahmoud, ridden by Charlie Smirke, in 1936. Kahyasi, ridden by Ray Cochrane, won the 1988 Derby in an electronically timed 2 minutes 33.84 seconds.

Most wins (jockey) Lester Piggott has won the Derby a record nine times: 1954, 1957, 1960, 1968, 1970, 1972, 1976–77 and 1983.

Grand National England's most famous steeplechase race, and most beloved sporting event, has been staged annually since 1839. The race is contested over a 4½ mile course of 30 fences at Aintree, Liverpool.

Fastest time The fastest time is 8 minutes 47.8 seconds, by Mr. Frisk, ridden by Marcus Armytage, in 1990.

Most wins (jockey) George Stevens won the National five times: 1856, 1863–64 and 1869–70.

Prix de l'Arc de Triomphe France's most prestigious classic race, and Europe's richest thoroughbred race, has been staged annually since 1920. The race is contested over 1 mile 864 yards at Longchamps, Paris.

Fastest time The fastest time is 2 minutes 26.3 seconds, by Trempolino, ridden by Pat Eddery, in 1987.

Most wins (jockey) Four jockeys have won the Arc four times: Jacques Doyasbere, 1942, 1944, 1950–51; Freddy Head, 1966, 1972, 1976, 1979; Yves Saint-Martin, 1970, 1974, 1982, 1984; Pat Eddery, 1980, 1985–87.

Irish Derby Ireland's most prestigious classic race has been staged annually since 1866. The race is contested over 1½ miles at The Curragh, County Kildare.

Fastest time The fastest time is 2 minutes 25.6 seconds, by St. Jovite, ridden by Christie Roche in 1992.

Most wins (jockey) Morny Wing has won the Irish Derby a record six times: 1921, 1923, 1930, 1938, 1942 and 1946.

HORSESHOE PITCHING

The object of the game of horseshoes is to toss a horseshoe over an iron stake so that it "comes to rest encircling the stake." The playing area, the horseshoe court, requires two stakes to be securely grounded 40 feet apart within a six-foot-square pitcher's box. Each contestant pitches two shoes in succession from the pitcher's box to the stake at the opposite end of the court. The pitching distance is 40 feet for men, and 30 feet for women. The winner is determined by a point system based on the shoe that is pitched closest to the stake. The pitcher with the most points wins the contest.

ORIGINS Historians claim that a variation of horseshoe pitching was first played by Roman soldiers to relieve the monotony of guard duty. Horseshoes was introduced to North America by the first settlers, and every town had its own horseshoe courts and competitions. The game was a popular pastime for soldiers during the Revolutionary War, and the famed British officer the Duke of Wellington wrote in his memoirs that "The War was won by pitchers of horse hardware!" The modern sport of horseshoes dates to the formation of the National Horseshoe Pitcher's Association (NHPA) in 1914.

WORLD CHAMPIONSHIPS First staged in 1909, the tournament was staged intermittently until 1946; since then it has been an annual event.

Most titles (men) Ted Allen (U.S.) has won 10 world titles: 1933–35, 1940, 1946, 1953, 1955–57 and 1959.

Most titles (women) Vicki Winston (née Chappelle) has won a record 10 women's titles: 1956, 1958–59, 1961, 1963, 1966–67, 1969, 1975 and 1981.

JUDO

ORIGINS Judo is a modern combat sport that developed from an amalgam of several old Japanese martial arts, the most popular of which was jujitsu (jiujitsu), which is thought to be of Chinese origin. Judo has developed greatly since 1882, when it was first devised by Dr. Jigoro Kano. The International Judo Federation was founded in 1951.

Highest grades The efficiency grades in judo are divided into pupil (*kyu*) and master (*dan*) grades. The highest grade awarded is the extremely rare red belt *judan* (10th dan), given to only 13 men so far. The judo protocol provides for an 11th dan (*juichidan*) who also would wear a red belt, a 12th dan (*junidan*) who would wear a white belt twice as wide as an ordinary belt, and the highest of all, *shihan* (doctor), but these have never been bestowed, save for the 12th dan, to the founder of the sport, Dr. Jigoro Kano.

OLYMPIC GAMES Judo was first included in the Games in 1964 in Tokyo, Japan, and has been included in every Games since 1972. Women's events were first included as official events at the Barcelona Games in 1992.

Most gold medals Four men have won two gold medals: Willem Ruska (Netherlands), open class and over 93 kilograms class, in 1972; Hiroshi Saito (Japan), over 95 kilograms class, in 1984 and 1988; Peter Seisenbacher (Austria), up to 86 kilograms class, in 1984 and 1988; and Waldemar Legien (Poland), up to 78 kilograms class, in 1988 and up to 86 kilograms class, in 1992.

Most medals (individual) Angelo Parisi has won a record four Olympic medals, while representing two countries. In 1972 Parisi won a bronze medal in the open class, representing Great Britain. In 1980 Parisi represented France and won a gold, over 95 kilograms class, and a silver, open class; and won a second silver in the open class in 1984.

WORLD CHAMPIONSHIPS The first men's world championships were held in Tokyo, Japan in 1956. The event has been staged biennially since 1965. A world championship for women was first staged in New York City in 1980.

JUDO THROWS ☞ GARY FOSTER AND LEE FINNEY (BOTH GREAT BRITAIN) EXECUTED 20,052 THROWING MOVES IN 10 HOURS AT THE FOREST JUDO CLUB, LEICESTER, ENGLAND ON AUGUST 22, 1992.

Most titles (men) Three men have won four world titles: Yasuhiro Yamashita (Japan), open class, 1981; over 95 kilograms class, 1979, 1981, 1983; Shozo Fujii (Japan), under 80 kilograms class, 1971, 1973, 1975; under 78 kilograms class, 1979; and Naoya Ogawa (Japan), open class, 1987, 1989, 1991 and over 95 kilograms class, 1989.

Most titles (women) Ingrid Berghmans (Belgium) has won a record six world titles: open class, 1980, 1982, 1984 and 1986; under 72 kilograms class, 1984 and 1989.

KARATE

ORIGINS Karate is a martial art developed in Japan. Karate (empty hand) techniques evolved from the Chinese art of shoalin boxing, known as kempo, which was popularized in Okinawa in the 16th century as a means of self-defense, and became known as Tang Hand. Tang Hand was introduced to Japan by Funakoshi Gichin in the 1920s, and the name karate was coined in the 1930s. Gichin's style of karate, known as shotokan, is one of five major styles adapted for competition, the others being wado-ryu, gojuryu, shito-ryu and kyokushinkai. Each style places different emphasis on the elements of technique, speed and power. Karate's popularity grew in the West in the late 1950s.

WORLD CHAMPIONSHIPS The first men's world championships were staged in Tokyo, Japan in 1970; a women's competition was first staged in 1980. Both tournaments are now staged biennially. The competition consists of two types: kumite, in which combatants fight each other, and kata events, in which contestants perform routines.

KUMITE CHAMPIONSHIPS (MEN)

Most titles (team) Great Britain has won six kumite world team titles, in 1975, 1982, 1984, 1986, 1988 and 1990.

Most titles (individual) Three men have won two individual world titles: Pat McKay (Great Britain) in the under 80 kilograms class, 1982, 1984; Emmanuel Pinda (France), in the open class, 1984, and the over 80 kilograms class, 1988; Theirry Masci (France), in the under 70 kilograms class, 1986 and 1988.

KATA CHAMPIONSHIPS (MEN)

Most titles (team) Japan has won two kata world team titles, in 1986 and 1988.

Most titles (individual) Tsuguo Sakumoto (Japan) has won three world titles, in 1984, 1986 and 1988.

KUMITE CHAMPIONSHIPS (WOMEN)

Most titles (individual) Guus van Mourik (Netherlands) has won four world titles in the over 60 kilograms class, in 1982, 1984, 1986 and 1988.

KATA CHAMPIONSHIPS (WOMEN)

Most titles (individual) Mie Nakayama (Japan) has won three world titles, in 1982, 1984 and 1986.

LACROSSE

LACROSSE (MEN)

ORIGINS The sport is of Native American origin, derived from the intertribal game of *baggataway*, which has been recorded as being played by Iroquois tribes as early as 1492. French settlers in North America coined the name "La Crosse" (the French word for a crozier or staff). The National Lacrosse Association was formed in Canada in 1867. The United States Amateur Lacrosse Association was founded in 1879. The International Federation of Amateur Lacrosse (IFAL) was founded in 1928.

WORLD CHAMPIONSHIPS The men's world championships were first staged in Toronto, Canada in 1967.

Most titles The United States has won five world titles, in 1967, 1974, 1982, 1986 and 1990.

NCAA CHAMPIONSHIPS (DIVISION I) The men's NCAA championship was first staged in 1971.

Most titles Johns Hopkins has won seven lacrosse titles, in 1974, 1978–80, 1984–85 and 1987.

LACROSSE (WOMEN)

ORIGINS Women were first reported to have played lacrosse in 1886. The women's game evolved separately from the men's, developing different rules; thus two distinct games were created: the women's game features 12-a-side and six-a-

MOST TITLES ■ IN 1992 THE UNIVERSITY OF MARYLAND WON ITS SECOND WOMEN'S LACROSSE TITLE, MATCHING THE SUCCESS OF TEMPLE AND PENN STATE.

side games, while men's games field 10-a-side teams.

WORLD CHAMPIONSHIPS A women's world championship was first held in 1969. Since 1982 the world championships have been known as the World Cup.

Most titles The United States has won three world titles, in 1974, 1982 and 1989.

NCAA CHAMPIONSHIPS (DIVISION I) The NCAA first staged a women's national championship in 1982.

Most titles Three teams have won two titles: Temple, 1984 and 1988; Penn State, 1987 and 1989; and Maryland, 1986 and 1992.

MODERN PENTATHLON

ORIGINS The modern pentathalon is comprised of five activities: fencing, horseback riding, pistol shooting, swimming and cross-country running. The sport derives from military training in the 19th century, which was based on a messenger's being able to travel across country on horseback, fighting his way through with sword and pistol, and being prepared to swim across rivers and complete his journey on foot. Each event is scored on points, determined either against other contestants or against scoring tables. There is no standard course; therefore, point totals are not comparable. *L'Union Internationale de Pentathlon*

Moderne (UIPM) was formed in 1948 and expanded to include the administration of the biathlon in 1957. (For further information on the biathlon, see pages 53–54.)

United States The United States Modern Pentathlon and Biathlon Association was established in 1971, but this body was split to create the U.S. Modern Pentathlon Association in 1978.

OLYMPIC GAMES Modern pentathlon was first included in the 1912 Games held in Stockholm, Sweden, and has been part of every Olympic program since.

Most gold medals Andras Balczo (Hungary) has won three gold medals in Olympic competition: team event, 1960 and 1968; individual title, 1972.

Most gold medals (team event) Two countries have won the team event four times: Hungary, 1952, 1960, 1968 and 1988; USSR, 1956, 1964, 1972 and 1980.

Most medals (individual) Pavel Lednev (USSR) has won a record seven medals in Olympic competition: two gold—team event, 1972 and 1980; two silver—team event, 1968; individual event, 1976; and three bronze—individual event, 1968, 1972 and 1980.

WORLD CHAMPIONSHIPS An official men's world championship was first staged in 1949, and has been held annually since. In Olympic years the Games are considered the world championships, and results from those events are included in world championship statistics. A women's world championship was inaugurated in 1981.

MEN'S CHAMPIONSHIP

Most titles (overall) Andras Balczo (Hungary) has won a record 13 world titles, including a record six individual titles: seven team, 1960, 1963, 1965–68 and 1970; six individual, 1963, 1965–67, 1969 and 1972.

Most titles (team event) The USSR has won 17 world championships: 1956–59, 1961–62, 1964, 1969, 1971–74, 1980, 1982–83, 1985 and 1991.

United States The United States won its only team world title in 1979, when Bob Nieman became the first American athlete, and so far the only man, to win an individual world championship.

WOMEN'S CHAMPIONSHIP

Most titles (individual event) Irina Kiselyeva (USSR) is the only woman to win the individual title twice, in 1986 and 1987.

Most titles (team event) Poland has won five world titles: 1985, 1988–91.

United States The best result for the U.S. in the team event is second place, which has been achieved twice, in 1981 and 1989. Lori Norwood won the individual championship in 1989.

UNITED STATES NATIONAL CHAMPIONSHIPS The men's championship was inaugurated in 1955, and the women's in 1977.

Most titles (men) Mike Burley has won four men's titles, in 1977, 1979, 1981 and 1985.

Most titles (women) Kim Arata (née Dunlop) has won nine titles, in 1979–80, 1984–89 and 1991.

MOTORCYCLE RACING

ORIGINS The first recorded motorcycle race took place in France on September 20, 1896, when eight riders took part in a 139-mile race from Paris to Nantes and back. The winner was M. Chevalier on a Michelin-Dion tricycle; he covered the course in 4 hours 10 minutes 37 seconds. The first race for two-wheeled motorcycles was held on a one-mile oval track at Sheen House, Richmond, England on November 29, 1897. The *Fédération Internationale Motorcycliste* (FIM) was founded in 1904 and is the world governing body.

WORLD CHAMPIONSHIPS The FIM instituted world championships in 1949 for 125, 250, 350 and 500cc classes. In 1962, a 50cc class was introduced, which was upgraded to 80cc in 1983. In 1982, the 350cc class was discontinued.

Most Championships

Overall 15, by Giacomo Agostini (Italy): 7—350cc (1968–74); 8—500cc (1966–72, 1975).

50cc 6, by Angel Nieto (Spain), 1969–70, 1972, 1975–77.

80cc 3, by Jorge Martinez (Spain), 1986–88.

125cc 7, by Angel Nieto (Spain), 1971–72, 1979, 1981–84.

LONG JUMP ■ THE APTLY NAMED DOUG DANGER JUMPED 251 FEET FROM RAMP TO RAMP ON JUNE 22, 1991.

250cc 4, by Phil Read (Great Britain), 1964–65, 1968, 1971.

350cc 7, by Giacomo Agostini (Italy), 1968–74.

500cc 8, by Giacomo Agostini (Italy), 1966–72, 1975.

Multiple titles The only rider to win more than one world championship in one year is Freddie Spencer (U.S.), who won the 250cc and 500cc titles in 1985.

United States The most world titles won by an American rider is four, by Eddie Lawson at 500cc in 1984, 1986, 1988–89.

Most Grand Prix Wins

Overall 122, by Giacomo Agostini (Italy): 54—350cc; 68—500cc.

50cc 27, by Angel Nieto (Spain).

80cc 21, by Jorge Martinez (Spain).

125cc 62, by Angel Nieto (Spain).

250cc 33, by Anton Mang (West Germany).

350cc 54, by Giacomo Agostini (Italy).

500cc 68, by Giacomo Agostini (Italy).

Most successful machines Japanese Yamaha machines won 44 world championships between 1964 and 1992.

LONGEST JUMP ☞ THE LONGEST DISTANCE EVER ACHIEVED FOR MOTORCYCLE RAMP JUMPING IS 251 FEET, BY DOUG DANGER AT LOUDON, N.H., ON JUNE 22, 1991.

Fastest circuits The highest average lap speed attained on any closed circuit is 160.288 mph, by Yvon du Hamel (Canada) on a modified 903cc four-cylinder Kawasaki Z1 at the 31-degree banked 2.5 mile Daytona International Speedway, Fla. in March 1973. His lap time was 56.149 seconds.

The fastest road circuit was the Francorchamps circuit near Spa, Belgium, then 8.74 miles long. It was lapped in 3 minutes 50.3 seconds (average speed 137.150 mph) by Barry Sheene (Great Britain) on a 495cc four-cylinder Suzuki during the Belgian Grand Prix on July 3, 1977. On that occasion he set a record time for this 10-lap (87.74-mile) race of 38 minutes 58.5 seconds (average speed 135.068 mph).

OLYMPIC GAMES

Records in this section include results from the Intercalated Games staged in 1906.

ORIGINS The exact date of the first Olympic Games is uncertain. The earliest date for which there is documented evidence is July 776 B.C. By order of Theodosius I, emperor of Rome, the

SUMMER OLYMPIC GAMES MEDAL WINNERS (1896–1992)

Country	Gold	Silver	Bronze	Total	Country	Gold	Silver	Bronze	Total
United States	789	603	518	1,910	Greece	24	40	39	103
USSR[1]	442	361	333	1,136	South Korea	31	27	41	99
Germany[2]	186	227	236	649	Yugoslavia[5]	26	30	30	86
Great Britain	177	224	218	619	Cuba	36	25	23	84
France	161	175	191	527	Austria	19	29	33	81
Sweden	133	149	171	453	New Zealand	27	10	28	65
East Germany[3]	154	131	126	411	South Africa	16	17	20	53
Italy	153	126	131	410	Turkey	26	15	12	53
Hungary	136	124	144	404	Argentina	13	19	15	47
Finland	98	77	112	287	Spain	17	19	10	46
Japan	90	83	93	266	Mexico	9	13	18	40
Australia	78	76	98	252	Brazil	9	10	21	40
Romania	59	70	90	219	Kenya	13	13	13	39
Poland	43	62	105	210	Iran	4	12	17	33
Canada	45	67	80	192	Jamaica	4	13	9	26
Netherlands	45	52	72	169	Estonia[6]	7	6	10	23
Switzerland	42	63	58	163	North Korea[7]	6	5	10	21
Bulgaria	38	69	55	162	Egypt	6	6	6	18
Czechoslovakia[4]	49	50	49	148	Ireland	5	5	5	15
Denmark	26	51	53	130	India	8	3	3	14
Belgium	35	47	44	126	Portugal	2	4	7	13
China	36	41	37	114	Mongolia	0	5	8	13
Norway	43	37	34	114	Ethiopia	6	1	6	13

[1] Includes Czarist Russia; Unified Team (1992)
[2] Germany 1896–1964, 1992; West Germany 1968–88
[3] 1968–88
[4] Includes Bohemia
[5] Includes I.O.P. (1992)
[6] Estonia and Latvia up to 1936
[7] North Korea from 1964

Games were prohibited in A.D. 394. The revival of the Olympic Games is credited to Pierre de Fredi, Baron de Coubertin, a French aristocrat, who was commissioned by his government to form a universal sports association in 1889. Coubertin presented his proposals for a modern Games on November 25, 1892 in Paris; this led to the formation of the International Olympic Committee (IOC) in 1894 and thence to the staging of the first modern Olympic Games, which were opened in Athens, Greece on April 6, 1896. In 1906, the IOC organized the Intercalated Games in Athens, to celebrate the 10th anniversary of the revival of the Games. In 1924, the first Winter Olympics were held in Chamonix, France.

OLYMPIC GAMES MEDAL RECORDS

INDIVIDUAL RECORDS

Most gold medals Ray Ewry (U.S.) has won 10 gold medals in Olympic competition: standing high jump, 1900, 1904, 1906 and 1908; standing long jump, 1900, 1904, 1906 and 1908; standing triple jump, 1900 and 1904. The most gold medals

SUMMER OLYMPIC GAMES MEDAL WINNERS (1896–1992)

Country	Gold	Silver	Bronze	Total	Country	Gold	Silver	Bronze	Total
Pakistan	3	3	4	10	Tanzania	0	2	0	2
Morocco	4	2	3	9	Cameroon	0	1	1	2
Uruguay	2	1	6	9	Haiti	0	1	1	2
Venezuela	1	2	5	8	Iceland	0	1	1	2
Chile	0	6	2	8	Israel	0	1	1	2
Nigeria	0	4	4	8	Panama	0	0	2	2
Philippines	0	1	7	8	Slovenia	0	0	2	2
Trinidad	1	2	4	7	Zimbabwe	1	0	0	1
Indonesia	2	3	1	6	Costa Rica	0	1	0	1
Latvia [8]	0	4	2	6	Ivory Coast	0	1	0	1
Colombia	0	2	4	6	Netherlands Antilles	0	1	0	1
Uganda	1	3	1	5	Senegal	0	1	0	1
Puerto Rico	0	1	4	5	Singapore	0	1	0	1
Tunisia	1	2	2	5	Sri Lanka	0	1	0	1
Peru	1	3	0	4	Syria	0	1	0	1
Algeria	1	0	3	4	Virgin Islands	0	1	0	1
Lebanon	0	2	2	4	Barbados	0	0	1	1
Taipei (Taiwan)	0	2	2	4	Bermuda	0	0	1	1
Ghana	0	1	3	4	Djibouti	0	0	1	1
Thailand	0	1	3	4	Dominican Republic	0	0	1	1
Bahamas	1	0	2	3	Guyana	0	0	1	1
Croatia	0	1	2	3	Iraq	0	0	1	1
Luxembourg	1	1	0	2	Malaysia	0	0	1	1
Lithuania	1	0	1	2	Niger	0	0	1	1
Suriname	1	0	1	2	Qatar	0	0	1	1
Namibia	0	2	0	2	Zambia	0	0	1	1

[8] Estonia and Latvia up to 1936

LARGEST GAMES ■ THE 1992 BARCELONA GAMES WAS THE BIGGEST SPORTS EVENT IN HISTORY. IT REQUIRED ONE OF THE WORLD'S LARGEST FLAGS TO WRAP IT ALL UP.

won by a woman is nine, by gymnast Larissa Latynina (USSR): all-around, 1956 and 1960; vault, 1956; floor exercise, 1956, 1960 and 1964; team title, 1956, 1960 and 1964.

Most medals Gymnast Larissa Latynina (USSR) has won 18 medals (nine gold, five silver and four bronze), 1956–64. The most medals won by a man is 15 (seven gold, five silver and three bronze), by gymnast Nikolai Andrianov (USSR), 1972–80.

Most gold medals at one Olympics Swimmer Mark Spitz (U.S.) won a record seven gold medals at Munich in 1972. His victories came in the 100-meter freestyle, 200-meter freestyle, 100-meter butterfly, 200-meter butterfly, and three relay events. The most gold medals won at one Games by a woman athlete is six, by swimmer Kristin Otto (East Germany), who won six gold medals at the 1988 Games. Her victories came in the 50-meter freestyle, 100-meter freestyle, 100-meter backstroke, 100-meter butterfly, and two relay events.

The most individual events won at one Games is five, by speed skater Eric Heiden (U.S.) in 1980. Heiden won the 500 meters, 1,000 meters, 1,500 meters, 5,000 meters, and 10,000 meters.

Most medals at one Olympics Gymnast Aleksandr Dityatin (USSR) won eight medals (three gold, four silver and one bronze) at Moscow, USSR in 1980. The most medals won by a woman athlete is seven (two gold and five silver), by gymnast Maria Gorokhovskaya (USSR) in 1952.

Most consecutive gold medals (same event) Al Oerter (U.S.) is the only athlete to win the same event, the discus, at four consecutive Games, 1956–68. Yachtsman Paul Elvstrom (Denmark) won four successive golds at monotype events, 1948–60, but there was a class change: Firefly in 1948; Finn class, 1952–60. Including the Intercalated Games of 1906, Ray Ewry (U.S.) won four consecutive gold medals in two events: standing high jump, 1900–1908; standing long jump, 1900–1908.

Oldest gold medalist Oscar Swahn (Sweden) was aged 64 years 258 days when he won an Olympic gold medal in 1912 as a member of the team that won the running deer shooting single-shot title. The oldest woman to win a gold medal was Queenie Newall (Great Britain), who won the 1908 national round archery event at age 53 years 275 days.

Youngest gold medalist The youngest-ever winner was an unnamed French boy who coxed the Netherlands pair to victory in the 1900 rowing event. He was believed to be 7–10 years old. The youngest-ever woman champion was Marjorie Gestring (U.S.), who at age 13 years 268 days won the 1936 women's springboard diving event.

Most Games Three Olympians have competed in eight Games: show jumper Raimondo d'Inzeo (Italy), 1948–76; yachtsman Paul Elvstrom (Denmark), 1948–60, 1968–72, 1984–88; yachtsman Durwood Knowles (Great Britain/Bahamas), 1948–72, 1988. The most appearances by a woman is seven, by fencer Kerstin Palm (Sweden), 1964–88.

Summer/Winter Games gold medalist The only person to have won gold medals in both Summer and Winter Olympiads is Edward Eagan (U.S.), who won the 1920 light-heavyweight boxing title and was a member of the 1932 winning four-man bobsled team.

Summer/Winter Games medalist (same year) The only athlete to have won medals at both the Winter and Summer Games held in the same year is Christa Rothenburger-Luding (East Germany). At the 1988 Winter Games in Calgary, Canada, Rothenburger-Luding won two speed skating medals: gold medal, 1,000 meters, and silver medal, 500 meters; and at the Seoul Games that summer she won a silver medal in the women's sprint cycling event.

UNITED STATES RECORDS

Most gold medals The records for most gold medals overall and at one Games are both held by American athletes (see above). The most gold medals won by an American woman is four, by three athletes: Patricia McCormick (née Keller), diving, 1952–1956; Evelyn Ashford, track and field, 1984–92; Janet Evans, swimming, 1988–92.

Most medals The most medals won by an American Olympian is 11, by three athletes: Carl Os-

MOST MEDALS ■ SWIMMER JANET EVANS WON HER FOURTH CAREER GOLD MEDAL AT BARCELONA, MATCHING THE U.S. WOMEN'S ALL-TIME RECORD.

burn, shooting—five gold, four silver and two bronze (1912–24); Mark Spitz, swimming—nine gold, one silver and one bronze (1968–72); Matt Biondi, swimming—eight golds, two silver and one bronze (1984–92). The most medals won by an American woman is eight, by Shirley Babashoff, swimming—two gold and six silver (1972–76).

Oldest gold medalist The oldest U.S. Olympic champion was Galen Spencer, who won a gold medal in the Team Round archery event in 1904, at age 64 years 2 days.

Youngest gold medalist The youngest gold medalist was Jackie Fields, who won the 1924 featherweight boxing title at age 16 years 162 days.

Oldest medalist The oldest U.S. medalist was Samuel Duvall, who was a member of the 1904 silver-medal-winning team in the team round archery event, at age 68 years 194 days.

Youngest medalist The youngest American medal winner, and the youngest-ever participant, was Dorothy Poynton, who won a silver medal in springboard diving at the 1928 Games at age 13 years 23 days. The youngest men's medalist was Donald Douglas Jr., who won a silver medal at six-meter yachting in 1932, at age 15 years 40 days.

WINTER GAMES MEDAL RECORDS

INDIVIDUAL RECORDS

Most gold medals Speed skater Lydia Skoblikova (USSR) has won six gold medals in Winter Games competition: 500 meters, 1964; 1,000 meters, 1964; 1,500 meters, 1960–64; 3,000 meters, 1960–64. The

LIGHTING THE WAY ■ THE LONGEST TORCH RELAY CULMINATED WITH THE LIGHTING OF THE OLYMPIC FLAME AT THE 1988 CALGARY WINTER GAMES.

most gold medals won by a man is five, by two speed skaters: Clas Thunberg (Finland), 500 meters, 1928;

1,500 meters, 1924–28; 5,000 meters, 1924; all-around title, 1924; Eric Heiden (U.S.), 500, 1,000, 1,500, 5,000 and 10,000 meters, all in 1980.

Most medals Cross-country skier Raisa Smetanina (USSR/Unified Team) has won 10 medals (four gold, five silver and one bronze), 1976–92. The most medals won by a man is nine (four gold, three silver and two bronze), by cross-country skier Sixten Jernberg (Sweden), 1956–64.

Oldest gold medalist Jay O'Brien (U.S.) was aged 48 years 359 days when he won an Olympic gold medal in 1932 in the 4-man bobsled event. The oldest woman to win a gold medal was Raisa Smetanina (Unified Team), who was a member of the 1992 4 x 5 km relay team at age 39 years 352 days.

Youngest gold medalist Maxi Herber (Germany) was aged 15 years 128 days when she won the 1936 figure skating title. The youngest-ever men's champion was Toni Neiminen (Finland), who at age 16 years 259 days was a member of the winning ski jumping team.

WINTER OLYMPIC GAMES MEDAL WINNERS (1924–1992)

Country	Gold	Silver	Bronze	Total
USSR[1]	88	63	67	218
Norway	63	66	59	188
United States	47	50	37	134
Austria	34	45	40	119
Finland	36	44	37	117
East Germany[2]	39	36	35	110
Germany[3]	36	36	29	101
Sweden	37	25	34	96
Switzerland	24	25	27	76
Canada	16	15	20	51
France	16	15	17	48
Italy	18	16	13	47
Netherlands	14	18	14	46
Czechoslovakia[4]	2	8	16	26
Great Britain	7	4	10	21
Japan	2	6	6	14
Liechtenstein	2	2	5	9
Hungary	0	2	4	6
South Korea	2	1	1	4
Belgium	1	1	2	4
Poland	1	1	2	4
Yugoslavia	0	3	1	4
China	0	3	0	3
Spain	1	0	1	2
Luxembourg	0	2	0	2
North Korea[5]	0	1	1	2
New Zealand	0	1	0	1
Bulgaria	0	0	1	1
Romania	0	0	1	1

[1] Includes Unified Team (1992)

[2] 1968–82

[3] Germany 1924–64, 1992, West Germany from 1968–88

[4] Includes Bohemia

[5] North Korea from 1964

OLYMPIAN EFFORT ■ AT THE '92 ALBERTVILLE GAMES, RAISA SMETANINA WON HER 10TH OLYMPIC MEDAL, THE MOST OF ANY ATHLETE IN WINTER GAMES HISTORY.

ORIENTEERING

Orienteering combines cross-country running with compass and map navigation. The object of the sport is for the competitor to navigate across a set course in the fastest time possible using a topographical map and a compass. The course contains designated locations called controls, identified by orange and white markers, which the runner must find and identify on a punch card that is handed to the official timer at the end of the race.

ORIGINS Orienteering can be traced to Scandinavia at the turn of the 20th century. Major Ernst Killander (Sweden) is regarded as the father of the sport, having organized the first large race in Saltsjobaden, Sweden in 1919. The Swedish federation, *Svenska Orienteringsforbundet*, was founded in 1936. The International Orienteering Federation was established in 1961.

United States Orienteering was introduced to the U.S. in the 1940s. The first U.S. Orienteering Championships were held on October 17, 1970. The U.S. Orienteering Federation (USOF) was founded on August 1, 1971.

WORLD CHAMPIONSHIPS The world championships were first held in 1966 in Fiskars, Finland, and are held biennially.

Most titles (relay) The men's relay has been won a record seven times by Norway—1970, 1978, 1981, 1983, 1985, 1987 and 1989. Sweden has won the women's relay nine times—1966, 1970, 1974, 1976, 1981, 1983, 1985, 1989 and 1991.

Most titles (individual) Three women's individual titles have been won by Annichen Kringstad (Sweden), in 1981, 1983 and 1985. The men's title has been won twice by three men: Age Hadler (Norway), in 1966 and 1972; by Egil Johansen (Norway), in 1976 and 1978; and by Oyvin Thon (Norway), in 1979 and 1981.

UNITED STATES NATIONAL CHAMPIONSHIPS First held on October 17, 1970, the nationals are held annually.

Most titles Sharon Crawford, New England Orienteering Club, has won a record 11 overall women's titles: 1977–82, 1984–87, and 1989. The men's title has been won five times by two men: Peter Gagarin, New England Orienteering Club, 1976–79, 1983; Mikell Platt, New England Orienteering Club, 1986, 1988–91.

MOST COMPETITORS ☛ THE LARGEST FIELD FOR AN ORIENTEERING RACE WAS 38,000 COMPETITORS FOR THE RUF DES HERBSTES AT SIBIU, ROMANIA IN 1982.

POLO

The playing field for polo is the largest of any sport, with a standard length of 300 yards and a width of 200 yards (without boards) or 160 yards (with boards). The object of the game is to score in the opponent's goals, the goalposts being eight yards wide, with the team scoring the most goals winning the game. Each side fields a team of four players; the game is played over six periods of seven minutes' duration each. A period is known as a chukka, and players must change their mount after each chukka. Polo players are assigned handicaps based on their skill, with a 10 handicap being the highest level of play.

ORIGINS Polo originated in Central Asia, possibly as early as 3100 B.C., in the state of Manipur. The name is derived from the Tibetan word *pulu*. The modern era began in India in the 1850s when British army officers were introduced to the game. The Cachar Club, Assam, India was founded in 1859, and is believed to be the first polo club of the modern era. The game was introduced in England in 1869. The world governing body, the Hurlingham Polo Association, was founded in London, England in 1874 and drew up the laws of the game in 1875.

United States Polo was introduced to the U.S. by James Gordon Bennett in 1876, when he arranged for the first indoor game at Dickel's Riding Academy, N.Y. The first game played outdoors was held on May 13, 1876 at the Jerome Park Racetrack in Westchester County, N.Y. The oldest existing polo club in the United States is Meadow Brook Polo Club, Jericho, N.Y., founded in 1879. The United States Polo Association was formed on March 21, 1890.

UNITED STATES OPEN POLO CHAMPIONSHIP The U.S. Open was first staged in 1904 and is an annual event.

Most wins The Meadow Brook Polo Club, Jericho, N.Y. has won the U.S. Open 28 times: 1916, 1920, 1923–41, 1946–51, and 1953.

Highest score The highest aggregate number of goals scored in an international match is 30, when Argentina beat the U.S. 21–9 at Meadowbrook, Long Island, N.Y. in September 1936.

ROOM TO ROAM ■ POLO IS PLAYED ON THE LARGEST PLAYING FIELD OF ANY TEAM SPORT. STANDARD MEASUREMENTS ARE 300 FEET BY 200 FEET.

TIMEOUT

POOL

ORIGINS Pool traces its ancestry to billiards, an English game introduced in Virginia in the late 17th century. During the 19th century the game evolved from one in which a mace was used to push balls around a table, to a game of precise skill using a cue, with the aim of pocketing numbered balls. The original form of pool in the United States was known as pyramid pool, with the object being to pocket eight out the 15 balls on the table. From this game, "61-pool" evolved: each of the 15 balls was worth points equal to its numerical value; the first player to score 61 points was the winner. In 1878 the first world championship was staged under the rules of 61-pool. In 1910, Jerome

NINE-BALL ■ EARL STRICKLAND (LEFT) AND ROBIN BELL (RIGHT) HAVE EACH WON THEIR RESPECTIVE WORLD TITLES TWICE.

Keogh suggested that the rules be adjusted to make the game faster and more attractive; he proposed that the last ball be left free on the table to be used as a target on the next rack; the result was 14.1 continuous pool (also known as American straight pool). The game of 14.1 was adopted as the championship form of pool from 1912 onwards. In the last 20 years, nine-ball pool and eight-ball pool have surpassed 14.1 in popularity. In 1990 the World Pool Billiard Association inaugurated the nine-ball world championship.

14.1 CONTINUOUS POOL (ALSO KNOWN AS AMERICAN STRAIGHT POOL)

WORLD CHAMPIONSHIPS The first official world championship was held in April 1912 and was won by Edward Ralph (U.S.).

Most titles Two players have won the world title six times: Ralph Greenleaf (U.S.) and Willie Mosconi (U.S.). From 1919–37, Greenleaf won the title six times and defended it 13 times. Between 1941 and 1956, Mosconi also won the title six times and defended it 13 times.

Longest consecutive run The longest consecutive run in 14.1 recognized by the Billiard Congress of America (BCA) is 526 balls, by Willie Mosconi in March 1954 during an exhibition in Springfield, Ohio. Michael Eufemia is reported to have pocketed 625 balls at Logan's Billiard Academy in Brooklyn, N.Y. on February 2, 1960; however, this run has never been ratified by the BCA.

NINE-BALL POOL

WORLD CHAMPIONSHIP In this competition, inaugurated in 1990, Earl Strickland (U.S.) has won the men's title twice, 1990–1991. Robin Bell (U.S.) has won the women's title twice, 1990–91.

TIMEOUT

POOL POCKETING ☞ THE FASTEST TIME FOR POCKETING ALL 15 BALLS IS 37.9 SECONDS BY ROB MCKENNA (GREAT BRITAIN) AT BLACKPOOL, ENGLAND ON NOVEMBER 7, 1987.

POWERBOAT RACING

ORIGINS A gasoline engine was first installed in a boat by Jean Lenoir on the River Seine, Paris, France in 1865. Organized powerboat races were first run at the turn of the 20th century. The first major international competition was the Harnsworth Trophy, launched in 1903. Modern powerboat racing is broken down into two main types: circuit racing in sheltered waterways, and offshore racing. Offshore events were initially for displacement (nonplaning) cruisers, but in 1958 the 170-mile Miami, Fla.-to-Nassau, Bahamas race was staged for planing cruisers.

POWERBOAT SPEED RECORDS

The following is a selection of speed records recognized by the APBA as of January 1, 1993.

Distance: One Kilometer

Type	Class	Speed (mph)	Driver	Location	Year
Inboard	GP	170.024	Kent MacPhail	Decatur, Ill.	1989
Inboard	KRR	146.649	Gordon Jennings	Lincoln City, Ore.	1989
Offshore	Super Boat	148.238	Thomas Gentry	New Orleans, La.	1987
Offshore	Open	138.512	Al Copeland	New Orleans, La.	1987
PR Outboard	500ccH	121.940	Daniel Kirts	Moore Haven, Fla.	1987
PR Outboard	700ccH	118.769	Billy Rucker Jr.	Waterford, Calif.	1992
Performance	Champ Boat	131.963	Jim Merten	Kaukauna, Wis.	1978
Performance	Mod U	142.968	Bob Wartinger	Moore Haven, Fla.	1989
Special Event	Formula 1	165.338	Robert Hering	Parker, Ariz.	1986
Special Event	Jet	317.600	Ken Warby	Tumut, Australia	1976

Unlimited in Competition

Type	Distance	Speed (mph)	Driver	Location	Year
Qual. Lap	2 miles	164.234	Chip Hanauer	Evansville, Ind.	1992
Lap	2 miles	154.872	Chip Hanauer	Evansville, Ind.	1992
Qual. Lap	2.5 miles	168.935	Chip Hanauer	Evansville, Ind.	1992
Lap	2.5 miles	154.573	Chip Hanauer	San Diego, Calif.	1990
Lap	3 miles	155.682	Mark Tate	San Diego, Calif.	1991

Source: APBA

United States The American Power Boat Association (APBA) was founded on April 22, 1903 in New York City. In 1913 the APBA issued the "Racing Commission" rules, which created its powers for governing the sport in North America. In 1924 the APBA set rules for boats propelled by outboard detachable motors and became the governing body for both inboard and outboard racing in North America. The APBA is currently based in East Detroit, Mich.

APBA GOLD CUP The APBA held its first Gold Cup race at the Columbia Yacht Club on the Hudson River, N.Y. in 1904, when the winner was *Standard*, piloted by C. C. Riotto at an average speed of 23.6 mph.

Most wins (driver) The most wins is eight, by two drivers: Bill Muncey, 1956–57, 1961–62, 1972 and 1977–79; Chip Hanauer, 1982–88 and 1992.

Most wins (boat) The most successful boat has been *Budweiser*, driven by Bill Sterett Sr. in 1969; by Dean Chenoweth in 1970, 1973 and 1980–81; by Tom D'Eath in 1989–90; and by Chip Hanauer in 1992.

Consecutive wins Chip Hanauer has won a record seven successive victories, 1982–88.

Longest races The longest offshore race has been the London (England) to Monte Carlo (Monaco) Marathon Offshore international event. The race extended over 2,947 miles in 14 stages from June 10–25, 1972. It was won by *H.T.S.* (Great Britain), piloted by Mike Bellamy, Eddie Chater and Jim Brooker in 71 hours 35 minutes 56 seconds, for an average speed of 41.15 mph. The longest circuit race is the 24-hour race held annually since 1962 on the River Seine at Rouen, France.

PROPELLING PROJECTILES

The longest independently authenticated throw of any inert object heavier than air is 1,257 feet, for a flying ring, by Scott Zimmerman on July 8, 1986 at Fort Funston, Calif. This illustration shows the distances achieved for a selection of miscellaneous identifiable, yet in some cases unlikely, flying objects. Zimmerman's ring fling mark is way off the page.

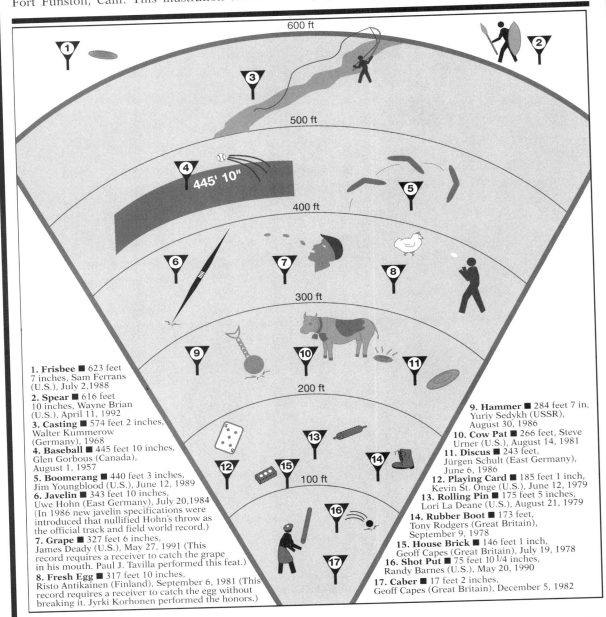

600 ft

500 ft

445' 10"

400 ft

300 ft

200 ft

100 ft

1. Frisbee ■ 623 feet 7 inches, Sam Ferrans (U.S.), July 2, 1988

2. Spear ■ 616 feet 10 inches, Wayne Brian (U.S.), April 11, 1992

3. Casting ■ 574 feet 2 inches, Walter Kummerow (Germany), 1968

4. Baseball ■ 445 feet 10 inches, Glen Gorbous (Canada), August 1, 1957

5. Boomerang ■ 440 feet 3 inches, Jim Youngblood (U.S.), June 12, 1989

6. Javelin ■ 343 feet 10 inches, Uwe Hohn (East Germany), July 20, 1984 (In 1986 new javelin specifications were introduced that nullified Hohn's throw as the official track and field world record.)

7. Grape ■ 327 feet 6 inches, James Deady (U.S.), May 27, 1991 (This record requires a receiver to catch the grape in his mouth. Paul J. Tavilla performed this feat.)

8. Fresh Egg ■ 317 feet 10 inches, Risto Antikainen (Finland), September 6, 1981 (This record requires a receiver to catch the egg without breaking it. Jyrki Korhonen performed the honors.)

9. Hammer ■ 284 feet 7 in, Yuriy Sedykh (USSR), August 30, 1986

10. Cow Pat ■ 266 feet, Steve Urner (U.S.), August 14, 1981

11. Discus ■ 243 feet, Jürgen Schult (East Germany), June 6, 1986

12. Playing Card ■ 185 feet 1 inch, Kevin St. Onge (U.S.), June 12, 1979

13. Rolling Pin ■ 175 feet 5 inches, Lori La Deane (U.S.), August 21, 1979

14. Rubber Boot ■ 173 feet, Tony Rodgers (Great Britain), September 9, 1978

15. House Brick ■ 146 feet 1 inch, Geoff Capes (Great Britain), July 19, 1978

16. Shot Put ■ 75 feet 10 1/4 inches, Randy Barnes (U.S.), May 20, 1990

17. Caber ■ 17 feet 2 inches, Geoff Capes (Great Britain), December 5, 1982

RACQUETBALL

ORIGINS Racquetball, using a 40-foot x 20-foot court, was invented in 1950 by Joe Sobek at the Greenwich YMCA, Greenwich, Conn. Sobek designed a "strung paddle racquet" and combined the rules of squash and handball to form the game of "paddle rackets." The International Racquetball Association (IRA) was founded in 1960 by Bob Kendler, and was renamed the American Amateur Racquetball Association (AARA) in 1979. The International Amateur Racquetball Federation (IARF) was founded in 1979 and staged its first world championship in 1981.

WORLD CHAMPIONSHIPS First held in 1981, the IARF world championships have been held biennially since 1984.

Most titles (team) The United States has won all six team titles, in 1981, 1984, 1986 (tie with Canada), 1988, 1990 and 1992.

Most titles (men) Egan Inoue (U.S.) has won two singles titles, in 1986 and 1990.

Most titles (women) Two women have won two world titles: Cindy Baxter (U.S.), 1981 and 1986; and Heather Stupp (Canada), 1988 and 1990.

UNITED STATES NATIONAL CHAMPIONSHIPS The first championships were held in 1968.

Most titles A record four men's open titles have been won by Ed Andrews of California, 1980–81 and 1985–86. Two players have won four women's open titles: Cindy Baxter of Pennsylvania, 1981, 1983, 1985–86; and Michelle Gilman-Gould of Idaho, 1989–92.

RODEO

ORIGINS Rodeo originated in Mexico, developing from 18th century fiestas, and moved north to the United States and Canada with the expansion of the North American cattle industry in the 18th and 19th centuries. There are several claims to the earliest organized rodeo. The Professional Rodeo Cowboys Association (PRCA) sanctions the West of the Pecos Rodeo, Pecos, Tex. as the oldest; it was first held in 1883. The development of rodeo as a regulated national sport can be traced to the formation of the Cowboys' Turtle Association in 1936. In 1945 the Turtles became the Rodeo Cowboy Association, which in 1975 was renamed the Professional Rodeo Cowboys Association (PRCA). The PRCA is recognized as the oldest and largest rodeo-governing body in the world.

Rodeo events are divided into two groups: roughstock and timed.

Roughstock The roughstock events are saddle bronc riding, bareback riding, and bull riding. In these events the cowboy is required to ride the mount for eight seconds to receive a score. The cowboy must use only one hand to grip the "rigging" (a handhold secured to the animal), and is disqualified if the free hand touches the animal or equipment during the round. The performance is judged on the cowboy's technique and the animal's bucking efforts.

Timed The timed events are calf roping, steer roping, team roping, and steer wrestling. In these events the cowboy chases the calf or steer, riding a registered quarter horse, catches up to the animal, and then captures the animal performing the required feat. The cowboy's performance is timed, with the fastest time winning the event.

WORLD CHAMPIONSHIPS The Rodeo Association of America organized the first world championships in 1929. The championship has been organized under several different formats and sponsored by several different groups throughout its existence. The current championship is a season-long competition based on PRCA earnings. The PRCA has organized the championship since 1945 (as the Rodeo Cowboy Association through 1975).

TOP BULL ☛ BUCKING BULL RED ROCK DISLODGED 312 RIDERS FROM 1980–88. HE WAS FINALLY RIDDEN TO THE EIGHT-SECOND BELL BY LANE FROST ON MAY 20, 1988.

OVER A BARREL ■ IN 1992, CHARMAYNE RODMAN WON HER NINTH CONSECUTIVE WOMEN'S BARREL RACING

Most titles (overall) Jim Shoulders has won 16 rodeo world championship events: all-around, 1949, 1956–59; bareback riding, 1950, 1956–58; bull riding, 1951, 1954–59.

INDIVIDUAL EVENTS

All-around Two cowboys have won six all-around titles: Larry Mahan, 1966–70, 1973; Tom Ferguson, 1974–79.

Saddle bronc riding Casey Tibbs won six saddle bronc titles, in 1949, 1951–54 and 1959.

Bareback riding Two cowboys have won five titles: Joe Alexander, 1971–75; Bruce Ford, 1979–80, 1982–83, 1987.

Bull riding Don Gay has won eight bullriding titles: 1975–81 and 1984.

Calf roping Dean Oliver has won eight titles: 1955, 1958, 1960–64 and 1969.

Steer roping Everett Shaw has won six titles: 1945–46, 1948, 1951, 1959 and 1962.

Steer wrestling Homer Pettigrew has won six titles: 1940, 1942–45 and 1948.

Team roping The team of Jake Barnes and Clay O'Brien Cooper has won five titles, 1985–89.

Women's barrel racing Charmayne Rodman has won nine titles, 1984–92.

Oldest world champion Ike Rude won the 1953 steer roping title at age 59 to became the oldest rodeo titleholder.

Youngest world champion Jim Rodriguez Jr. won the 1959 team roping title at age 18 to become the youngest rodeo titleholder.

RIDING RECORDS

HIGHEST SCORES (MAXIMUM POSSIBLE: 100 POINTS)

Bull riding Wade Leslie scored 100 points riding Wolfman Skoal at Central Point, Ore. in 1991.

Saddle bronc riding Doug Vold scored 95 points riding Transport at Meadow Lake, Saskatchewan, Canada in 1979.

Bareback riding Joe Alexander scored 93 points riding Marlboro at Cheyenne, Wyo. in 1974.

FASTEST TIMES

Calf roping The fastest time in this event is 5.7 seconds, by Lee Phillips at Assinobia, Saskatchewan, Canada in 1978.

Steer wrestling Without a barrier, the fastest time is reported to have been 2.2 seconds by Oral Zumwalt in the 1930s. With a barrier, the record time is 2.4 seconds, achieved by three cowboys: Jim Bynum at Marietta, Okla. in 1955; Gene Melton at Pecatonia, Ill. in 1976; and Carl Deaton at Tulsa, Okla. in 1976.

Team roping The team of Bob Harris and Tee Woolman performed this feat in a record 3.7 seconds at Spanish Fork, Utah in 1986.

Steer roping The fastest time in this event is 8.5 seconds, by Shaun Burchett at Fredonia, Kan. in 1987.

HIGHEST EARNINGS

Career Roy Cooper holds the career PRCA earnings mark at $1,374,953, 1976–92.

Season The single-season PRCA mark is $258,750 by Ty Murray in 1991.

ROLLER SKATING

ORIGINS Roller skates were invented by Joseph Merlin of Belgium. He demonstrated his new mode of transport at a masquerade party in London in 1760, with disastrous consequences—he was unable to stop and crashed into a large mirror, receiving near-fatal wounds. In 1863, James L. Plimpton of Medfield, Mass. patented the modern four-wheeled roller skate. In 1866, he opened the first public roller skating rink in the United States in Newport, R.I. The *Federation Internationale de Roller Skating* was founded in 1924 and is now headquartered in Spain. The Roller Skating Rink Operators' Association staged the first U.S. National Championship in 1937. Since 1973 the United States Amateur Confederation of Roller Skating has been the governing body of the sport in the United States. Three distinct sports have derived from roller skating: speed skating, artistic skating, and roller hockey.

SPEED SKATING

Speed skating events are divided into two categories: road racing and track racing. World championships are staged in alternate years for each discipline.

WORLD CHAMPIONSHIPS The first world championships were held in Monza, Italy in 1937. A women's championship was first staged in 1953.

Most titles Alberta Vianello (Italy) has won a record 19 world titles—eight track and 11 road—1953–65. Marco Cantarella (Italy) has won 15 men's titles—seven track and eight road—1964–80.

UNITED STATES NATIONAL CHAMPIONSHIPS The first U.S. championships were staged in 1937 for indoor competition, and contests have been held annually since. In 1985 a separate outdoor championship was initiated, and this is also staged annually.

Most titles Mary Merrell has won a record six overall champion titles, 1959–61, 1964, and 1966–67 (all indoors). Dante Muse has won six men's overall titles—three indoors, 1986, 1990 and 1992; three outdoors, 1987, 1989 and 1990.

ARTISTIC SKATING

WORLD CHAMPIONSHIPS The first world championships were held in Washington D.C. in 1947. The championships have been held annually since 1970.

Most titles Scott Cohen (U.S.) has won five men's free-skating titles, 1985–86 and 1989–91. Sandro Guerra (Italy) has won five men's combined titles, 1987–89, 1991–92. Rafaella del Vinaccio (Italy) has won five free-skating and five combined women's titles, 1988–92.

UNITED STATES NATIONAL CHAMPIONSHIPS The first U.S. championships were staged in 1939, and contests are now held annually.

Most titles Michael Jacques has won seven free-skating titles, 1966–72. Laurene Anselmi has won seven women's titles—three figure skating, 1951, 1953–54; four free-skating, 1951–54.

ROLLER HOCKEY

Roller hockey is played by two five-man teams over two twenty-minute periods.

WORLD CHAMPIONSHIPS First held in Stuttgart, Germany in 1936, the world championships have been held under several formats, both annual and biennial. Currently the tournament is an annual event.

Most titles Portugal has won 13 world titles: 1947–50, 1952, 1956, 1958, 1960, 1962, 1968, 1974, 1982 and 1991.

ROWING

ORIGINS Forms of rowing can be traced back to ancient Egypt; however, the modern sport of rowing dates to 1715, when the Doggett's Coat and Badge scull race was established in London, England. Types of regattas are believed to have taken place in Venice, Italy in 1300, but the modern regatta can also be traced to England, where races were staged in 1775 on the River Thames at Ranleigh Gardens, Putney. The world governing body is the *Federation Internationale des Sociétés d'Aviron* (FISA), founded in 1892. Rowing has been part of the Olympic Games since 1900.

United States The first organized boat races in the United States were reportedly races staged between boatmen in New York harbor in the late 18th century. The first rowing club formed in the United States was the Castle Garden Amateur Boat Club Association, New York City, in 1834. The oldest active boat club is the Detroit Boat Club, founded in 1839. The first and oldest collegiate boat club was formed at Yale University in 1843. The National Association of Amateur Oarsmen (NAAO) was formed in 1872. The NAAO merged with the National Women's Rowing Association in 1982 to form the United States Rowing Association.

OLYMPIC GAMES Men's rowing events have been included in the Olympic Games since 1900. In 1976 women's events were included.

Most gold medals Seven oarsmen have won three gold medals: John Kelly (U.S.), single sculls, 1920, double sculls, 1920 and 1924; Paul Costello (U.S.), double sculls, 1920, 1924 and 1928; Jack Beresford (Great Britain), single sculls, 1924, coxless fours, 1932, double sculls, 1936; Vyacheslav Ivanov (USSR), single sculls, 1956, 1960 and 1964; Siegfried Brietzke (East Germany), coxless pairs, 1972, coxless fours, 1976 and 1980; Pertti Karppinen (Finland), single sculls, 1976, 1980 and 1984; Steven Redgrave (Great Britain), coxed fours, 1984, coxless pairs, 1988 and 1992.

GOLDEN STROKE ■ AT THE 1992 OLYMPICS STEVEN REDGRAVE (RIGHT) WON HIS THIRD GOLD MEDAL.

Most medals Jack Beresford (Great Britain) won five medals in rowing competition: three gold (see above) and two silver (single sculls, 1920, and eights, 1928).

WORLD CHAMPIONSHIPS World rowing championships staged separately from the Olympic Games were first held in 1962. Since 1974 the championships have been staged annually. In Olympic years the Games are considered the world championships, and results from the Olympics are included in this section.

Most titles Giuseppe and Carmine Abbagnale (both Italy) have won nine coxed pairs titles, 1981–82, 1984–85 and 1987–91. Jutta Behrendt (née Hampe; East Germany) has won six titles: three single sculls, 1983, 1986 and 1988; three quadruple sculls, 1985, 1987 and 1989.

Single sculls Three oarsmen have won five single sculls titles: Peter-Michael Kolbe (West Germany), 1975, 1978, 1981, 1983 and 1986; Pertti Karppinen (Finland), 1976, 1979–80 and 1984–85; and Thomas Lange (Germany), 1988–92. Christine Hahn (née Scheiblich; East Germany) has won five women's titles, 1974–78.

Eights Since 1962, East German crews have won seven men's eights titles—1970, 1975–80. In women's competition the USSR has won seven titles—1978–79, 1981–83, 1985–86.

COLLEGIATE CHAMPIONSHIPS Harvard and Yale staged the first intercollegiate boat race in 1852. The Intercollegiate Rowing Association was formed in 1895, and in 1898 inaugurated the Varsity Challenge Cup, which was recognized as the national championship. In 1979 the United States Rowing Association introduced the women's National Collegiate Championship, which was extended to men's competition in 1982, supplanting the Varsity Cup as the men's national title.

Most wins (men) Cornell has won 24 titles: 1896–97 (includes two wins in 1897), 1901–03, 1905–07, 1909–12, 1915, 1930, 1955–58, 1962–63, 1971, 1977, and 1981. Since 1982, Harvard has won six titles, 1983, 1985, 1987–89, and 1992.

Most wins (women) Washington has won seven titles—1981–85, 1987–88.

Fastest speed The fastest recorded speed on nontidal water for 2,000 meters is by an American eight, in 5 minutes 27.14 seconds (13.68 mph) at Lucerne, Switzerland on June 17, 1984. A crew from Penn AC was timed in 5 minutes 18.8 seconds (14.03 mph) in the FISA Championships on the River Meuse, Liège, Belgium on August 17, 1930.

RUGBY

ORIGINS As with baseball in the United States, the origins of rugby are obscure—but a traditional "history" has become so embedded in the national psyche, in this case that of Great Britain, that any historical revision is either ignored or derided. The tradition is that the game began when William Webb Ellis picked up the ball during a soccer game at Rugby School in November 1823 and ran with it. Whether or not there is any truth to this legend, the "new" handling code of soccer developed, and the game was played at Cambridge University in 1839. The first rugby club was formed at Guy's Hospital, London, England in 1843, and the Rugby Football Union (RFU) was founded in January 1871. The International Rugby Football Board (IRFB) was founded in 1886.

OLYMPIC GAMES Rugby was played at four Games from 1900 to 1924. The only double gold medalist was the U.S., which won in 1920 and 1924.

WORLD CUP The World Cup is staged every four years and is the world championship for rugby.

24-HOUR ROWING ☛ THE GREATEST DISTANCE ROWED IN 24 HOURS (UPSTREAM AND DOWNSTREAM) IS 135.22 MILES, BY A COXED QUAD SCULL (PETER HALLIDAY, PAUL TURNBULL, MIKE SKERRY, BELINDA GOGLIA AND MARGARET MUNEKE) ON THE YARRA RIVER, MELBOURNE, AUSTRALIA ON JANUARY 26–27, 1992.

The first World Cup was hosted by Australia and New Zealand in 1987.

Most wins New Zealand won the first World Cup in 1987, and Australia won the second tournament in 1991.

WORLD CUP SCORING RECORDS

TEAM RECORDS

Most points (game) The most points in World Cup play is 74, scored by New Zealand against Fiji (13 points) at Christchurch, New Zealand on May 27, 1987.

Most points (game, aggregate score) The highest aggregate score in World Cup competition is 87 points, New Zealand defeating Fiji 74–13 (see above).

INDIVIDUAL RECORDS

Most points (game) Didier Camberabero (France) scored 30 points (three tries and nine conversions) *v.* Zimbabwe at Auckland, New Zealand on June 2, 1987.

Most points (tournament) Grant Fox (New Zealand) scored 126 points in 1987.

Most points (career) Grant Fox (New Zealand) scored 170 points in 1987 and 1991.

INTERNATIONAL RUGBY RECORDS

Highest score The highest score by a team in a full international game is 106 points, which has occurred twice: New Zealand 106, Japan 4, at Tokyo, Japan on November 1, 1987; France 106, Paraguay 12, at Asunción, Paraguay on June 28, 1988.

INDIVIDUAL RECORDS

Game

Most points Phil Bennett (Wales) scored 34 points (two tries, 10 conversions, two penalty goals) *v.* Japan at Tokyo on September 24, 1975.

Most tries Patrice Lagisquet (France) scored seven tries *v.* Paraguay at Asunción, Paraguay on June 28, 1988.

Most penalty goals Mark Wyatt (Canada) kicked eight penalty goals *v.* Scotland at St. John, New Brunswick on May 25, 1991.

Career

Most points Michael Lynagh (Australia) has scored a record 760 points in international rugby competition, 1984–92.

Most tries David Campese (Australia) is the leading try scorer in international competition with 52 tries, 1982–92.

Most internationals Serge Blanco (France) has played a record 93 international matches, 1980–91.

Consecutive internationals Two players played in 53 consecutive games: Gareth Edwards (Wales), 1967–78; Willie John McBride (Ireland), 1962–75.

SHOOTING

The National Rifle Association recognizes four categories of shooting competition: conventional, international, silhouette, and action pistol. This section reports records only for international style shooting—the shooting discipline used at the Olympic Games.

ORIGINS The earliest recorded shooting club is the Lucerne Shooting Guild (Switzerland), formed *c.* 1466. The first known shooting competition was held at Zurich, Switzerland in 1472. The international governing body, the *Union International de Tir* (UIT), was formed in Zurich in 1907.

United States The National Rifle Association (NRA) was founded in 1871, and is designated as the national governing body for shooting sports in the United States by the U.S. Olympic Committee.

TIMEOUT

HIGHEST GOALPOSTS ☛ THE WORLD'S HIGHEST GOALPOSTS ARE 110 FEET ½ INCH HIGH. THEY STAND AT THE ROAN ANTELOPE RUGBY UNION CLUB, LUANSHYA, ZAMBIA.

SHOOTING—INDIVIDUAL WORLD RECORDS

In 1986 the International Shooting Union introduced new regulations for determining major championships and world records. Now the leading competitors undertake an additional round with a target subdivided to tenths of a point for rifle and pistol shooting and an extra 25 shots for trap and skeet. The table below shows the world records for the 13 Olympic shooting disciplines, giving in parentheses the score for the number of shots specified plus the score in the additional round.

Men

Event	Points	Marksman (Country)	Date
Free rifle 50 m 3 x 40 shots	1,287.9 (1,186 + 101.9)	Rajmond Debevec (Slovenia)	August 29, 1992
Free rifle 50 m 60 shots prone	703.5 (599 + 104.5)	Jens Harskov (Denmark)	June 6, 1991
Air rifle 10 m 60 shots	699.4 (596 + 103.4)	Rajmond Debevec (Yugoslavia)	June 7, 1990
Free pistol 50 m 60 shots	671 (579 + 92)	Sergey Pyzhyanov (USSR)	May 30, 1990
	671 (577 + 94)	Spas Koprinkov (Bulgaria)	August 9, 1991
Rapid-fire pistol 25 m 60 shots	891 (594 +297)	Ralf Schumann (East Germany)	June 3, 1989
Air pistol 10 m 60 shots	695.1 (593 + 102.1)	Sergey Pyzhyanov (USSR)	October 3, 1989
Running target 10 m 30 + 30 shots	679 (582 + 97)	Lubos Racansky (Czechoslovakia)	May 30, 1991

Women

Event	Points	Markswoman (Country)	Date
Standard rifle 50 m 3 x 20 shots	689.3 (590 + 99.3)	Vessela Letcheva (Bulgaria)	August 28, 1992
Air rifle 10 m 40 shots	500.8 (399 + 101.8)	Valentina Cherkasova (USSR)	March 23, 1991
Sport pistol 25 m 60 shots	693 (593 + 100)	Nino Salukvadse (USSR)	July 13, 1989
Air pistol 10 m 40 shots	492.4 (392 + 100.4)	Lieselotte Breker (West Germany)	May 18, 1989

Open

Event	Points	Marksman (Country)	Date
Trap 200 targets	224 (200 + 24)	Jorg Damme (West Germany)	August 18, 1990
	224 (199 + 25)	Giovanni Pellielo (Italy)	August 30, 1992
Skeet 200 targets	225 (200 + 25)	Axel Wegner (Germany)	August 31, 1991
	225 (200 + 25)	Hennie Dompeling (Netherlands)	August 31, 1991

The first world record by a woman at any sport for a category in direct and measurable competition with men was by Margaret Murdock (née Thompson; U.S.), who set a world record for smallbore rifle (kneeling position) of 391 in 1967.

INTERNATIONAL STYLE SHOOTING

International or Olympic-style shooting is comprised of four disciplines: rifle, pistol, running target, and shotgun. Running target events are limited to male competitors. The targets for rifle, pistol, and running deer events are the same, but in running deer the target is moving. Shotgun shooting (also known as trap and skeet) requires the competitor to hit clay targets released from a skeet.

OLYMPIC GAMES Shooting has been part of the Olympic program since the first modern Games in 1896. Women were allowed to compete against men at the 1968 Games, and separate women's events were included in 1984.

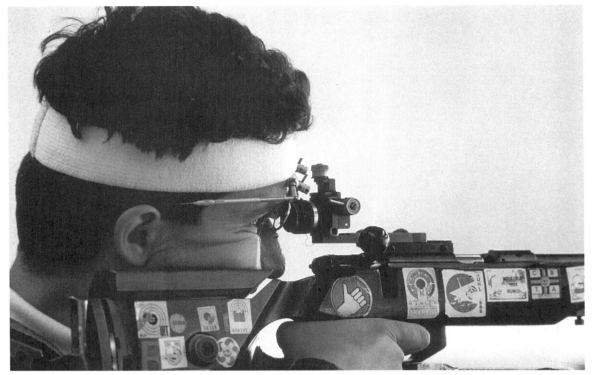

ON TARGET ■ RAJMOND DEBEVEC HOLDS THE WORLD RECORD FOR FREE RIFLE SHOOTING.

Most gold medals Seven marksmen have won five gold medals: Konrad Staheli (Switzerland), 1900–1906; Louis Richardet (Switzerland), 1900–06; Alfred Lane (U.S.), 1912–20; Carl Osburn (U.S.), 1912–24; Ole Lilloe-Olsen (Norway), 1920–24; Morris Fisher (U.S.), 1920–24; and Willis Lee (U.S.), 1920. Marina Logvinenko (Unified Team) is the only woman to win two gold medals: sport pistol and air pistol, both in 1992.

Most medals Carl Osburn (U.S.) has won 11 medals: five gold, four silver and two bronze. Four women have won two medals: Wu Xiaoxuan (China), one gold, one bronze in 1984; Nino Saloukvadze (USSR), one gold, one silver in 1988; Silvia Sperber (West Germany), one gold, one silver in 1988; Marina Logvinenko (Unified Team), two golds in 1992.

NCAA CHAMPIONSHIPS A combined NCAA rifle championship was inaugurated in 1980, and the contest is now held annually.

Most titles (team) West Virginia has won eight NCAA team titles, 1983–84, 1986, and 1988–92.

Most titles (individual) Seven competitors have won two individual titles: Rod Fitz-Randolph, Tennessee Tech, smallbore and air rifle, 1980; Kurt Fitz-Randolph, Tennessee Tech, smallbore, 1981–82; John Rost, West Virginia, air rifle, 1981–82; Pat Spurgin, Murray State, air rifle, 1984, smallbore, 1985; Web Wright, West Virginia, smallbore, 1987–88; Michelle Scarborough, South Florida, air rifle, 1989, smallbore, 1990; Ann-Marie Pfiffner, West Virginia, air rifle, 1991–92.

SKIING

ORIGINS Skiing traces its history to Scandinavia; *ski* is the Norwegian word for snowshoe. A ski discovered in a peat bog in Hoting, Sweden dates to c. 2500 B.C., and records note the use of skis at the Battle of Isen, Norway in A.D. 1200. The first ski races were held in Norway and Australia in the 1850s and 1860s. Two men stand out as pioneers of the development of skiing in the 19th century: Sondre Nordheim, a Norwegian, who designed equipment and developed skiing techniques; and Mathias Zdarsky, an Austrian, who pioneered Alpine skiing. The first national governing body was that of Norway, formed in 1833. The International Ski Commission was founded in 1910 and was succeeded as the world governing body in 1924 by the International Ski Federation (FIS).

United States The first ski club in the United States was formed at Berlin, N.H. in January 1872. The United States Ski Association was originally founded as the National Ski Association in 1905; in 1962, it was renamed the United States Ski Association, and in 1990 it was renamed U.S. Skiing.

In the modern era, skiing has evolved into two main categories, Alpine and Nordic. Alpine skiing encompasses downhill and slalom racing. Nordic skiing covers ski jumping events and cross-country racing.

ALPINE SKIING

OLYMPIC GAMES Downhill and slalom events were first included at the 1936 Olympic Games.

Most gold medals In men's competition, the most gold medals won is three, by three skiers: Anton Sailer (Austria), who won all three events, downhill, slalom and giant slalom, in 1956; Jean-Claude Killy (France), who matched Sailer's feat in 1968; and Alberto Tomba (Italy), who won the slalom and giant slalom in 1988 and the giant slalom in 1992. For women the record is two golds, achieved by seven skiers: Andrea Mead-Lawrence (U.S.), slalom, giant slalom, 1952; Marielle Goitschel (France), giant slalom 1964, slalom, 1968; Marie-Therese Nadig (Switzerland), downhill, giant slalom, 1972; Rosi Mittermaier (West Germany), downhill, slalom, 1976; Hanni Wenzel (Liechtenstein), giant slalom, slalom, 1980; Vareni Schneider (Switzerland), giant slalom, slalom, 1988; and Petra Kronberger (Austria), giant slalom and combined, 1992.

Most medals Hanni Wenzel (Liechtenstein) has won four Olympic medals: two gold, one silver and one bronze, 1976–80. The most medals won by a male skier is also four, by Alberto Tomba (Italy)—three golds and one silver, 1988–92.

SUPER SWISS ■ FOUR OVERALL WORLD CUP TITLES AND FOUR SUPER G TITLES MAKE PIRMIN ZURBRIGGEN THE MOST SUCCESSFUL SKIER IN HISTORY.

WORLD CHAMPIONSHIPS This competition was inaugurated in 1931 at Murren, Switzerland. From 1931–39 the championships were held annually; from 1950 they were held biennially. Up to 1980, the Olympic Games were considered the world championships, except in 1936. In 1985, the cham-

FASTEST SKIER ☛ THE OFFICIAL WORLD RECORD FOR A SKIER IS 142.165 MPH, BY MICHAËL PRÜFER (FRANCE), SET AT LES ARCS, FRANCE ON FEBRUARY 22, 1992.

THE BOMBA ■ IN 1992 ALBERTO TOMBA WON TWO OLYMPIC MEDALS, RAISING HIS CAREER TALLY TO FOUR, THE MOST OF ANY ALPINE SKIER.

pionship schedule was changed so as not to coincide with an Olympic year.

Most gold medals Christel Cranz (Germany) won a record 12 titles: four slalom, 1934, 1937–39; three downhill, 1935, 1937, 1939; five combined, 1934–35, 1937–39. Anton Sailer (Austria) holds the men's record with seven titles: one slalom, 1956; two giant slalom, 1956, 1958; two downhill, 1956, 1958; two combined, 1956, 1958.

WORLD CUP Contested annually since 1967, the World Cup is a circuit of races where points are earned during the season, with the champion being the skier with the most points at the end of the season.

INDIVIDUAL RACING RECORDS

Most wins (men) Ingemar Stenmark (Sweden) won a record 86 races (46 giant slalom, 40 slalom) from 287 contested, 1974–89.

Most wins (women) Annemarie Moser-Pröll (Austria) won a record 62 races, 1970–79.

Most wins (season) Ingemar Stenmark (Sweden) won 13 races in 1978–79 to set the men's mark. Vreni Schneider (Switzerland) won 13 races in 1988–89 to set the women's mark.

LONGEST SKI LIFT ☛ THE LONGEST GONDOLA SKI LIFT IS 3.88 MILES LONG AT GRINDELWALD-MÄNNLICHEN, SWITZERLAND. THE HIGHEST SKI LIFT IS LOCATED AT CHACALTAYA, BOLIVIA, AND RISES TO 16,500 FEET.

Consecutive wins Ingemar Stenmark (Sweden) won 14 successive giant slalom races from March 18, 1978 to January 21, 1980. The women's record is 11 wins by Annemarie Moser-Pröll (Austria) in the downhill from December 1972 to January 1974.

UNITED STATES NATIONAL CHAMPIONSHIPS

Most titles Tamara McKinney won seven slalom titles, 1982–84, 1986–89—the most by any skier in one discipline. Phil Mahre won five giant slalom titles, 1975, 1977–79, 1981—the most by a male skier in one event.

NCAA CHAMPIONSHIPS The NCAA skiing championship was introduced in 1954. Teams compete in both Alpine and cross-country events, with cumulative point totals determining the national champion. Teams are comprised of both men and women.

Most titles (team) Denver has won 14 titles, 1954–57, 1961–67, and 1969–71.

Most titles (individual) Chiharu Igaya of Dartmouth won a record six NCAA titles: Alpine, 1955–56; downhill, 1955; slalom, 1955–57.

NORDIC SKIING

CROSS-COUNTRY SKIING

OLYMPIC GAMES Cross-country racing has been included in every Winter Olympic Games.

Most gold medals In men's competition, three skiers have each won four gold medals: Sixten Jernberg (Sweden), 50 km, 1956; 30 km, 1960; 50 km and 4 x 10 km relay, 1964; Gunde Svan (Sweden), 15 km and 4 x 10 km relay, 1984; 50 km and 4 x 10 km relay, 1988; Thomas Wassberg (Sweden), 15 km, 1980; 50 km and 4 x 10 km relay, 1984; 4 x 10 km relay, 1988. The women's record is also four golds, won by two skiers: Galina Kulakova (USSR), 5 km, 10 km and 3 x 5 km relay, 1972; 4 x 5 km relay, 1976; Raisa Smetanina (USSR/Unified Team), 10 km and 4 x 5 km relay, 1976; 5 km, 1980; 4 x 5 km, 1992.

Most medals The most medals won in Nordic events is 10, by Raisa Smetanina (four gold, five silver and one bronze, 1976–92). Sixten Jernberg (Sweden) holds the men's record with nine (four gold, three silver, two bronze, 1956–64).

WORLD CUP A season series of World Cup races was instituted in 1981.

GATEMAN ■ PHIL MAHRE HAS WON A RECORD FIVE U.S. GIANT SLALOM TITLES.

NORDIC ACCELERATION ■ THE FASTEST AVERAGE SPEED ATTAINED BY A NORDIC SKIER IS 15.57 MPH, BY BILL KOCH IN MARCH 1981.

Most titles Gunde Svan (Sweden) has won five overall cross-country skiing titles, 1984–86 and 1988–89. Two women have won three overall ti-

tles: Marjo Matikainen (Finland), 1986–88; Yelena Vialbe (USSR/Russia), 1989, 1991–92.

UNITED STATES NATIONAL CHAMPIONSHIPS

Most titles Martha Rockwell has won a record 14 national titles, 1969–75. The record in men's competition is 12, by Audun Endestad, 1984–90.

SKI JUMPING

OLYMPIC GAMES Ski jumping has been included in every Winter Games.

Most gold medals Matti Nykanen (Finland) has won four gold medals: 70-meter hill, 1988; 90-meter hill, 1984 and 1988; 90-meter team, 1988.

Most medals Matti Nykanen has won five medals in Olympic competition: four gold (see above) and one silver, 70-meter hill, 1984.

WORLD CUP A season series of ski jumping events was instituted in 1981.

Most titles Matti Nykanen (Finland) has won four World Cup titles, 1983, 1985–86 and 1988.

UNITED STATES NATIONAL CHAMPIONSHIPS

Most titles Lars Haugen has won seven ski jumping titles, 1912–28.

SLED DOG RACING

ORIGINS Racing between harnessed dog teams (usually huskies) is believed to have been practiced by Inuits in North America, and also by the peoples of Scandinavia, long before the first recorded formal race, the All-America Sweepstakes, which took place in 1908. Sled dog racing

TIMEOUT

FASTEST SNOWSHOER ☛ JEREMY BADEAU (U.S.) SNOWSHOED 100 METERS IN 14.07 SECONDS AT CANASERAGA, N.Y. ON MAY 31, 1991.

FASTEST SLED ■ MARTIN BUSER WON THE 1992 IDITAROD IN A RECORD TIME OF 10 DAYS, 19 HOURS, 36 MINUTES, 17 SECONDS.

was a demonstration sport at the 1932 Olympic Games. The best known race is the Iditarod Trail Sled Dog Race, first run in 1973.

IDITAROD TRAIL SLED DOG RACE

The annual race from Anchorage to Nome, Alaska commemorates the 1925 midwinter emergency mission to get medical supplies to Nome during a diphtheria epidemic. Raced over alternate courses, the northern and southern trails, the Iditarod was first run in 1973.

IDITAROD WINNERS

Year	Musher	Elapsed Time
1973	Dick Wilmarth	20 days, 00:49:41
1974	Carl Huntington	20 days, 15:02:07
1975	Emmitt Peters	14 days, 14:43:45
1976	Gerald Riley	18 days, 22:58:17
1977	Rick Swenson	16 days, 16:27:13
1978	Rick Mackey	14 days, 18:52:24
1979	Rick Swenson	15 days, 10:37:47
1980	Joe May	14 days, 07:11:51
1981	Rick Swenson	12 days, 08:45:02
1982	Rick Swenson	16 days, 04:40:10
1983	Rick Mackey	12 days, 14:10:44
1984	Dean Osmar	12 days, 15:07:33
1985	Libby Riddles	18 days, 00:20:17
1986	Susan Butcher	11 days, 15:06:00
1987	Susan Butcher	11 days, 02:05:13
1988	Susan Butcher	11 days, 11:41:40
1989	Joe Runyan	11 days, 05:24:34
1990	Susan Butcher	11 days, 01:53:23
1991	Rick Swenson	12 days, 16:34:39
1992	Martin Buser	10 days, 19:36:17

Most wins Rick Swenson has won the event five times: 1977, 1979, 1981–82, 1991.

Record time The fastest recorded time is 10 days, 19 hours, 36 minutes, 17 seconds, by Martin Buser (Switzerland) in 1992.

SNOOKER

ORIGINS Neville Chamberlain, a British army officer, is credited with inventing the game in Jubbulpore, India in 1875. Snooker is a hybrid of pool and pyramids. Chamberlain added a set of colored balls to the 15 red ones used in pyramids and devised a scoring system based on pocketing the balls in sequence: red, color, red, color until all the reds have been cleared, leaving the colored balls to be pocketed in numerical order. The modern scoring system (a red ball is worth one point, yellow—2, green—3, brown—4, blue—5, pink—6 and black—7) was adopted in England in 1891. The sequence of pocketing the balls is called a break, the maximum possible being 147. The name *snooker* comes from the term coined for new recruits at the Woolwich Military Academy and was Chamberlain's label for anyone who lost at his game.

WORLD PROFESSIONAL CHAMPIONSHIPS This competition was first organized in 1927.

Most titles Joe Davis (England) won the title on the first 15 occasions it was contested, and this still stands as the all-time record for victories.

Maximum break The only 147 "maximum break" in world championship competition was compiled by Cliff Thorburn (Canada) on April 23, 1983.

SOARING

ORIGINS Research by Isadore William Deiches has shown evidence of the use of gliders in ancient Egypt *c.* 2500–1500 B.C. Emanuel Swedenborg of Sweden made sketches of gliders *c.* 1714. The earliest human-carrying glider was designed by Sir George Cayley and carried his coachman (possibly John Appleby) about 500 yards across a valley in Brompton Dale, North Yorkshire, England in the summer of 1853.

WORLD CHAMPIONSHIPS World championships were instituted in 1937.

Most individual titles The most individual titles won is four, by Ingo Renner (Australia) in 1976 (Standard class), 1983, 1985 and 1987 (Open).

Height gain 42,303 feet, Paul Bikle (U.S.), Mojave, Calif., February 25, 1961. The women's record is 33,506 feet, by Yvonne Loader (New Zealand) at Omarama, New Zealand on January 12, 1988.

SPEED OVER TRIANGULAR COURSE

100 km 121.35 mph, Ingo Renner (Australia), December 14, 1982.

300 km 105.32 mph, Jean-Paul Castel (France), November 15, 1986.

500 km 105.67 mph, Beat Bunzli (Switzerland), January 9, 1988.

750 km 98.43 mph, Hans-Werner Grosse (Germany), January 8, 1985.

1,000 km 90.32 mph, Hans-Werner Grosse (Germany), January 3, 1979.

1,250 km 82.79 mph, Hans-Werner Grosse (Germany), January 9, 1980.

United States The most titles won by an American pilot is two, by George Moffat, in the Open category, 1970 and 1974.

SOARING WORLD RECORDS (SINGLE-SEATERS)

DISTANCE AND HEIGHT

Straight distance 907.7 miles, Hans-Werner Grosse (Germany), Lubeck, Germany to Biarritz, France, April 25, 1972.

Declared goal distance 779.4 miles, by three pilots: Bruce Drake, David Speight and Dick Georgeson (all New Zealand), who each flew from Te Anau to Te Araroa, New Zealand, January 14, 1978.

Goal and return 1,023.2 miles, Tom Knauff (U.S.), Williamsport, Pa. to Knoxville, Tenn., April 25, 1983.

Absolute altitude 49,009 feet, Robert R. Harris (U.S.), over California, February 17, 1986. The women's record is 41,449 feet, by Sabrina Jackintell (U.S.) on February 14, 1979.

SOCCER

ORIGINS A game called *tsu chu* ("to kick a ball of stuffed leather") was played in China more than 2,500 years ago. However, the ancestry of the modern game is traced to England. In 1314, King Edward II prohibited the game because of excessive noise. Three subsequent monarchs also banned the game. Nevertheless, "football," the name by which soccer is known outside the United States, continued its development in England. In 1848, the first rules were drawn up at Cambridge University; in 1863, the Football Association (FA) was founded in England. The sport grew in popularity worldwide, and the *Fédération Internationale de Football Association* (FIFA), the world governing body, was formed in Paris, France in 1904. FIFA currently has more than 160 members.

WORLD CUP

The first World Cup for the Jules Rimet Trophy was held in Uruguay in 1930, and the contest has been staged quadrennially since, with a break from 1939–49 because of World War II. In 1970, Brazil won its third World Cup and was awarded permanent possession of the Jules Rimet Trophy. Countries now compete for the FIFA World Cup.

WORLD CUP FINALS (1930–1990)

Year	Winner	Loser	Score	Year	Winner	Loser	Score
1930	Uruguay	Argentina	4–2	1966	England	West Germany	4–2
1934	Italy	Czechoslovakia	2–1	1970	Brazil	Italy	4–1
1938	Italy	Hungary	4–2	1974	West Germany	Netherlands	2–1
1950	Uruguay	Brazil	2–1	1978	Argentina	Netherlands	3–1
1954	West Germany	Hungary	3–2	1982	Italy	West Germany	3–1
1958	Brazil	Sweden	5–2	1986	Argentina	West Germany	3–2
1962	Brazil	Czechoslovakia	3–1	1990	West Germany	Argentina	1–0

TEAM RECORDS

Most wins Three countries have won the World Cup on three occasions: Brazil (1958, 1962, 1970); Italy (1934, 1938, 1982); West Germany (1954, 1974, 1990).

Most appearances Brazil is the only country to qualify for all 14 World Cup tournaments.

Most goals The highest score by one team in a game is 10, by Hungary in a 10–1 defeat of El Salvador at Elche, Spain on June 15, 1982. The most goals in tournament history is 148 (from 66 games) by Brazil.

Highest-scoring game The highest-scoring game took place on June 26, 1954 when Austria defeated Switzerland 7–5.

INDIVIDUAL RECORDS

CHAMPIONSHIP GAME

Most wins Pelé (Brazil) is the only player to have played on three winning teams. Mario Zagalo (Brazil) was the first man to both play for (in 1958 and 1962) and be manager of (in 1970) a World Cup winning team. Franz Beckenbauer emulated Zagalo when he managed the West German team to victory in 1990. He had previously captained the 1974 winning team. Beckenbauer is the only man to have both captained and managed a winning side.

Most goals The most goals scored in a final is three, by Geoff Hurst for England *v*. West Germany on July 30, 1966.

FINALS TOURNAMENT

Most games played Two players have appeared in 21 games in the finals tournament: Uwe Seeler (West Germany, 1958–70); Wladyslaw Zmuda (Poland, 1974–86).

Most goals scored The most goals scored by a player in a game is four; this has occurred nine times. The most goals scored in one tournament is 13, by Just Fontaine (France) in 1958, in six games. The most goals scored in a career is 14, by Gerd Muller (West Germany), 10 goals in 1970 and four in 1974.

OLYMPIC GAMES There is some dispute among Olympic historians as to whether soccer became an official Olympic sport in 1900 or in 1908. Since most Olympic histories do include the results from 1900, those results are included in the statistics in this section.

BALL CONTROL ☛ HUH NAM JIN (SOUTH KOREA) JUGGLED A REGULATION SOCCER BALL FOR 17 HOURS 10 MINUTES 57 SECONDS NONSTOP, WITHOUT THE BALL EVER TOUCHING THE GROUND, ON MAY 24, 1991. JAN SKORKOVSKY (CZECHOSLOVAKIA) KEPT A SOCCER BALL ALOFT WHILE RUNNING THE PRAGUE MARATHON IN A TIME OF 7 HOURS 18 MINUTES 55 SECONDS ON JULY 8, 1990.

Most gold medals Two countries have won three Olympic titles: Great Britain, 1900, 1908 and 1912; Hungary, 1952, 1964 and 1968.

NCAA DIVISION I CHAMPIONSHIPS The NCAA Division I men's championship was first staged in 1959. A women's tournament was introduced in 1982.

Most titles (men) The University of St. Louis has won the most Division I titles with 10 victories, which includes one tie: 1959–60, 1962–63, 1965, 1967, 1969–70, 1972–73.

Most titles (women) The University of North Carolina has won a record 10 Division I titles. Its victories came in 1982–84 and 1986–92.

SOFTBALL

ORIGINS Softball, a derivative of baseball, was invented by George Hancock at the Farragut Boat Club, Chicago, Ill. in 1887. Rules were first codified in Minneapolis, Minn. in 1895 under the name kitten ball. The name softball was introduced by Walter Hakanson at a meeting of the National Recreation Congress in 1926. The name was adopted throughout the United States in 1930. Rules were formalized in 1933 by the International Joint Rules Committee for Softball and adopted by the Amateur Softball Association of America. The International Softball Federation was formed in 1950 as governing body for both fast pitch and slow pitch.

FAST PITCH SOFTBALL

WORLD CHAMPIONSHIPS A women's fast pitch world championship was first staged in 1965, and a men's tournament in 1966. Both tournaments are held quadrennially.

Most titles (men) The United States has won five world titles: 1966, 1968, 1976 (tied), 1980 and 1988.

Most titles (women) The United States has won four world titles: 1974, 1978, 1986, and 1990.

AMATEUR SOFTBALL ASSOCIATION NATIONAL CHAMPIONSHIP The first ASA national championship was staged in 1933 for both men's and women's teams.

Most titles (men) The Clearwater Bombers (Florida) won 10 championships between 1950 and 1973.

Most titles (women) The Raybestos Brakettes (Stratford, Conn.) have won 23 women's fast pitch titles from 1958 through 1992.

NCAA CHAMPIONSHIPS The first NCAA Division I women's championship was staged in 1982.

Most titles UCLA has won seven titles: 1982, 1984–85, 1988–90, and 1992.

SLOW PITCH SOFTBALL

WORLD CHAMPIONSHIPS A slow pitch world championship was staged for men's teams in 1987. The United States team won this event. So far a second tournament has not been scheduled. No world championship has been staged for women's teams.

AMATEUR SOFTBALL ASSOCIATION NATIONAL CHAMPIONSHIP The first men's ASA national championship was staged in 1953. The first women's event was staged in 1962.

Most titles (men—major slow pitch) Two teams have won three major slow pitch championships: Skip Hogan A.C. (Pittsburgh, Pa.), 1962, 1964–65; Joe Gatliff Auto Sales (Newport, Ky.), 1956–57, 1963.

Most titles (men—super slow pitch) Two teams have won three super slow pitch titles: Howard's Western Steer (Denver, Colo.), 1981, 1983–84; Steele's Silver Bullets (Grafton, Ohio), 1985–87.

Most titles (women) The Dots of Miami (Fla.) have won five major slow pitch titles, 1969, 1974–75, 1978–79.

SPEED SKATING

ORIGINS The world's longest skating race, the 124-mile "Elfstedentocht" ("Tour of the Eleven Towns"), is said to commemorate a similar race staged in the Netherlands in the 17th century. The first recorded skating race was staged in 1763, from Wisbech to Whittlesey, England. The International Skating Union (ISU) was founded at Scheveningen, Netherlands in 1892 and is the governing body for both speed skating and figure skating.

OLYMPIC GAMES Men's speed skating events have been included in the Olympic Games since 1924. Women's events were first staged in 1960.

Most gold medals Lidiya Skoblikova (USSR) has won six gold medals: 500-meter, 1964; 1,000-meter, 1964; 1,500-meter, 1960, 1964; 3,000-meter, 1960, 1964. The men's record is five, shared by two skaters: Clas Thunberg (Finland), 500-meter, 1928; 1,500-

ICE QUEEN ■ HER TWO GOLDS IN ALBERTVILLE RAISED BONNIE BLAIR'S CAREER TOTAL TO THREE, THE MOST FOR ANY U.S. WOMAN.

SPEED SKATING WORLD RECORDS

Men

Event	Time	Skater (Country)	Date
500 meters	36.41	Dan Jansen (U.S.)	January 25, 1992
1,000 meters	1:12.58	Pavel Pagov (USSR)	March 25, 1987
		Igor Zhelezovski (USSR)	February 25, 1989
1,500 meters	1:52.06	Andre Hoffman (East Germany)	February 20, 1988
5,000 meters	6:41.73	Johann Olav Koss (Norway)	February 9, 1991
10,000 meters	13:43.54	Johann Olav Koss (Norway)	February 10, 1991

Women

Event	Time	Skater (Country)	Date
500 meters	39.10	Bonnie Blair (U.S.)	February 22, 1988
1,000 meters	1:17.65	Christa Rothenburger (East Germany)	February 26, 1988
1,500 meters	1:59.30	Karin Kania (East Germany)	March 22, 1986
3,000 meters	4:10.89	Gunda Kleeman (Germany)	December 9, 1990
5,000 meters	7:14.13	Yvonne van Gennip (Netherlands)	February 28, 1988

Source: United States International Speedskating Association

meter, 1924, 1928; 5,000-meter, 1924; all-around title, 1924; and Eric Heiden (U.S.), 500-meter, 1,000-meter, 1,500-meter, 5,000-meter, and 10,000-meter, all in 1980.

WORLD CHAMPIONSHIPS Speed skating world championships were first staged in 1893.

Most titles Oscar Mathisen (Norway) and Clas Thunberg (Finland) have won a record five overall world titles. Mathisen won titles in 1908–09 and 1912–14; Thunberg won in 1923, 1925, 1928–29 and 1931. Karin Enke-Kania (East Germany) holds the women's mark, also at five. She won in 1982, 1984 and 1986–88.

UNITED STATES Eric Heiden won three overall world titles, 1977–79, the most by any U.S. skater. His sister Beth became the only American woman to win an overall championship in 1979.

SHORT TRACK SPEED SKATING

ORIGINS An indoor version of the more familiar outdoor speed skating races, short track speed skating was developed in North America in the 1960s. Besides being held indoors and on a shorter circuit, short track racing also differs from the longer version in that there are usually a pack of four skaters in a race, and a certain amount of bumping between the competitors as allowed. World championships were first staged unofficially in 1978, and the sport gained offical Olympic status at the 1992 Games.

Olympic Games Short track speed skating was included as a demonstration sport at the 1988 Calgary Games, and gained official status at the 1992 Games in Albertville.

ON TRACK ■ SHORT-TRACK SPEED SKATING BECAME AN OFFICIAL WINTER GAMES SPORT IN 1992.

Most gold medals Kim Ki-hoon (South Korea) won two gold medals at the 1992 Games: 1,000 meters and 5,000 meter relay.

SQUASH

ORIGINS Squash is an offshoot of rackets and is believed to have been first played at Harrow School, London, England in 1817. The International Squash Rackets Federation (ISRF) was founded in 1967. The Women's International Squash Rackets Federation was formed in 1976.

United States The U.S. Squash Racquets Association was formed in 1907, and staged the first U.S. amateur championships that year.

WORLD OPEN CHAMPIONSHIPS Both the men's and women's events were first held in 1976. The men's competition is an annual event, but the women's tournament was biennial until 1989, when it switched to the same system as the men's event. There was no championship in 1978.

Most titles Jahangir Khan (Pakistan) has won six titles, 1981–85 and 1988. Susan Devoy (New Zealand) holds the mark in the women's event with four victories, 1985, 1987, 1990 and 1991.

UNITED STATES AMATEUR CHAMPIONSHIPS The U.S. Amateur Championships were first held for men in 1907, and for women in 1928.

Most titles G. Diehl Mateer won 11 men's doubles titles between 1949 and 1966 with five different partners. Joyce Davenport won eight women's

AGAINST THE WALL ■ SUSAN DEVOY HAS WON FOUR WOMEN'S WORLD SQUASH TITLES.

doubles titles between 1969 and 1990 with two different partners.

Most titles (singles) Alicia McConnell has won seven women's singles titles, 1982–88. Stanley Pearson won a record six men's titles, 1915–17, 1921–23.

SURFING

ORIGINS The Polynesian sport of surfing in a canoe (*ehorooe*) was first recorded by the British explorer Captain James Cook in December 1771 during his exploration of Tahiti. The modern sport developed in Hawaii, California and Australia in the mid-1950s. Although Hawaii is one of the 50 states, it is allowed to compete separately from the U.S. in international surfing competition.

WORLD AMATEUR CHAMPIONSHIPS First held in May 1964 in Sydney, Australia, the open champi-onship is the most prestigious event in both men's and women's competition.

Most titles In the women's division the title has been won twice by two surfers: Joyce Hoffman (U.S.), 1965–66; and Sharon Weber (Hawaii), 1970 and 1972. The men's title has been won by different surfers on each occasion.

WORLD PROFESSIONAL CHAMPIONSHIPS First held in 1970, the World Championship has been organized by the Association of Surfing Professionals (ASP) since 1976. The World Championship is a circuit of events held throughout the year; the winning surfer is the one who gains the most points over the course of the year.

Most titles The most titles won by a professional surfer is five, by Mark Richards (Australia), 1975, 1979–82. The women's record is four, by two surfers: Frieda Zamba (U.S.), 1984–86, 1988; Wendy Botha (Australia), 1987, 1989, 1991–92.

SWIMMING

ORIGINS The earliest references to swimming races were in Japan in 36 B.C. The first national

ENDURANCE ■ KIEREN PERKINS SET WORLD REC-ORDS IN THE 800 AND 1,500 METERS DURING 1992.

SWIMMING—MEN'S WORLD RECORDS (set in 50-meter pools)

Freestyle

Event	Time	Swimmer (Country)	Date
50 meters	21.81	Tom Jager (U.S.)	March 24, 1990
100 meters	48.42	Matt Biondi (U.S.)	August 10, 1988
200 meters	1:46.69	Giorgio Lamberti (Italy)	August 15, 1989
400 meters	3:45.00	Yevgeni Sadovyi (Unified Team)	July 29, 1992
800 meters	7:46.60	Kieren Perkins (Australia)	February 14, 1992
1,500 meters	14:43.48	Kieren Perkins (Australia)	July 31, 1992
4 x 100-meter relay	3:16.53	U.S. (Chris Jacobs, Troy Dalbey, Tom Jager, Matt Biondi)	September 25, 1988
4 x 200-meter relay	7:11.95	Unified Team (Dmitri Lepikov, Vladimir Pychenko, Veniamin Taianovitch, Yevgeni Sadovyi)	July 27, 1992

Breaststroke

Event	Time	Swimmer (Country)	Date
100 meters	1:01.29	Norbert Kosza (Hungary)	August 20, 1991
200 meters	2:10.16	Michael Barrowman (U.S.)	July 29, 1992

Butterfly

Event	Time	Swimmer (Country)	Date
100 meters	52.84	Pablo Morales (U.S.)	June 23, 1986
200 meters	1:55.69	Melvin Stewart (U.S.)	January 12, 1991

Backstroke

Event	Time	Swimmer (Country)	Date
100 meters	53.86	Jeff Rouse (U.S.)	July 31, 1992
200 meters	1:56.57	Martin Zubero (Spain)	November 23, 1991

Individual Medley

Event	Time	Swimmer (Country)	Date
200 meters	1:59.36	Tamás Darnyi (Hungary)	January 13, 1991
400 meters	4:12.36	Tamás Darnyi (Hungary)	January 8, 1991
4 x 100-meter relay	3:36.93	U.S. (David Berkoff, Rich Schroeder, Matt Biondi, Chris Jacobs)	September 23, 1988
	3.36.93	U.S. (Jeff Rouse, Nelson Diebel, Pablo Morales, Jon Olsen)	July 31, 1992

swimming association, the Metropolitan Swimming Clubs Association, was founded in England in 1791. The international governing body for swimming, diving and water polo—the *Fédération Internationale de Natation Amateur* (FINA)—was founded in 1908.

OLYMPIC GAMES Swimming events were included in the first modern Games in 1896 and have been included in every Games since.

Most gold medals The greatest number of Olympic gold medals won is nine, by Mark Spitz (U.S.): 100-meter and 200-meter freestyle, 1972; 100-meter and 200-meter butterfly, 1972; 4 x 100-meter freestyle, 1968 and 1972; 4 x 200-meter freestyle, 1968 and 1972; 4 x 100-meter medley, 1972. The record number of gold medals won by a woman is six, by Kristin Otto (East Germany) at Seoul, South Korea in 1988: 100-meter freestyle, backstroke and butterfly, 50-meter freestyle, 4 x 100-meter freestyle and 4 x 100- meter medley.

Most medals The most medals won by a swimmer is 11, by two competitors: Mark Spitz (U.S.): nine gold (see above), one silver and one bronze, 1968–72; and Matt Biondi (U.S.), eight gold, two

SWIMMING—WOMEN'S WORLD RECORDS (set in 50-meter pools)

Freestyle

Event	Time	Swimmer (Country)	Date
50 meters	24.98	Yang Wenyi (China)	April 11, 1988
100 meters	54.48	Jenny Thompson (U.S.)	March 1, 1992
200 meters	1:57.55	Heike Freidrich (East Germany)	June 18, 1986
400 meters	4:03.85	Janet Evans (U.S.)	September 22, 1988
800 meters	8:16.22	Janet Evans (U.S.)	August 20, 1989
1,500 meters	15:52.10	Janet Evans (U.S.)	March 26, 1988
4 x 100-meter relay	3:39.46	U.S. (Nicole Haislett, Dara Torres, Angel Martino, Jenny Thompson)	July 28, 1992
4 x 200-meter relay	7:55.47	East Germany (Manuella Stellmach, Astrid Strauss, Anke Möhring, Heike Freidrich)	August 18, 1987

Breaststroke

100 meters	1:07.91	Silke Hörner (East Germany)	August 21, 1987
200 meters	2:25.35	Anita Nall (U.S.)	March 2, 1992

Butterfly

100 meters	57.93	Mary T. Meagher (U.S.)	August 16, 1981
200 meters	2:05.97	Mary T. Meagher (U.S.)	August 13, 1981

Backstroke

100 meters	1:00.31	Kristina Egerszegi (Hungary)	August 20, 1991
200 meters	2:06.82	Kristina Egerszegi (Hungary)	August 26, 1991

Individual Medley

200 meters	2:11.65	Lin Li (China)	July 30, 1992
400 meters	4:36.10	Petra Schneider (East Germany)	August 1, 1982
4 x 100-meter relay	4:02.54	U.S. (Lea Loveless, Anita Nall, Crissy Ahmann-Leighton, Jenny Thompson)	July 30, 1992

Source: USA Swimming

silver and one bronze, 1984–92. The most medals won by a woman is eight, by three swimmers: Dawn Fraser (Australia), four gold, four silver, 1956–64; Kornelia Ender (East Germany), four gold, four silver, 1972–76; Shirley Babashoff (U.S.), two gold, six silver, 1972–76.

Most medals (one Games) The most medals won at one Games is seven, by two swimmers: Mark Spitz (U.S.), seven golds in 1972; and Matt Biondi (U.S.), five gold, one silver and one bronze in 1988. Kristin Otto (East Germany) won six gold medals at the 1988 Games, the most for a woman swimmer.

IN HER WAKE ■ WORLD RECORD HOLDER KRISTINA EGERSZEGI WON TWO GOLD MEDALS IN

WORLD CHAMPIONSHIPS The first world swimming championships were held in Belgrade, Yugoslavia in 1973. The championships have been held quadrennially since 1978.

Most gold medals Kornelia Ender (East Germany) won eight gold medals, 1973–75. Jim Montgomery (U.S.) won six gold medals, 1973–75, the most by a male swimmer.

Most medals Michael Gross (West Germany) has won 13 medals: five gold, five silver and three bronze, 1982–90. The most medals won by a female swimmer is 10, by Kornelia Ender, who won eight gold and two silver, 1973–75.

Most medals (one championship) Matt Biondi (U.S.) won seven medals—three gold, one silver and three bronze—in 1986 at Madrid, Spain.

UNITED STATES NATIONAL CHAMPIONSHIPS The first United States swimming championships were staged by the Amateur Athletic Union on August 25, 1888.

Most titles Tracy Caulkins has won a record 48 national swimming titles, 1977–84. The most titles for a male swimmer is 36, by Johnny Weissmuller, 1921–28.

Fastest swimmer In a 25-yard pool, Tom Jager (U.S.) achieved an average speed of 5.37 mph, swimming 50 yards in 19.05 seconds at Nashville, Tenn. on March 23, 1990. The women's fastest time is 4.48 mph, by Yang Wenyi (China) in her 50-meter world record (see World Records table).

MANHATTAN SWIM ☞ THE FASTEST SWIM AROUND MANHATTAN ISLAND IN NEW YORK CITY WAS 5 HOURS 53 MINUTES 57 SECONDS, BY KRIS RUTFORD (U.S.) ON AUGUST 29, 1992.

SYNCHRONIZED SWIMMING

In international competition, synchronized swimmers compete in two disciplines: solo and duet. In both disciplines the swimmers perform to music a series of moves that are judged for technical skills and musical interpretation. In solo events the swimmer has to be synchronized with the music; in duet events the swimmers have to be synchronized with each other as well as with the music.

ORIGINS Annette Kellerman and Kay Curtis are considered the pioneers of synchronized swimming in the United States. Kellerman's water ballet performances drew widespread attention throughout the U.S. at the beginning of the 20th century. Curtis was responsible for establishing synchronized swimming as part of the physical education program at the University of Wisconsin. In the 1940s, film star Esther Williams again drew attention to the sport, and in 1945 the Amateur Athletic Union recognized the sport. In 1973 the first world championship was staged, and in 1984 synchronized swimming was recognized as an official Olympic sport. The governing body for the sport in this country is United States Synchronized Swimming, formed in 1978.

OLYMPIC GAMES Synchronized swimming was first staged as an official sport at the 1984 Games.

Most gold medals Two swimmers have won two gold medals: Tracie Ruiz-Conforto (U.S.), solo and duet, 1984; Carolyn Waldo (Canada), solo and duet, 1988.

Most medals Two swimmers have won three medals: Tracie Ruiz-Conforto (U.S.), two gold and one silver, 1984–88; Carolyn Waldo (Canada), two gold and one silver, 1984–88.

WORLD CHAMPIONSHIPS The world championships were first held in 1973, and have been held quadrennially since 1978.

Most titles The solo title has been won by a different swimmer on each occasion.

Most titles (team) The United States has won four team titles, 1973, 1975, 1978 and 1991.

UNITED STATES NATIONAL CHAMPIONSHIPS The first national championships were staged in 1946, and the competition is now an annual event.

Most titles Gail Johnson has won 11 national titles: six solo (two indoors, four outdoors), 1972–

IN SYNCH ■ TWINS KAREN AND SARAH JOSEPHSON HAVE WON FIVE U.S. DUET TITLES.

75; and five duet (two indoors, three outdoors), 1972–74.

Most titles (duet) The team of Karen and Sarah Josephson has won five national duet titles, 1985–88, and 1990.

TABLE TENNIS

ORIGINS The earliest evidence relating to a game resembling table tennis has been found in the catalogs of London sporting goods manufacturers in the 1880s. The International Table Tennis Federation (ITTF) was founded in 1926.

United States The United States Table Tennis Association was established in 1933. In 1971, a U.S. table tennis team was invited to play in the People's Republic of China, thereby initiating the first officially sanctioned Chinese-American cultural exchange in almost 20 years.

OLYMPIC GAMES Table tennis was included in the Olympic Games in 1988 for the first time.

Most medals Yoo Nam-Kyu (South Korea) has won three medals in Olympic competition: one gold, two bronze, 1988–92. Chin Jing (China) is the only woman to win two medals, one gold, one silver, in 1988.

WORLD CHAMPIONSHIPS The ITTF instituted European championships in 1926 and later designated this event the world championship. The tournament was staged annually until 1957, when the event became biennial.

TIMEOUT

PING PONG ☛ THE RECORD NUMBER OF HITS IN 60 SECONDS IS 172, BY THOMAS BUSIN AND STEFAN RENOLD (BOTH SWITZERLAND) ON NOVEMBER 4, 1989. WITH A BAT IN EACH HAND, GARY D. FISHER (U.S.) COMPLETED 5,000 CONSECUTIVE VOLLEYS OVER THE NET ON JUNE 25, 1975.

TOP SPIN ■ RICHARD MILLS HAS WON A RECORD 11 U.S. SINGLES TITLES.

SWAYTHLING CUP The men's team championship is named after Lady Swaythling, who donated the trophy in 1926.

Most titles The most wins is 12, by Hungary (1926, 1928–31, 1933 [two events were held that year, with Hungary winning both times], 1935, 1938, 1949, 1952, 1979).

CORBILLON CUP The women's team championship is named after M. Marcel Corbillon, president of the French Table Tennis Association, who donated the trophy in 1934.

Most titles China has won the most titles, with nine wins (1965, 1975, 1977, 1979, 1981, 1983, 1985, 1987, 1989).

Men's singles The most victories in singles is five, by Viktor Barna (Hungary), 1931, 1932–35.

Women's singles The most victories is six, by Angelica Rozeanu (Romania), 1950–55.

Men's doubles The most victories is eight, by Viktor Barna (Hungary), 1929–35, 1939. The partnership that has won the most titles is Viktor Barna and Miklos Szabados (Hungary), 1929–33, 1935.

Women's doubles The most victories is seven, by Maria Mednyanszky (Hungary), 1928, 1930–35. The team that has won the most titles is Maria Mednyanszky and Anna Sipos (Hungary), 1930–35.

Mixed doubles Maria Mednyanszky (Hungary) has won a record six mixed doubles titles: 1927–28, 1930–31, 1933 (twice). The pairing of Miklos Szabados and Maria Mednyanszky (Hungary) won the title a record three times: 1930–31, 1933.

UNITED STATES NATIONAL CHAMPIONSHIPS U.S. national championships were first held in 1931.

Most titles Leah Neuberger (née Thall) won a record 21 titles between 1941 and 1961: nine women's singles, 12 women's doubles. Richard Mills won a record 10 men's singles titles between 1945 and 1962.

TAEKWONDO

ORIGINS Taekwondo is a martial art, with all activities based on defensive spirit, developed over 20 centuries in Korea. It was officially recognized as part of Korean tradition and culture on April 11, 1955. The first World Taekwondo Championships were organized by the Korean Taekwondo Association and were held at Seoul, South Korea in 1973. The World Taekwondo Federation was then formed and has organized biennial championships.

United States The United States Taekwondo Union was founded in 1974.

OLYMPIC GAMES Taekwondo was included as a demonstration sport at the 1988 and 1992 Games.

WORLD CHAMPIONSHIPS These biennial championships were first held in Seoul, South Korea in 1973, when they were staged by the Korean Taekwondo Association. Women's events were first staged unofficially in 1983 and have been officially recognized since 1987.

Most titles Chung Kook-hyun (South Korea) has won a record four world titles: light middleweight, 1982–83; welterweight 1985, 1987.

TEAM HANDBALL

ORIGINS Team handball developed around the turn of the 20th century. It evolved from a game devised by soccer players in northern Germany and Denmark designed to keep them fit during the winter months. An outdoors version of the game was included in the 1936 Olympic Games as a demonstration sport. In 1946 the International Handball Federation (IHF) was formed. The growth of team handball has been rapid since its reintroduction into the Olympic Games in 1972 as an indoor game with seven players on each side. The IHF claims 4.2 million members from 88 countries, second only to soccer in terms of worldwide membership.

United States Team handball was first introduced to the United States in the 1920s, and a national team entered the 1936 Olympic demonstration competition. In 1959 the United States Team Handball Federation (USTHF) was formed, and it still governs the sport in this country.

OLYMPIC GAMES

Most wins In men's competition the USSR/Unified Team has won the Olympic gold medal three times—1976, 1988 and 1992. In women's competition, introduced in 1976, two countries have won the gold medal twice: the USSR in 1976 and 1980; and South Korea in 1988 and 1992.

WORLD CHAMPIONSHIP This competition was instituted in 1938.

Most titles (country) Romania has won four men's and three women's titles (two outdoor, one indoor) from 1956 to 1974. East Germany has also won three women's titles, in 1971, 1975 and 1978.

TENNIS

ORIGINS The modern game evolved from the indoor sport of real tennis. There is an account of a game called "field tennis" in an English sports periodical dated September 29, 1793; however, the "father" of lawn tennis is considered to be Major Walter Wingfield, who patented a type of tennis called "sphairistike" in 1874. The Marylebone Cricket Club, England revised Wingfield's initial rules in 1877, and the famed All-England Croquet Club (home of the Wimbledon Championships)

added the name Lawn Tennis to its title in 1877. The "open" era of tennis, when amateurs were permitted to play with and against professionals, was introduced in 1968.

GRAND SLAM

The grand slam is achieved by winning all four grand slam events—the Australian Open, French Open, Wimbledon and U.S. Open—in one calendar year.

GRAND SLAM WINNERS

Singles Don Budge (U.S.) was the first player to achieve the grand slam when he won all four events in 1938. The only player to have won the grand slam twice is Rod Laver (Australia), who accomplished this in 1962 and 1969. Three women have completed the grand slam: Maureen Connolly (U.S.), in 1953; Margaret Court (née Smith; Australia), in 1970; and Steffi Graf (West Germany), in 1988.

Doubles The only men to win the grand slam for doubles were Frank Sedgman and Ken McGregor (Australia) in 1951. Three women have won the grand slam: Maria Bueno (Brazil) in 1960; Martina Navratilova and Pam Shriver (U.S.) in 1984. Navratilova and Shriver won eight consecutive doubles titles from 1983–85.

Mixed doubles Ken Fletcher and Margaret Court (Australia) won all four legs of the grand slam in 1963. Owen Davidson (Australia) won all four events, with two partners, in 1967.

MOST GRAND SLAM TITLES

Singles The most singles championships won in grand slam tournaments is 24, by Margaret Court (née Smith; Australia): 11 Australian, five French, three Wimbledon, five U.S. Open between 1960 and 1973. The men's record is 12, by Roy Emerson (Australia): six Australian, two French, two Wimbledon, two U.S. Open between 1961 and 1967.

Doubles The most wins by a doubles partnership is 20, by two teams: Louise Brough (U.S.) and Margaret Du Pont (U.S.), who won three French, five Wimbledon and 12 U.S. Opens, 1942–57; and by Martina Navratilova (U.S.) and Pam Shriver (U.S.). They won seven Australian, four French, five Wimbledon, four U.S. Opens, 1981–89.

MARTINA NAVRATILOVA

Nine-time Wimbledon champion Martina Navratilova raised women's tennis to new heights in the early 1980s, changing the women's game forever. Her powerful, athletic style of play overwhelmed opponents, forcing rivals to copy her training techniques in order to compete with her. Chris Evert, in particular, worked to improve her stamina, and the legendary Navratilova–Evert matches helped define and popularize women's tennis. During her career Navratilova has set numerous records, including most career titles and match wins. She is also an outstanding doubles player, having won more Grand Slam doubles titles than any other woman.

WOMEN'S TENNIS RECORDS

GRAND SLAM EVENTS

- Most Wimbledon singles **9**
- Most French doubles **7**
- Most doubles (career) **31**

WTA CIRCUIT

- Most titles **161**
- Most matches won **1,359**
- Winning streak (singles) **74**
- Winning streak (doubles) **109***
- Best W–L record (season) **86–1**
- Career earnings **$18,396,526**

* With Pam Shriver

MILESTONES		
Win #	Opponent	Year
1	Iris Reidel	1973
100	Kathy Kuykendall	1975
500	Sherry Acker	1980
1,000	Nathalie Tauziat	1986
1,300	Laura Garrone	1991

IN 1983 NAVRATILOVA WON 16 TOURNAMENTS OUT OF 17 ENTERED, AND 86 MATCHES OF 87 PLAYED.

MOST SINGLES TITLES

Navratilova's first professional title was the 1973 Pilser Open. She defeated Renata Tomanova, 6–2, 6–1 in the final. At the end of the 1992 season, she has gone on to win a record 161 tournaments.

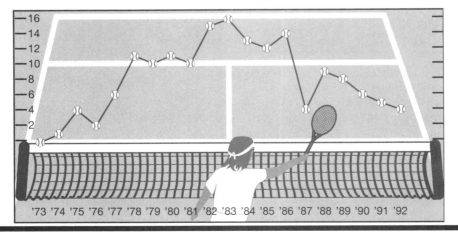

SOURCE: WTA MEDIA GUIDE

THE CHAMPIONSHIPS, WIMBLEDON

On July 7, 1990, Navratilova defeated Zina Garrison (U.S.) to win her ninth Wimbledon singles title, thus breaking her tie with Helen Wills Moody (U.S.) to become the most successful women's player in the history of the championship. Besides her record number of ladies' singles titles, Navratilova has also won a record 106 singles matches. Her overall record on the famed lawns is nine singles titles, seven doubles titles and one mixed doubles title.

NAVRATILOVA CELEBRATES
HER NINTH WIMBLEDON TRIUMPH IN 1990.

LADIES SINGLES CHAMPIONSHIP WINS

Year	Opponent	Score
1978	Chris Evert	2–6, 6–4, 7–5
1979	Chris Evert	6–4, 6–4
1982	Chris Evert	6–1, 3–6, 6–2
1983	Andrea Jaeger	6–0, 6–3
1984	Chris Evert	7–6, 6–2
1985	Chris Evert	4–6, 6–3, 6–2
1986	Hana Mandlikova	7–6, 6–3
1987	Steffi Graff	7–5, 6–3
1990	Zina Garrison	6–4, 6–1

DOUBLES

In the modern era very few high-ranked singles players have played doubles on a regular basis, and of those, none have come near the success of Navratilova. The team of Pam Shriver and Martina Navratilova dominated women's doubles in the 1980s, setting numerous records, among them: Most grand slam titles, 20* (Australian Open seven times, Wimbledon five times, U.S. Open four times, French Open four times); Most consecutive grand slam titles, eight (1983–85); Most consecutive match wins, 109 (June 23, 1983 to July 9, 1985). With other partners Navratilova has won 11 other grand slam doubles titles, the most by any woman player in history.

* Tied with Louise Brough and Margaret du Pont (née Osborne).

NAVRATILOVA AND SHRIVER WON EIGHT SUCCESSIVE
GRAND SLAM DOUBLES TITLES FROM 1983–85.

GRAND SLAM DOUBLES TITLES

AUSTRALIAN OPEN		FRENCH OPEN		WIMBLEDON		U.S. OPEN	
Year	Partner	Year	Partner	Year	Partner	Year	Partner
1980	Betsy Nagelsen	1975	Chris Evert	1976	Chris Evert	1977	Betty Stove
1982	Pam Shriver	1982	Anne Smith	1979	Billie Jean King	1978	Billie Jean King
1983	Pam Shriver	1984	Pam Shriver	1981	Pam Shriver	1980	Billie Jean King
1984	Pam Shriver	1985	Pam Shriver	1982	Pam Shriver	1983	Pam Shriver
1985	Pam Shriver	1986	Andrea Temesvari	1983	Pam Shriver	1984	Pam Shriver
1987	Pam Shriver	1987	Pam Shriver	1984	Pam Shriver	1986	Pam Shriver
1988	Pam Shriver	1988	Pam Shriver	1986	Pam Shriver	1987	Pam Shriver
1989	Pam Shriver					1989	Hana Mandlikova
						1990	Gigi Fernandez

WIMBLEDON CHAMPIONSHIPS

The "Lawn Tennis Championships" at the All-England Club, Wimbledon are generally regarded as the most prestigious in tennis and currently form the third leg of the grand slam events. They were first held in 1877 and, until 1922, were organized on a challenge round system (the defending champion automatically qualifies for the following year's final and plays the winner of the challenger event). Wimbledon became an open championship (professionals could compete) in 1968.

WIMBLEDON CHAMPIONS (1877–1932)

Men's Singles

Year	Player	Year	Player
1877	Spencer Gore	1905	Lawrence Doherty
1878	Frank Hadlow	1906	Lawrence Doherty
1879	Rev. John Hartley	1907	Norman Brookes
1880	Rev. John Hartley	1908	Arthur Gore
1881	William Renshaw	1909	Arthur Gore
1882	William Renshaw	1910	Tony Wilding
1883	William Renshaw	1911	Tony Wilding
1884	William Renshaw	1912	Tony Wilding
1885	William Renshaw	1913	Tony Wilding
1886	William Renshaw	1914	Norman Brookes
1887	Herbert Lawford	1915	not held
1888	Ernest Renshaw	1916	not held
1889	William Renshaw	1917	not held
1890	Willoughby Hamilton	1918	not held
1891	Wilfred Baddeley	1919	Gerald Patterson
1892	Wilfred Baddeley	1920	Bill Tilden
1893	Joshua Pim	1921	Bill Tilden
1894	Joshua Pim	1922	Gerald Patterson
1895	Wilfred Baddeley	1923	William Johnston
1896	Harold Mahoney	1924	Jean Borotra
1897	Reginald Doherty	1925	Rene Lacoste
1898	Reginald Doherty	1926	Jean Borotra
1899	Reginald Doherty	1927	Henri Cochet
1900	Reginald Doherty	1928	Rene Lacoste
1901	Arthur Gore	1929	Henri Cochet
1902	Lawrence Doherty	1930	Bill Tilden
1903	Lawrence Doherty	1931	Sidney Wood
1904	Lawrence Doherty	1932	Ellsworth Vines

Women's Singles

Year	Player	Year	Player
1877	no event	1905	May Sutton
1878	no event	1906	Dorothea Douglass
1879	no event	1907	May Sutton
1880	no event	1908	Charlotte Sterry[2]
1881	no event	1909	Dora Boothby
1882	no event	1910	Dorothea Lambert-Chambers[3]
1883	no event	1911	Dorothea Lambert-Chambers[3]
1884	Maud Watson	1912	Ethel Larcombe
1885	Maud Watson	1913	Dorothea Lambert-Chambers[3]
1886	Blanche Bingley	1914	Dorothea Lambert-Chambers[3]
1887	Lottie Dod	1915	not held
1888	Lottie Dod	1916	not held
1889	Blanche Hillyard[1]	1917	not held
1890	Helene Rice	1918	not held
1891	Lottie Dod	1919	Suzanne Lenglen
1892	Lottie Dod	1920	Suzanne Lenglen
1893	Lottie Dod	1921	Suzanne Lenglen
1894	Blanche Hillyard[1]	1922	Suzanne Lenglen
1895	Charlotte Cooper	1923	Suzanne Lenglen
1896	Charlotte Cooper	1924	Kathleen McKane
1897	Blanche Hillyard[1]	1925	Suzanne Lenglen
1898	Charlotte Cooper	1926	Kathleen Godfree[4]
1899	Blanche Hillyard[1]	1927	Helen Wills
1900	Blanche Hillyard[1]	1928	Helen Wills
1901	Charlotte Sterry[2]	1929	Helen Wills
1902	Muriel Robb	1930	Helen Moody[5]
1903	Dorothea Douglass	1931	Cilly Aussem
1904	Dorothea Douglass	1932	Helen Moody[5]

1–Blanche Hillyard (née Bingley)   2–Charlotte Sterry (née Cooper)   3–Dorothea Lambert-Chambers (née Douglass)   4–Kathleen Godfree (née McKane)
5–Helen Moody (née Wills)

Most titles (men) Overall, the most titles is seven, by William Renshaw (Great Britain), 1881–86, 1889. Since the abolition of the Challenge Round in 1922, the most wins is five, by Bjorn Borg (Sweden), 1976–80.

Most titles (women) Martina Navratilova has

WIMBLEDON CHAMPIONS (1933–1992)

	Men's Singles				Women's Singles		
Year	Player	Year	Player	Year	Player	Year	Player
1933	Jack Crawford	1963	Chuck McKinley	1933	Helen Moody[5]	1963	Margaret Smith
1934	Fred Perry	1964	Roy Emerson	1934	Dorothy Round	1964	Maria Bueno
1935	Fred Perry	1965	Roy Emerson	1935	Helen Moody[5]	1965	Margaret Smith
1936	Fred Perry	1966	Manuel Santana	1936	Helen Jacobs	1966	Billie Jean King
1937	Don Budge	1967	John Newcombe	1937	Dorothy Round	1967	Billie Jean King
1938	Don Budge	1968	Rod Laver	1938	Helen Moody[5]	1968	Billie Jean King
1939	Bobby Riggs	1969	Rod Laver	1939	Alice Marble	1969	Ann Jones
1940	not held	1970	John Newcombe	1940	not held	1970	Margaret Court[6]
1941	not held	1971	John Newcombe	1941	not held	1971	Evonne Goolagong
1942	not held	1972	Stan Smith	1942	not held	1972	Billie Jean King
1943	not held	1973	Jan Kodes	1943	not held	1973	Billie Jean King
1944	not held	1974	Jimmy Connors	1944	not held	1974	Chris Evert
1945	not held	1975	Arthur Ashe	1945	not held	1975	Billie Jean King
1946	Yvon Petra	1976	Bjorn Borg	1946	Pauline Betz	1976	Chris Evert
1947	Jack Kramer	1977	Bjorn Borg	1947	Margaret Osborne	1977	Virginia Wade
1948	Bob Falkenburg	1978	Bjorn Borg	1948	Louise Brough	1978	Martina Navratilova
1949	Ted Schroeder	1979	Bjorn Borg	1949	Louise Brough	1979	Martina Navratilova
1950	Budge Patty	1980	Bjorn Borg	1950	Louise Brough	1980	Evonne Cawley[7]
1951	Dick Savitt	1981	John McEnroe	1951	Doris Hart	1981	Chris Evert
1952	Frank Sedgman	1982	Jimmy Connors	1952	Maureen Connolly	1982	Martina Navratilova
1953	Vic Seixas	1983	John McEnroe	1953	Maureen Connolly	1983	Martina Navratilova
1954	Jaroslav Drobny	1984	John McEnroe	1954	Maureen Connolly	1984	Martina Navratilova
1955	Tony Trabert	1985	Boris Becker	1955	Louise Brough	1985	Martina Navratilova
1956	Lew Hoad	1986	Boris Becker	1956	Shirley Fry	1986	Martina Navratilova
1957	Lew Hoad	1987	Pat Cash	1957	Althea Gibson	1987	Martina Navratilova
1958	Ashley Cooper	1988	Stefan Edberg	1958	Althea Gibson	1988	Steffi Graf
1959	Alex Olmedo	1989	Boris Becker	1959	Maria Bueno	1989	Steffi Graf
1960	Neale Fraser	1990	Stefan Edberg	1960	Maria Bueno	1990	Martina Navratilova
1961	Rod Laver	1991	Michael Stich	1961	Angela Mortimer	1991	Steffi Graf
1962	Rod Laver	1992	Andre Agassi	1962	Karen Susman	1992	Steffi Graf

5 – Helen Moody (née Wills)   6 – Margaret Court (née Smith)   7 – Evonne Cawley (née Goolagong)

won a record nine titles: 1978–79, 1982–87, 1990.

Men's doubles Lawrence and Reginald Doherty (Great Britain) won the doubles title a record eight times: 1897–1901, 1903–05.

Women's doubles Suzanne Lenglen (France) and Elizabeth Ryan (U.S.) won the doubles a rec-

ord six times: 1919–23, 1925. Elizabeth Ryan was a winning partner on a record 12 occasions: 1914, 1919–23, 1925–27, 1930, 1933–34.

Mixed doubles The team of Ken Fletcher and Margaret Court (née Smith), both of Australia, won the mixed doubles a record four times: 1963,

U.S. OPEN CHAMPIONS (1881–1938)

Men's Singles				Women's Singles			
Year	Player	Year	Player	Year	Player	Year	Player
1881	Richard Sears	1910	William Larned	1881	no event	1910	Hazel Hotchkiss
1882	Richard Sears	1911	William Larned	1882	no event	1911	Hazel Hotchkiss
1883	Richard Sears	1912	Maurice McLoughlin	1883	no event	1912	Mary Browne
1884	Richard Sears	1913	Maurice McLoughlin	1884	no event	1913	Mary Browne
1885	Richard Sears	1914	Norris Williams	1885	no event	1914	Mary Browne
1886	Richard Sears	1915	William Johnston	1886	no event	1915	Molla Bjurstedt
1887	Richard Sears	1916	Norris Williams	1887	Ellen Hansell	1916	Molla Bjurstedt
1888	Henry Slocum Jr.	1917	Lindley Murray	1888	Bertha Townsend	1917	Molla Bjurstedt
1889	Henry Slocum Jr.	1918	Lindley Murray	1889	Bertha Townsend	1918	Molla Bjurstedt
1890	Oliver Campbell	1919	William Johnston	1890	Ellen Roosevelt	1919	Hazel Wightman[1]
1891	Oliver Campbell	1920	Bill Tilden	1891	Mabel Cahill	1920	Molla Mallory[2]
1892	Oliver Campbell	1921	Bill Tilden	1892	Mabel Cahill	1921	Molla Mallory[2]
1893	Robert Wrenn	1922	Bill Tilden	1893	Aline Terry	1922	Molla Mallory[2]
1894	Robert Wrenn	1923	Bill Tilden	1894	Helen Helwig	1923	Helen Wills
1895	Fred Hovey	1924	Bill Tilden	1895	Juliette Atkinson	1924	Helen Wills
1896	Robert Wrenn	1925	Bill Tilden	1896	Elisabeth Moore	1925	Helen Wills
1897	Robert Wrenn	1926	Rene Lacoste	1897	Juliette Atkinson	1926	Molla Mallory[2]
1898	Malcolm Whitman	1927	Rene Lacoste	1898	Juliette Atkinson	1927	Helen Wills
1899	Malcolm Whitman	1928	Henri Cochet	1899	Marion Jones	1928	Helen Wills
1900	Malcolm Whitman	1929	Bill Tilden	1900	Myrtle McAteer	1929	Helen Wills
1901	William Larned	1930	John Doeg	1901	Elisabeth Moore	1930	Betty Nuthall
1902	William Larned	1931	Ellsworth Vines	1902	Marion Jones	1931	Helen Moody[3]
1903	Lawrence Doherty	1932	Ellsworth Vines	1903	Elisabeth Moore	1932	Helen Jacobs
1904	Holcombe Ward	1933	Fred Perry	1904	May Sutton	1933	Helen Jacobs
1905	Beals Wright	1934	Fred Perry	1905	Elisabeth Moore	1934	Helen Jacobs
1906	William Clothier	1935	Wilmer Allison	1906	Helen Homans	1935	Helen Jacobs
1907	William Larned	1936	Fred Perry	1907	Evelyn Sears	1936	Alice Marble
1908	William Larned	1937	Don Budge	1908	Maud Bargar-Wallach	1937	Anita Lizana
1909	William Larned	1938	Don Budge	1909	Hazel Hotchkiss	1938	Alice Marble

1 – Hazel Wightman (née Hotchkiss)   2 – Molla Mallory (née Bjurstedt)   3 – Helen Moody (née Wills)

1965–66, 1968. Fletcher's four victories tie him for the men's record for wins, which is shared by two other players: Vic Seixas (U.S.), 1953–56; Owen Davidson (Australia), 1967, 1971, 1973–74. Elizabeth Ryan (U.S.) holds the women's record with seven wins: 1919, 1921, 1923, 1927–28, 1930, 1932.

Most titles (overall) Billie Jean King (U.S.) won a record 20 Wimbledon titles from 1961–79: six singles, 10 doubles and four mixed doubles.

Youngest champions The youngest champion was Lottie Dod (Great Britain), who was 15 years 285 days when she won in 1887. The youngest men's champion was Boris Becker (Ger-

U.S. OPEN CHAMPIONS (1939–1992)

	Men's Singles				Women's Singles		
Year	Player	Year	Player	Year	Player	Year	Player
1939	Bobby Riggs	1967	John Newcombe	1939	Alice Marble	1967	Billie Jean King
1940	Donald McNeil	1968	Arthur Ashe*	1940	Alice Marble	1968	Margaret Court*⁴
1941	Bobby Riggs	1968	Arthur Ashe†	1941	Sarah Cooke	1968	Virginia Wade†
1942	Ted Schroeder	1969	Stan Smith*	1942	Pauline Betz	1969	Margaret Court*⁴
1943	Joseph Hunt	1969	Rod Laver†	1943	Pauline Betz	1969	Margaret Court†⁴
1944	Frank Parker	1970	Ken Rosewall	1944	Pauline Betz	1970	Margaret Court⁴
1945	Frank Parker	1971	Stan Smith	1945	Sarah Cooke	1971	Billie Jean King
1946	Jack Kramer	1972	Ilie Nastase	1946	Pauline Betz	1972	Billie Jean King
1947	Jack Kramer	1973	John Newcombe	1947	Louise Brough	1973	Margaret Court⁴
1948	Pancho Gonzalez	1974	Jimmy Connors	1948	Margaret Du Pont	1974	Billie Jean King
1949	Pancho Gonzalez	1975	Manuel Orantes	1949	Margaret Du Pont	1975	Chris Evert
1950	Arthur Larsen	1976	Jimmy Connors	1950	Margaret Du Pont	1976	Chris Evert
1951	Frank Sedgman	1977	Guillermo Vilas	1951	Maureen Connolly	1977	Chris Evert
1952	Frank Sedgman	1978	Jimmy Connors	1952	Maureen Connolly	1978	Chris Evert
1953	Tony Trabert	1979	John McEnroe	1953	Maureen Connolly	1979	Tracy Austin
1954	Vic Seixas	1980	John McEnroe	1954	Doris Hart	1980	Chris Evert
1955	Tony Trabert	1981	John McEnroe	1955	Doris Hart	1981	Tracy Austin
1956	Ken Rosewall	1982	Jimmy Connors	1956	Shirley Fry	1982	Chris Evert
1957	Malcolm Anderson	1983	Jimmy Connors	1957	Althea Gibson	1983	Martina Navratilova
1958	Ashley Cooper	1984	John McEnroe	1958	Althea Gibson	1984	Martina Navratilova
1959	Neale Fraser	1985	Ivan Lendl	1959	Maria Bueno	1985	Hanna Mandlikova
1960	Neale Fraser	1986	Ivan Lendl	1960	Darlene Hard	1986	Martina Navratilova
1961	Roy Emerson	1987	Ivan Lendl	1961	Darlene Hard	1987	Martina Navratilova
1962	Rod Laver	1988	Mats Wilander	1962	Margaret Smith	1988	Steffi Graf
1963	Raphael Osuna	1989	Boris Becker	1963	Maria Bueno	1989	Steffi Graf
1964	Roy Emerson	1990	Pete Sampras	1964	Maria Bueno	1990	Gabriela Sabatini
1965	Manuel Santana	1991	Stefan Edberg	1965	Margaret Smith	1991	Monica Seles
1966	Fred Stolle	1992	Stefan Edberg	1966	Maria Bueno	1992	Monica Seles

4– Margaret Court (née Smith)   * Amateur championship   † Open championship

many), who was 17 years 227 days when he won in 1985.

UNITED STATES OPEN CHAMPIONSHIPS

The first official U.S. championships were staged in 1881. From 1884 to 1911, the contest was based on a challenger format. In 1968 and 1969, separate amateur and professional events were held. Since 1970, there has been only an Open competition. On the current schedule the U.S. Open is the fourth and final leg of the grand slam and is played at the U.S. National Tennis Center, Flushing Meadows, N.Y.

Most titles (men) The most wins is seven, by three players: Richard Sears (U.S.), 1881–87; William Larned (U.S.), 1901–02, 1907–11; Bill Tilden (U.S.), 1920–25, 1929.

Most titles (women) Molla Mallory (née Bjurstedt; U.S.) won a record eight titles: 1915–18, 1920–22, 1926.

Men's doubles The most wins by one pair is five, by Richard Sears and James Dwight (U.S.), 1882–84, 1886–87. The most wins by an individual player is six, by two players: Richard Sears, 1882–84, 1886–87 (with Dwight) and 1885 (with Joseph Clark); Holcombe Ward, 1899–1901 (with Dwight Davis), 1904–06 (with Beals Wright).

Women's doubles The most wins by a pair is 12, by Louise Brough and Margaret Du Pont (née Osborne), both of the U.S.. They won in 1942–50 and in 1955–57.

GOLDEN SET ☛ THE ONLY KNOWN EXAMPLE OF A "GOLDEN SET" (WINNING 6–0 WITHOUT DROPPING A SINGLE POINT) IN PROFESSIONAL TENNIS WAS ACHIEVED BY BILL SCANLON (U.S.) V. MARCOS HOCEVAR (BRAZIL). SCANLON WON THEIR FIRST-ROUND MATCH IN THE WCT GOLD COAST CLASSIC AT DEL RAY, FLA., ON FEBRUARY 22, 1983, 6–2, 6–0.

Margaret Du Pont holds the record for an individual player with 13 wins; adding to her victories with Brough was the 1941 title with Sarah Cooke.

Mixed doubles The most wins by one pair is four, by William Talbert and Margaret Osborne (U.S.), who won in 1943–46. The most titles won by any individual is nine, by Margaret Du Pont (née Osborne). She won in 1943–46, 1950, 1956, 1958–60. The most titles won by a man is four, accomplished by six players: Edwin Fischer (U.S.), 1894–96, 1898; Wallace Johnson (U.S.), 1907, 1909, 1911, 1920; Bill Tilden (U.S.), 1913–14, 1922–23; William Talbert (U.S.), 1943–46; Owen Davidson (Australia), 1966–67, 1971, 1973; and Marty Riessen (U.S.), 1969–70, 1972, 1980.

Most titles (overall) Margaret Du Pont (née Osborne) won a record 25 U.S. Open titles from 1941–60—three singles, 13 doubles, and nine mixed doubles.

Youngest champions The youngest singles champion was Tracy Austin (U.S.), who was 16 years 271 days when she won the women's singles in 1979. The youngest men's champion was Pete Sampras (U.S.), who was 19 years 28 days when he won the 1990 title.

FRENCH OPEN CHAMPIONSHIPS

The first French championships were held in 1891; however, entry was restricted to members of French clubs until 1925. Grand slam records include the French Open only from 1925. This event has been staged at the Stade Roland Garros since 1928 and currently is the second leg of the grand slam.

Most wins (men) Bjorn Borg (Sweden) has won the French title a record six times: 1974–75, 1978–81.

Most wins (women) Chris Evert has won a record seven French titles: 1974–75, 1979–80, 1983, 1985–86.

Men's doubles Roy Emerson (Australia) has won the men's doubles a record six times, 1960–65, with five different partners.

Women's doubles The pair of Martina Navratilova and Pam Shriver (both U.S.) have won the doubles title a record four times, 1984–85, 1987–88. The most wins by an individual player is seven, by Martina Navratilova—four times with Pam Shriver, 1984–85, 1987–88; and with three other players, in 1975, 1982 and 1986.

FRENCH OPEN CHAMPIONS (1925–1992)

Men's Singles

Year	Player	Year	Player
1925	Rene Lacoste	1959	Nicola Pietrangeli
1926	Henri Cochet	1960	Nicola Pietrangeli
1927	Rene Lacoste	1961	Manuel Santana
1928	Henri Cochet	1962	Rod Laver
1929	Rene Lacoste	1963	Roy Emerson
1930	Henri Cochet	1964	Manuel Santana
1931	Jean Borotra	1965	Fred Stolle
1932	Henri Cochet	1966	Tony Roche
1933	Jack Crawford	1967	Roy Emerson
1934	Gottfried Von Cramm	1968	Ken Rosewall
1935	Fred Perry	1969	Rod Laver
1936	Gottfried Von Cramm	1970	Jan Kodes
1937	Henner Henkel	1971	Jan Kodes
1938	Don Budge	1972	Andres Gimeno
1939	Donald McNeil	1973	Ilie Nastase
1940	not held	1974	Bjorn Borg
1941	not held	1975	Bjorn Borg
1942	not held	1976	Adriano Panatta
1943	not held	1977	Guillermo Vilas
1944	not held	1978	Bjorn Borg
1945	not held	1979	Bjorn Borg
1946	Marcel Bernard	1980	Bjorn Borg
1947	Jozsef Asboth	1981	Bjorn Borg
1948	Frank Parker	1982	Mats Wilander
1949	Frank Parker	1983	Yannick Noah
1950	Budge Patty	1984	Ivan Lendl
1951	Jaroslav Drobny	1985	Mats Wilander
1952	Jaroslav Drobny	1986	Ivan Lendl
1953	Ken Rosewall	1987	Ivan Lendl
1954	Tony Trabert	1988	Mats Wilander
1955	Tony Trabert	1989	Michael Chang
1956	Lew Hoad	1990	Andres Gomez
1957	Sven Davidson	1991	Jim Courier
1958	Mervyn Rose	1992	Jim Courier

Women's Singles

Year	Player	Year	Player
1925	Suzanne Lenglen	1959	Christine Truman
1926	Suzanne Lenglen	1960	Darlene Hard
1927	Kea Bouman	1961	Ann Haydon
1928	Helen Moody [1]	1962	Margaret Smith
1929	Helen Moody [1]	1963	Lesley Turner
1930	Helen Moody [1]	1964	Margaret Smith
1931	Cilly Aussem	1965	Lesley Turner
1932	Helen Moody [1]	1966	Ann Jones [3]
1933	Margaret Scriven	1967	Francoise Durr
1934	Margaret Scriven	1968	Nancy Richey
1935	Hilde Sperling	1969	Margaret Court [4]
1936	Hilde Sperling	1970	Margaret Court [4]
1937	Hilde Sperling	1971	Evonne Goolagong
1938	Simone Mathieu	1972	Billie Jean King
1939	Simone Mathieu	1973	Margaret Court [4]
1940	not held	1974	Chris Evert
1941	not held	1975	Chris Evert
1942	not held	1976	Sue Barker
1943	not held	1977	Mimi Jausovec
1944	not held	1978	Virginia Ruzici
1945	not held	1979	Chris Evert
1946	Margaret Osborne	1980	Chris Evert
1947	Pat Todd	1981	Hana Mandlikova
1948	Nelly Landry	1982	Martina Navratilova
1949	Margaret Du Pont [2]	1983	Chris Evert
1950	Doris Hart	1984	Martina Navratilova
1951	Shirley Fry	1985	Chris Evert
1952	Doris Hart	1986	Chris Evert
1953	Maureen Connolly	1987	Steffi Graf
1954	Maureen Connolly	1988	Steffi Graf
1955	Angela Mortimer	1989	Aranxta Sanchez Vicario
1956	Althea Gibson	1990	Monica Seles
1957	Shirley Bloomer	1991	Monica Seles
1958	Zsuzsi Kormoczy	1992	Monica Seles

1 – Helen Moody (née Wills)   2 – Margaret Du Pont (née Osborne)   3 – Ann Jones (née Haydon)   4 – Margaret Court (née Smith)

Mixed doubles Two teams have won the mixed title three times: Ken Fletcher and Margaret Smith (Australia), 1963–65; Jean-Claude Barclay and Francoise Durr (France), 1968, 1971, 1973. Margaret Court (née Smith) has won the title the most times, with four wins, winning with Marty Riessen (U.S.) in 1969, in addition to her three wins with Fletcher. Fletcher and Barclay share the men's record of three wins.

Most titles (overall) Margaret Court (née Smith) has won a record 13 French Open titles, 1962–73: five singles, four doubles and four mixed doubles.

Youngest champions The youngest singles champion at the French Open was Monica Seles (Yugoslavia) in 1990, at 16 years 169 days. The youngest men's winner is Michael Chang (U.S.), who was 17 years 109 days when he won the 1989 title.

AUSTRALIAN OPEN CHAMPIONSHIPS

The first Australasian championships were held in 1905, with New Zealand hosting the event in 1906 and 1912. A women's championship was

AUSTRALIAN OPEN CHAMPIONS (1905–1952)

Men's Singles				Women's Singles			
Year	Player	Year	Player	Year	Player	Year	Player
1905	Rodney Heath	1929	John Gregory	1905	no event	1929	Daphne Akhurst
1906	Tony Wilding	1930	Gar Moon	1906	no event	1930	Daphne Akhurst
1907	Horace Rice	1931	Jack Crawford	1907	no event	1931	Coral Buttsworth
1908	Fred Alexander	1932	Jack Crawford	1908	no event	1932	Coral Buttsworth
1909	Tony Wilding	1933	Jack Crawford	1909	no event	1933	Joan Hartigan
1910	Rodney Heath	1934	Fred Perry	1910	no event	1934	Joan Hartigan
1911	Norman Brookes	1935	Jack Crawford	1911	no event	1935	Dorothy Round
1912	J. Cecil Parke	1936	Adrian Quist	1912	no event	1936	Joan Hartigan
1913	E. F. Parker	1937	V. B. McGrath	1913	no event	1937	Nancye Wynne
1914	Pat O'Hara Wood	1938	Don Budge	1914	no event	1938	Dorothy M. Bundy
1915	Francis Lowe	1939	John Bromwich	1915	no event	1939	Emily Westacott
1916	not held	1940	Adrian Quist	1916	not held	1940	Nancye Wynne
1917	not held	1941	not held	1917	not held	1941	not held
1918	not held	1942	not held	1918	not held	1942	not held
1919	A. Kingscote	1943	not held	1919	no event	1943	not held
1920	Pat O'Hara Wood	1944	not held	1920	no event	1944	not held
1921	Rhys Gemmell	1945	not held	1921	no event	1945	not held
1922	Pat O'Hara Wood	1946	John Bromwich	1922	Margaret Molesworth	1946	Nancye Bolton[1]
1923	Pat O'Hara Wood	1947	Dinny Pails	1923	Margaret Molesworth	1947	Nancye Bolton[1]
1924	James Anderson	1948	Adrian Quist	1924	Sylvia Lance	1948	Nancye Bolton[1]
1925	James Anderson	1949	Frank Sedgman	1925	Daphne Akhurst	1949	Doris Hart
1926	John Hawkes	1950	Frank Sedgman	1926	Daphne Akhurst	1950	Louise Brough
1927	Gerald Patterson	1951	Dick Savitt	1927	Esna Boyd	1951	Nancye Bolton[1]
1928	Jean Borotra	1952	Ken McGregor	1928	Daphne Akhurst	1952	Thelma Long

1– Nancye Bolton (née Wynne)

not introduced until 1922. The tournament was changed to the Australian Open in 1925 and is counted as a grand slam event from that year. There were two championships in 1977 because the event was moved from early season (January) to December. It reverted to a January date in 1987, which meant there was no championship in 1986. Currently the tournament is held at the Australian Tennis Center in Melbourne and is the first leg of the grand slam.

Most wins (men) The most wins is six, by Roy Emerson (Australia), 1961, 1963–67.

Most wins (women) The most wins is 11, by Margaret Court (née Smith) of Australia, 1960–66, 1969–71, 1973.

Men's doubles The most wins by one pair is eight, by John Bromwich and Adrian Quist (Australia), 1938–40, 1946–50. In addition, Quist holds the record for most wins by one player with 10, winning in 1936–37 with Don Turnbull, to add to his triumphs with Bromwich.

Women's doubles The most wins by one pair is 10, by Nancye Bolton (née Wynne) and Thelma Long (née Coyne), both Australian. Their victories came in 1936–40, 1947–49, 1951–52. Long also holds the record for most wins with 12, winning in 1956 and 1958 with Mary Hawton.

Mixed doubles The most wins by one pair is four, by two teams: Harry Hopman and Nell Hopman

AUSTRALIAN OPEN CHAMPIONS (1953–1993)

	Men's Singles					Women's Singles			
Year	Player	Year	Player		Year	Player	Year	Player
1953	Ken Rosewall	1974	Jimmy Connors		1953	Maureen Connolly	1974	Evonne Goolagong
1954	Mervyn Rose	1975	John Newcombe		1954	Thelma Long	1975	Evonne Goolagong
1955	Ken Rosewall	1976	Mark Edmondson		1955	Beryl Penrose	1976	Evonne Cawley[3]
1956	Lew Hoad	1977	Roscoe Tanner*		1956	Mary Carter	1977	Kerry Reid*
1957	Ashley Cooper	1977	Vitas Gerulaitis*		1957	Shirley Fry	1977	Evonne Cawley*[3]
1958	Ashley Cooper	1978	Guillermo Vilas		1958	Angela Mortimer	1978	Christine O'Neill
1959	Alex Olmedo	1979	Guillermo Vilas		1959	Mary Reitano[1]	1979	Barbara Jordan
1960	Rod Laver	1980	Brian Teacher		1960	Margaret Smith	1980	Hana Mandlikova
1961	Roy Emerson	1981	Johan Kriek		1961	Margaret Smith	1981	Martina Navratilova
1962	Rod Laver	1982	Johan Kriek		1962	Margaret Smith	1982	Chris Evert
1963	Roy Emerson	1983	Mats Wilander		1963	Margaret Smith	1983	Martina Navratilova
1964	Roy Emerson	1984	Mats Wilander		1964	Margaret Smith	1984	Chris Evert
1965	Roy Emerson	1985	Stefan Edberg		1965	Margaret Smith	1985	Martina Navratilova
1966	Roy Emerson	1986	not held		1966	Margaret Smith	1986	not held
1967	Roy Emerson	1987	Stefan Edberg		1967	Nancy Richey	1987	Hana Mandlikova
1968	Bill Bowrey	1988	Mats Wilander		1968	Billie Jean King	1988	Steffi Graf
1969	Rod Laver	1989	Ivan Lendl		1969	Margaret Court[2]	1989	Steffi Graf
1970	Arthur Ashe	1990	Ivan Lendl		1970	Margaret Court[2]	1990	Steffi Graf
1971	Ken Rosewall	1991	Boris Becker		1971	Margaret Court[2]	1991	Monica Seles
1972	Ken Rosewall	1992	Jim Courier		1972	Virginia Wade	1992	Monica Seles
1973	John Newcombe	1993	Jim Courier		1973	Margaret Court[2]	1993	Monica Seles

1–Mary Reitano (née Carter)   2–Margaret Court (née Smith)   3–Evonne Cawley (née Goolagong)
* There were two championships in 1977 because the event was moved from early season (January) to December.

(née Hall; Australia), 1930, 1936–37, 1939; Colin Long and Nancye Bolton (née Wynne; Australia), 1940, 1946–48.

Most titles (overall) Margaret Court (née Smith) has won a record 21 Australian Open titles between 1960 and 1973—11 singles, eight doubles and two mixed doubles.

Youngest champions The youngest women's singles champion was Monica Seles, Yugoslavia, who won the 1991 event at age 17 years 55 days.

OLYMPIC GAMES Tennis was reintroduced to the Olympic Games in 1988, having originally been included at the Games from 1896 to 1924. It was also a demonstration sport in 1968 and 1984.

Most gold medals Max Decugis (France) won four gold medals: men's singles, 1906; men's doubles, 1906; mixed doubles, 1906 and 1920.

Most medals Max Decugis (France) won a record six medals in Olympic competition: four gold (see above), one silver and one bronze, 1900–1920. Kitty McKane (Great Britain) won a women's record five medals: one gold, two silver and two bronze, 1920–24.

DAVIS CUP The Davis Cup, the men's international team championship, was first held in 1900, and is held annually.

Most wins The U.S. team has won the Davis Cup a record 30 times, 1900–92.

Most matches (career) Nicola Pietrangeli (Italy) played a record 163 matches (66 ties), 1954 to

CLAY KILLER ■ CHRIS EVERT CELEBRATES HER SEVENTH FRENCH OPEN WIN IN 1986.

1972, winning 120. He played 109 singles (winning 78) and 54 doubles (winning 42).

Most matches (season) Ilie Nastase (Romania) set a singles season mark of 18 wins (with 2 losses) in 1971.

UNITED STATES TEAM RECORDS

Most selections John McEnroe has played for the U.S. team on 30 occasions, 1978–92.

Most wins John McEnroe has won 59 matches in Davis Cup competition—41 singles and 18 doubles.

FEDERATION CUP The Federation Cup, the women's international team championship, was first held in 1963 and is an annual event.

Most wins The United States has won the Federation Cup a record 14 times.

MEN'S PROFESSIONAL TOUR RECORDS (1968–92)

Most singles titles (career) Jimmy Connors (U.S.) has won 109 singles titles, 1972–89.

Most singles titles (season) Three players have won 15 titles in one season: Jimmy Connors (U.S.), 1977; Guillermo Vilas (Argentina), 1977; Ivan Lendl (Czechoslovakia), 1982.

Most doubles titles (career) Tom Okker (Netherlands) has won 78 doubles titles, 1968–79.

Most doubles titles (season) John McEnroe (U.S.) won 17 doubles titles in 1979.

Most consecutive match wins Guillermo Vilas (Argentina) won 46 consecutive matches, 1977–78.

Most weeks ranked number one Jimmy Connors (U.S.) held the number one ranking on the ATP computer from July 29, 1974 to August 16, 1977, a total of 159 weeks—the longest streak in tour history.

Highest earnings (career) Ivan Lendl (Czechoslovakia) has won a career record $19,172,627, 1978–92.

Highest earnings (season) Stefan Edberg (Sweden) earned a season record $2,363,575 in 1991.

WOMEN'S PROFESSIONAL TOUR RECORDS (1968–92)

Most singles titles (career) Martina Navratilova (U.S.) has won 161 titles, 1975–92.

Most singles titles (season) Martina Navratilova won 16 titles in 1983.

Most consecutive matches won Martina Navratilova won 74 consecutive matches in 1984.

Most consecutive weeks ranked number one Steffi Graf (Germany) held the number one computer ranking from August 17, 1987 to March 11, 1991, a total of 186 weeks.

Highest earnings (career) Martina Navratilova (U.S.) has won a career record $18,396,526 in prize money, 1972–92.

Highest earnings (season) Monica Seles (Yugoslavia) won a season record $2,622,352 in 1992.

TRACK AND FIELD

ORIGINS Competition in running, jumping and throwing must have occurred from the earliest days of humankind. The earliest evidence of organized running is from 3800 B.C. in Egypt. The ancient Olympic Games were cultural festivals that highlighted the ancient Greek ideal of perfection of mind and body. The first modern Olympic Games, staged in 1896, focused on athletic achievement and the spirit of competition, and the Games have provided the focus for track and field as a sport ever since. In 1983, a separate world championship was introduced.

OLYMPIC GAMES The first modern Olympic Games were staged in Athens, Greece, April 6–15, 1896. Fifty-nine athletes from 10 nations competed; women's events were not added until 1928.

Most gold medals Ray Ewry (U.S.) holds the all-time record for most appearances atop the winners' podium, with 10 gold medals: standing high jump (1900, 1904, 1906, 1908); standing long jump (1900, 1904, 1906, 1908); standing triple jump (1900, 1904). The women's record is four, shared by four athletes: Fanny Blankers-Koen (Netherlands): 100 m, 200 m, 80 m hurdles and 4 x 100 m relay in 1948; Betty Cuthbert (Australia): 100 m, 200 m, 4 x 100 m relay in 1956, and 400 m in 1964; Barbel Wockel (née

WORLD RECORDS—MEN

World records are for the men's events scheduled by the International Amateur Athletic Federation. Full automatic electronic timing is mandatory for events up to 400 meters.

Event	Time	Athlete (Country)	Place	Date
100 meters	9.86	Carl Lewis (U.S.)	Tokyo, Japan	August 25, 1991
200 meters	19.72	Pietro Mennea (Italy)	Mexico City, Mexico	September 12, 1979
400 meters	43.29	Butch Reynolds (U.S.)	Zürich, Switzerland	August 17, 1988
800 meters	1:41.73	Sebastian Coe (Great Britain)	Florence, Italy	June 10, 1981
1,500 meters	3:28.86	Noureddine Morceli (Algeria)	Rieti, Italy	September 6, 1992
1 mile	3:46.32	Steve Cram (Great Britain)	Oslo, Norway	July 27, 1985
5,000 meters	12:58.39	Saïd Aouita (Morocco)	Rome, Italy	July 22, 1987
10,000 meters	27:08.23	Arturo Barrios (Mexico)	Berlin, Germany	August 18, 1989
110 meter hurdles	12.92	Roger Kingdom (U.S.)	Zürich, Switzerland	August 16, 1989
400 meter hurdles	46.78	Kevin Young (U.S.)	Barcelona, Spain	August 6, 1992
3,000-meter steeplechase	8:02.08	Moses Kiptanui (Kenya)	Zürich, Switzerland	August 19, 1992
4 x 100 meters	37.40	United States (Mike Marsh, Leroy Burrell, Dennis Mitchell, Carl Lewis)	Barcelona, Spain	August 8, 1992
4 x 400 meters	2:55.74	United States (Andrew Valmon, Quincy Watts, Michael Johnson, Steve Lewis)	Barcelona, Spain	August 8, 1992

Event	Distance	Athlete (Country)	Place	Date
High jump	8' 0"	Javier Sotomayor (Cuba)	San Juan, Puerto Rico	July 29, 1989
Pole vault	20' 1½"	Sergey Bubka (Ukraine)	Tokyo, Japan	September 19, 1992
Long jump	29' 4½"	Mike Powell (U.S.)	Tokyo, Japan	August 30, 1991
Triple jump	58' 11½"	Willie Banks (U.S.)	Indianapolis, Ind.	June 16, 1985
Shot	75' 10¼"	Randy Barnes (U.S.)	Los Angeles, Calif.	May 20, 1990
Discus	243' 0"	Jürgen Schult (East Germany)	Neubrandenburg, Germany	June 6, 1986
Hammer	284' 7"	Yuriy Sedykh (USSR)	Stuttgart, Germany	August 30, 1986
Javelin	300' 1"	Steve Backley (Great Britain)	Auckland, New Zealand	January 25, 1992

Time	Decathlon
8,891 points	Dan O'Brien (U.S.) (1st day: 100m 10.43 sec, Long jump 26' 6¼", Shot put 54' 9¼", High jump 6' 9½", 400 m 48.51 sec), (2nd day: 110 m hurdles 13.98 sec, Discus 159' 4", Pole vault 16' 4¾", Javelin 205' 4", 1,500 m 4:42.10 sec), Talence, France, September 4–5, 1992

Walking

Event	Time	Athlete (Country)	Place	Date
20 km	1:18.35.2	Stefan Johansson (Sweden)	Fana, Norway	May 15, 1992
50 km	3:41.38.4	Raul Gonzales (Mexico)	Bergen, Norway	May 27, 1979

HIGH HURDLES ■ KEVIN YOUNG WON THE '92 OLYMPIC 400 METER HURDLES AND SMASHED THE WORLD RECORD IN THE PROCESS.

Eckert; East Germany): 200 m and 4 x 100 m relay in both 1976 and 1980; Evelyn Ashford (U.S.): 100 m and 4 x 100 m relay in 1984, 4 x 100 m relay in 1988, 4 x 100 m relay in 1992.

Most gold medals (one Games) Paavo Nurmi (Finland) won five gold medals at the 1924 Games. His victories came in the 1,500 m, 5,000 m, 10,000 m cross-country, 3,000 m team, and cross-country team. The most wins at individual events (not including relay or other team races) is four, by Alvin Kraenzlein (U.S.) in 1900 at 60 m, 110 m hurdles, 200 m hurdles and the long jump.

Most medals won Paavo Nurmi (Finland) won a record 12 medals (nine gold, three silver) in the Games of 1920, 1924 and 1928. The women's record is seven, shared by two athletes: Shirley de la Hunty (Australia), three gold, one silver, three bronze in the 1948, 1952 and 1956 Games; Irena

Szewinska (Poland), three gold, two silver, two bronze in the 1964, 1968, 1972 and 1976 Games.

INDIVIDUAL RECORDS (U.S. ATHLETES)

Most medals Ray Ewry's 10 gold medals are the most won by any U.S. athlete (see above). Florence Griffith-Joyner has won a women's record five medals in track and field—three golds, two silver in the 1984 and 1988 Games.

Most gold medals Ray Ewry holds the Olympic mark for most golds (see above). The women's record for gold medals is four, by Evelyn Ashford—100m and 4 x 100 m relay in 1984, 4 x 100 m relay in 1988, 4 x 100 m relay in 1992.

Most gold medals (one Games) The most gold medals won at one Olympics is four, by three men: Alvin Kraenzlein (see above); Jesse Owens, 100 m, 200 m, long jump and 4 x 100 m relay in 1936; Carl Lewis, 100 m, 200 m, long jump and 4 x 100 m relay in 1984. The women's record is three golds, held by Wilma Rudolph, Valerie Brisco and Florence Griffith-Joyner (see above).

WORLD CHAMPIONSHIPS Quadriennial world championships distinct from the Olympic Games were first held in 1983 at Helsinki, Finland.

Most medals The most medals won is nine: seven gold, two silver by Carl Lewis (U.S.), 1983–91. The most medals won by a woman is five, by Heike Drechsler (East Germany/Germany): two silver, three bronze, 1983–91.

UNITED STATES NATIONAL CHAMPIONSHIPS

Most titles The most American national titles won at all events, indoors and out, is 65, by Ronald

BACKWARDS SPRINT ☛ FERDIE ATO ADOBOE (GHANA) RAN 100 METERS BACKWARDS IN 12.7 SECONDS AT NORTHAMPTON, MASS., ON JULY 25, 1991.

WORLD RECORDS—WOMEN

World records are for the women's events scheduled by the International Amateur Athletic Federation. The same stipulation about automatically timed events applies in the six events up to 400 meters as in the men's list.

Event	Time	Athlete (Country)	Place	Date
100 meters	10.49	Florence Griffith-Joyner (U.S.)	Indianapolis, Ind.	July 16, 1988
200 meters	21.34	Florence Griffith-Joyner (U.S.)	Seoul, South Korea	September 29, 1988
400 meters	47.60	Marita Koch (East Germany)	Canberra, Australia	October 6, 1985
800 meters	1:53.28	Jarmila Kratochvilová (Czechoslovakia)	Münich, Germany	July 26, 1983
1,500 meters	3:52.47	Tatyana Kazankina (USSR)	Zürich, Switzerland	August 13, 1980
1 mile	4:15.61	Paula Ivan (Romania)	Nice, France	July 10, 1989
3,000 meters	8:22.62	Tatyana Kazankina (USSR)	Leningrad, USSR	August 26, 1984
5,000 meters	14:37.33	Ingrid Kristiansen (Norway)	Stockholm, Sweden	August 5, 1986
10,000 meter	30:13.74	Ingrid Kristiansen (Norway)	Oslo, Norway	July 5, 1986
100 meter hurdles	12.21	Yordanka Donkova (Bulgaria)	Stara Zagora, Bulgaria	August 20, 1988
400 meter hurdles	52.94	Marina Styepanova (USSR)	Tashkent, USSR	September 17, 1986
4 x 100 meters	41.37	East Germany (Silke Gladisch, Sabine Rieger, Ingrid Auerswald, Marlies Göhr)	Canberra, Australia	October 6, 1985
4 x 400 meters	3:15.17	USSR (Tatyana Ledovskaya, Olga Nazarova, Maria Pinigina, Olga Bryzgina)	Seoul, South Korea	October 1, 1988

Event	Distance	Athlete (Country)	Place	Date
High jump	6' 10¼"	Stefka Kostadinova (Bulgaria)	Rome, Italy	August 30, 1987
Long jump	24' 8¼"	Galina Chistyakova (USSR)	Leningrad, USSR	June 11, 1988
Triple jump	49' ¾"	Inessa Kravets (USSR)	Moscow, USSR	June 10, 1991
Shot	74' 3"	Natalya Lisovskaya (USSR)	Moscow, USSR	June 7, 1987
Discus	252' 0"	Gabriele Reinsch (East Germany)	Neubrandenburg, Germany	July 9, 1988
Javelin	262' 5"	Petra Felke (East Germany)	Potsdam, Germany	September 9, 1988

Heptathlon

Time	Heptathlon
7,291 points	Jacqueline Joyner-Kersee (U.S.) (100 m hurdles 12.69 sec; High jump 6' 1¼"; Shot put 51' 10"; 200 m 22.56 sec; Long jump 23' 10 "; Javelin 149' 9"; 800 m 2:08.51 sec), Seoul, South Korea, September 23–24, 1988

Walking

Event	Time	Athlete (Country)	Place	Date
5 km	20:17.19	Kerry Saxby (Australia)	Sydney, Australia	January 14, 1990
10 km	41:56.21	Nadezhda Ryashkina (USSR)	Seattle, Wash.	July 24, 1990

JACKIE JOYNER-KERSEE

With back-to-back victories at the 1988 and 1992 Olympics, Jackie Joyner-Kersee can justifiably claim to be "the world's greatest female athlete." Joyner-Kersee has suffered from asthma since childhood, yet remarkably, she has not only dominated the most arduous of womens' endurance events but has also won the Olympic and world championship long jump titles. In 1986 she set her first heptathlon world record, in the process becoming the first person to break the 7,000-point barrier. She has surpassed 7,000 points on five occasions, a feat only achieved once by one other athlete. Joyner-Kersee set the current world record at the 1988 Olympics. Currently she has the five highest points scores of all time, and six of the top ten.

JOYNER-KERSEE TRACK & FIELD RECORDS

WORLD RECORDS
- Heptathlon record, **7,291 points**
- Consecutive heptathlon wins **13**
- Most Olympic heptathlon golds **2**

U.S. RECORDS
- Long jump, outdoors **24'5½"**
- Long jump, indoors **23'1¼"**
- 55 meter hurdles, indoors **7.37**
- 60 meter hurdles, indoors **7.81**
- Most Olympic medals by a woman in track events **5***

* Shared with four other athletes

WITH HER SECOND OLYMPIC HEPTATHLON VICTORY IN 1992, JOYNER–KERSEE CEMENTED HER REPUTATION AS THE WORLD'S GREATEST WOMEN ATHELETE.

HEPTATHLON WORLD RECORD

The heptathlon is a two-day competition consisting of seven events: 100 meter hurdles, high jump, shot put, 200 meters, long jump, javelin and 800 meters. Joyner-Kersee set the world record for the first time at the 1986 Goodwill Games, scoring 7,148 points; she also became the first to break the 7,000-point barrier. She has extended her record on three other occasions, the current world record being 7,291 points set at the 1988 Seoul Olympics.

Event 1	100m Hurdles		12.69 secs	1,172 points
Event 2	High Jump		6 feet 1 1/4 inches	1,054 points
Event 3	Shot Put		51 feet 10 inches	915 points
Event 4	200 Meters		22.56 secs	1,123 points
Event 5	Long Jump		23 feet 10 inches	1,264 points
Event 6	Javelin		149 feet 9 inches	776 points
Event 7	800 Meters		2 min 08.51 secs	987 points
Total	Seoul, S. Korea, Sept. 23–24, 1988	**World Record**		7,291 points

SOURCE: THE ATHLETICS CONGRESS, JJK & ASSOCIATES, INC.

Owen Laird at various walking events between
1958 and 1976. Excluding the walks, the record is
41, by Stella Walsh (née Walasiewicz), who won
41 women's events between 1930 and 1954: 33
outdoors and eight indoors.

Longest winning sequence Iolanda Balas (Romania) won a record 140 consecutive competitions at high
jump from 1956 to 1967. The record at a track event
was 122, at 400 meter hurdles, by Edwin Moses (U.S.)
between his loss to Harald Schmid (West Germany) at
Berlin, Germany on August 26, 1977 and that to Danny
Harris (U.S.) at Madrid, Spain on June 4, 1987.

ROAD RUNNING

MARATHON

The marathon is run over a distance of 26 miles
385 yards. This distance was the one used for the

race at the 1908 Olympic Games, run from Windsor to the White City stadium, London, England,
and it became standard from 1924 on. The marathon was introduced at the 1896 Olympic Games
to commemorate the legendary run of
Pheidippides (or Philippides) from the battlefield
of Marathon to Athens in 490 B.C. The 1896 Olympic marathon was preceded by trial races that year.
The first Boston Marathon, the world's oldest annual marathon race, was held on April 19, 1897 at
24 miles 1,232 yards, and the first national marathon championship was that of Norway in 1897.

The first championship marathon for women
was organized by the Road Runners Club of America on September 27, 1970.

WORLD RECORDS There are as yet no official records
for the marathon, and it should be noted that courses
may vary in severity. The following are the best times
recorded, all on courses with verified distances: for
men, 2 hours 6 minutes 50 seconds, by Belayneh
Dinsamo (Ethiopia) at Rotterdam, Netherlands on
April 17, 1988; for women, 2 hours 21 minutes 6
seconds, by Ingrid Kristiansen (née Christensen;
Norway) at London, England on April 21, 1985.

United States The Athletics Congress recognizes
the following U.S. records: for men, Pat Peterson,
2 hours 10 minutes 4 seconds, at London, England
on April 23, 1989; for women, Joan Benoit Samuelson, 2 hours 21 minutes 21 seconds, at Chicago,
Ill., on October 20, 1985.

OLYMPIC GAMES The marathon has been run at every
Olympic Games of the modern era; however, a
women's race wasn't included in the Games until 1984.

Most gold medals The record for most wins in the
men's race is two, by two marathoners: Abebe Bikila
(Ethiopia), 1960 and 1964; Waldemar Cierpinski
(East Germany), 1976 and 1980. The women's event
has been run twice, with different winners.

BOSTON MARATHON The world's oldest annual
running race, the Boston Marathon was first
staged on April 19, 1897.

Most wins Clarence De Mar (U.S.) has won the
race seven times—1911, 1922–24, 1927–28, 1930.
Rosa Mota (Portugal) has won the women's division three times—1987–88, 1990.

Fastest time The course record for men is 2
hours 7 minutes 51 seconds, by Rob de Castella
(Australia) in 1986. The women's record is 2 hours

LONGEST LEAPS

On July 10, 1969, astronaut Neil Armstrong made the most famous "giant leap" in history. Back here on Earth, other leapers have captured the world's attention. Evil Knievel spawned a stunt industry; Bob Beamon jumped beyond 29 feet; and no Christmas holiday season would be complete with-

out the fabled "ten lords a-leaping." The motivation for the yuletide aristocrats is something of a mystery, but for Armstrong, Knievel, Beamon and the record-holders below, the reason is clear: they all sought the thrill experienced by head ing out into the unknown.

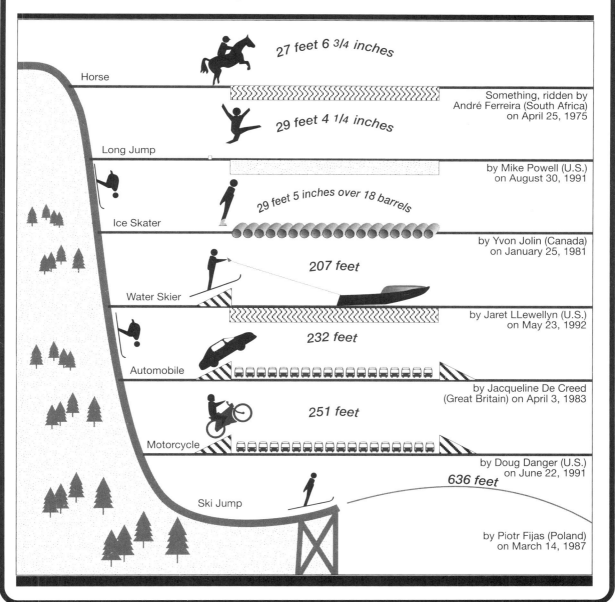

Horse
27 feet 6 3/4 inches
Something, ridden by André Ferreira (South Africa) on April 25, 1975

Long Jump
29 feet 4 1/4 inches
by Mike Powell (U.S.) on August 30, 1991

Ice Skater
29 feet 5 inches over 18 barrels
by Yvon Jolin (Canada) on January 25, 1981

Water Skier
207 feet
by Jaret LLewellyn (U.S.) on May 23, 1992

Automobile
232 feet
by Jacqueline De Creed (Great Britain) on April 3, 1983

Motorcycle
251 feet
by Doug Danger (U.S.) on June 22, 1991

Ski Jump
636 feet
by Piotr Fijas (Poland) on March 14, 1987

UPS AND DOWNS ■ STEVE SILVA (ABOVE) CLIMBED
45,708 STEPS (39 ASCENTS, DESCENDING BY ELEVA-
TOR) OF THE WESTIN PEACHTREE PLAZA HOTEL IN
ATLANTA, GA., IN 9 HOURS 50 MINUTES 43 SECONDS
JANUARY 27–28, 1990. FLIPPING A PANCAKE THE EN-
TIRE RACE, DOMINIC CUZZACREA (RIGHT) COMPLETED
THE BUFFALO MARATHON IN 3 HOURS 6 MINUTES 22
SECONDS ON MAY 6, 1990.

TIMEOUT

BACKWARDS MARATHON ☞ BUD
BADYANA HOLDS THE FASTEST TIME
FOR COMPLETING A FULL MARATHON
RUNNING BACKWARDS. ON NOVEMBER
10, 1991 HE RAN THE COLUMBUS
(OHIO) MARATHON IN A TIME OF 4
HOURS 15 SECONDS.

22 minutes 43 seconds, by Joan Benoit (now Samuelson; U.S.) in 1983.

NEW YORK CITY MARATHON The race was run in Central Park each year from 1970 to 1976, when, to celebrate the U.S. Bicentennial, the course was changed to a route through all five boroughs of the city. From that year, when there were 2,090 runners, the race has become one of the world's great sporting occasions; in 1992 there were a record 27,797 finishers.

Most wins Grete Waitz (Norway) has won nine times—1978–80, 1982–86 and 1988. Bill Rodgers has a men's record four wins—1976–79.

Fastest time The course record for men is 2 hours 8 minutes 1 second, by Juma Ikangaa (Tanzania), and for women, 2 hours 25 minutes 30 seconds, by Ingrid Kristiansen (Norway), both set in 1989. On a course subsequently remeasured as about 170 yards short, Grete Waitz was the 1981 women's winner in 2 hours 25 minutes 29 seconds.

LONG-DISTANCE RUNNING RECORDS

Longest race (distance) The longest races ever staged were the 1928 (3,422 miles) and 1929 (3,665 miles) transcontinental races from New York City to Los Angeles, Calif. Johnny Salo (U.S.) was the winner in 1929 in 79 days, from March 31 to June 18. His elapsed time of 525 hours 57 minutes 20 seconds (averaging 6.97 mph) left him only 2 minutes 47 seconds ahead of Englishman Peter Gavuzzi.

The longest race staged annually is Australia's Westfield Run from Paramatta, New South Wales to Doncaster, Victoria (Sydney to Melbourne). The distance run has varied slightly, but the record is by Yiannis Kouros (Greece) in 5 days 2 hours 27

WALKING ON HANDS ☞ THE DISTANCE RECORD FOR WALKING ON HANDS IS 870 MILES, BY JOHANN HURLINGER (AUSTRIA). IN 55 DAILY 10-HOUR STINTS, HURLINGER WALKED FROM VIENNA, AUSTRIA TO PARIS, FRANCE IN 1900.

minutes 27 seconds in 1989, when the distance was 658 miles.

Longest runs The longest run by an individual is one of 11,134 miles around the United States, by Sarah Covington-Fulcher (U.S.), starting and finishing in Los Angeles, Calif., between July 21, 1987 and October 2, 1988. Robert J. Sweetgall (U.S.) ran 10,608 miles around the perimeter of the United States, starting and finishing in Washington D.C., between October 1982 and July 15, 1983.

WALKING

OLYMPIC GAMES Walking races have been included in the Olympic events since 1906.

Most gold medals The only walker to win three gold medals has been Ugo Frigerio (Italy), with the 3,000 meter in 1920, and the 10,000 meter in 1920 and 1924.

Most medals The record for most medals is four, by two walkers: Ugo Frigerio (Italy), three gold, one bronze, 1920–32; Vladimir Golubnichiy (USSR), two gold medals, one silver and one bronze, 1960–68.

TRAMPOLINING

ORIGINS Trampolining has been part of circus acts for many years. The sport of trampolining dates from 1936, when the prototype "T" model trampoline was designed by George Nissen of the United States. The first official tournament took place in 1947.

WORLD CHAMPIONSHIPS Instituted in 1964, championships have been staged biennially since 1968. The world championships recognize champions, both men and women, in four events: individual, synchronized pairs, tumbling, and double mini trampoline.

Most titles Judy Wills (U.S.) has won a record five individual world titles, 1964–68. The men's record is two, shared by six trampolinists: Wayne Miller (U.S.), 1966 and 1970; Dave Jacobs (U.S.), 1967–68; Richard Tisson (France), 1974 and 1976; Yevgeniy Yanes (USSR), 1976 and 1978; Lionel Pioline (France), 1984 and 1986; and Alexander Maskalenko (USSR/Russia), 1990 and 1992 .

IRON MAN ■ THE RECORD TIME FOR THE HAWAII IRONMAN TRIATHLON IS 8 HOURS 9 MINUTES 8 SECONDS, BY MARK ALLEN IN 1992.

UNITED STATES NATIONAL CHAMPIONSHIPS The American Trampoline & Tumbling Association staged the first national championship in 1947. The inaugural event was open only to men; a women's event was introduced in 1961.

Most titles Stuart Ransom has won a record 12 national titles: six individual, 1975–76, 1978–80, 1982; three synchronized, 1975, 1979–80; three double mini-tramp, 1979–80, 1982. Leigh Hennessy has won a record 10 women's titles: one individual, 1978; eight synchronized, 1972–73, 1976–78, 1980–82; one double mini-tramp, 1978.

TRIATHLON

ORIGINS The triathlon combines long distance swimming, cycling, and running. The sport was developed by a group of dedicated athletes who founded the Hawaii "Ironman" in 1974. After a series of unsuccessful attempts to create a world governing body, *L'Union Internationale de Triathlon* (UIT) was founded in Avignon, France in 1989. The UIT staged the first official world championships in Avignon on August 6, 1989.

WORLD CHAMPIONSHIPS An unofficial world championship has been held in Nice, France since 1982. The three legs comprise a 3,200 meter swim (4,000 meter since 1988), 120 kilometer bike ride, and 32 kilometer run.

Most titles Mark Allen (U.S.) has won a record eight times, 1982–86, 1989–91. Paula Newby-Fraser (Zimbabwe) has won a record three women's titles, 1989–91.

Fastest times The men's record is 5 hours 46 minutes 10 seconds, by Mark Allen (U.S.) in 1988. The women's record is 6 hours 27 minutes 6 seconds, by Erin Baker (New Zealand) in 1988.

HAWAII IRONMAN This is the first, and best known, of the triathlons. Instituted on February 18, 1978, the first race was contested by 15 athletes. The Ironman grew rapidly in popularity, and 1,000 athletes entered the 1984 race. Contestants must first swim 2.4 miles, then cycle 112 miles, and finally run a full marathon of 26 miles 385 yards.

Most titles Dave Scott (U.S.) has won the Ironman a record six times, 1980, 1982–84, 1986–87. The women's event has been won a record five times by Paula Newby-Fraser (Zimbabwe) in 1986, 1988–89, and 1991–92.

Fastest times Mark Allen (U.S.) holds the course record at 8 hours 9 minutes 8 seconds in 1992. Paula Newby-Fraser holds the women's record at 8 hours 55 seconds in 1992.

Fastest time The fastest time ever recorded over the Ironman distances is 8 hours 1 minute 32 seconds, by Dave Scott (U.S.) at Lake Biwas, Japan on July 30, 1989.

Largest field The most competitors to finish a triathlon race were the 3,888 who completed the 1987 Bud Lite U.S. Triathlon in Chicago, Ill.

VOLLEYBALL

ORIGINS The game was invented as *mintonette* in 1895 by William G. Morgan at the YMCA gymnasium at Holyoke, Mass. The International Volleyball Association (IVA) was formed in Paris, France in April 1947. The United States Volleyball Association was founded in 1922 and is the governing body for the sport in this country. The United States National Championships were inaugurated for men in 1928, and for women in 1949.

OLYMPIC GAMES Volleyball became an official Olympic sport in 1964, when both men's and women's tournaments were staged in Tokyo, Japan.

Most gold medals (country) The USSR has won three men's titles, 1964, 1968 and 1980; and four women's titles, 1968, 1972, 1980 and 1988.

Most medals (individual) Inna Ryskal (USSR) has won four medals in Olympic competition: two gold, 1968, 1972; and two silver, 1964, 1976. The men's record is three, won by three players: Yuriy Poyarkov (USSR), two golds, 1964 and 1968, one bronze, 1972; Katsutoshi Nekoda (Japan), one gold, 1972, one silver, 1968, and one bronze, 1964; and Steve Timmons

SPIKE ■ RANDY STOKLOS IS THE LEADING MONEY WINNER ON THE AVP/MILLER LITE TOUR.

(U.S.), two gold, 1984 and 1988, and one bronze, 1992.

WORLD CHAMPIONSHIPS World championships were instituted in 1949 for men and in 1952 for women.

Most titles The USSR has won six men's titles, 1949, 1952, 1960, 1962, 1978 and 1982, and five women's titles, 1952, 1956, 1960, 1970 and 1990.

BEACH VOLLEYBALL

In professional beach volleyball the court dimensions are the same as in the indoor game: 30 feet x 60 feet, or 30 feet x 30 feet on each side, with the net set at a height of eight feet. In beach volleyball, teams play two-a-side, as opposed to six-a- side for the indoor game.

ORIGINS Beach volleyball originated in California in the 1940s. The sport grew rapidly in the 1960s, and the first world championships were staged in

1976. In 1981 the Association of Volleyball Professionals was founded, and the AVP/Miller Lite Tour was formed that year.

AVP/MILLER LITE TOUR RECORDS (1977–92)

Most tour wins Sinjin Smith has won 125 tour events, 1977–92.

Highest earnings Randy Stoklos has a earned a career record $1,131,289, 1982–92.

WATER POLO

ORIGINS This game was originally played in England as "water soccer" in 1869. The first rules were drafted in 1876. Water polo has been an Olympic event since 1900. In 1908, FINA (see Swimming) became the governing body for water polo. The first world championships were held in 1973.

OLYMPIC GAMES Water polo was first included at the 1900 Games, and has been included in every Games since.

Most gold medals (country) Hungary has won six Olympic titles, 1932, 1936, 1952, 1956, 1964 and 1976.

Most gold medals (players) Five players have won three gold medals: George Wilkinson (Great Britain), 1900, 1908, 1912; Paul Radmilovic (Great Britain), 1908, 1912, 1920; Charles Smith (Great Britain), 1908, 1912, 1920; Deszo Gyarmati (Hungary), 1952, 1956, 1964; Gyorgy Karpati (Hungary), 1952, 1956, 1964.

WORLD CHAMPIONSHIPS A competition was first held at the World Swimming Championships in 1973. A women's event was included from 1986.

Most titles Two countries have won two men's titles: USSR, 1975 and 1982; Yugoslavia, 1986 and 1991. The women's competition was won by Australia in 1986, and by the Netherlands in 1991.

UNITED STATES NATIONAL CHAMPIONSHIPS The first men's national championship was held in 1891. A women's tournament was first held in 1926.

Most titles The New York Athletic Club has won 25 men's titles: 1892–96, 1903–04, 1906–08, 1922, 1929–31, 1933–35, 1937–39, 1954, 1956, 1960–61, and 1971. The Industry Hills Athletic Club (Calif.) has won nine women's titles: 1980–81 and 1984–88 (outdoors), 1987–88 (indoors).

MAKING A SPLASH ■ WATER POLO DATES TO THE MID-19TH CENTURY. IT HAS BEEN INCLUDED IN EVERY OLYMPICS SINCE 1900.

WATERSKIING

ORIGINS Modern waterskiing was pioneered in the 1920s. Ralph Samuelson, who skied on Lake Pepin, Minn. in 1922 using two curved pine boards, is generally credited as being the father of the sport. Forms of skiing on water can be traced back centuries to people attempting to walk on water with planks. The development of the motorboat to tow skiers was the largest factor in the sport's growth. The world governing body is the World Water Ski Union (WWSU), which succeeded the *Union Internationale de Ski Nautique* that had been formed in Geneva, Switzerland in 1946. The American Water Ski Association was founded in 1939 and held the first national championships that year.

WORLD CHAMPIONSHIPS The first world championships were held in 1949.

Most titles Sammy Duvall (U.S.) has won four overall titles, in 1981, 1983, 1985 and 1987. Two women have won three overall titles: Willa McGuire (née Worthington; U.S.), 1949–50 and 1955; Liz Allan-Shetter (U.S.), 1965, 1969 and 1975.

Most individual titles Liz Allan-Shetter has won a record eight individual championship events and is the only person to win all four titles—slalom, jumping, tricks, and overall in one year, at Copenhagen, Denmark in 1969.

UNITED STATES NATIONAL CHAMPIONSHIPS National championships were first held at Marine Stadium, Jones Beach State Park, Long Island, N.Y. on July 22, 1939.

TIMEOUT

MOST SKIERS TOWED ☛ A RECORD 100 WATERSKIERS WERE TOWED ON DOUBLE SKIS OVER A NAUTICAL MILE BY THE CRUISER REEF CAT AT CAIRNS, AUSTRALIA ON OCTOBER 18, 1986.

LONG JUMP ■ JARET LLEWELLYN JUMPED A RECORD 207 FEET ON MAY 23, 1992.

Most titles The most overall titles is eight, by Willa Worthington McGuire, 1946–51 and 1954–55, and by Liz Allan-Shetter, 1968–75. The men's record is six titles, by Chuck Stearns, 1957–58, 1960, 1962, 1965 and 1967.

WEIGHTLIFTING

There are two standard lifts in weightlifting: the "snatch" and the "clean and jerk." Totals of the two lifts determine competition results. The "press," which had been a standard lift, was abolished in 1972.

ORIGINS Competitions for lifting weights of stone were held at the ancient Olympic Games. In the 19th century, weightlifting consisted of professional exhibitions in which some of the advertised poundages were open to doubt. The *Fédération Internationale Haltérophile et Culturiste*, now the International Weightlifting Federation (IWF), was established in 1905, and its first official championships were held in Tallinn, Estonia on April 29–30, 1922.

OLYMPIC GAMES Weightlifting events were included in the first modern Games in 1896.

WORLD WEIGHTLIFTING RECORDS (MEN)
Bantamweight 56 kg (123¼ lb)

Event	Weight	Lifter (Country)	Date
Snatch	135.0 kg	Liu Shoubin (China)	September 28, 1991
Jerk	171.0 kg	Neno Terziiski (Bulgaria)	September 6, 1987
Total	300.0 kg	Naim Suleimanov (Bulgaria)	May 11, 1984

Featherweight 60 kg (132¼ lb)

Event	Weight	Lifter (Country)	Date
Snatch	152.5 kg	Naim Suleymanoglü (Turkey)*	September 20, 1988
Jerk	190.0 kg	Naim Suleymanoglü (Turkey)*	September 20, 1988
Total	342.5 kg	Naim Suleymanoglü (Turkey)*	September 20, 1988

Lightweight 67.5 kg (148¾ lb)

Event	Weight	Lifter (Country)	Date
Snatch	160.0 kg	Israil Militosyan (USSR)	September 18, 1989
Jerk	200.5 kg	Mikhail Petrov (Bulgaria)	September 8, 1987
Total	355.0 kg	Mikhail Petrov (Bulgaria)	December 5, 1987

Middleweight 75 kg (165¼ lb)

Event	Weight	Lifter (Country)	Date
Snatch	170.0 kg	Angel Guenchev (Bulgaria)	December 11, 1987
Jerk	215.5 kg	Aleksandr Varbanov (Bulgaria)	December 5, 1987
Total	382.5 kg	Aleksandr Varbanov (Bulgaria)	February 20, 1988

Light-Heavyweight 82.5 kg (181¾ lb)

Event	Weight	Lifter (Country)	Date
Snatch	183.0 kg	Asen Zlatev (Bulgaria)	December 7, 1986
Jerk	225.0 kg	Asen Zlatev (Bulgaria)	November 12, 1986
Total	405.0 kg	Yuri Vardanyan (USSR)	September 14, 1984

Middle-Heavyweight 90 kg (198¼ lb)

Event	Weight	Lifter (Country)	Date
Snatch	195.5 kg	Blagoi Blagoyev (Bulgaria)	May 1, 1983
Jerk	235.0 kg	Anatoliy Khrapatliy (USSR)	April 29, 1988
Total	422.5 kg	Viktor Solodov (USSR)	September 15, 1984

First-Heavyweight 100 kg (220¼ lb)

Event	Weight	Lifter (Country)	Date
Snatch	200.5 kg	Nicu Vlad (Romania)	November 14, 1986
Jerk	242.5 kg	Aleksandr Popov (USSR)	March 5, 1988
Total	440.0 kg	Yuriy Zakharevich (USSR)	March 4, 1983

Heavyweight 110 kg (242½ lb)

Event	Weight	Lifter (Country)	Date
Snatch	210.0 kg	Yuriy Zakharevich (USSR)	September 27, 1988
Jerk	250.5 kg	Yuriy Zakharevich (USSR)	April 30, 1988
Total	455.0 kg	Yuriy Zakharevich (USSR)	September 27, 1988

Super-Heavyweight—over 110 kg (242½ lb)

Event	Weight	Lifter (Country)	Date
Snatch	216.0 kg	Antonio Krastev (Bulgaria)	September 13, 1987
Jerk	266.0 kg	Leonid Taranenko (USSR)	November 26, 1988
Total	475.0 kg	Leonid Taranenko (USSR)	November 26, 1988

* Formerly Naim Suleimanov or Neum Shalamanov of Bulgaria

TURKISH TITAN ■ FEATHERWEIGHT NAIM SULEYMANOGLÜ DOMINATES HIS WEIGHT CLASS. HE HOLDS ALL THREE WORLD RECORDS AND HAS WON THE LAST TWO OLYMPIC TITLES.

Most gold medals Four lifters have won two gold medals: John Davis Jr. (U.S.), heavyweight, 1942 and 1952; Tommy Kono (U.S.), lightweight, 1952, light heavyweight, 1956; Chuck Vinci Jr. (U.S.), bantamweight, 1956 and 1960; and Naim Suleymanoglü (Turkey), featherweight, 1988 and 1992.

Most medals Norbert Schemansky (U.S.) has won four medals: one gold, one silver and two bronze, 1960–64.

WORLD CHAMPIONSHIPS The IWF held its first world championships at Tallinn, Estonia in 1922, but has subsequently recognized 18 championships held in Vienna, Austria between 1898 and 1920. The championships have been held annually since 1946, with the Olympic Games recognized as world championships in the year of the Games until 1988, when a championship separate from the Olympics was staged. A women's championship was introduced in 1987.

Most titles The record for most titles is eight, held by three lifters: John Davis (U.S.), 1938, 1946–52; Tommy Kono (U.S.), 1952–59; and Vasiliy Alekseyev (USSR), 1970–77.

BENCH PRESS ☞ A 24-HOUR TOTAL WEIGHT BENCH PRESS RECORD OF 8,529,699 LBS WAS SET BY A NINE-MAN TEAM FROM THE HOGARTH BARBELL CLUB, CHISWICK, ENGLAND ON JULY 18–19, 1987.

Most titles The most titles won is 13, by Anthony Terlazzo at 137 pounds, 1932 and 1936, and at 148 pounds, 1933, 1935, 1937–45.

WRESTLING

ORIGINS Wrestling was the most popular sport in the ancient Olympic Games; wall drawings dating to *c.* 2600 B.C. show that the sport was popular long before the Greeks. Wrestling was included in the first modern Games. The International Amateur Wrestling Association (FILA) was founded in 1912. There are two forms of wrestling at the international level: freestyle and Greco-Roman. The use of the legs and holds below the waist are prohibited in Greco-Roman.

OLYMPIC GAMES Wrestling events have been included in all the Games since 1896.

FREESTYLER ■ THE MOST WORLD TITLES WON BY ANY U.S. WRESTLER IS SIX, BY JOHN SMITH.

Most gold medals Three wrestlers have won three Olympic titles: Carl Westergren (Sweden) in 1920, 1924 and 1932; Ivar Johansson (Sweden) in 1932 (two) and 1936; and Aleksandr Medved (USSR) in 1964, 1968 and 1972.

Most medals (individual) Wilfried Dietrich (Germany) has won five medals in Olympic competition: one gold, two silver and two bronze, 1956–68.

WORLD CHAMPIONSHIPS

Most titles The freestyler Aleksandr Medved (USSR) won a record 10 world championships, 1962–64 and 1966–72, in three weight categories. The most world titles won by any U.S. wrestler is six by the freestyler John Smith, 1987–92.

NCAA DIVISION I CHAMPIONSHIP Oklahoma State University was the first unofficial national champion, in 1928.

Most titles Including five unofficial titles, Oklahoma State has won a record 29 NCAA titles, in 1928–31, 1933–35, 1937–42, 1946, 1948–49, 1954–56, 1958–59, 1961–62, 1964, 1966, 1968, 1971, 1989–90.

Consecutive titles The University of Iowa has won the most consecutive titles, with nine championships from 1978–86.

SUMO WRESTLING

Sumo bouts are fought between two wrestlers (*rikishi*) inside a 14.9-foot-diameter earthen circle (*dohyo*), covered by a roof, symbolizing a Shinto shrine. The wrestlers try to knock each other out of the ring or to the ground. The wrestler who steps out of the dohyo or touches the ground with any part of his body except the soles of his feet loses the contest. Sumo wrestlers are ranked according to their skills; the highest rank is *Yokozuma* (Grand Champion).

ORIGINS Sumo wrestling traces its origins to the development of the Shinto religion in Japan in the eighth century A.D. Sumo matches were staged at Shinto shrines to honor the divine spirits (known as *kami*) during planting and harvesting ceremonies. During the Edo era (1600–1868) sumo wrestling became a professional sport. Currently, sumo wrestling is governed by Nihon Sumo Kyokai (Japan Sumo Association), which stages six 15-day tournaments (*basho*) throughout the year.

Most wins (bouts) Kenji Hatano, known as Oshio, won a record 1,107 bouts in 1,891 contests, 1962–88.

Highest winning percentage Tameemon Torokichi, known as Raiden, compiled a .961 winning percentage—244 wins in 254 bouts—from 1789 to 1810.

YACHTING

ORIGINS Sailing as a sport dates from the 17th century. Originating in the Netherlands, it was introduced to England by Charles II, who participated in a 23 mile race along the River Thames in 1661. The oldest yacht club in the world is the Royal Cork Yacht Club, which claims descent from the Cork Harbor Water Club, founded in Ireland in 1720. The oldest continuously existing yacht club in the United States is the New York Yacht Club, founded in 1844.

AMERICA'S CUP The America's Cup was originally won as an outright prize by the schooner *America* on August 22, 1851 at Cowes, England and was later offered by the New York Yacht Club as a challenge trophy. On August 8, 1870, J. Ashbury's *Cambria* (Great Britain) failed to capture the trophy from *Magic*, owned by F. Osgood (U.S.). The Cup has been challenged 27 times. The U.S. was undefeated until 1983, when *Australia II*, skippered by John Bertrand and owned by a Perth syndicate headed by Alan Bond, beat *Liberty* 4–3, the narrowest series victory, at Newport, R.I.

Most wins (skipper) Three skippers have won the cup three times: Charlie Barr (U.S.), who defended in 1899, 1901 and 1903; Harold S. Vanderbilt (U.S.), who defended in 1930, 1934 and 1937; and Dennis Conner (U.S.), who defended in 1980, challenged in 1987, and defended in 1988.

Largest yacht The largest yacht to have competed in the America's Cup was the 1903 defender, the gaff-rigged cutter *Reliance*, with an overall length of 144 feet, a record sail area of 16,160 square feet and a rig 175 feet high.

OLYMPIC GAMES Bad weather caused the abandonment of yachting events at the first modern Games in 1896. However, the weather has stayed "fair" ever since, and yachting has been part of every Games.

Most gold medals Paul Elvstrom (Denmark) won a record four gold medals in yachting, and in the process became the first competitor in Olympic history to win individual gold medals in four successive Games. Elvstrom's titles came in the Firefly class in 1948, and in the Finn class in 1952, 1956 and 1960.

HIGH TECH ■ THE 1992 AMERICA'S CUP WAS THE MOST EXPENSIVE YACHTING REGATTA IN HISTORY. THE BIGGEST SPENDER, BILL KOCH, SKIPPERED HIS BOAT AMERICA^3 TO VICTORY.

Most medals Paul Elvstrom's four gold medals are also the most medals won by any Olympic yachtsman.

ROUND-THE-WORLD RACING

Longest race (nonstop) The world's longest nonstop sailing race is the Vendée Globe Challenge, the first of which started from Les Sables

LONGEST SAILBOARD ☞ THE WORLD'S LONGEST SAILBOARD, 165 FEET, WAS BUILT AT FREDRIKSTAD, NORWAY AND FIRST SAILED ON JUNE 28, 1986.

AMERICA'S CUP WINNERS (1851–1992)

Year	Cup Winner	Skipper	Challenger	Series
1851	America	Richard Brown	—	—
1870	Magic	Andrew Comstock	Cambria (England)	—
1871	Columbia	Nelson Comstock	Livonia (England)	4–1
1876	Madeleine	Josephus Williams	Countess of Dufferin (Canada)	2–0
1881	Mischief	Nathaniel Cook	Atalanta (Canada)	2–0
1885	Puritan	Aubrey Crocker	Genesta (England)	2–0
1886	Mayflower	Martin Stone	Galatea (England)	2–0
1887	Volunteer	Henry Haff	Thistle (Scotland)	2–0
1893	Vigilant	William Hansen	Valkyrie II (England)	3–0
1895	Defender	Henry Haff	Valkyrie III (England)	3–0
1899	Columbia	Charlie Barr	Shamrock I (England)	3–0
1901	Columbia	Charlie Barr	Shamrock II (England)	3–0
1903	Reliance	Charlie Barr	Shamrock III (England)	3–0
1920	Resolute	Charles Adams	Shamrock IV (England)	3–2
1930	Enterprise	Harold Vanderbilt	Shamrock V (England)	4–0
1934	Rainbow	Harold Vanderbilt	Endeavour (England)	4–2
1937	Ranger	Harold Vanderbilt	Endeavour II (England)	4–0
1958	Columbia	Briggs Cunningham	Sceptre (England)	4–0
1962	Weatherly	Emil Mosbacher Jr.	Gretel (Australia)	4–1
1964	Constellation	Bob Bavier Jr.	Sovereign (England)	4–0
1967	Intrepid	Emil Mosbacher Jr.	Dame Pattie (Australia)	4–0
1970	Intrepid	Bill Fricker	Gretel II (Australia)	4–1
1974	Courageous	Ted Hood	Southern Cross (Australia)	4–0
1977	Courageous	Ted Turner	Australia (Australia)	4–0
1980	Freedom	Dennis Conner	Australia (Australia)	4–1
1983	Australia II	John Bertrand	Liberty (U.S.)	4–3
1987	Stars & Stripes	Dennis Conner	Kookaburra III (Australia)	4–0
1988	Stars & Stripes	Dennis Conner	New Zealand (New Zealand)	2–0
1992	America[3]	Bill Koch	Il Moro di Venezia (Italy)	4–1

d'Olonne, France on November 26, 1989. The distance circumnavigated without stopping was 22,500 nautical miles. The race is for boats between 50–60 feet, sailed single-handed. The record time on the course is 109 days 8 hours 48 minutes 50 seconds, by Titouan Lamazou (France) in the sloop *Ecureuil d'Aquitaine*, which finished at Les Sables on March 19, 1990.

Longest race (total distance) The longest and oldest regular sailing race around the world is the quadrennial Whitbread Round the World race (instituted August 1973), organized by the Royal Naval Sailing Association (Great Britain). It starts in England, and the course around the world and the number of legs with stops at specified ports are varied from race to race. The distance for 1989–90 was 32,000 nautical miles from Southampton, England and return, with stops and restarts at Punta del Este, Uruguay; Fremantle, Australia; Auckland, New Zealand; Punta del Este, Uruguay, and Fort Lauderdale, Fla.

1992, SEASONS IN REVIEW

A listing of world champions, Olympic champions, national champions, tournament winners and leading money winners of the 1992 sports season. A complete listing of the medalists at the 1992 Winter and Summer Olympic Games can be found on pages 235–246. A country abbreviation code is included on page 235 and 237.

ARCHERY

UNITED STATES NATIONAL OUTDOOR CHAMPIONSHIPS STAGED AT OXFORD, OHIO

Men's Champion ■ Allen Rasor
Women's Champion ■ Sherry Block

AUTO RACING

CART PPG-INDY CAR WORLD SERIES

Champion ■ Bobby Rahal, Lola-Chevy A, 196 points

NASCAR WINSTON CUP CHAMPIONSHIP

Champion ■ Alan Kulwicki, Ford Thunderbird, 4,078 points

FORMULA ONE DRIVERS CHAMPIONSHIP

Champion ■ Nigel Mansell (GB), Williams, 108 points

NHRA WINSTON CUP CHAMPIONSHIP

Top Fuel Champion ■ Joe Amato, Valvoline dragster, 12,232 points
Funny Car Champion ■ Cruz Pedregon, MacDonald's/Larry Minor Motor Sports Olds Cutlass, 15,246 points
Pro Stock Champion ■ Warren Johnson, AC Delco Olds Cutlass, 15,868 points

BADMINTON

UNITED STATES NATIONAL CHAMPIONSHIPS STAGED AT COLORADO SPRINGS, COLO.

Men's Singles ■ Chris Jogis
Women's Singles ■ Joy Kitzmiller
Men's Doubles ■ Ben Lee/Tom Reidy
Women's Doubles ■ Joy Kitzmiller/Linda French
Mixed Doubles ■ Andy Chong/Linda French

BASEBALL

MAJOR LEAGUES

1992 FINAL STANDINGS

AMERICAN LEAGUE EAST				
Team	W	L	Pct.	GB
Toronto	96	66	.593	—
Milwaukee	92	70	.568	4
Baltimore	89	73	.549	7
Cleveland	76	86	.469	20
New York	76	86	.469	20
Detroit	75	87	.463	21
Boston	73	89	.451	23

AMERICAN LEAGUE WEST				
Team	W	L	Pct.	GB
Oakland	96	66	.593	—
Minnesota	90	72	.556	6
Chicago	86	76	.531	10
Texas	77	85	.475	19
California	72	90	.444	24
Kansas City	72	90	.444	24
Seattle	64	98	.395	32

NATIONAL LEAGUE EAST				
Team	W	L	Pct.	GB
Pittsburgh	96	66	.593	—
Montreal	87	75	.537	9
St. Louis	83	79	.512	13
Chicago	78	84	.481	18
New York	72	90	.444	24
Philadelphia	70	92	.432	26

NATIONAL LEAGUE WEST				
Team	W	L	Pct.	GB
Atlanta	98	64	.605	—
Cincinnati	90	72	.556	8
San Diego	82	80	.506	16

NATIONAL LEAGUE WEST (cont'd)				
Houston	81	81	.500	17
San Francisco	72	90	.444	26
Los Angeles	63	99	.389	35

1992 STATISTICAL LEADERS

AMERICAN LEAGUE

Batting Average	.343	Edgar Martinez, Seattle
Runs Batted In	124	Cecil Fielder, Detroit
Home Runs	43	Juan Gonzalez, Texas
Triples	12	Lance Johnson, Chicago
Doubles	46	Edgar Martinez, Seattle
Hits	210	Kirby Puckett, Minnesota
Runs Scored	114	Tony Phillips, Detroit
Stolen Bases	66	Kenny Lofton, Cleveland
Earned Run Average	2.41	Roger Clemens, Boston
Victories	21	Jack Morris, Toronto (21–6)
	21	Kevin Brown, Texas (21–11)
Strikeouts	241	Randy Johnson, Seattle
Saves	51	Dennis Eckersley, Oakland

NATIONAL LEAGUE

Batting Average	.330	Gary Sheffield, San Diego
Runs Batted In	109	Darren Daulton, Philadelphia
Home Runs	35	Fred McGriff, San Diego
Triples	14	Deion Sanders, Atlanta
Doubles	45	Andy Van Slyke, Pittsburgh
Hits	199	Terry Pendleton, Atlanta Andy Van Slyke, Pittsburgh
Runs Scored	109	Barry Bonds, Pittsburgh
Stolen Bases	78	Marquis Grissom, Montreal
Earned Run Average	2.08	Bill Swift, San Francisco
Victories	20	Tom Glavine, Atlanta (20–8) Greg Maddux, Chicago (20–11)
Strikeouts	215	John Smoltz, Atlanta
Saves	43	Lee Smith, St. Louis

AWARDS

American League

Most Valuable Player ■ Dennis Eckersley, Oakland

Cy Young Award ■ Dennis Eckersley, Oakland

Rookie of the Year ■ Pat Listach, Milwaukee

Manager of the Year ■ Tony La Russa, Oakland

National League

Most Valuable Player ■ Barry Bonds, Pittsburgh

Cy Young Award ■ Greg Maddux, Chicago

Rookie of the Year ■ Eric Karros, Los Angeles

Manager of the Year ■ Jim Leyland, Pittsburgh

1992 PLAYOFFS

AMERICAN LEAGUE CHAMPIONSHIP SERIES

Toronto Blue Jays 4, Oakland A's 2

Game 1 (at Toronto) ■ Oakland 4, Toronto 3

Game 2 (at Toronto) ■ Toronto 3, Oakland 1

Game 3 (at Oakland) ■ Toronto 7, Oakland 5

Game 4 (at Oakland) ■ Toronto 7, Oakland 6*

Game 5 (at Oakland) ■ Oakland 6, Toronto 2

Game 6 (at Toronto) ■ Toronto 9, Oakland 2

* 11-inning game

Most Valuable Player ■ Roberto Alomar, Toronto

NATIONAL LEAGUE CHAMPIONSHIP SERIES

Atlanta Braves 4, Pittsburgh Pirates 3

Game 1 (at Atlanta) ■ Atlanta 5, Pittsburgh 1

Game 2 (at Atlanta) ■ Atlanta 13, Pittsburgh 5

Game 3 (at Pittsburgh) ■ Pittsburgh 3, Atlanta 2

Game 4 (at Pittsburgh) ■ Atlanta 6, Pittsburgh 4

Game 5 (at Pittsburgh) ■ Pittsburgh 7, Atlanta 1

Game 6 (at Atlanta) ■ Pittsburgh 13, Atlanta 4

Game 7 (at Atlanta) ■ Atlanta 3, Pittsburgh 2

Most Valuable Player ■ John Smoltz, Atlanta

WORLD SERIES

Toronto Blue Jays 4, Atlanta Braves 2

Game 1 (at Atlanta) ■ Atlanta 3, Toronto 1

Game 2 (at Atlanta) ■ Toronto 5, Atlanta 4

Game 3 (at Toronto) ■ Toronto 3, Atlanta 2

Game 4 (at Toronto) ■ Toronto 2, Atlanta 1

Game 5 (at Toronto) ■ Atlanta 7, Toronto 2

OH! CANADA ■ THE TORONTO BLUE JAYS CELE-BRATE THEIR WORLD SERIES VICTORY OVER AT-LANTA. IT WAS THE FIRST TIME THE PENNANT WENT OUTSIDE THE U.S.

Game 6 (at Atlanta) ■ Toronto 4, Atlanta 3*
* 11–inning game

Most Valuable Player ■ Pat Borders, Toronto

ALL-STAR GAME (AT JACK MURPHY STADIUM, SAN DIEGO, CALIF.)

American League 13, National League 6
Most Valuable Player ■ Ken Griffey Jr.

COLLEGE BASEBALL

COLLEGE WORLD SERIES
(AT ROSENBLATT STADIUM, OMAHA, NEB.)

Pepperdine 3, Cal-State Fullerton 2

NCAA DIVISION II CHAMPIONSHIP
(AT PATERSON STADIUM, MONTGOMERY, ALA.)

Tampa 11, Mansfield 8

NCAA DIVISION III CHAMPIONSHIP
(AT BATTLE CREEK, MICH.)

William Patterson (NJ) 3, Cal Lutheran 1

LITTLE LEAGUE WORLD SERIES
(AT WILLIAMSPORT, PA.)

Philippines 15, Long Beach (Calif.) 4*
* On September 17, 1992 the Philippines were stripped of the title for fielding ineligible players. The championship was awarded as a 6–0 forfeit to Long Beach.

BASKETBALL

NATIONAL BASKETBALL ASSOCIATION (NBA)

1991–92 FINAL STANDINGS

EASTERN CONFERENCE
Atlantic Division

Team	W	L	Pct.	GB
Boston	51	31	.622	—
New York	51	31	.622	—
New Jersey	40	42	.488	11
Miami	38	44	.463	13
Philadelphia	35	47	.427	16
Washington	25	57	.305	26
Orlando	21	61	.256	30

Central Division

Team	W	L	Pct.	GB
Chicago	67	15	.817	—
Cleveland	57	25	.695	10
Detroit	48	34	.585	19
Indiana	40	42	.488	27
Atlanta	38	44	.463	29
Charlotte	31	51	.378	36
Milwaukee	31	51	.378	36

WESTERN CONFERENCE
Midwest Division

Team	W	L	Pct.	GB
Utah	55	27	.671	—
San Antonio	47	35	.573	8
Houston	42	40	.512	13
Denver	24	58	.293	31
Dallas	22	60	.268	33
Minnesota	15	67	.183	40

Pacific Division

Team	W	L	Pct.	GB
Portland	57	25	.695	—
Golden State	55	27	.671	2
Phoenix	53	29	.646	4
Seattle	47	35	.573	10
LA Clippers	45	37	.549	12
LA Lakers	43	39	.524	14
Sacramento	29	53	.354	28

1991–92 STATISTICAL LEADERS

Category	Total	Average	Player
Scoring	2,404 pts	30.1 pts	Michael Jordan, Chicago
Assists	1,126	13.7	John Stockton, Utah
Rebounds	1,530	18.7	Dennis Rodman, Detroit
Steals	244	2.98	John Stocktan, Utah
Blocked Shots	305	4.49	David Robinson, San Antonio

AWARDS

Most Valuable Player ■ Michael Jordan, Chicago
Coach of the Year ■ Don Nelson, Golden State
Rookie of the Year ■ Larry Johnson, Charlotte

1992 PLAYOFFS

EASTERN CONFERENCE (SERIES SCORE)
First Round
Chicago Bulls 3, Miami Heat 0
New York Knicks 3, Detroit Pistons 2
Boston Celtics 3, Indiana Pacers 0

Cleveland Cavaliers 3, New Jersey Nets 1

Semifinals

Chicago Bulls 4, New York Knicks 3

Cleveland Cavaliers 4, Boston Celtics 3

Finals

Chicago Bulls 4, Cleveland Cavaliers 2

WESTERN CONFERENCE (SERIES SCORE)

First Round

Portland Trail Blazers 3, Los Angeles Lakers 1

Phoenix Suns 3, San Antonio Spurs 0

Utah Jazz 3, Los Angeles Clippers 2

Seattle SuperSonics 3, Golden State Warriors 1

Semifinals

Portland Trail Blazers 4, Phoenix Suns 1

Utah Jazz 4, Seattle SuperSonics 1

Finals

Portland Trail Blazers 4, Utah Jazz 2

NBA CHAMPIONSHIP FINALS

Chicago Bulls 4, Portland Trail Blazers 2

Game 1 (at Chicago) ■ Chicago 122, Portland 89

Game 2 (at Chicago) ■ Portland 115, Chicago 104

Game 3 (at Portland) ■ Chicago 94, Portland 84

Game 4 (at Portland) ■ Portland 93, Chicago 88

Game 5 (at Portland) ■ Chicago 119, Portland 106

Game 6 (at Chicago) ■ Chicago 97, Portland 93

NBA Finals MVP ■ Michael Jordan, Chicago

COLLEGE BASKETBALL (MEN)

NCAA DIVISION I

1991–92 CONFERENCE WINNERS

Conference	Season	Tournament
Atlantic Coast	Duke	Duke
Atlantic 10	Massachusetts	Massachusetts
Big East	Seton Hall* Georgetown*	Syracuse
Big Eight	Kansas	Kansas
Big Sky	Montana	Montana
Big South	Radford	Campbell
Big Ten	Ohio State	None
Big West	UNLV	New Mexico State
Colonial Athletic Assoc.	Richmond* James Madison*	Old Dominion
East Coast	Hofstra	Towson
Great Midwest	Cincinnati* DePaul*	Cincinnati

Conference	Season	Tournament
Ivy League	Princeton	None
Metro	Tulane	NC–Charlotte
Metro Atlantic	Manhattan	La Salle
Mid-American	Miami, Ohio	Miami, Ohio
Mid-Continent	Wisconsin–Green Bay	Eastern Illinois
Mid-Eastern Athletic	Howard* N. Carolina A&T*	Howard
Midwestern Collegiate	Evansville	Evansville
Missouri Valley	Southern Illinois* Illinois State*	SW Missouri State
North Atlantic	Delaware	Delaware
Northeast	Robert Morris	Robert Morris
Ohio Valley	Murray State	Murray State
Pacific-10	UCLA	None
Patriot League	Fordham* Bucknell*	Fordham
Southeastern (East)	Kentucky	Kentucky†
Southeastern (West)	Arkansas	
Southern	East Tennessee St* Tenn–Chattanooga*	East Tennessee State
Southland	Texas–San Antonio	NE Louisiana
Southwest	Texas* Houston*	Houston
Southwestern Althletic	Miss. Valley State* Texas Southern*	Miss. Valley State
Sun Belt	Louisiana Tech	SW Louisiana
Trans America Athletic	Georgia Southern	Georgia Southern
West Coast	Pepperdine	Pepperdine
Western Athletic	Brigham Young* UTEP*	Brigham Young

* Tied
† Southeastern Conference tournament

NCAA DIVISION I TOURNAMENT

EAST REGIONAL

First Round

Duke 82, Campbell 56

Iowa 98, Texas 92

Missouri 89, West Virginia 78

Seton Hall 78, La Salle 76

Syracuse 51, Princeton 43

Massachusetts 85, Fordham 58

Iowa State 76, NC–Charlotte 74

Kentucky 88, Old Dominion 69

Second Round

Duke 75, Iowa 62

Seton Hall 88, Missouri 71

Massachusetts 77, Syracuse 71 (OT)

Kentucky 106, Iowa State 98

Regionals

Duke 81, Seton Hall 69

Kentucky 87, Massachusetts 77

Regional Final

Duke 104, Kentucky 103 (OT)

East Regional Final Four Qualifier ■ Duke

WEST REGIONAL

First Round

UCLA 73, Robert Morris 53

Louisville 81, Wake Forest 58

New Mexico State 81, DePaul 73

SW Louisiana 87, Oklahoma 83

Georgetown 75, South Florida 60

Florida State 78, Montana 68

Louisiana State 94, Brigham Young 83

Indiana 94, Eastern Illinois 55

Second Round

UCLA 85, Louisville 69

New Mexico State 81, SW Louisiana 73

Florida State 78, Georgetown 68

Indiana 89, Louisiana State 79

Regionals

UCLA 85, New Mexico State 78

Indiana 85, Florida State 74

Regional Final

Indiana 106, UCLA 79

West Regional Final Four Qualifier ■ Indiana

MIDWEST REGIONAL

First Round

Kansas 100, Howard 67

UTEP 55, Evansville 50

Michigan State 61, SW Missouri State 54

Cincinnati 85, Delaware 47

Memphis State 80, Pepperdine 70

Arkansas 80, Murray State 69

Georgia Tech 65, Houston 60

Southern Cal 84, NE Louisiana 54

Second Round

UTEP 66, Kansas 60

Cincinnati 77, Michigan State 65

Memphis State 82, Arkansas 80

Georgia Tech 79, Southern Cal 78

Regionals

Cincinnati 69, UTEP 67

Memphis State 83, Georgia Tech 79 (OT)

Regional Final

Cincinnati 88, Memphis 57

Midwest Regional Final Four Qualifier ■ Cincinnati

SOUTHEAST REGIONALS

First Round

Ohio State 83, Mississippi Valley State 56

Connecticut 86, Nebraska 65

Alabama 80, Stanford 75

North Carolina 68, Miami, Ohio 63

Michigan 73, Temple 66

East Tennessee State 87, Arizona 80

Tulane 61, St. John's 57

Oklahoma State 100, Georgia Southern 73

Second Round

Ohio State 78, Connecticut 55

North Carolina 64, Alabama 55

Michigan 102, East Tennessee State 90

Oklahoma State 87, Tulane 71

Regionals

Ohio State 80, North Carolina 73

Michigan 75, Oklahoma State 72

Regional Final

Michigan 75, Ohio State 71 (OT)

Southeast Regional Final Four Qualifier ■ Michigan

FINAL FOUR (AT THE HUBERT H. HUMPHREY METRODOME, MINNEAPOLIS, MINN.)

SEMIFINALS

Michigan 76, Cincinnati 72

Duke 81, Indiana 78

CHAMPIONSHIP GAME

Duke 71, Michigan 51

Final Four MVP ■ Bobby Hurley, Duke

NCAA DIVISION II CHAMPIONSHIP

Virginia Union 100, Bridgeport (Conn.) 75

NCAA DIVISION III CHAMPIONSHIP

Calvin (Mich.) 63, Rochester (NY) 49

COLLEGE BASKETBALL (WOMEN)

NCAA DIVISION I TOURNAMENT

First Round

George Washington 70, Vermont 69
Clemson 76, Tenn–Chattanooga 72
Connecticut 83, St. Peter's 66
North Carolina 60, Old Dominion 54
UC Santa Barbara 80, Houston 69
Santa Clara 73, California 71
Montana 85, Wisconsin 74
Creighton 79, Long Beach State 66
Southwest Missouri St. 75, Kansas 59
UCLA 93, Notre Dame 72
DePaul 67, Arizona State 65
Southern Ill. 84, Colorado 80 (OT)
Rutgers 93, Southern Mississippi 63
Alabama 100, Tennessee Tech 87
Northern Illinois 77, Louisiana Tech 71 (OT)
Toledo 74, Providence 64

Second Round

Virginia 97, George Washington 58
West Virginia 73, Clemson 72
Vanderbilt 75, Connecticut 47
Miami, Fla. 86, North Carolina 72
Stanford 82, UC Santa Barbara 73
Texas Tech 64, Santa Clara 58
Southern Cal 71, Montana 59
Stephen F. Austin 75, Creighton 74
Southwest Missouri State 61, Iowa 60 (OT)
UCLA 82, Texas 81
Penn State 77, DePaul 54
Mississippi 72, Southern Illinois 56
Tennessee 97, Rutgers 56
Western Kentucky 98, Alabama 68
Purdue 98, Northern Illinois 62
Maryland 73, Toledo 60

REGIONAL SEMIFINALS

Virginia 103, West Virginia 83
Vanderbilt 77, Miami, Fla. 67
Stanford 75, Texas Tech 63

Southern Cal 61, Stephen F. Austin 57
Southwest Missouri State 83, UCLA 57
Mississippi 75, Penn State 72
Western Kentucky 75, Tennessee 70
Maryland 64, Purdue 58

REGIONAL CHAMPIONSHIPS

Virginia 70, Vanderbilt 58
Stanford 82, Southern Cal 62
Southwest Missouri State 94, Mississippi 71
Western Kentucky 75, Maryland 70

FINAL FOUR (AT LOS ANGELES SPORTS ARENA, CALIF.)

SEMIFINALS

Stanford 66, Virginia 65
Western Kentucky 84, Southwest Missouri State 72

CHAMPIONSHIP GAME

Stanford 78, Western Kentucky 62
Final Four MVP ■ Molly Goodenbour, Stanford

NCAA DIVISION II CHAMPIONSHIP

Delta State 64, North Dakota State 63

NCAA DIVISION III CHAMPIONSHIP

Alma (Mich.) 79, Moravian (Pa.) 75

BIATHLON

UNITED STATES NATIONAL CHAMPIONSHIPS STAGED AT LAKE PLACID, N.Y.

Men's 10 km ■ Duncan Douglas
Men's 20 km ■ Josh Thompson
Women's 7.5 km ■ Joan Smith
Women's 15 km ■ Beth Coats

BOBSLED AND LUGE

UNITED STATES NATIONAL CHAMPIONSHIPS (LUGE) STAGED AT LAKE PLACID, N.Y.

Men's Singles ■ Duncan Kennedy
Men's Doubles ■ Chris Thorpe/Gordy Sheer
Women's Singles ■ Cammy Myler

BOWLING

PBA TOUR

Leading Money Winner ■ Mike McDowell, $176,215

AMERICAN BOWLING CONGRESS

ABC CHAMPIONSHIP TOURNAMENT
STAGED AT CORPUS CHRISTI, TEX.

Singles ■ Bob Youker Jr., Gary Blatchford, 801 pins

Doubles ■ Gene Stuf/David Bernhardt, 1,487 pins

Individual All-Events ■ Mike Tucker, 2,158 pins

Team ■ Coors Light, Reading, Pa., 3,344 pins

Booster Team ■ Suburban Lanes, Meade, Kan., 2,888 pins

Team All-Event ■ Reeb's Funeral Home, Toledo, Ohio, 9,939 pins

WOMEN'S INTERNATIONAL BOWLING CONGRESS

WIBC CHAMPIONSHIP TOURNAMENT
STAGED AT LANSING, MICH.

Singles ■ Patty Ann, 680 pins

Doubles ■ Nancy Fehr/Lisa Wagner 1,325 pins

Team ■ Hoinke Classic, Cincinnati, 2,983 pins

All-Events ■ Mitsuko Tokimito (Japan), 1,928 pins

BOXING

WORLD CHAMPIONS (AS OF DECEMBER 30, 1992)

Division	Boxer	Recognition
Heavyweight	Riddick Bowe (U.S.)	W.B.A., I.B.F.
	Lennox Lewis (GB)	W.B.C.
Cruiserweight	Bobby Czyz (U.S.),	W.B.A.
	Anaclet Wamba (FRA)	W.B.C.
	Alfred Cole (U.S.)	I.B.F.
Light-Heavyweight	Virgil Hill (U.S.)	W.B.A.
	Jeff Harding (AUS)	W.B.C.
	Charles Williams (U.S.)	I.B.F.
Super-Middleweight	Michael Nunn (U.S.)	W.B.A.
	Nigel Benn (GB)	W.B.C.
	Iran Barkley (U.S.)	I.B.F.
Middleweight	Reggie Johnson (U.S.)	W.B.A.
	Julian Jackson (VI)	W.B.C.
	James Toney (U.S.)	I.B.F.
Jr. Middleweight	Julio Cesar Vasquez (ARG)	W.B.A.
	Terry Norris (U.S.)	W.B.C.
	Gianfranco Rossi (ITA)	I.B.F.

Division	Boxer	Recognition
Welterweight	Cristanto Espana (VEN)	W.B.A.
	James McGirt (U.S.)	W.B.C.
	Maurice Blocker (U.S.)	I.B.F.
Jr. Welterweight	Morris East (PHI)	W.B.A.
	Julio César Chavez (MEX)	W.B.C.
	Pernell Whitaker (U.S.)	I.B.F.
Lightweight	Tony Lopez (U.S.)	W.B.A.
	Miguel Angel Gonzalez (MEX)	W.B.C.
	Vacant	I.B.F.
Jr. Lightweight	Ganaro Hernandez (U.S.)	W.B.A.
	Azumah Nelson (GHA)	W.B.C.
	Juan Molina (PR)	I.B.F.
Featherweight	Yung-Kyun Park (SK)	W.B.A.
	Paul Hodkinson (GB)	W.B.C.
	Manuel Medina (MEX)	I.B.F.
Jr. Featherweight	Wilfredo Vazquez (MEX)	W.B.A.
	Tracy Patterson (U.S.)	W.B.C.
	Kennedy McKinney (U.S.)	I.B.F.
Bantamweight	Jorge Eliecer Julio (COL)	W.B.A.
	Victor Rabanales (MEX)	W.B.C.
	Orlando Canizales (U.S.)	I.B.F.
Jr. Bantamweight	Katzuya Onizuka (JAP)	W.B.A.
	Sungkill Moon (SK)	W.B.C.
	Robert Quiroga (U.S.)	I.B.F.
Flyweight	Aquiles Guzman (VEN)	W.B.A.
	Yuri Arvachakov (RUS)	W.B.C.
	Pichit Sitbangphacan (THA)	I.B.F.
Jr. Flyweight	Myung-Woo Yuh (SK)	W.B.A.
	Humberto Gonzalez (MEX)	W.B.C.
	Michael Carbajal (U.S.)	I.B.F.
Strawweight	Choi Hi-yong (SK)	W.B.A.
	Ricardo Lopez (MEX)	W.B.C.
	Manny Melchor (PHI)	I.B.F.

W.B.A.: World Boxing Association; W.B.C.: World Boxing Council; I.B.F.: International Boxing Federation.

CRICKET

WORLD CUP STAGED AT SYDNEY, AUSTRALIA

Champion ■ Pakistan

CROQUET

WORLD CHAMPIONSHIPS STAGED AT NEWPORT, R.I.

Singles ■ Robert Fulford (ENG)

USCA NATIONAL CHAMPIONSHIPS
STAGED AT SOUTHAMPTON, N.Y.

Singles (Open) ■ Reid Fleming

Doubles (Open) ■ Robert Yount/Harold Brown

Singles (Amateur) ■ Alan Wollman

Doubles (Amateur) ■ Jerry Ball/Matt Burris

USCA NATIONAL CLUB TEAM CHAMPIONSHIPS STAGED AT PALM BEACH GARDENS, FLA.

Champion Flight ■ Palm Beach Croquet Club (Jack R. Osborn & Jay Rossbach)

CROSS-COUNTRY RUNNING

WORLD CHAMPIONSHIPS STAGED AT BOSTON, MASS.

Men's Champion ■ John Ngugi (Kenya)

Team event ■ Kenya

Women's Champion ■ Lynn Jennings (U.S.)

Team event ■ Kenya

UNITED STATES NATIONAL CHAMPIONSHIPS

Men's Champion ■ Todd Williams

Women's Champion ■ Lynn Jennings

NCAA DIVISION I CHAMPIONSHIPS

Men's Team ■ Arkansas

Men's Individual ■ Bob Kennedy (Indiana)

Women's Team ■ Villanova

Women's Individual ■ Carole Zajac (Villanova)

CURLING

WORLD CHAMPIONSHIPS

Men's team ■ Switzerland, Markus Eggler (skip)

Women's team ■ Sweden, Elisebet Johansson (skip)

UNITED STATES CHAMPIONSHIPS

Men's team ■ Seattle, Doug Jones (skip)

Women's team ■ Madison (Wisc.), Lisa Schoeneberg (skip)

THE LABATT BRIER

Men's team ■ Manitoba, Vic Peters (skip)

CYCLING

PROFESSIONAL EVENTS

TOUR DE FRANCE (2,380 MILES)

Winner ■ Miguel Indurain (SPA), 100 hours, 49 minutes, 30 seconds

OTHER MAJOR TOUR RACE RESULTS

Tour Du Pont ■ Greg LeMond (U.S.)

Tour of Italy ■ Miguel Indurain (SPA)

Tour of Spain ■ Tony Rominger (SWI)

Milk Race ■ Conor Henry (IRE)

Tour of Switzerland ■ Giorgio Furlan (ITA)

Tour of Catalan ■ Miguel Indurain (SPA)

WORLD CHAMPIONSHIPS STAGED AT VALENCIA, SPAIN

Sprint ■ Michael Huebner (GER)

Pursuit ■ Michael McCarthy (U.S.)

Road Race ■ Gianni Bugno (ITA)

Points Race ■ Bruno Risi (SWI)

Keirin ■ Michael Huebner (GER)

DARTS

WORLD CHAMPIONSHIPS STAGED AT FRIMLEY GREEN, ENGLAND

Champion ■ Phil Taylor (ENG)

UNITED STATES CHAMPIONSHIPS

Men's Champion ■ Dave Kelly

Women's Champion ■ Stacy Bromberg

DIVING

UNITED STATES INDOOR CHAMPIONSHIPS STAGED AT ANN ARBOR, MICH.

MEN'S RESULTS

1-meter springboard ■ Mark Lenzi

3-meter springboard ■ Mark Lenzi

Platform ■ Patrick Jeffrey

WOMEN'S RESULTS

1-meter springboard ■ Julie Ovenhouse

3-meter springboard ■ Julie Ovenhouse

Platform ■ Cokey Smith

UNITED STATES OUTDOOR CHAMPIONSHIPS

MEN'S RESULTS
1-meter springboard ■ Mark Lenzi
3-meter springboard ■ Mark Lenzi
Platform ■ Scott Donie
WOMEN'S RESULTS
1-meter springboard ■ Kristen Kane
3-meter springboard ■ Veronica Ribot-Canales
Platform ■ Mary Ellen Clark

EQUESTRIAN SPORTS

WORLD CUP (SHOW JUMPING)

Champion ■ Thomas Fruhmann (AUT)

WORLD CUP (DRESSAGE)

Champion ■ Isabell Werth (GER)

FENCING

UNITED STATES FENCING ASSOCIATION CHAMPIONSHIPS

Men's Foil ■ Nick Bravin
Men's Épée ■ Rob Stull
Men's Sabre ■ Michael Lofton
Women's Épée ■ Barbara Turpin

NCAA CHAMPIONSHIPS STAGED AT SOUTH BEND, IND.

Team Event ■ Columbia/Columbia–Barnard
Men's Foil ■ Nick Bravin, Stanford
Men's Épée ■ Harald Bauder, Wayne State
Men's Sabre ■ Tom Strzalkowski, Penn State
Women's Foil ■ Heidi Piper, Notre Dame

FIELD HOCKEY

NCAA CHAMPIONSHIPS

Champion ■ Old Dominion

FIGURE SKATING

WORLD CHAMPIONSHIPS STAGED AT OAKLAND, CALIF.

Men ■ Viktor Petrenko (CIS)
Women ■ Kristi Yamaguchi (U.S.)
Pairs ■ Natalia Mishkutlenok/Artur Dmitriev (CIS)
Dance ■ Marina Klimova/Sergei Ponomarenko(CIS)

UNITED STATES NATIONAL CHAMPIONSHIPS STAGED AT ORLANDO, FLA.

Men ■ Christopher Bowman
Women ■ Kristi Yamaguchi
Pairs ■ Calla Ubanski/Rocky Marval
Dance ■ April Sargent/Thomas-Russ Witherby

FOOTBALL

NATIONAL FOOTBALL LEAGUE (NFL)

1992 NFL FINAL STANDINGS

AMERICAN CONFERENCE
Eastern Division

Team	W	L	Pct.
Miami	11	5	.688
Buffalo	11	5	.688
Indianapolis	9	7	.563
N.Y. Jets	4	12	.250
New England	2	14	.125

Central Divison

Team	W	L	Pct.
Pittsburgh	11	5	.688
Houston	10	6	.625
Cleveland	7	9	.438
Cincinnati	5	11	.313

Western Division

Team	W	L	Pct.
San Diego	11	5	.688
Kansas City	10	6	.625
Denver	8	8	.500
L.A. Raiders	7	9	.438
Seattle	2	14	.125

NATIONAL CONFERENCE
Eastern Division

Team	W	L	Pct.
Dallas	13	3	.813
Philadelphia	11	5	.688
Washington	9	7	.563
N.Y. Giants	6	10	.375
Phoenix	4	12	.250

Central Division

Team	W	L	Pct.
Minnesota	11	5	.688
Green Bay	9	7	.563
Detroit	5	11	.313
Tampa Bay	5	11	.313
Chicago	5	11	.313

Western Division

Team	W	L	Pct.
San Francisco	14	2	.875
New Orleans	12	4	.750
Atlanta	6	10	.375
L.A. Rams	6	10	.375

NFL 1992 STATISTICAL LEADERS

Passing yardage	4,116	Dan Marino, Miami
Rushing yardage	1,713	Emmitt Smith, Dallas
Total yardage	2,113	Thurman Thomas, Buffalo
Points scored	124	Pete Stoyanovich, Miami
Touchdowns scored	19	Emmitt Smith, Dallas
Touchdowns thrown	25	Steve Young, San Francisco
Quarterback rating	107.0	Steve Young, San Francisco
Receptions	108	Sterling Sharpe, Green Bay
Sacks	19	Clyde Simmons, Philadelphia
Interceptions	8	Henry Jones, Buffalo Audray McMillian, Minnesota

SUPER BOWL XXVII PLAYOFFS

AMERICAN CONFERENCE

Wildcard Games

Buffalo Bills 41, Houston Oilers 38 (OT)

San Diego Chargers 17, Kansas City Chiefs 0

Second Round

Miami Dolphins 31, San Diego Chargers 0

Buffalo Bills 24, Pittsburgh Steelers 3

A.F.C. CHAMPIONSHIP GAME (at Miami)

Buffalo Bills 29, Miami Dolphins 10

NATIONAL CONFERENCE

Wildcard Games

Philadelphia Eagles 36, New Orleans Saints 20

Washington Redskins 24, Minnesota Vikings 7

Second Round

Dallas Cowboys 34, Philadelphia Eagels 10

San Francisco 49ers 20, Washington Redskins 13

N.F.C. CHAMPIONSHIP GAME (at San Francisco)

Dallas Cowboys 30, San Francisco 49ers 20

SUPER BOWL XXVII (AT THE ROSE BOWL, PASADENA, CALIF.)

Dallas Cowboys 52, Buffalo Bills 17

Super Bowl MVP ■ Troy Aikman, Dallas

COLLEGE FOOTBALL

NCAA DIVISION I-A

1992 FINAL NATIONAL POLLS

Poll	No. 1 Ranked	Record
A.P.	Alabama	13–0–0
USA Today/CNN	Alabama	13–0–0

BOWL GAME RESULTS (1992 SEASON)

BIG FOUR

Orange ■ Florida State 27, Nebraska 14

Rose ■ Michigan 38, Washington 31

Sugar ■ Alabama 34, Miami 13

Cotton ■ Notre Dame 28, Texas A&M 3

OTHER BOWL RESULTS

Aloha ■ Kansas 23, Brigham Young 20

Blockbuster ■ Stanford 24, Penn State 3

Citrus ■ Georgia 21, Ohio State 14

Copper ■ Washington State 31, Utah 28

Fiesta ■ Syracuse 26, Colorado 22

Freedom ■ Fresno State 24, Southern Cal. 7

Gator ■ Florida 27, North Carolina State 10

Hall of Fame ■ Tennessee 38, Boston College 23

Holiday ■ Hawaii 27, Illinois 17

Independence ■ Wake Forest 39, Oregon 35

John Hancock ■ Baylor 20, Arizona 15

Liberty ■ Mississippi 13, Air Force 0

Peach Bowl ■ North Carolina 21, Mississippi State 17

AWARDS

Heisman Trophy ■ Gino Torretta (Miami, Fla.)
Lombardi Trophy ■ Marvin Jones (Florida)
Outland Trophy ■ Will Shields (Nebraska)

NCAA DIVISION I-AA CHAMPIONSHIP

Marshall 31, Youngstown (Ohio) 28

NCAA DIVISION II CHAMPIONSHIP

Jacksonville State (Ala.) 17, Pittsburg (Kan.) State 13

NCAA DIVISION III CHAMPIONSHIP GAME

Wisconsin–La Crosse 16, Washington & Jefferson (Pa.) 12

CANADIAN FOOTBALL LEAGUE (CFL)

1992 CFL FINAL STANDINGS

EASTERN DIVISION

Team	W	L	Pct.
Winnipeg	11	7	.611
Hamilton	11	7	.611
Ottawa	9	9	.500
Toronto	6	12	.333

WESTERN DIVISION

Team	W	L	Pct.
Calgary	13	5	.722
Edmonton	10	8	.556
Saskatchewan	9	9	.500
B.C. Lions	3	15	.167

1992 GREY CUP PLAYOFFS

EASTERN DIVISION
Semifinal
Hamilton 29, Ottawa 28
Final
Winnipeg 59, Hamilton 11
WESTERN DIVISION
Semifinal
Edmonton 22, Saskatchewan 20
Final
Calgary 23, Edmonton 22
GREY CUP FINAL (at Sky Dome, Toronto)
Calgary Stampeders 24, Winnipeg Blue Bombers 10
Grey Cup MVP ■ Doug Flutie, Calgary

WORLD LEAGUE OF AMERICAN FOOTBALL

WORLD BOWL II STAGED AT OLYMPIC STADIUM, MONTREAL, CANADA

Sacramento Surge 21, Orlando Thunder 17
MVP ■ David Archer, Sacramento

ARENA FOOTBALL

ARENA BOWL STAGED AT ORLANDO, FLA.

Detroit Drive 56, Orlando Predators 38

GOLF

PGA TOUR

GRAND SLAM RESULTS
The Masters ■ Fred Couples (U.S.)
U.S. Open ■ Tom Kite (U.S.)
British Open ■ Nick Faldo (GB)
P.G.A. Championship ■ Nick Price (ZIM)
Leading Money Winner ■ Fred Couples, $1,156,000

OTHER TOURNAMENT RESULTS
Skins Game ■ Payne Stewart
Johnnie Walker Championship ■ Nick Faldo (GB)

EUROPEAN PGA TOUR

Leading Money Winner ■ Nick Faldo (GB), £707,567

LPGA TOUR

GRAND SLAM RESULTS
Nabisco Dinah Shore ■ Dottie Mochrie
LPGA Championship ■ Betsy King
U.S. Open ■ Patty Sheehan
du Maurier Classic ■ Sherri Steinhauer
Leading Money Winner ■ Dottie Mochrie, $693,335

PGA SENIOR TOUR

SENIOR SLAM
The Tradition ■ Lee Trevino
Senior PGA Championship ■ Lee Trevino
Senior Players Championship ■ Dave Stockton
U.S. Senior Open ■ Larry Laoretti
Leading Money Winner ■ Lee Trevino, $1,027,002

AMATEUR GOLF

U.S Amateur (men) ■ J. Leonard
U.S Amateur (women) ■ Vicki Goetze
NCAA (individual, men) ■ Phil Mickelson, Arizona State
NCAA (team, men) ■ Arizona
NCAA (individual, women) ■ Vicki Goetze, Georgia
NCAA (team, women) ■ San Jose State

GYMNASTICS

WORLD CHAMPIONSHIPS STAGED AT PARIS, FRANCE

Men's Results
Floor Exercise ■ Igor Korubchinski (U.T.)
Rings ■ Vitaliy Scherbo (U.T.)
Pommel Horse ■ Pae Gil Su (NK)/Vitaliy Scherbo (U.T.)
Vault ■ You Ok Youl (SK)
Parallel Bars ■ Alexei Voropaev (U.T.)/Li Jing (CHI)
Horizontal Bar ■ Grigori Misioutine (U.T.)
Women's Results
Vault ■ Henrietta Onodi (HUN)
Floor Exercise ■ Kim Zmeskal (U.S.)
Uneven Bars ■ Lavinia Milosovici (ROM)
Balance Beam ■ Kim Zmeskal (U.S.)

NCAA CHAMPIONSHIPS (MEN) STAGED AT LINCOLN, NEBR.

All-Around ■ John Roethlisberger, Minnesota
Team ■ Stanford

NCAA CHAMPIONSHIPS (WOMEN) STAGED AT MINNEAPOLIS, MINN.

All-Around ■ Missy Malone, Utah
Team ■ Utah

HARNESS RACING

TRIPLE CROWN WINNERS

TROTTERS

Race	Horse
Yonkers Trot	McCluckey*
	Magic Lobell*

* Dead Heat

TROTTERS (cont'd)

Race	Horse
Hambletonian	Alf Palema
Kentucky Futurity	Armbro Keepsake

PACERS

Cane Pace	Western Hanover
Little Brown Jug	Fake Left
Messenger Stakes	Western Hanover

Leading Money Winners
Trotter ■ Alf Palema, $1,049,167
Pacer ■ Western Hanover, $1,844,315

HOCKEY

NATIONAL HOCKEY LEAGUE (NHL)

1991–92 FINAL STANDINGS

WALES CONFERENCE
Adams Division

Team	W	L	T	Pts.
Montreal	41	28	11	93
Boston	36	32	12	84
Buffalo	31	37	12	74
Hartford	26	41	13	65
Quebec	20	48	12	52

Patrick Division

Team	W	L	T	Pts.
N.Y. Rangers	50	25	5	105
Washington	45	27	8	98
Pittsburgh	39	32	9	87
New Jersey	38	31	11	87
N.Y. Islanders	34	35	11	79
Philadelphia	32	37	11	75

CAMPBELL CONFERENCE
Norris Division

Team	W	L	T	Pts.
Detroit	43	25	12	98
Chicago	36	29	15	87
St. Louis	36	33	11	83
Minnesota	32	42	6	70
Toronto	30	43	7	67

Smythe Division

Team	W	L	T	Pts.
Vancouver	42	26	12	96
Los Angeles	35	31	14	84
Edmonton	36	34	10	82

CAMPBELL CONFERENCE
Smythe Division

Team	W	L	T	Pts.
Winnipeg	33	32	15	81
Calgary	31	37	12	74
San Jose	17	58	5	39

NHL 1991–92 Statistical Leaders

Points	131	Mario Lemieux, Pittsburgh
Goals	70	Brett Hull, St. Louis
Assists	90	Wayne Gretzky, Los Angeles
Wins	38	Kirk McLean, Vancouver (38–17)
	38	Tim Cheveldae, Detroit (38–23)
Shutouts	5	Bob Essensa, Winnipeg
	5	Ed Belfour, Chicago
	5	Kirk McLean, Vancouver
	5	Patrick Roy, Montreal

AWARDS

Hart Trophy (MVP) ■ Mark Messier, N.Y. Rangers

Norris Trophy (Best defenseman) ■ Brian Leetch, N.Y. Rangers

Vezina Trophy (Best goaltender) ■ Patrick Roy, Montreal

STANLEY CUP PLAYOFFS 1992

WALES CONFERENCE (SERIES SCORE)
ADAMS DIVISION

First Round

Montreal Canadiens 4, Hartford Whalers 3

Boston Bruins 4, Buffalo Sabres 3

Semifinals

Boston Bruins, 4, Montreal Canadiens 0

Adams Division Champion ■ Boston Bruins

PATRICK DIVISION

First Round

New York Rangers 4, New Jersey Devils 3

Pittsburgh Penguins 4, Washington Capitals 3

Semifinals

Pittsburgh Penguins 4, New York Rangers 2

Patrick Division Champion ■ Pittsburgh Penguins

WALES CONFERENCE FINAL

Pittsburgh Penguins 4, Boston Bruins 0

CAMPBELL CONFERENCE (SERIES SCORE)
NORRIS DIVISION

First Round

Detroit Red Wings 4, Minnesota North Stars 3

Chicago Blackhawks 4, St. Louis Blues 2

Semifinals

Chicago Blackhawks 4, Detroit Red Wings 0

Norris Division Champion ■ Chicago Blackhawks

SMYTHE DIVISION

First Round

Vancouver Canucks 4, Winnipeg Jets 3

Edmonton Oilers 4, Los Angeles Kings 2

Semifinals

Edmonton Oilers 4, Vancouver 2

Smythe Division Champion ■ Edmonton Oilers

CAMPBELL CONFERENCE FINAL

Chicago Blackhawks 4, Edmonton Oilers 0

STANLEY CUP FINAL

Pittsburgh Penguins 4, Boston Bruins 0

Game 1 (at Pittsburgh) ■ Pittsburgh 5, Chicago 4

Game 2 (at Pittsburgh) ■ Pittsburgh 3, Chicago 1

Game 3 (at Chicago) ■ Pittsburgh 1, Chicago 0

Game 4 (at Chicago) ■ Pittsburgh 6, Chicago 5

Conn Smythe Trophy (Playoffs MVP) ■ Mario Lemieux, Pittsburgh

WORLD CHAMPIONSHIP Staged at Prague, Czechoslovakia

Sweden 5, Finland 2

NCAA DIVISION 1 CHAMPIONSHIP Staged at Albany, N.Y.

Lake Superior State 5, Wisconsin 3

HORSE RACING

TRIPLE CROWN WINNERS

Kentucky Derby ■ Lil E. Tee

The Preakness ■ Pine Buff

Belmont Stakes ■ A.P. Indy

THE BREEDER'S CUP WINNERS

Sprint ■ Thirty Slews

Juvenile Fillies ■ Eliza

Distaff ■ Pasaena

Mile ■ Lure

Juvenile ■ Gilded Time

Turf ■ Fraise

Classic ■ A.P. Indy

INTERNATIONAL RACES

Prix de l'Arc de Triomphe (France) ■ Subotica

Epsom Derby (England) ■ Dr. Devious

Irish Derby (Ireland) ■ St. Jovite

The Grand National (England) ■ Party Politics

HORSESHOE PITCHING

WORLD CHAMPIONSHIPS

Men's Champion ■ Kevin Cone (U.S.)

Women's Champion ■ Sue Snyder (U.S.)

LACROSSE

NCAA DIVISION I (MEN)

Princeton

NCAA DIVISION III (MEN)

Nazareth

NCAA DIVISION I (WOMEN)

Maryland

NCAA DIVISION III (WOMEN)

Trenton State

MODERN PENTATHLON

UNITED STATES NATIONAL CHAMPIONSHIPS

Men's Champion ■ Mike Gostigian

Women's Champion ■ Terry Lewis

MODERN RHYTHMIC GYMNASTICS

WORLD CHAMPIONSHIPS

All-Around ■ Oksana Kostina (RUS)

Rope ■ Oksana Kostina (RUS)*
Larissa Lukyanenko (RUS)*

Hoop ■ Oksana Kostina (RUS)*
Larissa Lukyanenko (RUS)*

Ball ■ Oksana Kostina (RUS)

Clubs ■ Oksana Kostina (RUS)

* Tie

MOTORCYCLE RACING

WORLD CHAMPIONS

125 cc ■ Alessandro Gramigni (ITA)

250 cc ■ Luca Cadalora (ITA)

500 cc ■ Wayne Rainey (U.S.)

POLO

U.S. OPEN CHAMPIONSHIP STAGED AT LEXINGTON, KY.

Hana Lei Bay (Calif.) 13, Fish Creek 6

POWERBOAT RACING

APBA GOLD CUP STAGED AT DETROIT, MICH.

Champion ■ Chip Hanauer, *Miss Budweiser*

RACQUETBALL

UNITED STATES AMATEUR CHAMPIONSHIPS

Men's Champion ■ Chris Cole

Women's Champion ■ Michelle Gould

UNITED STATES PROFESSIONAL CHAMPIONSHIPS

Men's Champion ■ Drew Kachtik

Women's Champion ■ Jackie Paraiso-Gibson

RODEO

PRCA All-Around Champion ■ Ty Murray (U.S.)

ROWING

NATIONAL COLLEGIATE CHAMPIONSHIPS
STAGED AT CINCINNATI, OHIO

Men's eight ■ Harvard
Women's eight ■ Boston University

SKIING

WORLD CUP (ALPINE)

MEN'S RESULTS
Overall Champion ■ Paul Accola (SWI)
Downhill ■ Franz Heinzer (SWI)
Slalom ■ Alberto Tomba (ITA)
Giant Slalom ■ Alberto Tomba (ITA)
Super G ■ Paul Accola (SWI)

WOMEN'S RESULTS
Overall Champion ■ Petra Kronberger (AUT)
Downhill ■ Katja Seizinger (GER)
Slalom ■ Vreni Schneider (SWI)
Giant Slalom ■ Carole Merle (FRA)
Super G ■ Carole Merle (FRA)

UNITED STATES ALPINE CHAMPIONSHIPS
STAGED AT WINTER PARK, COLO.

MEN'S RESULTS
Downhill ■ Jeff Olson
Slalom ■ Matt Grosjean
Giant Slalom ■ Erik Schlopy
Super G ■ Erik Schlopy

WOMEN'S RESULTS
Downhill ■ Kate Pace
Slalom ■ Diann Roffe-Steinrotter
Giant Slalom ■ Diann Roffe-Steinrotter
Super G ■ Diann Roffe-Steinrotter

UNITED STATES CROSS-COUNTRY CHAMPIONSHIPS STAGED AT BIWABIK, MINN.

Men's 10 km Classical ■ John Aalberg

Women's 5 km Classical ■ Nancy Fiddler

NCAA CHAMPIONSHIPS STAGED AT WATERVILLE VALLEY, N.H.

Team Champion ■ Vermont

SLED DOG RACING

THE IDITAROD

Winner ■ Martin Buser (SWI), 10 days, 19 hours, 17 minutes

SOCCER

INTERNATIONAL TOURNAMENTS

EUROPEAN CHAMPIONSHIP STAGED IN SWEDEN

CHAMPIONSHIP GAME
Denmark 2, Germany 0

AFRICAN NATIONS' CUP STAGED IN SENEGAL

CHAMPIONSHIP GAME
Ivory Coast 0, Ghana 0*
* Ivory Coast wins on penalty kicks, 11–10

INTERNATIONAL CLUB TEAM COMPETITIONS

TOYOTA WORLD CUP CHAMPIONSHIP STAGED AT TOKYO, JAPAN

Sao Paulo (BRA) 2, Barcelona (SPA) 1

EUROPEAN CUP FINAL STAGED AT LONDON, ENGLAND

Barcelona (SPA) 1, Sampdoria (ITA) 0

EUROPEAN CUP WINNERS CUP FINAL STAGED AT LISBON, PORTUGAL

Werder Bremen (GER) 2, AS Monaco (FRA) 0

UEFA CUP (2-GAME/AGGREGATE GOALS SERIES)

Torino (ITA) 2, Ajax Amsterdam (NET) 2
Ajax Amsterdam 0, Torino 0*
* Series tied 2–2, Ajax wins on away goals

COPA LIBERTADORES
(2-GAME/AGGREGATE GOALS SERIES)

Newell's Old Boys (ARG) 1, Sao Paulo (BRA) 0

Sao Paulo 1, Newell's Old Boys 0
Series tied 1–1, Sao Paulo wins on penalty kicks

NCAA CHAMPIONSHIPS

DIVISION I (MEN) STAGED AT DAVIDSON, N.C.

Virginia 2, San Diego 0

DIVISION 1 (WOMEN) STAGED AT CHAPEL HILL, N.C.

North Carolina 9, Duke 1

SOFTBALL

AMERICAN SOFTBALL ASSOCIATION CHAMPIONSHIPS

Men's Major Fast Pitch ■ National Health Care, Sioux City, Iowa

Men's Major Slow Pitch ■ Vernon's, Jacksonville, Fla.

Men's Super Slow Pitch ■ Rich's/Superior, Windsor Locks, Conn.

Women's Major Fast Pitch ■ Raybestos Brakettes, Stratford, Conn.

Women's Major Slow Pitch ■ Universal Plastics, Cookeville, Tenn.

SWIMMING

NCAA CHAMPIONSHIPS (MEN) STAGED AT INDIANAPOLIS, IND.

Men's Team ■ Stanford

NCAA CHAMPIONSHIPS (WOMEN) STAGED AT AUSTIN, TEX.

Women's Team ■ Stanford

TENNIS

GRAND SLAM EVENTS

AUSTRALIAN OPEN

Men's Singles ■ Jim Courier (U.S.)

Women's Singles ■ Monica Seles (YUG)

Men's Doubles ■ Todd Woodbridge/Mark Woodforde (AUS)

Women's Doubles ■ Arantxa Sanchez-Vicario (SPA)/Helena Sukova (CZE)

Mixed Doubles ■ Arantxa Sanchez-Vicario (SPA)/Todd Woodbridge (AUS)

FRENCH OPEN

Men's Singles ■ Jim Courier (U.S.)

Women's Singles ■ Monica Seles (YUG)

Men's Doubles ■ Jakob Hlasek/Marc Rosset (SWI)

Women's Doubles ■ Gigi Fernandez (U.S.)/Natalia Zvereva (RUS)

Mixed Doubles ■ Arantxa Sanchez-Vicario (SPA)/Todd Woodbridge (AUS)

WIMBLEDON

Men's Singles ■ Andre Agassi (U.S.)

Women's Singles ■ Steffi Graf (GER)

Men's Doubles ■ John McEnroe (U.S.)/Michael Stich (GER)

Women's Doubles ■ Gigi Fernandez (U.S.)/Natalia Zvereva (RUS)

Mixed Doubles ■ Larisa Savchenko-Neiland (RUS)/Cyril Suk (CZE)

U.S. OPEN

Men's Singles ■ Stefan Edberg (SWE)

Women's Singles ■ Monica Seles (YUG)

Men's Doubles ■ Jim Grabb (U.S.)/Richey Reneberg (SAF)

Mixed Doubles ■ Nicole Provis/Mark Woodforde (AUS)

I.B.M./APT TOUR
Leading Money Winner ■ Stefan Edberg (SWE) $2,341.804

KRAFT GENERAL FOODS WORLD TOUR
Leading Money Winner ■ Monica Seles (YUG), $2,622,352

TEAM COMPETITIONS

DAVIS CUP FINAL (AT FORT WORTH, TEX.)

United States 3, Switzerland 1

TEAM TENNIS ■ THE U.S. TEAM SAVORS ITS 1992 DAVIS CUP VICTORY.

FEDERATION CUP FINAL (AT FRANKFURT, GERMANY)

Germany 2, Spain 1

NCAA CHAMPIONSHIPS (MEN) STAGED AT ATHENS, GA.

Team ■ Stanford
Singles ■ Alex O'Brien (Stanford)

NCAA CHAMPIONSHIPS (WOMEN) STAGED AT STANFORD, CALIF.

Team ■ Florida
Singles ■ Lisa Raymond (Florida)

TRACK AND FIELD

MAJOR MARATHONS

MEN'S RESULTS
Boston ■ Ibrahim Hussein (KEN)
New York ■ Willie Mtolo (SAF)
Los Angeles ■ John Treacy (IRE)
Rotterdam ■ Salvador Garcia (MEX)

London ■ Antonio Pinto (POR)

WOMEN'S RESULTS
Boston ■ Olga Markova (CIS)
New York ■ Lisa Ondieki (AUS)
Los Angeles ■ Madina Biktagirova (CIS)
Rotterdam ■ Aurora Cunha (POR)
London ■ Katrin Dorre (GER)

TRIATHLON

IRONMAN CHAMPIONSHIP

Men's Champion ■ Mark Allen (U.S.)
Women's Champion ■ Paula Newby-Fraser (ZIM)

WORLD CHAMPIONSHIP STAGED AT HUNTSVILLE, OHIO

Men's Champion ■ Simon Lessing (GB)
Women's Champion ■ Michelle Jones (AUS)

WATERSKIING

WORLD BAREFOOT CHAMPIONSHIPS

Men's Overall ■ Ron Scarpa (U.S.)
Women's Overall ■ Jennifer Calleri (U.S.)

WRESTLING

NCAA CHAMPIONSHIPS

Team ■ Iowa

YACHTING

AMERICA'S CUP STAGED AT SAN DIEGO, CALIF.

America[3] (U.S.) 4, *Il Moro di Venezia* (Italy) 1

THE 1992 OLYMPIC GAMES

The marquee sports event of 1992 was the Olympic Games. The Winter Games were staged in Albertville, France from February 8–23, and Barcelona, Spain provided the magnificent backdrop for the Summer Games, held from July 25–August 9. These Olympics saw the last hurrah of the Soviet sports machine (known at these Games as the Unified Team), the arrival on court of the "dream team," and many new records. Highlighted below are some of the record-setters of 1992. The following pages list a complete catalogue of the results for every event of the 1992 Olympic Games.

CARL LEWIS WON HIS THIRD OLYMPIC LONG JUMP TITLE.

MAGIC JOHNSON LED THE DREAM TEAM TO BASKETBALL GOLD

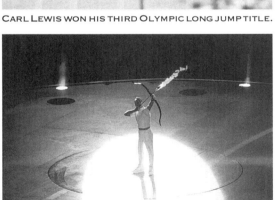

ANTONIO REBOLLO LIT THE OLYMPIC FLAME IN BARCELONA WITH A FLAMING ARROW SHOT INTO THE TORCH BOWL.

KRISTI YAMAGUICHI BECAME THE FIFTH AMERICAN TO CAPTURE THE WOMEN'S SINGLES TITLE.

1992 WINTER GAMES RESULTS (STAGED AT ALBERTVILLE, FRANCE, FEBRUARY 8–23, 1992)

Country Abbreviation Codes: AUT, Austria; CAN, Canada; CHI, China; CZE, Czechoslovakia; FIN, Finland; FRA, France; GER, Germany; ITA, Italy; JAP, Japan; LUX, Luxembourg; NK, North Korea; NL, Netherlands; NOR, Norway; NZ, New Zealand; SK, South Korea; SPA, Spain; SWE, Sweden; SWI, Switzerland; U.S., United States of America; U.T., Unified Team.

EVENT	GOLD	SILVER	BRONZE
		ALPINE SKIING (Men)	
Downhill	Patrick Ortlieb (AUT)	Franck Piccard (FRA)	Guenther Mader (AUT)
Slalom	Finn Christian Jagge (NOR)	Alberto Tomba (ITA)	Michael Tritscher (AUT)
Giant Slalom	Alberto Tomba (ITA)	Marc Girardelli (LUX)	Kjetil-Andre Aamodt (NOR)
Super Giant Slalom	Kjetil-Andre Aamodt (NOR)	Marc Girardelli (LUX)	Jan Einar Thorsen (NOR)
Combined	Josef Polig (ITA)	Gianfranco Martin (ITA)	Steve Locher (SWI)
		(Women)	
Downhill	Kerrin Lee-Gartner (CAN)	Hilary Lindh (U.S.)	Veronika Wallinger (AUT)
Slalom	Petra Kronberger (AUT)	Annelise Coberger (NZ)	Blanca Fernandez Ochoa (SPA)
Giant Slalom	Pernilla Wiberg (SWE)	Diann Roffe (U.S.)*[Tie] Anita Wachter (AUT)*[Tie]	
Super Giant Slalom	Deborah Compagnoni (ITA)	Carole Merle (FRA)	Katja Seizinger (GER)
Combined	Petra Kronberger (AUT)	Anita Wachter (AUT)	Florence Masnada (FRA)
		BIATHLON (Men)	
10 km	Mark Kirchner (GER)	Ricco Gross (GER)	Harri Eloranta (FIN)
20 km	Yevgeny Redkine (U.T.)	Mark Kirchner (GER)	Mikael Lofgren (SWE)
4 x 7.5 km relay	Germany	Unified Team	Sweden
		(Women)	
7.5 km	Anfissa Restzova (U.T.)	Antje Misersky (GER)	Yelena Belova (U.T.)
15 km	Antje Misersky (GER)	Svetlana Pecherskaia (U.T.)	Myriam Bedard (CAN)
3 x 7.5 km relay	France	Germany	Unified Team
		BOBSLED	
2–man	Gustav Weder/Donat Acklin (SWI)	Rudi Lochner/Markus Zimmerman (GER)	Christoph Langen/Gunther Eger (GER)
4–man	Austria I	Germany I	Switzerland I
		CROSS-COUNTRY SKIING (Men)	
10 km	Vegard Ulvang (NOR)	Marco Alvarello (ITA)	Christer Majback (SWE)
15 km	Bjorn Dahlie (NOR)	Vegard Ulvang (NOR)	Giorgio Vanzetta (ITA)
30 km	Vegard Ulvang (NOR)	Bjorn Dahlie (NOR)	Terje Langli (NOR)
50 km	Bjorn Dahlie (NOR)	Maurilio De Zolt (ITA)	Giorgio Vanzetta (ITA)
4 x 10 km relay	Norway	Italy	Finland
		(Women)	
5 km	Marjut Lukkarinen (FIN)	Lyubov Egorova (U.T.)	Elena Valbe (U.T.)
10 km	Lyubov Egorova (U.T.)	Stefania Belmondo (ITA)	Elena Valbe (U.T.)
15 km	Lyubov Egorova (U.T.)	Marjut Lukkarinen (FIN)	Elena Valbe (U.T.)
30 km	Stefania Belmondo (ITA)	Lyubov Egorova (U.T.)	Elena Valbe (U.T.)
4 x 5 km relay	Unified Team	Norway	Italy
		FIGURE SKATING	
Men	Viktor Petrenko (U.T.)	Paul Wylie (U.S.)	Petr Barna (CZE)
Women	Kristi Yamaguchi (U.S.)	Midori Ito (JAP)	Nancy Kerrigan (U.S.)
Pairs	Natalya Mishkutienok & Artur Dmitriev (U.T.)	Elena Bechke & Denis Petrov (U.T.)	Isabelle Brasseur & Lloyd Eisler (CAN)
Ice Dance	Marina Klimova & Sergei Ponomarenko (U.T.)	Isabelle & Paul Duchesnay (FRA)	Maia Usova & Aleksandr Zhulin (U.T.)
		FREESTYLE SKIING (Moguls)	
Men	Edgar Grospiron (FRA)	Olivier Allamand (FRA)	Nelson Carmichael (U.S.)
Women	Donna Weinbrecht (U.S.)	Elizaveta Kojevnikova (U.T.)	Stine Hattestad (NOR)

EVENT	GOLD	SILVER	BRONZE
	HOCKEY		
Team	Unified Team	Canada	Czechoslovakia
	LUGE (Men)		
Singles	Georg Hackl (GER)	Markus Prock (AUT)	Markus Schmidt (AUT)
2–man	Stefan Krausse & Jan Behrendt (GER)	Yves Mankel & Thomas Rudolph (GER)	Hansjorg Raffi & Norbert Huber (ITA)
	(Women)		
Singles	Doris Neuner (AUT)	Angelika Neuner (AUT)	Susi Erdmann (GER)
	NORDIC COMBINED		
Individual	Fabrice Guy (FRA)	Sylvain Guillaume (FRA)	Klaus Sulzenbacher (AUT)
Combined-team	Japan	Norway	Austria
	SHORT TRACK SPEEDSKATING (Men)		
1,000 m	Kim Ki-Hoon (SK)	Frederic Blackburn (CAN)	Lee Yoon-Ho (SK)
5,000 m relay	South Korea	Canada	Japan
	(Women)		
500 m	Cathy Turner (U.S.)	Li Yan (CHI)	Hwang Ok Sil (NK)
3,000 m relay	Canada	United States	Unified Team
	SKI JUMPING		
Normal Hill	Ernst Vettori (AUT)	Martin Hollwarth (AUT)	Toni Nieminen (FIN)
Large Hill	Toni Nieminen (FIN)	Martin Hollwarth (AUT)	Heinz Kuttin (AUT)
Team	Finland	Austria	Czechoslovakia
	SPEED SKATING (Men)		
500 m	Uwe-Jens Mey (GER)	Toshiyuki Kuroiwa (JAP)	Junichi Inoue (JAP)
1,000 m	Olaf Zinke (GER)	Kim Yoon-Man (SK)	Yukinori Miyabe (JAP)
1,500 m	Johann Olav Koss (NOR)	Adne Sondral (NOR)	Leo Visser (NL)
5,000 m	Geir Karlstad (NOR)	Falco Zandstra (NL)	Leo Visser (NL)
10,000 m	Bart Veldkamp (NL)	Johann Olav Koss (NOR)	Geir Karlstad (NOR)
	(Women)		
500 m	Bonnie Blair (U.S.)	Ye Qiaobo (CHI)	Christa Luding (GER)
1,000 m	Bonnie Blair (U.S.)	Ye Qiaobo (CHI)	Monique Gatbrecht (GER)
1,500 m	Jacqueline Boerner (GER)	Gunda Niemann (GER)	Seiko Hashimoto (JAP)
3,000 m	Gunda Niemann (GER)	Heiko Warnicke (GER)	Emese Hunyady (AUT)
5,000 m	Gunda Niemann (GER)	Heiko Warnicke (GER)	Claudia Pechstein (GER)

1992 WINTER GAMES MEDAL TABLE

COUNTRY	GOLD	SILVER	BRONZE	TOTAL	COUNTRY	GOLD	SILVER	BRONZE	TOTAL
Germany	10	10	6	26	South Korea	2	1	1	4
Unified Team*	9	6	8	23	Netherlands	1	1	2	4
Austria	6	7	8	21	Sweden	1	0	3	4
Norway	9	6	5	20	Switzerland	1	0	2	3
Italy	4	6	4	14	China	0	3	0	3
United States	5	4	2	11	Czechoslovakia	0	0	3	3
France	3	5	1	9	Luxembourg	0	2	0	2
Finland	3	1	3	7	New Zealand	0	1	0	1
Canada	2	3	2	7	North Korea	0	0	1	1
Japan	1	2	4	7	Spain	0	0	1	1

* Representing the former Soviet republics of Russia, Belarus, Ukraine, Kazakhstan and Uzbekistan.

Country Abbreviation Codes: ALG, Algeria; ARG, Argentina; AUS, Australia; AUT, Austria; BAH, Bahamas; BEL, Belgium; BRA, Brazil; BUL, Bulgaria; CAN, Canada; CHI, China; COL, Colombia; CRO, Croatia; CUB, Cuba; CZE, Czechoslovakia; DEN, Denmark; EST, Estonia; ETH, Ethiopia; FIN, Finland; FRA, France; GB, Great Britain; GER, Germany; GHA, Ghana; GRE, Greece; HUN, Hungary; IND, Indonesia; IRA, Iran; IRE, Ireland; ISR, Israel; ITA, Italy; JAM, Jamaica; JAP, Japan; KEN, Kenya; LAT, Latvia; LIT, Lithuania; LUX, Luxembourg; MAL, Malaysia; MEX, Mexico; MON, Mongolia; MOR, Morocco; NAM, Namibia; NIG, Nigeria; NK, North Korea; NL, Netherlands; NOR, Norway; NZ, New Zealand; PAK, Pakistan; PER, Peru; PHI, Philippines; POL, Poland; PR, Puerto Rico; QAT, Qatar; ROM, Romania; SAF, South Africa; SK, South Korea; SLO, Slovenia; SPA, Spain; SUR, Suriname; SWE, Sweden; SWI, Switzerland; TAI, Taiwan; THAI, Thailand; TUR, Turkey; U.S., United States of America; U.T., Unified Team.

EVENT	GOLD	SILVER	BRONZE
		ARCHERY	
		Men	
70 meter	Sebastien Flute (FRA)	Chung Jae Hun (SK)	Simon Terry (GB)
Team	Spain	Finland	Great Britain
		Women	
70 meter	Cho Youn Jeong (SK)	Kim Soo Nyung (SK)	Natalya Valyeva (U.T.)
Team	South Korea	China	Unified Team
		BADMINTON	
		Men	
Singles	Alan Budi Kusuma (IND)	Ardy Wiranata (IND)	Thomas Stuer-Lauridsen (DEN) Hermawan Susanto (IND)
Doubles	Kim Moon-Soo & Park Joo-Bong (SK)	Eddy Hartono & Rudy Gunawan (IND)	Li Yongbo & Tian Bingyi (CHI) Sidek Razif & Sidek Jalani (MAL)
		Women	
Singles	Susi Susanti (IND)	Bang Soo Hyun (SK)	Huang Hua (CHI) Tang Jiuhong (CHI)
Doubles	Hwang Hye Young & Chung So-Young (SK)	Guan Weizhen & Nong Qunhua (CHI)	Gil Young-Ah & Shim Eun-Jung (SK) Lin Yanfen & Yao Fen (CHI)
		BASEBALL	
Team	Cuba	Taiwan	Japan
		BASKETBALL	
		Men	
Team	United States	Croatia	Lithuania
		Women	
Team	Unified Team	China	United States
		BOXING	
Light Flyweight	Rogelio Marcelo (CUB)	Daniel Bojinov (BUL)	Jan Quast (GER) Roel Velasco (PHI)
Flyweight	Su Choi Chol (NK)	Raul Gonzalez (CUB)	Timothy Austin (U.S.) Istvan Kovacs (HUN)
Bantamweight	Joel Casamayor (CUB)	Wayne McCullough (IRE)	Li Gwang Sik (NK) Mohammed Achik (MOR)
Featherweight	Andreas Tews (GER)	Faustino Reyes (SPA)	Hocine Soltani (ALG) Ramazi Paliani (U.T.)
Lightweight	Oscar De La Hoya (U.S.)	Marco Rudolph (GER)	Hong Sung Sik (SK) Namjil Bayarsaikhan (MON)
Light Welterweight	Hector Vincent (CUB)	Mark Leduc (CAN)	Jyri Kjall (FIN) Leonard Doroftei (ROM)
Welterweight	Michael Carruth (IRE)	Juan Hernandez (CUB)	Anibal Santiago (PR) Arkom Chenglai (THA)

EVENT	GOLD	SILVER	BRONZE
		BOXING (cont'd)	
Light middleweight	Juan Lemus (CUB)	Orhan Delibas (NL)	Gyorgy Mizsei (HUN)
Middleweight	Ariel Hernandez (CUB)	Chris Byrd (U.S.)	Chris Johnson (CAN)
			Lee Seung Bae (SK)
Light Heavyweight	Torsten May (GER)	Rostislav Zaoulitchnyi (U.T.)	Zoltan Beres (HUN)
			Wojciech Bartnik (POL)
Heavyweight	Felix Savon (CUB)	David Izonritei (NIG)	Arnold Van Der Lijde (NL)
			David Tua (NZ)
Super Heavyweight	Roberto Balado (CUB)	Richard Igbineghu (NIG)	Brian Nielsen (DEN)
			Svilen Roussinov (BUL)

CANOE AND KAYAK
Men

EVENT	GOLD	SILVER	BRONZE
C-1 500 m	Nikolai Bukhalov (BUL)	Mikhail Slivinski (U.T.)	Olaf Heukrodt (GER)
C-1 1,000 m	Nikolai Bukhalov (BUL)	Ivans Klementjevs (LAT)	Gyorgy Zala (HUN)
C-2 500 m	Unified Team	Germany	Bulgaria
C-2 1,000 m	Germany	Denmark	France
C-1 slalom	Lukas Pollert (CZE)	Gareth Marriott (GB)	Jacky Avril (FRA)
C-2 slalom	United States	Czechoslovakia	France
K-1 500 m	Mikko Kolehmainen (FIN)	Zsolt Gyulay (HUN)	Knut Holmann (NOR)
K-1 1,000 m	Clint Robinson (AUS)	Knut Holmann (NOR)	Greg Barton (U.S.)
K-2 500 m	Germany	Poland	Italy
K-2 1,000 m	Germany	Sweden	Poland
K-4 1,000 m	Germany	Hungary	Australia
K-1 slalom	Pierpaolo Ferrazzi (ITA)	Sylvain Curinier (FRA)	Jochen Lettmann (GER)

Women

EVENT	GOLD	SILVER	BRONZE
K-1 500 m	Birgit Schmidt (GER)	Rita Koban (HUN)	Izabella Dylewska (POL)
K-2 500 m	Germany	Sweden	Hungary
K-4 500 m	Hungary	Germany	Sweden
K-1 slalom	Elisabeth Micheler (GER)	Danielle Woodward (AUS)	Dana Chladek (U.S.)

CYCLING
Men

EVENT	GOLD	SILVER	BRONZE
Ind. Road Race	Fabio Casartelli (ITA)	Erik Dekker (NL)	Dainis Ozols (LAT)
Road Race	Germany	Italy	France
Ind. Points Race	Giovanni Lombardi (ITA)	Leon Van Bon (NL)	Cedric Mathy (BEL)
Ind. Pursuit	Chris Boardman (GB)	Jens Lehmann (GER)	Gary Anderson (NZ)
Team Pursuit	Germany	Australia	Denmark
Time Trial	Jose Moreno (SPA)	Shane Kelly (AUS)	Erin Hartwell (U.S.)
Sprint	Jens Fiedler (GER)	Garry Neiwand (AUS)	Curtis Harnett (CAN)

Women

EVENT	GOLD	SILVER	BRONZE
Ind. Road Race	Kathryn Watt (AUS)	Jeannie Longo (FRA)	Monique Knol (NL)
Sprint	Erika Salumae (EST)	Annett Neumann (GER)	Ingrid Haringa (NL)
Ind. Pursuit	Petra Rossner (GER)	Kathryn Watt (AUS)	Rebecca Twigg (U.S.)

DIVING
Men

EVENT	GOLD	SILVER	BRONZE
Springboard	Mark Lenzi (U.S.)	Tan Liangde (CHI)	Dmitri Saoutine (U.T.)
Platform	Sun Shuwei (CHI)	Scott Donie (U.S.)	Xiong Ni (CHI)

Women

EVENT	GOLD	SILVER	BRONZE
Springboard	Gao Min (CHI)	Irina Lachko (U.T.)	Brita Baldus (GER)
Platform	Fu Mingxia (CHI)	Elena Mirochina (U.T.)	Mary Ellen Clark (U.S.)

EVENT	GOLD	SILVER	BRONZE
		EQUESTRIAN	
		Dressage	
Individual	Nicole Uphoff (GER)	Isabelle Werth (GER)	Klaus Balkenhol (GER)
Team	Germany	Netherlands	United States
		Three-day Event	
Individual	Matthew Ryan (AUS)	Herbert Blocker (GER)	Robert Tait (NZ)
Team	Australia	New Zealand	Germany
		Show Jumping	
Individual	Ludger Beerbaum (GER)	Piet Raymakers (NL)	Norman Joio (U.S.)
Team	Netherlands	Austria	France
		FENCING	
		Men	
Épée	Eric Srecki (FRA)	Paul Kolobkov (U.T.)	Jean-Michel Henry (FRA)
Épée (Team)	Germany	Hungary	Unified Team
Foil	Philippe Omnes (FRA)	Sergei Goloubitski (U.T.)	Elvis Gil (CUB)
Foil Team	Germany	Cuba	Poland
Sabre	Bence Szabo (HUN)	Marco Marin (ITA)	Jean-Francois Lamour (FRA)
Sabre (Team)	Unified Team	Hungary	France
		Women	
Foil	Giovanna Trillini (ITA)	Wang Huifeng (CHI)	Tatyana Sadovskaya (U.T.)
Team Foil	Italy	Germany	Romania
		FIELD HOCKEY	
		Men	
Team	Germany	Australia	Pakistan
		Women	
Team	Spain	Germany	Great Britain
		GYMNASTICS	
		Men	
All Around	Vitaly Shcherbo (U.T.)	Grigory Misutin (U.T.)	Valery Belenki (U.T.)
Team	Unified Team	China	Japan
Horizontal Bar	Trent Dimas (U.S.)	Grigory Misutin (U.T.) Andreas Wecker (GER)	
Pommel Horse	Vitaly Shcherbo (U.T.) Pae Gil Su (NK)		Andreas Wecker (GER)
Floor Exercise	Li Xiaosahuang (CHI)	Grigory Misutin (U.T.) Yukio Iketani (JAP)	
Parallel Bars	Vitaly Shcherbo (U.T.)	Li Jing (CHI)	Guo Linyao (CHI) Igor Korobtchinski (U.T.) Masayuki Matsunaga (JAP)
Rings	Vitaly Shcherbo (U.T.)	Li Jing (CHI)	Li Xiaosahuang (CHI) Andreas Wecker (GER)
Vault	Vitaly Shcherbo (U.T.)	Grigory Mustin (U.T.)	Yoo Ok Ryul (SK)
		Women	
All-Around	Tatyana Gutsu (U.T.)	Shannon Miller (U.S.)	Lavinia Milosovici (ROM)
Team	Unified Team	Romania	United States
Balance beam	Tatyana Lyssenko (U.T.)	Shannon Miller (U.S.) Lu Li (CHI)	
Uneven bars	Lu Li (CHI)	Tatyana Gutsu (U.T.)	Shannon Miller (U.S.)
Floor Exercise	Lavinia Milosovici (ROM)	Henrietta Onodi (HUN)	Tatyana Gutsu (U.T.) Shannon Miller (U.S.) Cristina Bontas (ROM)

EVENT	GOLD	SILVER	BRONZE
	GYMNASTICS (cont'd) Women		
Vault	Henrietta Onodi (HUN) Lavinia Milosovici (ROM)		Tatyana Lyssenko (U.T.)
	JUDO Men		
132 lb	Nazim Gusseinov (U.T.)	Yoon Hyun (SK)	Tadanori Koshino (JAP) Richard Trautmann (GER)
143 lb	Rogerio Cardoso (BRA)	Josef Csak (HUN)	Udo Quellmalz (GER) Israel Planas (CUB)
157 lb	Toshihiko Koga (JAP)	Bertalan Hajtos (HUN)	Chung Hoon (SK) Shay Oren Smadga (ISR)
172 lb	Hidehiko Yoshida (JAP)	Jason Morris (U.S.)	Bertrand Damaisin (FRA) Kim Byung Joo (SK)
198 lb	Waldemar Legien (POL)	Pascal Tayot (FRA)	Hirotaka Okada (JAP) Nicolas Gill (CAN)
209 lb	Antal Kovacs (HUN)	Raymond Stevens (GB)	Dmitri Sergeyev (U.T.) Theo Meijer (NL)
Heavyweight	David Khakhaleichvili (U.T.)	Naoya Ogawa (JAP)	David Douillet (FRA) Imre Csosz (HUN)
	Women		
106 lb	Cecile Nowak (FRA)	Ryoko Tamura (JAP)	Amarilis Savon (CUB) Hulya Senyurt (TUR)
115 lb	Almudena Munoz Martinez (SPA)	Noriko Mizoguchi (JAP)	Li Zhongyun (CHI) Sharon Rendle (GB)
123 lb	Miriam Blasco Soto (SPA)	Nicola Fairbrother (GB)	Chiyori Tateno (JAP) Driulis Gonzalez (CUB)
134 lb	Catherine Fleury (FRA)	Yael Arad (ISR)	Zhang Di (CHI) Yelena Petrova (U.T.)
146 lb	Odalis Reve Jimenez (CUB)	Emanuela Pierantozzi (ITA)	Kate Howey (GB) Heidi Rakels (BEL)
159 lb	Kim Mi Jung (SK)	Yoko Tanabe (JAP)	Irene de Kok (NL) Laetitia Meignan (FRA)
Over 159 lb	Zhuang Xiaoyan (CHI)	Estella Villanueva (CUB)	Natalia Lupino (FRA) Yoko Sakaue (JAP)
	MODERN PENTATHLON		
Ind.	Arkadiusz Skrzypaszek (POL)	Atilla Mizser (HUN)	Eduard Zenovka (U.T.)
Team	Poland	Unified Team	Italy
	ROWING Men		
Single Sculls	Thomas Lange (GER)	Vaclav Chalupa (CZE)	Kajetan Broniewski (POL)
Double Sculls	Australia	Austria	Netherlands
Coxless Pairs	Great Britain	Germany	Slovenia
Coxed Pairs	Great Britain	Italy	Romania
Coxless Fours	Australia	United States	Slovenia
Coxed Fours	Romania	Germany	Poland
Quadruple Sculls	Germany	Norway	Italy
Coxed Eights	Canada	Romania	Germany
	Women		
Single Sculls	Elisabeta Lipa (ROM)	Annelies Bredael (BEL)	Silken Laumann (CAN)
Double Sculls	Germany	Romania	China

EVENT	GOLD	SILVER	BRONZE
		ROWING (cont'd)	
		Women	
Coxless Pairs	Canada	Germany	United States
Coxless Fours	Canada	United States	Germany
Quadruple Sculls	Germany	Romania	Unified Team
Coxed Eights	Canada	Romania	Germany
		RHYTHMIC GYMNASTICS	
Ind.	Aleksandra Rimoshenko (U.T.)	Carolina Pascual (SPA)	Oksana Skaldina (U.T.)
		SHOOTING	
		Men	
Air Pistol	Wang Yifu (CHI)	Sergei Pyzhanov (U.T.)	Sorin Babii (ROM)
Air Rifle	Iouri Fedkine (U.T.)	Franck Badiou (FRA)	Johann Riederer (GER)
Free Pistol	Konstantine Loukachik (U.T.)	Wang Yifu (CHI)	Ragnar Skanaker (SWE)
Free Rifle	Lee Eun Chul (SK)	Harald Stenvaag (NOR)	Stevan Pletikosic (IOP)
		Three Position	
Rifle	Gratchia Petikiane (U.T.)	Bob Froth (U.S.)	Ryohei Koba (Jap)
		Rapid Fire	
Pistol	Ralf Schumann (GER)	Afanasijs Kuzmins (LAT)	Vladimir Vokhmanin (U.T.)
		Running Game	
Target	Michael Jakosits (GER)	Anatoly Asrabaev (U.T.)	Lubos Racansky (CZE)
		Women	
Air Pistol	Marina Logvinenko (U.T.)	Jasna Sekaric (IOP)	Maria Grousdeva (BUL)
Air Rifle	Yeo Kab-soon (SK)	Vesela Letcheva (BUL)	Aranka Binder (IOP)
		Three Position	
Rifle	Launi Meili (U.S.)	Nonka Matova (BUL)	Malgorzata Ksiazkiewicz (POL)
Sport Pistol	Marina Logvinenko (U.T.)	Li Duihong (CHI)	Dorzhsuren Munkhbayer (MON)
		Open	
Skeet	Zhang Shan (CHI)	Juan Yarur (PER)	Bruno Rossetti (ITA)
Trap	Petr Hrdlicka (CZE)	Kazumi Watanabe (JAP)	Marco Venturini (ITA)
		SOCCER	
Team	Spain	Poland	Ghana
		SWIMMING	
		Men	
		Backstroke	
100 m	Mark Tewksbury (CAN)	Jeff Rouse (U.S.)	David Berkoff (U.S.)
200 m	Martin Lopez-Zubero (SPA)	Vladimir Selkov (U.T.)	Stefano Battistelli (ITA)
		Breaststroke	
100 m	Nelson Diebel (U.S.)	Norbert Rozsa (HUN)	Philip Rogers (AUS)
200 m	Mike Barrowman (U.S.)	Norbert Rozsa (HUN)	Nick Gillingham (GB)
		Butterfly	
100 m	Pablo Morales (U.S.)	Rafal Szukala (POL)	Anthony Nesty (SUR)
200 m	Melvin Stewart (U.S.)	Danyon Loader (NZ)	Franck Esposito (FRA)
		Freestyle	
50 m	Aleksandr Popov (U.T.)	Matt Biondi (U.S.)	Tom Jager (U.S.)
100 m	Aleksandr Popov (U.T.)	Gustavo Borges (BRA)	Stephane Caron (FRA)
200 m	Yevgeny Sadovyi (U.T.)	Anders Holmertz (SWE)	Antti Kasvio (FIN)
400 m	Yevgeny Sadovyi (U.T.)	Kieren Perkins (AUS)	Anders Holmertz (SWE)
1,500 m	Kieren Perkins (AUS)	Glen Housman (AUS)	Jorg Hoffman (GER)

EVENT	GOLD	SILVER	BRONZE
		SWIMMING (cont'd)	
		Men	
		Ind. Medley	
200 m	Tamas Darnyi (HUN)	Greg Burgess (U.S.)	Attila Czene (HUN)
400 m	Tamas Darnyi (HUN)	Eric Namesnik (U.S.)	Luca Sacchi (ITA)
		Relays	
4 x 100 m freestyle	United States	Unified Team	Germany
4 x 200 m freestyle	Unified Team	Sweden	United States
4 x 100 m medley	United States	Unified Team	Canada
		Women	
		Backstroke	
100 m	Kristina Egerszegi (HUN)	Tunde Szabo (HUN)	Lea Loveless (U.S.)
200 m	Kristina Egerszegi (HUN)	Dagmar Hase (GER)	Nicole Stevenson (AUS)
		Breaststroke	
100 m	Yelena Roudkovskaya (U.T.)	Anita Nall (U.S.)	Samantha Riley (AUS)
200 m	Kyoko Iwasaki (JAP)	Lin Li (CHI)	Anita Nall (U.S.)
		Butterfly	
100 m	Qian Hong (CHI)	Christine Ahmann-Leighton (U.S.)	Catherine Plewinski (FRA)
200 m	Summer Sanders (U.S.)	Wang Xiaohong (CHI)	Susan O'Neill (AUS)
		Freestyle	
50 m	Yang Wenyi (CHI)	Zhuang Yong (CHI)	Angel Martino (U.S.)
100 m	Zhuang Yong (CHI)	Jenny Thompson (U.S.)	Franziska van Almsick (GER)
200 m	Nicole Haislett (U.S.)	Franzika van Almsick (GER)	Kerstin Kielgass (GER)
400 m	Dagmar Hase (GER)	Janet Evans (U.S.)	Hayley Lewis (AUS)
800 m	Janet Evans (U.S.)	Hayley Lewis (AUS)	Jana Henke (GER)
		Ind. Medley	
200 m	Lin Li (CHI)	Summer Sanders (U.S.)	Daniela Hunger (GER)
400 m	Kristina Egerszegi (HUN)	Lin Li (CHI)	Summer Sanders (U.S.)
		Relays	
4 x 100 m freestyle	United States	China	Germany
4 x 100 m medley	United States	Germany	Unified Team
		SYNCHRONIZED SWIMMING	
Solo	Kristen Babb-Sprague (U.S.)	Sylvie Frechette (CAN)	Sumiko Okuno (JAP)
Duet	Karen Josephson & Sarah Josephson (U.S.)	Penny Vilagos & Vicky Vilagos (CAN)	Fumiko Okuno & Aki Takayama (JAP)
		TABLE TENNIS	
		Men	
Singles	Jan Ove Waldner (SWE)	Jean-Philippe Gatien (FRA)	Kim Taek Soo (SK)
Doubles	Lu Lin & Wang Tao (CHI)	Steffan Fetzner & Jorg Rosskopf (GER)	Kang Hee Chan & Lee Chul Seung (SK) Kim Taek Soo & Yoo Nam Kyu (SK)
		Women	
Singles	Deng Yaping (CHI)	Qiao Hong (CHI)	Hyun Jung Hwa (SK) Li Bun Hui (NK)
Doubles	Deng Yaping & Qiao Hong (CHI)	Chen Zihe & Gao Jun (CHI)	Li Bun Hui & Yu Sun Bok (NK) Hong Cha Ok & Hyun Jung Hwa (SK)

EVENT	GOLD	SILVER	BRONZE
		TEAM HANDBALL	
		Men	
Team	Unified Team	Sweden	France
		TEAM HANDBALL	
		Women	
Team	South Korea	Norway	Unified Team
		TENNIS	
		Men	
Singles	Marc Rosset (SWI)	Jordi Arrese (SPA)	Goran Ivanisevic (CRO) Andrei Cherkasov (U.T.)
Doubles	Boris Becker & Michael Stich (GER)	Wayne Ferreira & Piet Norval (SAF)	Goran Ivanisevic & Goran Prpic (CRO) Javier Frana & Christian Miniussi (ARG)
		Women	
Singles	Jennifer Capriati (U.S.)	Steffi Graf (GER)	Arantxa Sanchez-Vicario (SPA) Mary Joe Fernandez (U.S.)
Doubles	Gigi Fernandez & Mary Joe Fernandez (U.S.)	Conchita Martinez & Arantxa Sanchez-Vicario (SPA)	Natalia Zvereva & Leila Meskhi (U.T.) Rachel McQuillan & Nicole Provis (AUS)
		TRACK AND FIELD	
		Men	
100 m	Linford Christie (GB)	Frank Fredericks (NAM)	Dennis Mitchell (U.S.)
200 m	Michael Marsh (U.S.)	Frank Fredericks (NAM)	Michael Bates (U.S.)
400 m	Quincy Watts (U.S.)	Steve Lewis (U.S.)	Samson Kitur (KEN)
800 m	William Tanui (KEN)	Nixon Kiprotich (KEN)	Johnny Grey (U.S.)
1,500 m	Fermin Cacho (SPA)	Rachid el-Basir (MOR)	Mohammed Sulaiman (QAT)
5,000 m	Dieter Baumann (GER)	Paul Bitok (KEN)	Fita Bayisa (ETH)
10,000 m	Khalid Skah (MOR)	Richard Chelimo (KEN)	Addis Abebe (ETH)
110 m Hurdles	Mark McCoy (CAN)	Tony Dees (U.S.)	Jack Pierce (U.S.)
400 m Hurdles	Kevin Young (U.S.)	Winthrop Graham (JAM)	Kriss Akabusi (GB)
3,000 m Steeplechase	Matthew Birir (KEN)	Patrick Sang (KEN)	William Mutwol (KEN)
Marathon	Hwang Young Cho (SK)	Koichi Morishita (JAP)	Stephan Freigang (GER)
4 x 100 m Relay	United States	Nigeria	Cuba
4 x 400 m Relay	United States	Cuba	Great Britain
20 K m Walk	Daniel Plaza (SPA)	Guillaume Leblanc (CAN)	Giovanni de Benedictis (ITA)
50 K m Walk	Andrei Perlov (U.T.)	Carlos Mercenario (MEX)	Ronald Weigel (GER)
Discus	Romas Ubartas (LIT)	Jurgen Schult (GER)	Roberto Moya (CUB)
Hammer	Andrei Abduvaliyev (U.T.)	Igor Astapkovich (U.T.)	Igor Nikulin (U.T.)
High Jump	Javier Sotomayor (CUB)	Patrik Sjoeberg (SWE)	Artur Partyka (POL) Tim Forsythe (AUS) Hollis Conway (U.S.)
Javelin	Jan Zelezny (CZE)	Seppo Raty (FIN)	Steve Backley (GB)
Long Jump	Carl Lewis (U.S.)	Mike Powell (U.S.)	Joe Green (U.S.)
Pole Vault	Maksim Tarasov (U.T.)	Igor Trandenkov (U.T.)	Javier Gracia (SPA)
Shot Put	Mike Stulce (U.S.)	James Doehrin (U.S.)	Vyacheslav Lykho (U.T.)
Triple Jump	Mike Conley (U.S.)	Charles Simpkins (U.S.)	Frank Rutherford (BAH)
Decathlon	Robert Zmelik (CZE)	Antonio Penalver (SPA)	Dave Johnson (U.S.)
		Women	
100 m	Gail Devers (U.S.)	Juliet Cuthbert (JAM)	Irina Privalova (U.T.)
200 m	Gwen Torrence (U.S.)	Juliet Cuthbert (JAM)	Merlene Ottey (JAM)
400 m	Marie-Jose Perec (FRA)	Olga Bryzgina (U.T.)	Ximena Restrepo (COL)

EVENT	GOLD	SILVER	BRONZE
		TRACK AND FIELD (cont'd)	
		Women	
800 m	Ellen van Langen (NL)	Liliya Nurutdinova (U.T.)	Ana Quirot (CUB)
1,500 m	Hassiba Boulmerka (ALG)	Lyudmila Rogacheva (U.T.)	Qu Yunxia (CHI)
3,000 m	Yelina Romanova (U.T.)	Tatyana Dorovskikh (U.T.)	Angela Chalmers (CAN)
10,000 m	Derartu Tulu (U.T.)	Elena Meyer (SAF)	Lynn Jennings (U.S.)
110 m Hurdles	Paraskevi Patoulidou (GRE)	LaVonna Martin (U.S.)	Yordanka Donkova (BUL)
400 m Hurdles	Sally Gunnell (GB)	Sandra Farmer-Patrick (U.S.)	Janeene Vickers (U.S.)
Marathon	Valentina Yegorova (U.T.)	Yuko Arimori (JAP)	Lorraine Moller (NZ)
4 x 100 m relay	United States	Unified Team	Nigeria
4 x 400 m relay	Unified Team	United States	Great Britain
10K m Walk	Chen Yueling (CHI)	Yelina Nikolayeva (U.T.)	Li Chunxiu (CHI)
Discus	Maritza Marten Garcia (CUB)	Tsvetanka Khristova (BUL)	Daniela Costian (AUS)
High Jump	Heike Henkel (GER)	Galina Astafei (ROM)	Joanet Quintero (CUB)
Javelin	Silke Renke (GER)	Natalya Shikolenko (U.T.)	Karen Forkel (GER)
Long Jump	Heike Drechsler (GER)	Inessa Kravets (U.T.)	Jackie Joyner-Kersee (U.S.)
Shot Put	Svetlana Kriveleva (U.T.)	Huang Zhihong (CHI)	Kathrin Neimke (GER)
Heptathlon	Jackie Joyner-Kersee (U.S.)	Irena Belova (U.T.)	Sabine Braun (GER)
		VOLLEYBALL	
		Men	
Team	Brazil	Netherlands	United States
		Women	
Team	Cuba	Unified Team	United States
		WATER POLO	
Team	Italy	Spain	Unified Team
		WEIGHTLIFTING	
115 lb	Ivan Ivanov (BUL)	Lin Qisheng (CHI)	Traian Ciharean (ROM)
123 lb	Chun Byung-Kwan (SK)	Liu Shoubin (CHI)	Luo Jianming (CHI)
132 lb	Naim Suleymanoglü (TUR)	Nikolai Peshalov (BUL)	He Yingqiang (CHI)
148 lb	Israel Militossyan (U.T.)	Yoto Yotov (BUL)	Andreas Behm (GER)
165 lb	Fyodor Kassapu (U.T.)	Pablo Lara (CUB)	Kim Myong Nam (NK)
180 lb	Pyrros Dimas (GRE)	Krysztof Siemion (POL)	Ibrahim Samadov (U.T.)
198 lb	Kakhi Kakhiashvili (U.T.)	Sergei Syrtsov (U.T.)	Sergiusz Wolczaniecki (POL)
220 lb	Viktor Tregubov (U.T.)	Timur Taimazov (U.T.)	Waldemar Malak (POL)
243 lb	Ronny Weller (GER)	Artur Akoyev (U.T.)	Stefan Botev (BUL)
Over 243 lb	Aleksandr Kurlovich (U.T.)	Leonid Taranenko (U.T.)	Manfred Nerlinger (GER)
		WRESTLING	
		Greco-Roman	
106 lb	Oleg Koutherenko (U.T.)	Vincenzo Maenza (ITA)	Wilber Sanchez (CUB)
115 lb	Jon Ronningen (NOR)	Alfred Ter-Mkrttychyan (U.T.)	Min Kyung Kap (SK)
126 lb	An Han Bong (SK)	Rifat Yildiz (GER)	Sheng Zetian (CHI)
137 lb	M. Akif Oirim (TUR)	Sergei Martynov (U.T.)	Juan Luis Delis (CUB)
150 lb	Attila Repka (HUN)	Isalm Dougoutchyev (U.T.)	Rodney Smith (U.S.)
163 lb	Mnatsakan Iskandaryan (U.T.)	Jozef Tracz (POL)	Torbjom Johansson (SWE)
182 lb	Peter Farkas (HUN)	Piotr Stepien (POL)	Daulet Turlykhanov (U.T.)
198 lb	Miak Bullmann (GER)	Hakki Basar (TUR)	Gogui Kogouachvili (U.T.)
220 lb	Hector Milian Perez (CUB)	Dennis Koslowski (U.S.)	Sergei Demyachkyevich (U.T.)
286 lb	Aleksandr Karelin (U.T.)	Tomas Johansson (SWE)	Ioan Grigoras (ROM)
		WRESTLING	
		Freestyle	
106 lb	Kim il (NK)	Kim Jong Shin (SK)	Vugar Orudzhov (U.T.)

EVENT	GOLD	SILVER	BRONZE
WRESTLING (cont'd)			
Freestyle			
115 lb	Li Hak Son (NK)	Zeke Jones (U.S.)	Valentin Jordanov (BUL)
126 lb	Alejandro Diaz (CUB)	Sergei Smal (U.T.)	Kim Yong Sik (NK)
137 lb	John Smith (U.S.)	Asgari Mohammadian (IRA)	Lazaro Martinez (CUB)
150 lb	Arsen Fadzyev (U.T.)	Valentin Getzov (BUL)	Kosei Akaishi (JAP)
163 lb	Park Jang Sun (SK)	Kenny Monday (U.S.)	Amir Reza Khadem Azghadi (IRA)
182 lb	Kevin Jackson (U.S.)	Elmadi Dzhabrailov (U.T.)	Rasul Azghadi (IRA)
198 lb	Makharbek Khadartsev (U.T.)	Kenan Simsek (TUR)	Chris Campbell (U.S.)
220 lb	Lery Khabelov (U.T.)	Heiko Balz (GER)	Ali Kayali (TUR)
286 lb	Bruce Baumgartner (U.S.)	Jeff Thue (CAN)	David Gobedzhichvili (U.T.)
YACHTING			
Men			
Sailboard	Franck David (FRA)	Mike Gebhardt (U.S.)	Lars Kleppich (AUS)
Flying Dutchman	Spain	United States	Denmark
Star	United States	New Zealand	Canada
Finn	Jose van der Ploeg (SPA)	Brian Ledbetter (U.S.)	Craig Monk (NZ)
470	Spain	United States	Estonia
Soling	Denmark	United States	Great Britain
		Women	
Europe	Linda Anderson (NOR)	Natalia Via Dufrense (SPA)	Julia Trotman (U.S.)
Sailboard	Barbara Kendall (NZ)	Xiaodong Zhang (CHI)	Dorien de Vries (CHI)
470	Spain	New Zealand	United States
		Open	
Tornado	France	United States	Australia

EVELYN ASHFORD (SECOND LEFT) WON HER FOURTH CAREER OLYMPIC GOLD MEDAL IN BARCELONA, MATCHING THE ALL-TIME MARK FOR AN AMERICAN WOMAN.

1992 SUMMER GAMES MEDAL TABLE

COUNTRY	GOLD	SILVER	BRONZE	TOTAL		COUNTRY	GOLD	SILVER	BRONZE	TO'.
Unified Team*	45	38	29	112		Ethiopia	1	0	2	3
United States	37	34	37	108		Latvia	0	2	1	3
Germany	33	21	28	82		Croatia	0	1	2	3
China	16	22	16	54		Belgium	0	1	2	3
Cuba	14	6	11	31		Iran	0	1	2	3
Hungary	11	12	7	30		I.O.P.**	0	1	2	3
South Korea	12	5	12	29		Greece	2	0	0	2
France	8	5	16	29		Ireland	1	1	0	2
Australia	7	9	11	27		Algeria	1	0	1	2
Spain	13	7	2	22		Estonia	1	0	1	2
Japan	3	8	11	22		Lithuania	1	0	1	2
Great Britain	5	3	12	20		Austria	0	2	0	2
Italy	6	5	8	19		Namibia	0	2	0	2
Poland	3	6	10	19		South Africa	0	2	0	2
Canada	6	5	7	18		Israel	0	1	1	2
Romania	4	6	8	18		Mongolia	0	0	2	2
Bulgaria	3	7	6	16		Slovenia	0	0	2	2
Netherlands	2	6	7	15		Switzerland	1	0	0	1
Sweden	1	7	4	12		Mexico	0	1	0	1
New Zealand	1	4	5	10		Peru	0	1	0	1
North Korea	4	0	5	9		Taiwan	0	1	0	1
Kenya	2	4	2	8		Argentina	0	0	1	1
Czechoslovakia	4	2	1	7		Bahamas	0	0	1	1
Norway	2	4	1	7		Colombia	0	0	1	1
Turkey	2	2	2	6		Ghana	0	0	1	1
Denmark	1	1	4	6		Malaysia	0	0	1	1
Indonesia	2	2	1	5		Pakistan	0	0	1	1
Finland	1	2	2	5		Philippines	0	0	1	1
Jamaica	0	3	1	4		Puerto Rico	0	0	1	1
Nigeria	0	3	1	4		Qatar	0	0	1	1
Brazil	2	1	0	3		Suriname	0	0	1	1
Morocco	1	1	1	3		Thailand	0	0	1	1

* Athletes from 12 former Soviet republics
** Independent Olympic Participants (athletes from Serbia, Montenegro and Macedonia)

INDEX

Boldface type indicates main subjects. *Italic* type indicates "Timeout" features. With the exception of names listed under "record files," names of sports figures appear only in the main body of the text.

domed stadium, largest, *85*
drag racing, 12–14
  NHRA Winston Cup, 13–14, 217
dressage—*See equestrian sports*
dribbling (of basketball), *41*

E

earnings, highest
  in auto racing
    Daytona 500, 9
    Indianapolis 500, 5
    Indy car series, 7
    NASCAR, 8
  in bowling
    LPBT, 57
    PBA, 57, 222
  in golf
    LPGA tour, 118, 227
    PGA European tour, 115, 227
    PGA tour, 115, 227
    Senior PGA tour, 115, 227
  in harness racing
    by driver, 125
    by pacer, 124, 228
    by trotter, 124, 228
  in horse racing
    by horse, 141, 146
    by jockey (female), 144
    by jockey (male), 143, 146
  in rodeo (PRCA), 165
  in tennis
    men's circuit, 199
    women's circuit, 199
egg throw, 162
Epsom Derby (England), 146–147, 230
equestrian sports, 69–71
  1992 results, 225
  Olympic Games, 239
  dressage, 70–71, 225, 239
  miscellaneous records
    highest jump, *70*
    longest jump, 205
  show jumping, 69–70, 225, 239
  three-day event, 70, 239

F

Federation Cup, 198, 232
fencing, 71–72
  1992 results, 225
  Olympic Games, 239
field hockey, 72
  1992 results, 225
  Olympic Games, 239
figure skating, 72–73
  1992 results, 225
  Olympic Games, 235
fishing, 74–76
flight shooting (archery), 3
flying disc throwing—*See frisbee*

footbag, 76
  largest circle, 76
football, 76–107
  1992 season results, 225–227
  collegiate (NCAA), 91–102, 226–227
    attendance records, 101–102
    bowl games, 100–101, 102, 226
    championship games (divisions 1-AA/II/III) (1992), 227
    Heisman Trophy winners, 100–101, 227
    national champions, 98–99, 226
    statistical leaders (all divisions), 91, 96
    statistical leaders (Div. 1-A), 92–95, 96–99
    team records (Div. 1-A), 99
  miscellaneous records
    longest field goal, 97
  professional (CFL), 102–107, 227
    regular season individual records, 103–104
    regular season team records, 102, 105
    Grey Cup, 105–107, 227
  professional (NFL), 77–90, 225–226
    championships (1920-65), 85, 86–87
    coaches, 85, 88
    regular season individual records, 78–84
    regular season team records, 84
    Super Bowl records, 85, 88–90
    Super Bowl results, 87, 226
    trades, 85
  professional (World League), 227
Formula One (Grand Prix), 9, 12, 217
forward rolls, *121*
French Open (tennis), 194–196, 232
frisbee, 107, 162
Funny Car (drag racing), 12–13
  NHRA Winston Series, 14, 217

G

golf, 107–119
  1992 results, 227–228
  age records—*See age records*
  amateur (men), 119, 228
  amateur (women), 228

  miscellaneous records
    ball balancing, 114
    longest hole, *110*
    one-club lowest score, *114*
  professional (men), 108–115, 227
    British Open, 110–112, 227
    grand slam titles, 108
    Johnnie Walker Championship (1992), 227
    Masters, 108–109, 227
    PGA Championship, 111, 113, 227
    PGA European tour, 115, 227
    PGA tour, 112–115, 227
    Senior PGA tour, 115, 227
    Skins Game (1992), 227
    US Open, 109–110, 227
  professional (women), 115–119, 227
    du Maurier Classic, 118, 227
    grand slam titles, 115–116
    LPGA Championship, 117, 227
    LPGA tour, 118–119, 227
    Nabisco Dinah Shore, 117, 227
    US Open, 116–117, 227
Grand National, 147, 230
grape throw, 162
Grey Cup, 105–107, 227
gymnastics, 119–121
  1992 results, 228
  Olympic Games, 239–240

H

hammer throw, 162, 200, 243
handball (team)—*See team handball*
hands, walking on, *207*
hang gliding, 121–123
harness racing, 123–125
  1992 results, 228
  Hart Trophy (hockey MVP award), 130, 229
  Hawaii Ironman, 208–209, 233
Heisman Trophy, 100–101, 227
high diving, 69
hockey, 125–140
  1992 results, 229, 236
  miscellaneous records
    fastest hat trick, *140*
  National Hockey League (NHL)—*See National Hockey League*
  NCAA championships, 138, 229

Olympic Games, 140
  Albertville (1992), 236
  Stanley Cup—*See National Hockey League*
  world championships, 140, 229
hockey, field—*See field hockey*
hockey, roller—*See roller hockey*
horse racing, 140–147
  1992 results, 229–230
  Belmont Stakes, 145, 146, 229
  Breeders' Cup, 141, 146, 229–230
  international events, 146–147, 230
  Kentucky Derby, 143, 144–145, 229
  miscellaneous records
    biggest payout, *141*
  Preakness Stakes, 144, 146, 229
  Triple Crown winners, 142, 144
  U.S. records
    for horses, 141
    for jockeys, 141, 143–144
horseshoe pitching, 147
  1992 results, 230

I

ice skates, longest leap on, 205
ice skating—*See figure skating; speed skating*
Iditarod Trail Sled Dog Race, 175, 231
Indianapolis 500, 4–6
Irish Derby, 147, 230
Ironman Championship—*See Hawaii Ironman*

J

javelin throw, 162, 200, 202, 243, 244
judo, 147–148
  Olympic Games (1992), 240
  throws completed, *148*
jumping—*See equestrian sports; leaps, longest; motorcycle ramp jumping; track and field*

K

karate, 148–149
kayaking—*See canoeing*
Kentucky Derby, 143, 144–145, 229

L

lacrosse, 149
  1992 results, 230